LOOKING CLOSER 4
CRITICAL WRITINGS
ON GRAPHIC DESIGN

EDITED BY

Michael Bierut, William Drenttel,
and Steven Heller

ALLWORTH PRESS
NEW YORK

07 06 05 04 03 02   5 4 3 2 1

Co-published with The American Institute of Graphic Arts
Published by Allworth Press, an imprint of Allworth Communications, Inc.
10 East 23rd Street, New York, NY 10010

LIBRARY OF CONGRESS CATALOGING-IN-PUBLICATION DATA
Looking closer 4, critical writings on graphic design / edited by
Michael Bierut, William Drenttel, and Steven Heller.
p. cm.
Includes bibliographical references and index.
ISBN 1-58115-235-3
1. Commercial art. 2. Graphic design. 3. Art and society.
I. Bierut, Michael. II. Drenttel, William. III. Heller, Steven.
NC997 .L6333 2002
741.6—dc21
2002002908

Cover design by Pentagram, New York, NY
Page composition/typography by Sharp Des!gns, Lansing, MI

Printed in Canada

CONTENTS

ACKNOWLEDGMENTS

The editors wish to thank all the writers who have allowed us to republish their essays in this book. Without their support neither this book nor graphic design criticism would be possible.

Much gratitude goes to Tad Crawford, publisher of Allworth Press, for his continued and unflagging support of Looking Closer. He has long understood the need for these and other volumes of graphic design criticism. Thanks and warmth also go to Liz Van Hoose, Jamie Kijowski, Nicole Potter, Bob Porter, Michael Madole, Cynthia Rivelli, and Kate Lothman.

Michael Bierut, William Drenttel, Steven Heller.

INTRODUCTION
Steven Heller

The first two volumes of *Looking Closer* measured two important phenomena: the key concerns of the graphic design field—professional and social—and the level of intellectual rigor evidenced through critical writing from the mid-Eighties through the mid-Nineties. The third volume was then the prequel that addressed these same phenomena from the inception of the field up to when the recent floodgates of critical writing were opened. With these criteria we bring you *Looking Closer 4*, surveying the development of our critical vocabulary since 1997.

There have been various hot-button issues since then. The First Things First Manifesto 2000 spawned fervent debate over the role of designers as agents of corporate greed and global dominion. In addition, a less vociferous discussion about the designer as "author" or "auteur" captured a segment of interest, inspiring criticism in the design and mainstream presses. Of course, there are also academic discussions balancing form and content and content and aesthetics. And critiques about the nature of criticism itself have been put forth. Yet, despite some very astute and readable commentaries on these and other concerns, the most surprising issue of the past few years is the decline of critical writing on graphic design.

This does not impugn the quality but rather the quantity of good writing. Compared to the late Eighties and early Nineties, an era of prodigious engagement among older and younger generations representing opposing aesthetic and philosophical points of view, the amount of passionate discourse, at least in print, has tapered off considerably. Sure, Internet chat sites and designer newsgroups have increased the amount of unedited musings and ramblings, and design organizations have not shied away from mounting events on controversial themes. Nonetheless, the editors of *Looking Closer* have found fewer texts published since 1997 in the design press by even some of the most prolific veteran commentators. This does not, however, suggest that the writing collected in *Looking Closer 4* is in any way inferior to that of the two earlier contemporary volumes. Included here are some excellent essays by a number of familiar commentators, and some by those who are outside the design orbit, as well as a few gems by newcomers. Yet the makeup of the writers who have appeared in these volumes has definitely changed.

The reason is twofold: While the editors purposely sought writers who were not included in previous volumes of *Looking Closer*, we were abetted by a genuine paucity of writing by certain known figures. The consistent venues for criticism, such as *Print, Eye, Emigre, Communication Arts*, and the former *AIGA Journal of Graphic Design*, are represented here, but the editors also looked to broader design and non-design journals, academic papers, the Internet, and lectures for fresh material. In the end, we had more than enough to fill this volume, but at the same time we concluded that there had been a diminution of critical writing on graphic design, especially in the graphic design magazines, while popular visual culture in general was receiving more attention.

The reader will decide whether or not this is a valid conclusion, but the following are some reasons to support it.

1. SHOCK OF THE ONCE NEW

After a period of charged professional and academic activity from the early- to mid-Nineties, stimulated by the intersecting computer and information revolutions, when old ideas and philosophies were challenged by new schools and movements, now comes the inevitable cooling-down period. The rebellion against modernism's dictum on the so-called rightness of form, the adaptation of new technological tools—their implications on form and function—and the acceptance of unique linguistic theoretical concepts inspired a torrent of visible and verbal response in the trade press, academic journals, and other zines. Yet now that postmodernism, deconstruction, and grunge are history, the next new thing has yet to emerge, and graphic design's current evolution has resulted in a new sobriety that has yet to inspire a comparable surge of intellectual excitement.

2. LIMITED DISCOURSE

Years before First Things First Manifesto 2000, designers routinely addressed ethics and social responsibility (in 1986 the AIGA devoted its national conference to this), but without a heartfelt cause or social crisis this theme is often too theoretical and rhetorical. First Things First was an attack on complacency designed to rekindle the "responsibility debate" within the field and was linked to the growing movement against corporate branding presented in *Adbusters* magazine, which has focused considerable attention on graphic design. Coincidentally, it was also concurrent with the widely covered and decidedly violent protest during the World Trade Organization's meeting in Seattle, Washington in 1999. As the essays herein attest, FTF certainly did its job in stimulating arguments, but owing to its inherent idealism it curiously polarized the debate, creating a black and white issue. FTF is undeniably the lynchpin in this volume, but arguably it is also a transitory issue in a field that inevitably reconciles itself to the requisites of commerce.

3. INFLATION AND RECESSION

The graphic design press had a remarkable growth spurt in the late-Eighties through mid-Nineties that was proportionate to outside interest in graphic design as a business tool. Generally, design earned greater popular understanding through the rise of newspaper style sections and lifestyle magazines, and graphic design was likewise elevated from a virtually transparent service to a cultural force. But that was during a strong economy. Today, the design press is faltering in terms of advertising, publications have been suspended, and, as a result, the venues for critical writing have returned to trade journalism.

4. NEW PRIORITIES

The business of doing business has supplanted the desire for viable criticism. This does not mean that criticism is entirely shunned, but the old ambivalence about how the design field wants to portray itself and be portrayed by others is a problem. Even in the best of times criticism was something that everyone said they wanted—in theory. Intelligent writing that truly captured the intent of a designer, or imposed a flattering point of view, was fine. But the proverbial, subjective, closer look has never been totally accepted. Hence, without the sincere support of the field, few professional critics have emerged, and some of the better designer-critics have retreated back into their design work.

5. NEW CULTURAL FORCES

Finally, as the spate of *big* monographs on graphic designers testifies, graphic design is not enough to carry a book, and so it is transforming into a broader discipline that involves everything from print to architecture and much new media in between. As a consequence, critical writing on graphic design will doubtless have to address larger concerns within visual culture to stay relevant.

This is something that the editors have attempted to reflect in the current volume. But implied in this move towards broader cultural criticism are questions about the future of critical writing on graphic design. Is the graphic design sphere wide enough and is our language expansive enough to include the panoply of design disciplines? Will graphic design continue to have enough weight to sustain meaningful criticism within and without the profession? Over the next few years, will the field produce enough objects *and* stimulate enough interest to make publishing another volume of *Looking Closer* viable? The editors know that the contents of this book will stimulate the reader to think, discuss and debate. Hopefully it will also inspire the next stage of critical dialogue.

TO THE
BARRICADES

The Nineties ended with violent assaults on an affluent consumer world by anti-globalists and culture-jammers who held that proliferation of multinational product brands was injurious to the cultural health of every nation. This, however, was not really a new complaint. Decades of forced obsolescence encouraged by business and promoted through advertising led to the birth of the mid-Fifties' Situationist International, a European movement of radical artists and social critics who took aim at the excesses of an encroaching consumer culture and the artist-designer's role in its perpetuation. Action was called to protest governments and corporations that prescribed a new and dangerous conformity. In an era of economic growth, the Western world was ostensibly oblivious, but the Situationists nonetheless made an impact. In 1963, as a counterculture emerged throughout Europe and the United States, British graphic designer Ken Garland wrote the First Things First manifesto, calling upon designers to take responsibility for their collective contribution to society replete with unnecessarily wasteful products.

Arguing that the lemming-like following of current trends enabled the shallowest forms of design to be celebrated, First Things First became a rallying point for practitioners who sought to balance profit-making business with profitable social responsibility. That designers could exert any significant influence seemed far-fetched, but FTF was a wakeup call that passivity could no longer be tolerated. Of course, design is a service, and FTF left an imprint on conscience but not on overall production. In fact, despite pockets of supporters, the document itself was virtually forgotten for over three decades until 1999 when, in response to another upsurge in anti-globalism, a revised First Things First manifesto was signed by a younger generation of signatories and published simultaneously in design journals in the United States, England, and Holland, as well as in *Adbusters*, the watchdog of consumer culture's immoderation. It became the topic of many design debates, and its moral high-ground tone immediately became a flashpoint for critics who called it hypocritical and adherents who read it as marching orders.

As a statement of principles, FTF 2000 sparked more controversy than any "design issue" since the modern-versus-postmodern style wars of the early Nineties, and it continues to resonate. In this section are published some of the key documents and responses, pro and con, to the manifesto; collectively, they address the dilemma inherent in design as a service and design with a conscience.

Steven Heller

FIRST THINGS FIRST MANIFESTO 2000

We, the undersigned, are graphic designers, art directors, and visual communicators who have been raised in a world in which the techniques and apparatus of advertising have persistently been presented to us as the most lucrative, effective, and desirable use of our talents. Many design teachers and mentors promote this belief; the market rewards it; a tide of books and publications reinforces it.

Encouraged in this direction, designers then apply their skill and imagination to sell dog biscuits, designer coffee, diamonds, detergents, hair gel, cigarettes, credit cards, sneakers, butt toners, light beer, and heavy-duty recreational vehicles. Commercial work has always paid the bills, but many graphic designers have now let it become, in large measure, what graphic designers do. This, in turn, is how the world perceives design. The profession's time and energy are used up manufacturing demand for things that are inessential at best.

Many of us have grown increasingly uncomfortable with this view of design. Designers who devote their efforts primarily to advertising, marketing, and brand development are supporting, and implicitly endorsing, a mental environment so saturated with commercial messages that it is changing the very way citizen-consumers speak, think, feel, respond, and interact. To some extent we are all helping draft a reductive and immeasurably harmful code of public discourse.

There are pursuits more worthy of our problem-solving skills. Unprecedented environmental, social, and cultural crises demand our attention. Many cultural interventions, social marketing campaigns, books, magazines, exhibitions, educational tools, television programs, films, charitable causes, and other information-design projects urgently require our expertise and help.

We propose a reversal of priorities in favor of more useful, lasting, and democratic forms of communication—a mind shift away from product marketing and toward the exploration and production of a new kind of meaning. The scope of debate is shrinking; it must expand. Consumerism is running uncontested; it must be challenged by other perspectives expressed, in part, through the visual languages and resources of design.

In 1964, twenty-two visual communicators signed the original call for our skills to be put to worthwhile use. With the explosive growth of global commercial culture,

Originally published in *AIGA Journal of Graphic Design* Vol. 17, no. 2 (1999).

their message has only grown more urgent. Today, we renew their manifesto in expectation that no more decades will pass before it is taken to heart.

Jonathan Barnbrook
Nick Bell
Andrew Blauvelt
Hans Bockting
Irma Boom
Sheila Levrant de Bretteville
Max Buinsma
Siân Cook
Linda van Deursen
Chris Dixon
William Drenttel

Gert Dumbar
Simon Esterson
Vince Frost
Ken Garland
Milton Glaser
Jessica Helfand
Steven Heller
Andrew Howard
Tibor Kalman
Jeffery Keedy
Zuzana Licko

Ellen Lupton
Katherine McCoy
Armand Mevis
J. Abbott Miller
Rick Poynor
Lucienne Roberts
Erik Spiekermann
Jan van Toorn
Teal Triggs
Rudy VanderLans
Bob Wilkinson

FIRST THINGS FIRST, A BRIEF HISTORY
Rick Poynor

When Ken Garland published his First Things First manifesto in London in 1964, he threw down a challenge to graphic designers and other visual communicators that refuses to go away. As the twenty-first century begins, this brief message, dashed off in the heat of the moment and signed by twenty-one of his colleagues, is more urgent than ever; the situation it lamented incalculably more extreme.

It is no exaggeration to say that designers are engaged in nothing less than the manufacture of contemporary reality. Today, we live and breathe design. Few of the experiences we value at home, at leisure, in the city or the mall are free of its alchemical touch. We have absorbed design so deeply into ourselves that we no longer recognize the myriad ways in which it prompts, cajoles, disturbs and excites us. It's completely natural. It's just the way things are.

We imagine that we engage directly with the "content" of the magazine, the TV commercial, the pasta sauce or perfume, but the content is always mediated by design, and it is design that helps direct how we perceive it and how it makes us feel. The brand-meisters and marketing gurus understand this only too well. The product may be little different in real terms from its rivals. What seduces us is its "image." This

Originally published in *Adbusters* no. 27 (Fall 1999). © 1999 Rick Poynor.

image reaches us first as a visual entity—shape, color, picture, type. But if it is to work its effect on us it must become an idea. This is the tremendous power of design.

The original First Things First was written at a time when the British economy was booming. People of all classes were better off than ever before and jobs were easily had. Consumer goods such as TVs, washing machines, fridges, record players and cars, which North Americans were the first to take for granted, were transforming everyday life in the wealthier European nations—and changing consumer expectations forever. Graphic design, too, had emerged from the austerity of the post-war years, when four-color printing was a rarity, and designers could only dream of American clients' lavish production budgets and visual panache. Young designers were vigorous and optimistic. They organized meetings, debates and exhibitions promoting the value of design. Professional associations were started and many leading figures, still active today, began their careers.

Ken Garland studied design at the Central School of Arts and Crafts in London in the early 1950s and for six years was art editor of *Design* magazine, official mouth-piece of the Council of Industrial Design. In 1962, he set up his own company, Ken Garland & Associates, and the same year began a fruitful association (a "do-it-for-love consultancy," as he once put it) with the Campaign for Nuclear Disarmament. He was a committed campaigner against the bomb, and his "Aldermaston to London Easter 62" poster, with its huge, marching CND symbol, is a classic piece of protest graphics from the period. Always outspoken, in person and in print, he was an active member of the socialist Labour Party.

Garland penned his historic statement on 29 November 1963, during a crowded meeting of the Society of Industrial Artists at London's Institute of Contemporary Arts. At the end he asked the chairman whether he could read it out. "As I warmed to the task I found I wasn't so much reading it as declaiming it," he recalled later; "it had become, we all realized simultaneously, that totally unfashionable device, a Manifesto." There was prolonged applause and many people volunteered their signatures there and then.

Four hundred copies of First Things First were published in January 1964. Some of the other signatories were well-established figures. Edward Wright, in his early for-ties and the oldest, taught experimental typography at the Central School; Anthony Froshaug was also a Central typographer of great influence. Others were teachers, students or just starting out as designers. Several were photographers.

The manifesto received immediate backing from an unexpected quarter. One of the signatories passed it to Caroline Wedgwood Benn, wife of the Labour Member of Parliament, Anthony Wedgwood Benn (now Tony Benn). On 24 January, Benn reprinted the manifesto in its entirety in his weekly *Guardian* newspaper column. "The responsibility for the waste of talent which they have denounced so vehemently is one we must all share," he wrote. "The evidence for it is all around us in the ugliness with which we have to live. It could so easily be replaced if only we consciously decided as a community to engage some of the skill which now goes into the frills of an affluent society."

That evening, as a result of the *Guardian* article, Garland was invited onto a BBC TV news program to read out a section of First Things First and discuss the manifesto. It was subsequently reprinted in *Design*, the *SIA Journal* (which built an issue round it), the Royal College of Art magazine *Ark* and the yearbook *Modern Publicity 1964/65*, where it was also translated into French and German. This publicity meant that many people, not just in Britain but abroad, heard about and read First Things First. Garland has letters in his files from designers, design teachers and other interested parties as far afield as Australia, the United States and the Netherlands requesting copies, affirming support for the manifesto's message or inviting him to come and speak about it.

That First Things First struck a nerve is clear. It arrived at a moment when design was taking off as a confident, professionalized activity. The rapid growth of the affluent consumer society meant there were many opportunities for talented visual communicators in advertising, promotion and packaging. The advertising business itself had experienced a so-called creative revolution in New York, and several influential American exponents of the new ideas-based graphic design were working for London agencies in the early 1960s. A sense of glamour and excitement surrounded this well-paid line of work. From the late 1950s onwards, a few skeptical designers began to ask publicly what this nonstop tide of froth had to do with the wider needs and problems of society. To some, it seemed that the awards with which their colleagues liked to flatter themselves attracted and celebrated only the shallowest and most ephemeral forms of design. For Garland and the other concerned signatories of First Things First, design was in danger of forgetting its responsibility to struggle for a better life for all.

The critical distinction drawn by the manifesto was between design as communication (giving people necessary information) and design as persuasion (trying to get them to buy things). In the signatories' view, a disproportionate amount of designers' talents and effort was being expended on advertising trivial items, from fizzy water to slimming diets, while "more useful and more lasting" tasks took second place: street signs, books and periodicals, catalogues, instruction manuals, educational aids and so on. The British designer Jock Kinneir (not a signatory) agreed: "Designers oriented in this direction are concerned less with persuasion and more with information, less with income brackets and more with physiology, less with taste and more with efficiency, less with fashion and more with amenity. They are concerned in helping people to find their way, to understand what is required of them, to grasp new processes and to use instruments and machines more easily."

Some dismissed the manifesto as naïve, but the signatories were absolutely correct in their assessment of the way that design was developing. In the years that followed, similar misgivings were sometimes voiced by other designers, but most preferred to keep their heads down and concentrate on questions of form and craft. Lubricated by design, the juggernaut rolled on. In the gentler, much less invasive commercial climate of the early 1960s, it was still possible to imagine that if a few more designers would only move across to the other side of the vehicle, balance would be restored. In its wording, the manifesto did not acknowledge the extent to which this might, in reality, be a political issue, and Garland himself made a point of explaining that the underlying political and economic system was not being called into question. "We do not," he wrote, "advocate the abolition of high pressure consumer advertising: this is not feasible."

But the decision to concentrate one's efforts as a designer on corporate projects, or advertising, or any other kind of design, is a political choice. "Design is not a neutral value-free process," argues the American design educator Katherine McCoy, who contends that corporate work of even the most innocuous content is never devoid of political bias. Today, the imbalance identified by First Things First is greater than ever. The vast majority of design projects—and certainly the most lavishly funded and widely disseminated—address corporate needs, a massive overemphasis on the commercial sector of society, which consumes most of graphic designers' time, skills and creativity. As McCoy points out, this is a decisive vote for economic considerations over other potential concerns, including society's social, educational, cultural, spiritual and political needs. In other words, it is a political statement in support of the status quo.

Design's love affair with form to the exclusion of almost everything else lies at the heart of the problem. In the 1990s, advertisers were quick to co-opt the supposedly "radical" graphic and typographic footwork of some of design's most celebrated and ludicrously self-regarding stars, and these designers, seeing an opportunity to reach national and global audiences, were only too happy to take advertising's dollar. Design styles lab-tested in youth magazines and obscure music videos became the stuff of sneaker, soft drink and bank ads. Advertising and design are closer today than at any point since the 1960s. For many young designers emerging from design schools, they now appear to be one and the same. Obsessed with how cool an ad looks, rather than with what it is really saying, or the meaning of the context in which it says it, these designers seriously seem to believe that formal innovations alone are somehow able to effect progressive change in the nature and content of the message communicated. Exactly how, no one ever manages to explain.

Meanwhile, in the sensation-hungry design press, in the judging of design competitions, in policy statements from design organizations, in the words of design's senior figures and spokespeople (on the few occasions they have a chance to address the public) and even in large sections of design education, we learn about very little these days other than the commercial uses of design. It's rare to hear any strong point of view expressed by most of these sources, beyond the unremarkable news that design really can help to make your business more competitive. When the possibility is tentatively raised that design might have broader purposes, potential and meanings, designers who have grown up in a commercial climate often find this hard to believe. "We have trained a profession," says McCoy, "that feels political or social concerns are either extraneous to our work or inappropriate."

The new signatories' enthusiastic support for *Adbusters's* updated First Things First reasserts its continuing validity, and provides a much-needed opportunity to debate these issues before it is too late. What is at stake in contemporary design, the artist and critic Johanna Drucker suggests, is not so much the look or form of design practice as the life and consciousness of the designer (and everybody else, for that matter). She argues that the process of unlocking and exposing the underlying ideological basis of commercial culture boils down to a simple question that we need to ask, and keep on asking: "In whose interest and to what ends? Who gains by this construction of reality, by this representation of this condition as 'natural'?"

This is the concern of the designer or visual communicator in at least two senses. First, like all of us, as a member of society, as a citizen (a word it would be good to revive), as a punch-drunk viewer on the receiving end of the barrage of commercial images. Second, as someone whose sphere of expertise is that of representation, of two-dimensional appearances, and the construction of reality's shifting visual surface, interface and expression. If thinking individuals have a responsibility to withstand the proliferating technologies of persuasion, then the designer, as a skilled professional manipulator of those technologies, carries a double responsibility. Even now, at this late hour, in a culture of rampant commodification, with all its blind spots, distortions, pressures, obsessions and craziness, it is possible for visual communicators to discover alternative ways of operating in design.

At root, it's about democracy. The escalating commercial takeover of everyday life makes democratic resistance more vital than ever.

FIRST THINGS FIRST: NOW MORE THAN EVER
Matt Soar

It is in the nature of manifestos to attempt to speak truth to power; to commit heresies against the prevailing wisdom of the day in the name of a higher public good. Documents such as the Futurist Manifesto and even the Communist Manifesto were written during times when capitalism was not a sure thing, let alone a ubiquitous force in society. So what of First Things First, also a self-described "manifesto" (*AIGA Journal* 17, no. 2), which has emerged once again with renewed vigor after its British debut in 1964? Rick Poynor, one of the signatories, suggested to me that "it's very easy for a profession to take its current concerns and obsessions and assumptions for granted; to assume these are natural, that this is the way things are." Another, Milton Glaser, pointed out that "at the end of every century in human history—not to mention the millennium itself—there's been this sense that the world is used up, that things have gone wrong, that the wrong people are in power, that it's time for a fresh vision of reality." For Glaser, this actually makes matters all the more urgent, particularly in light of what he called an "oppressive" contemporary mood in which "you can do anything to an

Originally published in *AIGA Journal of Graphic Design* Vol. 17, no. 3 (1999).

audience as long as it sells the goods." So, at the very least, it seems that the First Things First fire has been rekindled in an attempt to set off a debate where none—or not enough—existed before, at least in recent memory. And the enterprise initially got off to an unprecedented start, enjoying initial exposure in six design-oriented journals in Europe and North America and numerous follow-up commentaries, articles and letters to the editor.

In the revised document, thirty-three of the most familiar names in design (let's call them the "usual suspects") together made a public statement about their commitment to social responsibility. In part, they "propose a reversal of priorities in favor of more useful, lasting and democratic forms of communication" through design. This is hardly a profound heresy, however, since First Things First is aimed at the individual consciences of a professional cadre, rather than taking to task the fundamental power structures of the day. So, in this sense at least, its revolutionary language belies the essential modesty of its claims. Reading between the lines, however, we find that social class—a key component in historical struggles for social and political power—is an essential element here, too: the usual suspects might be understood as the "upper class," or professional elite, perhaps speaking above the heads of, or merely down to, the rank and file. This lower level consists in a "middle class" of designers who make up the bulk of AIGA's membership and, finally, the "proletariat": the tens of thousands of anonymous designers whose efforts we implicitly choose to demarcate as uninspired or, worse, uninformed; work that guarantees the rest of us our superior perspective on all things aesthetic. Surely what ultimately matters here is whether the manifesto resonates with these humbler practitioners?

Alex Callinicos has recently described those of us who work in design and advertising as "the children of Marx and Coca-Cola." The phrase—borrowed from Jean-Luc Godard—reflects a belief that, as a cultural group, graphic designers and art directors and copywriters have sensibilities formed by, or inflected with, the radical politics of the 1960s. Callinicos argues that now, for them, "'resistance' is reduced to the knowing consumption of consumer goods." (Can any of us look back honestly at our own career choices and distinguish a desire to design from a tantalizing perception of the lifestyle that might go with it?) To be sure, words such as "revolution," "resistance" and "rebellion" are today far more likely to be found describing computers, perfume or jeans than popular political movements. All told, there is some comfort in knowing that the return of First Things First has not gone unnoticed: at the very least it is evidence that there is still enough critical space available to us to be able to genuinely differentiate between calls for entries and calls to arms. Of course, there will always be fundamental issues about which most designers do actually agree, if only tacitly: for example, who wouldn't want to be publicly recognized as a socially responsible individual?

Michael Bierut, as partner at Pentagram and president of the AIGA, initially reported that he found the manifesto "intelligently written" and a welcome provocation. However, his sense was that the dominant response "out there" in the first weeks of its appearance had been frustration and alienation: a "that's-easy-for-them-to-say" kind of response. (Indeed, Bierut subsequently wrote a stinging—and somewhat facetious—

attack on the manifesto in *Print* magazine, although he has recently moderated his position once more.) Another prominent individual suggested that the manifesto's new architects were being somewhat disingenuous in claiming—surprise!—the moral high ground over advertising. Although Glaser signed only after the manifesto's "all-or-nothing" language had been toned down, some comments from the field suggest that its polemic still has an absolutist ring to it. Sarah Forbes, creative director of the in-house design department at Ben & Jerry's in Vermont, welcomed the appearance of First Things First 2000 but balked at its slightly "preachy" tone. Reflecting on her own career choices, she also took the view that those who follow their consciences really "don't need permission" in order to do the right thing—or, as Glaser puts it, "to do no harm."

Further afield, students at North Carolina State University, under the tutelage of Professor Austin Lowery, investigated the manifesto's credentials: part of their task was to chase down all of the signatories to find out exactly what level of practical commitment they have to the values espoused in First Things First. Perhaps, as Bierut and even Lowery's students suggested, the list of signatories could have been broader and less predictable. Indeed, Lorraine Wild said that inviting everyone to add their signatures would help to stem the creeping sense of alienation that may ultimately be the manifesto's Achilles' heel. Chris Dixon, who was *Adbusters*'s art director at the time, responded positively to this suggestion, and soon incorporated a response mechanism into the First Things First feature on the *Adbusters* Web site (*www.adbusters.org*).

Aside from dwelling on the manifesto or its venerable messengers, there are those who suggest that we hijack the language of the marketplace itself. For example, *Adbusters*, which was instrumental in the resurrection of First Things First, advocates in its magazine a form of activism called culture jamming. According to Kalle Lasn, *Adbusters*'s co-founder and editor, jamming's lofty aims begin with spoof ads and the creation of social marketing campaigns aimed at "taking the piss out of consumer capitalism." Furthermore, Lasn is asking designers and ad folk to be the "foot soldiers" in this revolution. But do the boots fit? As for "taking the piss," cultural critic Mark Crispin Miller (a professor at New York University) has argued that "the system is the ultimate ironist"; further, "in the great contest of ironies, the idealist will always lose out to the nihilist." Lasn, for his part, has seemed intent on promoting jamming as the only credible way forward, since, for him, "lefties," "academics" and "feminists" appear to be intellectually and programmatically bankrupt forces. Ultimately, though, using the frothy language of the marketplace to try to incite a genuine revolution might be a foolhardy project indeed. (Then again, perhaps Lasn is right, and the revolution *will* be art directed.)

Richard Wilde has been chair of the advertising and design departments at the School of Visual Arts since the early 1970s. As the owner of a design company and a senior vice president at an ad agency, he is also one of those rare individuals: the design/ad man. Wilde was unequivocal in his disdain for the manifesto's "totally idealistic" and "unmanageable" claims. For him, "virtually *any* product is unethical" if one scrutinizes it hard enough. Further, Wilde found it significant that it is ad people—not designers—who contribute millions of dollars in time and resources annually to create public service messages. And why *wouldn't* ad people object to the manifesto's clarion call, since advertising is surely the implicit enemy here? Why not take a real risk and have a combined AIGA and Art Directors Club conference? Wilde is in fact a board member of both organizations and thought the idea had merit.

At the very least, designers should perhaps work to address their many audiences as citizens rather than mere consumers. For example, as Jessica Helfand has argued so forcefully with respect to new media, this means recognizing audiences as people rather than "eyeballs." The former are (potentially, at least) participants in the democratic process; the latter merely a notional function of market economics. Miller suggests that the best answer lies in providing the population at large with the information and options that are theirs by right—and which are systematically lost or distorted in the fluff and clutter of our mega-corporate entertainment state. Surely this is a task at which all designers can excel—and do so with moral and ethical certitude—even if, as we all know, speaking truth to power doesn't generally pay the bills.

Contradictions are a necessary part of the human condition: from time to time we are all faced with dilemmas about which clients to work for, which to drop, and where to draw the line. Milton Glaser maintains that it is exceedingly difficult to spend a lifetime in the business "without having sinned": "the question is how to balance the reality of professional life" with "one's desire not to cause harm." First Things First, at its core, simply asks that we check in with our ethical and moral selves before making new decisions—rather than going ahead anyway, in the hope that our consciences won't connect up the dots. (It may also alleviate the resigned thought that goes something like: "Hell, I might as well work with this client, because if I don't someone else will.") At the limit, whether through culture jamming or some other flavor of social activism, the manifesto could offer some of us that final prod we needed begin thinking outside the biggest box of them all.

Since 1999, well over a thousand "visual communicators" have joined the original thirty-three signatories to call into question a "mental environment so saturated with commercial messages that it is changing the very way citizen-consumers speak, think, feel, respond and interact." If we ever had cause to doubt these words, surely much that has happened since September 11 should serve to underscore the predictive power of the manifesto: the hubris of the government and advertisers in conflating shopping with freedom; the laughable foreign policy initiative of attempting merely to *re-brand* America; and, the refusal by Michael Powell, the chairman of the FCC, to recognize that the "public interest" is not synonymous with the free market.

First Things First 2000 deserves to be remembered—and sustained—as a visionary initiative on the part of America's graphic designers. Those who still see it as nothing more than an embarrassingly elitist (and by now anachronistic) screed about dog biscuits and butt toners should take a moment to re-read the remaining 373 well-chosen words that help to make the manifesto's argument so much more vital today than it was even three years ago.

JUST SAY NO . . . QUIETLY
Monika Parrinder

Towards the end of 1999, when some of us were still clinging to the idea that a complete change in the digits of the calendar might magically constitute a new beginning, a conference was held in Sunderland, England, called "The Creative Summit." The intention was to provide a vision of the future of "creativity." John Hegarty of Bartle Bogle Hegarty presented e-commerce as the heart of this future and only stopped to draw breath from trumpeting its promise when a member of the audience dared to question its wider impact on society.

A more uneasy view of the future came from a graphic design perspective. Ralph Ardill, head of marketing at Imagination, offered a dystopian vision of a "brand-scape" of information overload. If Ardill's proposal left our minds in self-examination mode, then Michael Wolff of The Forth Room (his new company) led us into crisis. Wolff's lecture followed a moving session by Roger Graef, the documentary maker. Graef had lost his voice, forcing the audience to lean forward and concentrate hard to hear his harrowing, whispered accounts of human suffering. Following this, Wolff launched into a humorous tale about the brands we all encounter in our daily routines. Within a few minutes, he began to falter and ditched the script, ad-libbing for a while, but increasingly uncomfortable. In the end he stopped talking, apologized first for stopping, and then for having started at all. He explained that it seemed excruciatingly, embarrassingly trivial to be talking about brands in the wake of Graef's lecture. Wolff left the stage. Silence ensued.

Now that the year 2000 is here, we know that it is really not that much different from last year. The future still needs to be shaped, and creativity may not be enough. And it does not go without saying that creativity produces good things. In retrospect, and in the light of the recent First Things First Manifesto 2000 the importance of the conference and its performances have become clearer. In Wolff's personal moment of crisis, he was expressing a sentiment felt by many designers—free-spirited creatives—on an international scale.

Yet from the arguments and counter-arguments that have filled the letters pages of several international design journals in the wake of the manifesto's re-issue, it appears that the main criticism is that the First Things First Manifesto 2000 locks its supporters to an idealism that is impossible and impractical to live up to on an everyday scale.

"Consumerism is running uncontested," states the manifesto; "it must be challenged by other perspectives expressed, in part, through the visual languages and

Originally published in *Eye*, no. 35 (Spring 2000).

resources of design." The crux is that graphic design needs to get its priorities straight in the face of "unprecedented environmental, social, and cultural crises [that] demand our attention," advocating "a *mind shift* away from product marketing and towards the exploration and production of a new kind of meaning."

I stress the words "mind shift" because it is this word that seems to be at the heart of the confusion. From the correspondence, both heated and thoughtful, that has spread from *Eye* and *Emigre* to *Design Week* and *Graphis*, it appears that many designers are unclear whether the manifesto simply wishes to effect an "awakening of conscience" or whether they advocate a wholesale rejection of commercial work. The manifesto suggests that the challenge to consumerism should be made by drowning it out, or belittling it by placing importance on other spheres. Challenge *within* advertising, marketing or brand development does not appear to be of interest, for the manifesto berates these designers for "implicitly endorsing" the saturation of the mental environment with commercial messages. Some designers disagree with the broadly leftist, liberal position of the manifesto—temperamentally in agreement, but unable to square instinctive idealism with the need to earn a living. FTF2000 provokes questions but doesn't supply tangible solutions.

This "stalemate" need not get in the way at all. The re-issue of the manifesto is timely and inspiring but ultimately reductionist in the way it sets up socially responsible work as something separate—something in opposition to the commercial sphere of graphic design. The corporate network of capitalist culture is hard to characterize in a unified way and therefore difficult to oppose. Not all corporate work is trivial or in the business of flogging us with things we do not want. Many of the less commercial, more socially useful organizations and media are still bound up in bureaucratic power structures that invariably depend upon consumer goods to function. And even someone who decides to jack in a job promoting deodorant to work for a good cause may go home to a beer and "inessential" products such as sneakers and detergents. The manifesto admits that we all play a part in fueling the consumer economy, but does not recognize that there is no simple, unified system which one can legitimately set up as a "bad thing" and therefore clearly oppose or defect from to a "worthy thing."

Michel Foucault's investigations of the ways in which power operates in society tell us that power does not flow in one direction and simply oppress its subjects in a negative way. Power, which can be positive or negative, is everywhere, and if power is everywhere it can be addressed and disrupted everywhere. The fact that we are involved in the power structures we oppose does not negate opposition—it refocuses it. In each scenario, the individual needs to understand how power acts and through which methods. Rather than making individual voices feel lost in the mire, this empowers them because it means they can draw upon their own knowledge and intervene on their own terms, on their own ground.

So rather than having to dump the day job, or even stay in the job and say "no" to the client, designers can challenge the current "reductive and immeasurably harmful code of public discourse" from their position as mediators for commercial clients. To do this we need to understand the specific cultural contexts in which we work and our effect as mediators in their process.

In an article in *Zed* magazine that explored "Design, Intervention and the Situationist Approach," Russell Bestley suggests that designers *do* have some degree of control over the images they produce. Writing in 1996, he predicts what seems to be FTF2000's Achilles' heel: he points out the danger of debates about intervention getting side-tracked into discussions about "issues" or "responsibility," which usually result in the objectives of political affiliation (usually leftist or liberal) of the designer being fore-grounded at the expense of the act of intervening. He discusses intervention in relation to "a personal political or ideological standpoint," which he says can take place not only through overtly social or political work but through corporate work, too. In agreeing with Bestley, I would like to add to his position by advocating that the kind of challenge to consumerism advocated by FTF2000 not only requires intervention both inside and out-side the corporate sphere, but should also use as a tactic the empowering act of refusal.

Refusal is nothing new, born of the idea that doing nothing, inaction, is a polit-ical decision in itself. It draws its lifeblood from the idea that our culture is one of par-ticipation, and not participating is one of the most subversive and disturbing things you can do. Apathy, which is the response of many to the contemporary hyper-production of meaning, is often decried as symptomatic of its triumph. In the book *In the Shadow of the Silent Majorities,* Jean Baudrillard argues that apathy is the *solution* of the masses to their colonization. Having been surveyed, categorized and targeted endlessly, their response is to refuse to answer at all. He suggests that apathetic silence is their absolute weapon, because it is a problem for no one but those in power.

Baudrillard may have a point, but refusal is most effective when it is deliberate and intentional. Knowing when to stop, and deliberately doing so, is invaluable, and very different from what might be construed as despair. In this light we can readdress the despair that seemed to loom over "The Creative Summit." In his dignified exit from the stage and the silence that ensured, Michael Wolff offered us a partial but practical solu-tion to the "crisis" in graphic design. Silence is a particularly apt tactic for a culture only too aware of what it likes to call information overload. The usual "designer response" is either to create design which attempts to make sense of information overload, or to cre-ate design that attempts to block it out by delivering "experiences" not information. A better option might be just to shut up for a bit.

On the flipside of silence we have a sort of active, loud non-participation: say-ing NO. Graphic designers are constantly surrounded by people who see the rather vague concept of "some graphics" as being the solution to every empty bit of wall and space in people's brains that they spot: "Empty space, mmm . . . perhaps we could do some graphic panels. . . ." Sometimes the solution might be to say: "But why? I don't think it needs that at all." The problem is not that this kind of graphic design is inessen-tial or trivial (for who doesn't need trivia at times?) but that sometimes it is just so point-less—there for no other reason than that the budget or space can accommodate it.

And there lies the root of why our priorities so often get distorted. Because graphic design so often operates in the money-rich commercial sphere, the importance of many aspects of it become mistakenly index-linked to the budget it wields. Sometimes it takes moments of clarity, which arise in situations where issues about branding and marketing have to stand on the same podium as issues of human suffering and justify themselves, to get our priorities straight. In addition to considered intervention, silence and refusal are important because they challenge rampant consumerism without adding to it. They are empowering because anyone can use these tactics within their own experiences without having to shift elsewhere. Sometimes less is more. Sometimes silence is . . . sssshhh.

CAN DESIGNERS SAVE THE WORLD? (AND SHOULD THEY TRY?)

Nico Macdonald

L ate in May [in 2001] over four hundred of the great and the good from in and around the design world came together in Westminster at Church House, traditional meeting place of Church of England bishops, to discuss the role of design in society and listen to the High Priestess of anti-branding herself, Naomi Klein. This was the most high-profile discussion of this theme in over a decade. With Richard Seymour (of Seymour Powell fame) and Mark Leonard (onetime Demos-ite, author of *Britain TM* and New Labour favorite) at the helm, and the FT's Creative Business section behind it, expectations for "SuperHumanism" could hardly have been greater.[1]

Designers are clearly more self-conscious about their social role today than they have been at any time in the last twenty years, yet the lack of substance of the critics who have come to the fore, and the issues on which they have chosen to take a stand, reflect a political agenda that is set elsewhere. There are many areas of life in which designers can make a real difference, but we need to look first at why they are taking themselves so seriously in the naughties.

This self-consciousness among designers mirrors the increasing depoliticization of society, although it is driven by many of the same forces: primarily the end of ideology and the rise of individual politics. Most people are understandably frustrated by the disjuncture between presentation and reality in politics, and more broadly in commerce, and many—including designers—have taken to questioning authority more, as those who represent it have appeared less confident about their position. The current defensiveness of corporations was captured in an advertising campaign earlier this year by the Lattice Group, one of the successor companies to energy behemoth British Gas and a

Originally published in *New Design*, no. 6 (September/October 2001). This essay can also be found at *www.spy.co.uk/Articles/NewDesign/Superhumanism*.

sponsor of the Royal College of Art degree show. "We do need to benefit all our stake-holders," it stated sheepishly, "so while we operate safely and economically . . . we also make a profit."

There is also a sense of impotence, a result of the lack of apparent forces for change in society. This is a point that graphic designer Alex Cameron expresses well in the anthology *Becoming Designers*. "Ethical design in some sense is a response to a sense of political powerlessness: designers are urged to get off the fence and act."[2]

A greater awareness of the world around design—politics, business, economics, science and technology—can only be a good thing, but the reality of the new design ethics shouldn't be taken at face value.

There are a number of themes that have become the focus for the discussion of design in society, all of which draw from wider discussions.

The idea that "consumerism is running uncontested" was a key assertion in the reissued First Things First Manifesto—2000[3] (originally penned by British design lumi-nary Ken Garland in 1964)[4] and chimes with concerns about the role of designers in helping companies that simply want to push more products on us by "manufacturing demand for things that are inessential at best." The flip side of these concerns is that design is not being put to useful social ends, a point made by First Things First—2000 as it chided the application of designers' time to selling sport utility vehicles, butt ton-ers and dog food.

A broader challenge is leveled at advertising and branding, which, it is claimed, are co-opting and remaking our culture and blurring the distinction between public and private. This is of course one of the critiques found in *No Logo* (2000) and was rein-forced at the "SuperHumanism" conference 2001 where *pensioner terrible* Neville Brody claimed that the effects of brands on consumers "takes away their self respect."

Then at the macro level considerable concern has been exercised about the environment and sustainability, and the role design can play in creating products that are environmentally friendly and in discouraging waste.

While the design debate draws on concerns in wider society it has also adopted the "many Noes but not one Yes" approach that Klein has endorsed,[5] essentially becom-ing one big umbrella for the smorgasbord of dissatisfactions. Theodore Zeldin wryly applauded some "jolly good complaining" from the speakers who preceded him at "SuperHumanism," though his remark that "we have done this since the beginning of time" missed the point that in the past complaining usually expressed a desire for social improvement, not social restraint, and was allied with a force that could do something about it.

Dan Wieden, co-founder of Nike agency-of-record Wieden & Kennedy, noted this lack of focus at "SuperHumanism," asking whether "we are trying to save the world for capitalism, socialism, technology, or ourselves?"

The lack of focus for discussion is very telling. The end of any substantial social conflict has made it very easy to be a critic and to be against any and everything. Being anti-capitalist or anti-globalization these days sounds radical, but in an age when George Soros is one of the more articulate critics of capitalism, and the police treat anti-capitalist protestors with kid gloves, it seems to have rather lost its edge. (Genoa may have been an exception here, but anti-capitalists *anywhere* in Europe in the 1930s, or even the 1980s, received a good deal more beatings and shootings than their economy-class namesakes will ever experience.)

The disconnection between holding a view and acting on it means that most politics in designland is simply posturing, as ideas never have to be tested and justified in the real world. Neville Brody berated the audience at "SuperHumanism" about the evils of the world for forty-five minutes, but his opinions had no consequences by which he might be held to account. (One delegate commented that she had "heard it all before," and two exclaimed, "Why doesn't he just go and do something about it?" while another described the talk as a "PC string of stock images and stock phrases.")

So much of what passes for politics in the design world is really a discussion of tactics, and so much the more boring for it. The key issues—global warming, consumerism, sustainability, equality, restriction of choice—remain unsullied by debate as our self-appointed, and self-righteous, spokespeople don't consider that anyone might disagree with the received wisdom, treating doubters much as the Catholic Church in the Middle Ages treated anyone questioning the existence of God.

In reality the debate about global warming is far from settled, but the only discussion we are treated to is "what should we do about it," while the interesting debate about our relationship to the environment is considered superfluous. The obligatory use of "dramatic" statistics about the environment out of context and without reference is just the most insulting aspect of views that have no coherent foundation and only a shaky understanding of science. (And is there any discussion of how design might be used to address global warming if it really is a problem? The silence is deafening.)

This self-righteous attitude to debate extends to designers' ultimate clients, the real people who drive 4×4s and keep pet dogs (during those moments they aren't working, engaging with the world and being creative). Brody proudly claimed of his company that "we won't work for petrol companies,[6] cigarette companies, or drinks companies," leaving open the question of where he got the right to judge how other people should live their lives or how he manages to remain inured to the terrible influences that he believes the rest of us should be protected from, when in the same speech he constantly referred to the need to respect people.[7] (His respect for the audience can be judged by his decision to run over his allotted slot and reduce the already limited time for discussion.)

Brody's attitude is akin to the middle-class terrorists who came to prominence in Germany and the United States in the 1970s to liberate the oppressed and exploited while refraining from actually engaging in a debate about the beliefs they held with such certainty. As Pentagram partner Michael Bierut commented in a critique of First Things First in *I.D.* magazine in spring 2000, "Its vision of consumer capitalism is a stark one: Human beings have little or no critical faculties. They embrace the products of Disney, GM, Calvin Klein and Philip Morris not because they like them or because the products have any intrinsic merit, but because designer puppetmasters have hypnotized them with things like colors and typefaces."[8]

For designers to make a difference in broader political activity they would have to have a core of common interests that in fact doesn't exist. Being a designer doesn't pre-dispose you to having the same outlook on society in the way that historic social movements did. Designers are a diverse population and are individually oriented towards their clients; all they have in common is their skills and their professionalism. Expressing political views in design work that are beyond, or even contradictory to, the client brief simply makes for bad design work, however well intended the action.

In an odd way the ethical design movement over- and under-estimates the power of design. It over-estimates the power of design and advertising to influence people (most of whom can deconstruct an ad more effectively than their grandparents could take apart a Ford engine), but in concentrating on its message, rather than the best way to get it across, it doesn't treat the craft of design seriously enough. Alex Cameron notes that in this low view of humanity, "On the one hand people are [considered to be] sheep who will believe what they are shown and, on the other, not intelligent enough to warrant someone who concentrates his skills and effort in the process of effectively getting ideas across."

This isn't to say that designers shouldn't be political *as people*. However, we should be aware that effective political discussion is a battle of ideas, not tactics; aware that it is underpinned by theory and rhetoric, which is informed by, and contextualizes, facts; that while we may feel strongly about issues, emotion can't substitute for a well-considered argument. We should also be aware that *as designers* we can indeed make a great difference to the world by building on what we know how to do already.

Key skills in the design process include being able to conceptualize and weigh up a multi-dimensional problem, consider scenarios of use, think laterally and creatively, evaluate ideas and communicate effectively. As society's needs become more sophisticated, people want to do and achieve more and a larger population has access to more of society's resources, designerly thinking will become even more important as a skill for anticipating and working through problems and opportunities.

Secondly, design has at its core the concept of human agency: the idea that nothing in the external world is a given, and the problems we experience (sometimes unknowingly) and the opportunities we see are often design challenges waiting to be addressed. This is a key concept missing from social life and one that designers effectively propagate in their work.

Thirdly, for designers to be more effective at ensuring that their skills are applied to products that actually make a difference to people's lives they would do well do understand better the world around us, from a political, business, social trends, economic and technological perspective. Design, being a discipline that orients itself around the experience of the user, is uniquely positioned to mediate between all the parties in product development, and bringing a wider understanding of the world would help designers understand the interests of each group in this process more acutely.

To achieve this, we need to take users seriously and not impose our perceptions, values or prejudices on them, and treat them as robust individuals needing effective and satisfying design solutions, while critically assessing what they tell us. As Malcolm

Garrett—speaking at "SuperHumanism"—put it, we should "use our intelligence as designers so that people can use theirs." ("SuperHumanism" was notable for its lack of discussion of design, design process, or clients, which was remarkable considering Richard Seymour's admirable track record in effective communication on all these subjects. Irene McAra-McWilliam, the recently appointed head of Computer Related Design at the RCA, was the notable exception,[9] while Garrett addressed some of these themes but described a model of design development one rung above technology-push.)

To be more effective we should also consider improving the relationship we will have with our clients (and our collaborators) in the product development process. If we can apply some good design thinking to the experience clients have working with designers, we can guarantee that our insights will be taken more seriously, and real people will benefit at the end of the day.

As products, services and businesses become indistinguishable, one of the great challenges for design is to apply its processes and methods to the design of organizations. This is an area of application that could provide immeasurable value to the rest of us who interact on an hourly basis with increasingly dysfunctional companies and institutions. This idea was hinted at in the promotional material for "SuperHumanism," but the only speaker who addressed it at the event was Irene McAra-McWilliam, who noted that creatives "design the future of certain technologies, and to an extent the businesses of the future." Neither should we forget that we still live in a very physical world and that the physical design of spaces where objects are produced and services delivered (offices, factories and the like), rather than consumed, will be of continuing if not greater importance.

In September this year [2001][10] over two thousand designers and design critics will descend on the humid avenues of Washington, D.C., for the American Institute of Graphic Arts's "Voice" conference,[11] to "explore the ways in which designers can use their voices to make a difference to society now and in the future," and to ask "what kinds of meaningful things they have to say." The AIGA was in at the start of the current discussion of design ethics with its "Dangerous Ideas" event in the late 1980s. The secular capital is a spiritual world away from Church House but the discussion may be only a confessional apart.

Enough hand-wringing. Let's put down the rosary beads and pick up our tools.

Notes
1. The conference is very well documented on the D&AD Web site *www.dandad.org/content/super*
2. Alex Cameron, "'Ethical Design': The End of Graphic Design?" in *Becoming Designers EDS*, edited by Esther Dudley and Stuart Mealing (London: Intellect Books, 2000). This volume can be purchased at *www.amazon.co.uk/exec/obidos/ISBN=1841500321*.
3. "Consumerism is running uncontested and must be challenged through design," retorts Ken Garland in First Things First.
4. The 1964 publication of First Things First is best documented in *Adbusters* (adbusters.org/campaigns/first)
5. This approach was also adopted by Ken Garland back at the launch of the original First Things First: "We do not advocate the abolition of high pressure consumer advertising for this is not feasible."
6. Neville Brody at "SuperHumanism": There is no clear line on this. But we won't work for petrol companies, cigarette companies or drinks companies."

7. "If we are to survive as a species we must recognize the human race as a brand. Embrace respect not power."

8. Michael Bierut, "A Manifesto with Ten Footnotes," *I.D.* 47, no. 2 (March/April 2000): 76–79. *http://www. idonline.com/backissues.asp?2000*

9. "Find out what the ideal might be and talk engineers into reverse-engineering it down today. First implementation is just the first step."

10. *Editors' note*: Owing to the events of September 11, the conference was postponed until March 2002.

11. See voice.aiga.org

THE PEOPLE V. THE CORPORATE COOL MACHINE
Kalle Lasn

Has the Wild Human Spirit Been Tamed? Is an Oppositional Culture Still Possible?
Can We Launch Another Revolution?

The next revolution—World War III—will be waged inside your head. It will be, as Marshall McLuhan predicted, a guerrilla information war fought not in the sky or on the streets, not in the forests or around international fishing boundaries on the high seas, but in newspapers and magazines, on the radio, TV and in cyberspace. It will be a dirty, no-holds-barred propaganda war of competing world views and alternative visions of the future. We culture jammers can win this battle for ourselves and for planet Earth. Here's how. We build our own meme factory, put out a better product and beat the corporations at their own game. We identify the macromemes and the metamemes—the core ideas without which a sustainable future is unthinkable—and deploy them. Here are the five most potent metamemes in the culture jammers arsenal:

- *True Cost:* In the global marketplace of the future, the price of every product will tell the ecological truth.
- *Demarketing:* It's time to unsell the product and turn the incredible power of marketing against itself.
- *The Doomsday Meme:* The global economy is a doomsday machine that must be stopped and reprogrammed.
- *No Corporate "I":* Corporations are not legal "persons" with constitutional rights and freedoms of their own, but legal fictions that we ourselves created and must control.

Originally published in *Emigre*, no. 49 (Winter 1999). Originally published in *Adbusters*, no. 23 (Autumn 1998). Excerpted from the author's book *Culture Jam* (New York: HarperCollins, 2000).

- *Media Carta:* Every human being has the "right to communicate"—to receive and impart information through any media.

Meme warfare—not race, gender or class warfare—will drive the next revolution.

Only the vigilant can maintain their liberties, and only those who are constantly and intelligently on the spot can hope to govern themselves effectively by democratic procedures. A society, most of whose members spend a great deal of their time not on the spot, not here and now in the calculable future, but somewhere else, in the irrelevant other worlds of sport and soap opera, of mythology and metaphysical fantasy, will find it hard to resist the encroachments of those who would manipulate and control it.

Aldous Huxley was on the spot in the foreword of his revised 1946 edition of *Brave New World*—which, perhaps more than any other work of twentieth-century fiction, predicted the psychological climate of our wired age. There's a clear parallel between "soma"—the pleasure drug issued to citizens of *BNW*—and the mass media as we know it today. Both keep the hordes tranquilized and pacified, and maintain the social order. Both chase out reason in favor of entertainment and disjointed thought. Both encourage uniformity of behavior. Both devalue the past in favor of sensory pleasures now. Residents of Huxley's realm willingly participate in their manipulation. They happily take soma. They're in the loop and, by God, they love it. The pursuit of happiness becomes its own end—there's endless consumption, free sex and perfect mood management. People believe they live in Utopia. Only you, the reader (and a couple of "imperfect" characters in the book who somehow ended up with real personalities), know it's Dystopia. It's a hell that can only be recognized by those outside the system. Our own dystopia, too, can only be detected from the outside—by "outsiders" who did not watch too much TV when they were young; who read a few good books and then, perhaps, had a Satori-like awakening while hiking through Mexico or India; who by some lucky twist of fate were not seduced by The Dream and recruited into the consumer cult of the insatiables. Although most of us are still stuck in the cult, our taste for soma is souring. Through the haze of manufactured happiness, we're realizing that our only escape is to stop the flow of soma, to break the global communication cartel's monopoly on the production of meaning.

Next time you're in a particularly soul-searching mood, ask yourself these simple questions: What would it take for me to make a spontaneous, radical gesture in support of something I believe in? Do I believe in *anything* strongly enough? What would it take for me to say, this may not be nice, it may not be considerate, it may not even be rational—but damn it, I'm going to do it anyway because it feels right? Direct action is a proclamation of personal independence. It happens, for the first time, at the intersection of your self-consciousness and your tolerance for being screwed over. You act. You thrust yourself forward and intervene. And then you hang loose and deal with whatever comes. Once you start relating to the world as an empowered human being instead of a hapless consumer drone, something remarkable happens. Your cynicism dissolves. Your interior world is suddenly vivid. You're like my cat on the prowl: alive, alert and still a little wild. Guy Debord, the leader of the Situationist movement, said, "Revolution is not showing life to people, but making them live." This desire to be free and unfettered is hard-wired into each one of us. It's a drive almost as strong as sex or hunger, an irresistible force that, once harnessed, is almost impossible to stop. With that irresistible force on our side, we will strike. We will strike by smashing the postmodern hall of mirrors and redefining what it means to be alive. We will reframe the battle in the grandest terms. The old political battles that have consumed humankind during most of the twentieth century—black versus white, Left versus Right, male versus female—will fade into the background. The only battle still worth fighting and winning, the only one that can set us free, is *The People v. The Corporate Cool Machine.*

First we kill all the economists (figuratively speaking). We prove that despite the almost religious deference society extends to them, they are not untouchable. We launch a global media campaign to discredit them. We show how their economic models are fundamentally flawed, how their "scientifically" managed cycles of "growth" and "progress" are wiping out the natural world. We reveal their science as a dangerous pseudo-science. We ridicule them on TV. We pop up in unexpected places like the local business news, on commercial breaks during the midnight movie, and randomly on national prime-time. At the same time, we lay a trap for the G-8 leaders. Our campaign paints them as Lear-like figures, deluded kings unaware of the damage their deepening madness is doing. We demand to know why the issue of overconsumption in the First World is not even on their agenda. In the weeks leading up to their yearly summit meetings, we buy TV spots on stations around the world that ask, "Is Economic Progress Killing the Planet?" Bit by bit we maneuver the leaders into a position where suddenly, in a worldwide press conference, they are forced to respond to a question like this: "Mr. President, how do you measure economic progress? How do you tell if the economy is robust or sick?" Then we wait for them to give some pat answer about rising GDP. And that will be the decisive moment. We will have given our leaders a simple pop quiz and they will have flunked. This escalating war of nerves with the heads of state is the top jaw of our strategic pincer. The bottom jaw of the pincer is the work that goes on at a grassroots level, where neoclassical dogma is still being propagated every day. Within university economics departments worldwide, a wholesale mind shift is about to take place. The tenured professors who run those departments, the keepers of the neoclassical flame, are as proud and stubborn as high-alpine goats, and they don't take well to being challenged. But challenge them we must, fiercely and with the conviction that we are right and they are wrong. At critical times throughout history, university students have sparked massive protests, called their leaders on their lies and steered nations in brave new directions. It happened on campuses around the world in the 1960s, and more recently in Korea, China and Indonesia. Now we have reached another critical historical moment. Are the students up to it? Can they chase the old goats out of power? Will they be able to catalyze a paradigm shift in the science of economics and jam the doomsday machine?

A corporation has no soul, no morals. It cannot feel love or pain or remorse. You cannot argue with it. A corporation is nothing but a process—an efficient way of generating revenue. We demonize corporations for their unwavering pursuit of growth, power and wealth. Yet let's face it: they are simply carrying out genetic orders. This is exactly what corporations were designed—by us—to do. Trying to rehabilitate a corporation, urging it to behave responsibly, is a fool's game. The only way to change the behavior of a corporation is to recode it; rewrite its charter; reprogram it. In 1886, the U.S. Supreme Court brought down a decision that changed the course of American history. In *Santa Clara County v. Southern Pacific Railroad*, a dispute over a railbed route, the judge ruled that a private corporation was a "natural person" under the U.S. Constitution and therefore entitled to protection under the Bill of Rights. The judgment was one of the great legal blunders of the century. Sixty years after it was inked, Supreme Court Justice William O. Douglas said of Santa Clara that it "could not be supported by history, logic, or reason." With Santa Clara, we granted corporations "personhood" and the same rights and privileges as private citizens. But given their vast financial resources, corporations now had far *more* rights and powers than any private citizen. In a single legal stroke, the whole intent of the Constitution—that all citizens have one vote and exercise an equal voice in public debates—had been undermined. In 1886, we, the people, lost control of our affairs and sowed the seeds of the Corporate State we now live in. There is only one way to regain control. We must challenge the corporate "I" in the courts and ultimately reverse Santa Clara. It will be a long and vicious battle for the soul of America. Will the people or the corporations prevail? In the next century, will we live and work on Planet Earth or Planet Inc.? The critical task will be for each of us to relearn how to think and act as a sovereign citizen. Let's start by doing something so bold it chills the spine of corporate America. Let's make an example of the biggest corporate criminal in the world. Let's take on Philip Morris Inc., getting the truth out, applying pressure and never letting up until the State of New York revokes the company's charter.

    This is how the revolution begins: a few people start breaking their old patterns, embracing what they love (and in the process discovering what they hate), daydreaming, questioning, rebelling. What happens naturally then, according to the Situationists, is a groundswell of support for this new way of being, with more and more people empowered to perform new gestures "unencumbered by history." The new generation, Guy Debord believed, "would leave nothing to chance." These words still haunt us. The "society of spectacle" the Situationists railed against has triumphed. The American dream has devolved into exactly the kind of vacant obliviousness they talked about—a "have-a-nice-day" kind of happiness that close examination tends to disturb. If you keep up appearances, keep yourself diverted with new acquisitions and constant entertainments, keep yourself pharmacologized and recoil the moment you feel real life seeping in between the cracks, you'll be all right.

    Some dream.

    If the old America was about prosperity, maybe the new America will be about spontaneity. The Situationists maintained that ordinary people have all the tools they need for revolution. The only thing missing is a perceptual shift—a tantalizing glimpse of a new way of being—that suddenly brings everything into focus.

A MANIFESTO WITH TEN FOOTNOTES
Michael Bierut

FIRST THINGS FIRST MANIFESTO 2000[1]

1. In 1963, British designer Ken Garland wrote a 324-word manifesto titled "First Things First." It condemned the still-nascent graphic design profession for its obsession with the production of inconsequential commercial work, and suggested instead an emphasis on more worthy projects of benefit to humanity. It was signed by twenty-two designers and other visual artists, acquired some notoriety, and then dropped from view.

In fall 1998, Chris Dixon and Kalle Lasn reprinted the thirty-five-year-old document in their admirable and provocative self-described "journal of the mental environment," *Adbusters*. They had an opportunity to show it to Tibor Kalman, who was seriously ill with the cancer which would kill him within a year. "You know, we should do this again," Kalman said.

Adbusters, with help from journalist Rick Poynor, rewrote the statement, updating the references and sharpening the argument but otherwise leaving the spirit intact, and it was circulated by Lasn, Dixon and *Emigre*'s Rudy VanderLans to an international group of designers, many of whom signed it.

And who wouldn't? Published in the Autumn 1999 "Graphic Agitation" issue of *Adbusters*, bearing Kalman's now-ghostly imprimatur, the revamped manifesto was preceded by a historical overview of thoughtfully captioned political posters and other cause-related graphics. These in turn were contrasted with examples of contemporary commercial work, including packaging for the Gillette Mach 3 razor, Kellogg's Smart Start cereal and Winston cigarettes. Each of these examples was presented without comment, no doubt with the assumption that its surpassing vileness spoke for itself. Given all this, could someone seriously be *against* "more useful, lasting and democratic forms of communication" and in *favor* of the "reductive and immeasurably harmful code of public discourse" represented by Healthy Start cereal?

Good question. As for me, I wasn't asked to sign it.

We, the undersigned, are graphic designers, art directors and visual communicators.[2]

2. Most of the thirty-three signatories are names that will be unfamiliar to the average rank-and-file American graphic designer. Many of them built their reputations by doing "cultural work" on the fringes of commercial graphic design practice as critics, curators and academics. As designers, their clients generally have been institutions like

---

Originally published in *I.D.* Vol. 47, no. 2 (March/April 2000).

museums and publishers rather than manufacturers of nasty things like triple-edged razors, cigarettes and cereal. So it's likely your mom's probably never seen anything ever designed by these people, unless your mom is a tenured professor of culturalstudies at a state university somewhere.

In short, with some exceptions (including a glaring one, the prolific and populist Milton Glaser, who sticks out here like a sore thumb) the First Things First 2000 thirty-three have specialized in extraordinarily beautiful things for the cultural elite. They've resisted manipulating the proles who trudge the aisles of your local 7-Eleven for the simple reason that they haven't been invited to. A cynic, then, might dismiss the impact of the manifesto as no more than that of witnessing a group of eunuchs take a vow of chastity.

Techniques and apparatus of advertising.[3]

3. The phrases in the opening sentence have a tone of urgency that suits the ambitions of a millennial manifesto. But they have been lifted almost verbatim from the thirty-five-year-old original. In effect, the invidious influence of advertising has been haunting the graphic design profession since before most of the signatories were born.

It's hard to say exactly what's meant by this particular phrase. The most obvious interpretation is that graphic designers do work that informs, and that advertising agencies do work that persuades. In the First Things First universe the former is good and the latter is bad. But some of the most effective work on behalf of social causes has appropriated nothing more and nothing less than these same "techniques and apparatus": think of Gran Fury's work in the fight against HIV, or the Guerrilla Girls' agitation for gender equality in the fine arts.

Graphic designers, in truth, view the advertising world with a measure of envy. Whereas the effect of design is secretly feared to be cosmetic, vague and unmeasurable, the impact of advertising on a client's bottom line has a ruthless clarity to it. At the same time, ad agencies have treated designers as stylists for hire, ready to put the latest gloss on the sales pitch. Revolutions often begin with the politicizing of the most oppressed. And in the ecosystem of the design disciplines, graphic designers have long dwelled at the bottom of the pond.

Dog biscuits, designer coffee, diamonds, detergents, hair gel, cigarettes, credit cards, sneakers, butt toners, light beer and heavy-duty recreational vehicles.[4]

4. This litany of gruesome products has one thing in common: they are all things with which normal people are likely to be familiar. Yet haven't such common products comprised the subject matter of graphic designers throughout history? What is our design canon but a record of how messages about humble things like shoes, fountain pens, rubber flooring, booze and cigars have been transformed by designers like Bernhard,

Lissitzky, Zwart, Cassandre and Rand? What makes dog-biscuit packaging an unworthy object of our attention, as opposed to, say, a museum catalog or some other cultural project? Don't dachshund owners deserve the same measure of beauty, wit or intelligence in their lives?

If today's principled designers truly believe the role of commercial work is simply to "pay the bills," it should be pointed out it was not "always" so. "In the monotony and drudgery of our work-a-day world there is to be found a new beauty and a new aesthetic," declared Alexey Brodovich in 1930, summing up what was for him the essence of the modern condition. Graphic designers in mid-century America were passionately committed to the idea that good design was not simply an esoteric ideal, but could be used as a tool to ennoble the activities of everyday life, including commercial life.

This vision of design making the world a better place by marrying art and commerce is no longer a compelling vision for many designers. Tibor Kalman's quote, "Consumer culture is an oxymoron," is one of those aphorisms so pleasing one accepts it unthinkingly. Yet a centerpiece of his valedictory exhibition Tiborocity was a "shop" stocked with selections from his vast collection of unabashedly commercial detritis: packaging for Chinese gum, Mexican soda pop, Indian cigarettes. Is there a contradiction here? Or is this kind of work okay as long as it's performed anonymously and, if possible, in a third-world country?

Manufacturing demand.[5]

5. Many downtrodden graphic designers will read these damning words with a secret thrill. After countless years of attempting to persuade skeptical clients that "design is good business," or, failing that, that it has any measurable affect on sales whatsoever, here we stand accused of something no less delicious than *manufacturing demand* for otherwise useless products! If but it were so.

The First Things First vision of consumer capitalism is a stark one. Human beings have little or no critical faculties. They embrace the products of Disney, GM, Calvin Klein and Philip Morris not because they like them or because the products have any intrinsic merit, but because their designer puppetmasters have hypnotized them with things like colors and typefaces. Judging by the published response, First Things First has been received most gratefully by underpaid toilers in the boiler rooms of the twenty-first-century communications revolution. In the manifesto they discover that in deciding between circles or lozenges for the design of those goddamned home-page navigation buttons, they are in fact participants in a titanic struggle for the very future of humanity. When it comes to graphic designers, flattery will get you everywhere.

To some extent we are all helping draft a reductive and immeasurably harmful code of public discourse.[6]

6. To another extent, however, human beings have always used the marketplace as a forum for communication and culturization. "As we enter the twenty-first century, the urban condition is defined more and more by tourism, leisure and consumption, the hallmark of an evolved capitalist society wherein economic affluence allows personal freedom to seek pleasure," wrote architects Susan Nigra Snyder and Steven Izenour on the (re)commercialization of Times Square. They concluded, "If your model is the cultural mish-mash of the everyday landscape, then commerce is the very glue—visually, socially and economically—of American civic space." What will happen when the best designers withdraw from that space, as First Things First demands? If they decline to fill it with passion, intelligence and talent, who will fill the vacuum? Who benefits? And what exactly are we supposed to do instead?

Many cultural interventions, social marketing campaigns, books, magazines, exhibitions, educational tools, television programs, films, charitable causes and other information design projects.[7]

7. Finally, here the prescription is delivered, and note the contrast. Gone is the bracing specificity of butt toners and heavy-duty recreational vehicles, replaced by vague "tools," "campaigns" and "causes." The puzzling construction "cultural interventions" will be less baffling to readers of *Adbusters*, who will recognize it as code for the kind of subversive "culture jamming" activities the magazine has long advocated. From other contextual clues we can infer by this point that the books advocated here will deal with subjects other than the Backstreet Boys, that the magazines will feature models less appealing than Laetitia Casta on their covers, and that the television shows will not involve Regis Philbin.

The issue of *Adbusters* that introduced the First Things First Manifesto 2000 included a range of classic examples of design as a tool of protest. Almost all of these were historical antecedents to that glamorous old standby beloved by right-thinking graphic designers everywhere, the dramatic poster for the pro bono cause. Although Lasn and Dixon in that same issue paint a vivid, knowing picture of the awards and fame that accrue to the creator of "a stunning package design for a killer product," any seasoned designer can tell you that it's a hell of a lot easier to win a prize for a pro bono poster than for a butt toner brochure. What designers can't figure out is whether any of our worthy posters really work.

Illustrated nowhere are examples of some things that absolutely *do* work, those otherwise unexplained "information design projects." Too bad: designers actually *can* change the world for the better by making the complicated simple and finding beauty in truth. But things like the F.D.A. Nutrition Facts label, probably the most useful and widely reproduced piece of graphic design of the twentieth century, generally receive neither awards nor accolades from the likes of *Adbusters* or Rick Poynor: too humble, too accessible, too unshocking, too *boring*.

We propose a reversal of priorities.[8]

8. Manifestos are simple; life is complicated. One of my favorite personal clients is the Brooklyn Academy of Music, a fantastic non-profit organization that courageously supports forward-looking performers and is a first-class citizen of its decidedly heterogeneous urban neighborhood. Yet, like many cultural institutions, it is supported by philanthropy from many large corporations, including the generous Philip Morris Companies. So am I supporting an admirable effort to bring the arts to new audiences? Am I helping to buff the public image of a corporation that sells things that cause cancer? And come to think of it, don't I know a lot of graphic designers who smoke?

A new kind of meaning.[9]

9. "Designers: stay away from corporations that want you to lie for them," exhorted Tibor Kalman. But that High Noon moment when we're asked to consciously misrepresent the truth comes only rarely for most designers. We're seldom asked to *lie*. Instead, every day, we're asked to make something a little more stupid, or a little more ugly, or a little more blithely contemptuous of its audience. Is the failure of contemporary graphic design rooted in the kind of clients we work for, or in our inability to do our jobs as well, as persuasively, as we should?

The greatest designers have always found ways to align the aims of their corporate clients with their own personal interests and, ultimately, with the public good. Think of Charles and Ray Eames, who created a lifetime of extraordinary exhibitions and films that informed, entertained and educated millions of people while advancing the commercial aims of the IBM Corporation. Or Kalman himself, who struggled firsthand with the contradictions—and lies, perhaps?—inherent in the ongoing marketing challenge of portraying a sweater company, Benetton, as an ethically engaged global citizen.

What would happen if instead of "a new kind of meaning," the single most ambiguous phrase in the manifesto, we substituted "meaning," period? For injecting meaning to into *every* part of their work is what Kalman and Eames and designers like them have always done best.

Today, we renew their manifesto in expectation that no more decades will pass before it is taken to heart.[10]

10. Kalle Lasn and Chris Dixon have a dream. "We wait for that inevitable day of reckoning when the stock market crashes, or the world is otherwise destabilized," Lasn declares in the Autumn 1999 issue of *Adbusters*.

> On that day we storm the TV and radio stations and the Internet with our accumulated mindbombs. We take control of the streets, the billboards, the bus stops and the whole urban environment. Out of the despair and anarchy that follows, we crystallize a new vision of the future—a new style and way of being—a sustainable agenda for Planet Earth.

What a disappointment to learn that this revolution is aimed at replacing mass manipulation for commercial ends with mass manipulation for cultural and political ends.

I have a dream as well. I am the president of a national association of graphic designers and a principal in a large firm that works on occasion for the Disneys and Nikes of the world, so you can dismiss me as someone hopelessly invested in the status quo, and no fit person to lead us into the endless promise of the new millennium. Yet I take inspiration from something designer Bill Golden, the creator of the CBS eye, wrote over forty years ago. You can consider it a twenty-one-word-manifesto: "I happen to believe that the visual environment . . . improves each time a designer produces a good design—and in no other way."

Golden's manifesto, unlike First Things First, is easy to understand. Yet, if anything, it's harder to execute. As any working designer can tell you, commercial work is a bitch. If you do it for the awards, it's a hard way to get them. If you do it for the money, you've got to earn every penny twice over. Make no mistake, there is much to be alarmed about in the contemporary world, from the continuing establishment of the corporation as global superstate, to the idiotic claims of marketing mavens seeking to elevate brand loyalty to the status of world religions. Lasn, Dixon, Poynor and the signers of First Thing First are right that graphic design can be a potent tool to battle these trends. But it can be something else, something more. For in the end, the promise of design is about a simple thing: common decency.

About four years after the original First Things First, Ken Garland wrote, "What I am suggesting . . . is that we make some attempt to identify, and to identify with, our real clients: the public. They may not be the ones who pay us, nor the ones who give us our diplomas and degrees. But if they are to be the final recipients of our work, they're the ones who matter." And, I would submit, they deserve at the very least the simple, civic-minded gift of a well-designed dog-biscuit package.

If you think that's so easy, just try.

A NEW KIND OF DIALOGUE
Andrew Howard

Searching for values, design looks in the usual place—inward, never outward

"Don't make something unless it is both necessary and useful," goes the Shaker adage, "but if it is, don't hesitate to make it beautiful." There is a simple equilibrium to this philosophy, and in today's world of commodity production, equilibrium is in short supply. It is precisely what the market economy and its supporting ideology robs us of. We are submerged in excess—a futile abundance, high in material use but low in spiritual substance, which, in its inability to satiate us, subjects us instead to a continual hunger. The Shakers would perhaps nod their heads knowingly to see so much materialism producing so little sustenance. Equilibrium is a state of balance to which excess is antithetical.

Far from the isolationist world of the Shakers, the debate taking place within the world of design is also about need, use and aesthetics. It, too, has been addressing notions of excess, and although these issues have been recently placed on the agenda through the publication of the First Things First Manifesto 2000, it is not a new debate.

What should be self-evident by now is that talking about contemporary design practice draws us inevitably into a wider social discourse. Design is not an abstract theoretical discipline—it produces tangible artifacts, expresses social priorities and carried cultural values. Exactly whose priorities and values are at the core of this debate.

Many designers do find contemporary design practice problematic. We are drawn to design because we are excited by the visual and all its creative possibilities, by our fascination for language made visible, our pleasure in understanding how to craft a work, our sense of satisfaction in organizing ideas. We are sustained by the possibility of exercising skill and of creating beauty, and not least of all, because we have a talent for all these things. In parallel, we are troubled by the thought that the results of our efforts may be trivial, or worse, that they may serve damaging, ultimately antisocial, interests.

We can uncover the roots of some of the problems we identify by looking inside the design profession, but others clearly spring from the nature of the wider social framework within which we function. Defining the range of our skills and knowledge is one thing; controlling how they are applied socially is another. Learning to understand what comes with the territory, and what we can bring to it, is one step in elaborating strategies that aim to redefine our practice.

Learning to understand the territory itself means learning to sift through what

Originally published in *Adbusters*, no. 37 (September/October 2001).

John Berger has described as the modern rhetoric of bourgeois politics, the purpose of which is to conceal the true nature of the underlying economic practice. Marx's genius, wrote Berger, was his resolute insistence on the practice, refusing to be deceived or diverted by the rhetoric. The rhetoric tells us that the marketplace is natural, that ultimately it is the most efficient way to meet the needs of the majority while rewarding individual initiative and skill and developing human potential.

It is none of these. At the heart of capitalism lies a pitiless logic, an economic imperative rooted in material acquisition and possession. It is a logic that celebrates self-interest. It has constructed a system which contains no concept of sufficiency because its function is no longer concerned with satisfying human need, but satisfying the appetite for personal wealth. And since there is no such thing as sufficient wealth, there can be no such thing as sufficient production. Human needs have material limits. This is not good for the economic imperative. New demands have to be created so that they can match the profitable output of industrialized production. This is the inversion of supply-and-demand. It is best done by dividing our needs, desires, and activities into the smallest possible units so that products and services can be created to satisfy them.

So much has been written about this that it is tiresome to cover the same ground. Those still in doubt about the extent of our manipulation should read Vance Packard's *Hidden Persuaders*. First published in 1957, Packard's work remains a powerful exposé of the advertising industry and its attempts to "invade the privacy of our minds."

If this is not enough then try Stuart Ewen's *Captains of Consciousness* (1976) or the more recent *No Logo* by Naomi Klein (2000)—the list is long. These works look beneath the veneer of "normality" and uncover the real priorities and values of our economic system and the culture that springs from it. But there are other things, those that lie beyond our view or are simply ignored. There are acts of heroism, of self-sacrifice, of courage and of resistance by countless millions who are the necessary victims of simple greed explained away as "natural law."

The division of our needs and desires fragments our consciousness. We are kept from being complete. Social activity, including thought, is subject to specialization and compartmentalization. We are encouraged to concentrate on the details of our activity—to develop its internal logic. This is what it means to be a good professional. Thus we lose track of how things fit together. In our allocated areas of professional concern there is little time for the wider picture.

It is this disconnection which makes possible Michael Bierut's now famous dog-biscuit argument, referred to by Rick Poynor in the last issue of *Adbusters*. "What makes dog-biscuit packaging an unworthy subject of our attention," asks Poynor, "as opposed to, say, a Walker Art Center catalog?" Though Rick is right to point out the disparity for those whose dose of wit and beauty has to come in the form of dog-biscuit boxes, a more obvious reply springs to mind—dog-biscuits? It's difficult to pinpoint exactly where and when it happened, but sometime over the last thirty years, the priority life goal of dogs seems to have become the taking of vitamins. Only the apparently ill-informed could contemplate depriving their dogs of the vitamin-rich, teeth-sharpening, bowel-regulating, hair-shining dog-biscuits that are so essential to their health and happiness. It is the same sort of invention that persuades us that we need eight types (pick a number) of shampoo, depending on our age, gender, profession, activity level, and the texture, coloring and sheen of our hair.

There are points in the work of a designer at which it is necessary to become completely immersed in the internal logic of our work. Creative work is not possible without the intimacy of close proximity. But sooner or later the process has to reconnect to a larger, external logic. There has to be a set of reference points that lie beyond individual works or clients, some sort of guide that can locate your activity within a collective value system. Without this, dog-biscuit boxes are undoubtedly as worthy as anything else.

When I received the first draft of the FTF 2000 manifesto, I expressed my reservations about adding my name. I felt something more comprehensive was needed. Like some other signatories, I questioned the call for "a new kind of meaning." This has nothing to do with a distaste for ambiguity. On the contrary, ambiguity often has the power to disturb because it gives the imagination what it needs—an idea free of fixed associations or interpretations. But I believe that in calling for "a new kind of meaning," the manifesto just misses the mark. If there is a problem about the role that graphic design plays in what Jan van Toorn describes as "the circulation of material and symbolic commodities," then it's related not just to the content of these cultural messages, but also to the forms of communication which carry them.

The endless streams of messages that invade every corner of our lives are not open-ended; they are monologues. A call for "a new kind of dialogue" has the advantage of suggesting that we need to address form as well as content. Replacing billboards by car manufacturers with ones by Greenpeace doesn't amount to much more than swapping one monopoly of perception for another. Better not to have any billboards at all.

Thinking about forms of communication also helps to avoid the compilation of lists of "politically correct" clients—coming to be seen as a central task. The nature of the dialogue is as important as what is being expressed. In theory this does not exclude anyone. In practice, however, those whose interests lie in the commodification of our lives will have nothing to gain in creating the sorts of dialogues that are essential to democratic society.

The cult of the instant permeates our ability to imagine. Immediacy is primary; efficiency is equated with speed. We scan for quick responses and quick solutions. The extent to which extreme, usually violent, action is celebrated in much of our popular culture is a reflection of the dominant predilection to eliminate obstacles rather than resolve problems. "Slow" solutions, which involve approaches that are local and accumulative, lack the thrust of modernity. They seem somehow less appealing, less convincing. To suggest that a daily, continual questioning of our priorities and our social ambitions is a strategy may not seem earth-shattering. It is nevertheless necessary, linked to a more far-reaching process. "Democracy," wrote John Berger, "is a political demand. But it is something more. It is a moral demand for the individual right to decide by what criteria an action is called right or wrong. Democracy was born of the principle of conscience. Not, as the free market would have us believe, from the principle of choice which—if it is a principle at all—is a relatively trivial one." Most of us do not have the power, or even the economic independence, to challenge head on the priorities of those who pay for our skills. But we do have the possibility of defining, in collaboration with each other, a design agenda which provides a set of social references hostile to the commodification of our society and in defense of democratic values.

Rick Poynor has characterized my position as calling for "nothing less than the politicization of all design discourse and practice," in a way that suggests that I lie at one end of the spectrum. Perhaps this is true, for I do argue that a social analysis of design's cultural and political impact should be at the core of our practice. This means encouraging the socialization of design rather than its professionalization. It means learning to stand back from the daily routine and building habits in which we persistently evaluate what we communicate, to whom, in what ways and for what purpose. The sorts of strategies and policies that might arise from this will be dependent on context—there are no "off-the-shelf" solutions to be handed down from above. The politicization of design in this sense amounts to the creation of a methodological framework, a way of localizing our activity within a wider social spectrum, a mode of thinking which is the basis for acting. It is based on the idea that effective action is impossible without understanding.

Many designers are uncomfortable about the social application of their skills and energies. They recognize how problematic is the search for alternatives. None of us should be castigated for not being genial enough to find quick answers, but there is simply no excuse anymore for not looking.

THE SPECTACLE: A REEVALUATION
OF THE SITUATIONIST THESIS
Véronique Vienne

Mesmerized by the computer or television screen, most of us are docile spectators, our idle hands forever deprived of the tactile satisfaction of actually making things. This enforced passivity has dire consequences for the brain. Our hands are connected to our gray matter by a crisscrossing network of nerve pathways that travel back and forth from the right brain to the left hand and from the left brain to the right hand. There is evidence that toolmaking is linked to the development of language. Recent studies on the mind-body connection suggest that

Originally published in *Communication Arts* Vol. 42, no. 2 (March/April 2000).

the development (or atrophy, as the case may be) of parts of the body can in turn affect corresponding parts of the brain. So, while manual dexterity stimulates our central nervous system, simple spectatorship has a tendency to numb the mind.

But with nothing to fabricate, the majority of people are reduced to buying ready-made products—examining them, poking them and fondling them in the process just to satisfy the yearning in their fingers. Shopping is a substitute for producing. When my daughter was a teenager, she would often say, like so many of her contemporaries, "Mom, I have nothing to do. I am bored. Let's go shopping!" It soon became a family joke. We worked out a couple of silly variations, including, "Mom, my closet is full of clothes. I have nothing to wear. Let's go shopping," and, "Mom, I have too many pairs of sneakers. I am confused. Let's go shopping."

From time to time, I indulged her shopping impulses, but I also suggested fun alternatives: fix toys, repaint the bathroom, make jam, wax the furniture. One of her favorite mood-uppers, it turned out, was doing the silver. I will always cherish the memory of her sitting at the kitchen table, a big apron secured around her chest, happily polishing our odd collection of forks and spoons.

"In his or her day-dreams the passive worker becomes an active consumer," wrote John Berger, Britain's eminent critic and novelist, in his 1972 best-seller *Ways of Seeing*. Acquiring things, Berger believes, is a poor alternative for fashioning objects. The spectator-self, no longer involved with the making of artifacts, envies the consumer-self who gets to touch and use new gadgets, appliances, devices and goods. Deprived of the sensual pleasure of manual creation, we satisfy our tactile cravings by purchasing more and more ready-made objects and products.

This perception is not new. More than forty years ago in Paris, an obscure group of cultural critics calling themselves "Situationists" began protesting against the escalating commercial takeover of everyday life, and against the artists, illustrators, photographers, art directors and graphic designers who manufactured this fake gee-whiz reality. In his book *The Society of Spectacle*, French Situationist leader Guy Debord wrote: "In our society where modern conditions of production prevail, all of life presents itself as an immense accumulation of spectacles." Yet, by today's standards, the spectacle hadn't even begun. This was before the Cuban revolution, before the invasion of Tibet, before the Pill, before *La Dolce Vita*, before Pop Art. In the 1958 Paris of the early Situationists, Edith Piaf was singing "Milord," François Truffaut was shooting *The 400 Blows*, and demure Danish modern *was* the cutting edge.

Yet, with a clairvoyance that's startling in hindsight, the short-lived (1957–1972) Situationist International movement predicted our most serious current predicament. According to recent findings, we spend 58 percent of our waking time interacting with the media; people sleep less and spend less time with their family in order to watch more television; megaplexes and superstores are increasingly designed to resemble theme parks; and the Mall of America in Minneapolis hosts more visitors than Walt Disney World, Disneyland and the Grand Canyon combined. In his book *The Entertainment Economy: How Mega-Media Forces Are Transforming Our Lives*, Michael J. Wolf asserts: "We have come to expect that we will be entertained all the time. Products and brands that deliver on this expectation are succeeding. Products that do not will disappear."

No wonder the Situationists ethos has become the mantra of critics and detractors of our imagineering culture. Everyone who is anyone these days is dropping their name—from *Adbusters* to *Emigre* magazines, and from Greil Marcus to J. Abbott Miller. Debord's seminal book, *The Society of Spectacle*, is on the list of the trendy Zone Books, and M.I.T. Press has recently published *The Situationist City*, a comprehensive investigation of the Situationists' urbanist theories, written by Simon Sadler. Move over Paul Virilio; SI, as the Situationist International movement is now labeled, is the latest French intellectual import.

An underground movement that shunned the limelight—the members of this elusive group lived by the precepts they preached—SI's subversive ideology at first defies comprehension. Unless you understand the specific context of the period, many of their assertions make little sense today. Influenced by Lettrist International, a radical group of the 1950s that sought to revitalize urban life through the fusion of poetry and music, Debord and his colleague Raoul Vaneigem used Dada slogans to spread their message. "The more you consume, the less you live," and, "Be realistic, demand the impossible," are two of the most memorable SI pronouncements.

Yet in spite of its so-called anarchist mentality, the SI methodology was precisely constructed. The name of the group was born out of the realization that participants had to create in their everyday life special conditions—special "situations"—in order to resist the insidious appeal of the pseudo-needs of increased consumption and overcome the mounting sense of alienation that have characterized the postmodern age. They conducted open-ended experiments that involved playful constructive behavior aimed at scrambling mental expectations. Most popular of these strategies was taking aimless strolls through a busy neighborhood, deliberately rearranging the furniture in their apartments to create as many obstacles as possible, systematically rejecting labor-saving devices and voluntarily disorienting themselves by consulting the map of London when visiting Amsterdam. Called "Drifting"—*Dérive* in French—the technique was an effective way to "reclaim the night," to momentarily defy the white patriarchy of traditional space-time.

Like most rational people today, I would find this approach naïve and dogmatic if I hadn't experienced it firsthand. In 1960, as a student at the Paris Beaux-Arts school of architecture, I was unwittingly part of an SI experiment. The very first day I showed up at the studio with a dozen other new recruits, the young instructor announced that we should reconvene at "La Palette," a bistro across the street. At nine in the morning, the sidewalk had just been washed and the waiter was trundling the cast-iron tables out in the open. We each grabbed a wicker chair from a tall stack in a corner, picked our spot on the terrace, angled our seats to catch the morning sun, stretched our legs, yawned and ordered a round of black coffee.

"This is your first lesson in architecture," said the instructor, a gaunt young man in a black turtleneck—the trademark look of the avant-garde back then. "For the next three months, we will spend six hours a day sitting right here. I want you to learn about space-time—particularly how to use space in order to waste time. Unless you understand that, you'll never be good architects."

I now know that this is straightforward SI doctrine. Embracing Arthur Rimbaud's assertion that laziness is a refusal to compartmentalize time, Situationists advocated "living without restrictions or dead time," and "never work—never risk dying of boredom." They wasted time deliberately—and playfully—as a guerrilla strategy against the sense of emptiness imposed by the relentless spectacle of consumption that was quickly subsuming French culture.

And so, for the first semester, we sat at the bistro from 9:00 A.M. to 2:00 P.M., five days a week. Except for mornings when we would drift through Paris, sketchpads in hand, making detailed drawings of whatever caught our fancy—a stairway leading to the river bank, an abandoned gazebo in a park, the monumental gate of a hospital—you would find us huddled at the terrace of La Palette. This was *in situ* urban anthropology. I learned to observe how people choose the best spot to sit; how lovers fight, how couples brood and how friends compete; how everyone sits straighter when a pretty girl walks in; how people celebrate on payday—and how they scrutinize a menu when they are broke.

Sometimes we would get into conversations, sometimes we would draw, sometimes we would read, sometimes we would argue—and often we would simply daydream. As promised, the space-time equation became a reality, one rich in surprises and discoveries. We became familiar with the angles of the various streets, the movements of the sun, the sounds of the city, the rhythm of life around us. No two minutes were ever alike. As we sat there, absorbing what felt like vital information, we developed a perception of the human scale—a critical notion for architects. And then, almost reluctantly, after lunch, we drifted across the street to the studio where we worked late into the night to acquire the rudiments of the classical orders of architecture.

I never completed my architectural studies. Instead, I moved to the States and eventually became a magazine art director. During my career in design, I often used the *dérive* technique to avoid the pitfalls of linear thinking. Instead of focusing on a thorny design conundrum, the solution would come to me unsolicited if I patiently listened to a photographer rant on the phone about his mid-life crisis, or when I watched a five-year-old play with her baby brother. Another Situationist construct also came handy. Called *détournement*, translated as "rerouting," it consists in transforming images by interpreting them to mean something of your own making. SI theorists liked to describe the method as "hijacking, misappropriation, corruption of preexisting aesthetic elements." I simply call it sticking words on top of images.

Rerouting images is the basic modus operandi of graphic communication. The minute you caption a photograph, or place a headline next to a picture, or create a collage, or single out a pull-quote, or write cover lines, you subvert the significance of both word and image. I believe that most of the creative tensions between editors and art directors, or between clients and designers, evolve from a misunderstanding of how visual artifacts can be reconfigured into constructed situations.

Chris Dixon, art director of *Adbusters* magazine, the anti-consumerism publication that has whole-heartedly embraced the SI legacy, is probably one of the few North-American designers to consciously uses *détournement*. "Often the captions we use in the magazine are much more provocative than the images themselves," he says. "In fact, we deliberately use rather conventional photographs to let our readers know that we speak the same language they do." Even though its overall message is anti-commercial and anti-advertising, *Adbusters* is surprisingly well-designed, as if to mock the very aesthetic that drives the advertising community.

Where *Adbusters* and SI part ways is on the discourse they have chosen to promote similar ideas. "We link anti-consumerism to the environmental movement," explains Dixon. "Readers understand the correlation between buying too many useless products and depleting the natural resources of the planet." Concern for the environment never appears in the newspapers, journals, tracks, graffiti or manifestos left behind by the SI. They didn't have much of a social agenda either. Their mandate was to resist the cultural imperialism that drains human beings of that most French of concepts, their *joie de vivre*. Boredom was their enemy; happiness their goal. Another of their maxims was: "They are buying your happiness—steal it back."

The Situationist idea of happiness is very different from the "hedonomics" of the buying experience, as defined by Michael J. Wolf in *The Entertainment Economy*.

Whereas Americans equate feeling good with having "fun," the French in general, and the SI in particular, describe happiness as liberating—as being euphoric, mischievous, prankish. It's the feeling that swept over France during the first weeks of the May 1968 general strike, when all Paris took to the streets in what was at first a festival more than a student revolt.

The Situationists were responsible for initiating the construction of barricades in the streets of Paris that month. Pull up some cobblestones, add a half-dozen trash cans, more cobblestones, some discarded lumber, maybe a broken bicycle. Borrow chairs from a café, sit and wait. They also encouraged students to cover the walls of the city with Lettrist-inspired graffiti ("It is forbidden to forbid"). Last but not least, they were credited with giving the rebellion its upbeat and high-spirited signature.

But the events of 1968—not only in France but all over the world—were eventually "rerouted" by the establishment. As Thomas Frank, editor in chief of *The Baffler* explains in his book *The Conquest of Cool*, the anti-consumerism rebellion of the post-war era was commodified by Madison Avenue into what is now known as the "Youth Culture"—one of the greatest marketing tools of the second part of the twentieth century. The Society of Spectacle was here to stay. Blaming themselves for their failure to change society, but also grieving for the millions of consumers who would only experience euphoria through shopping, Debord and his troops dispersed in 1972. However, their ideas continued to resonate, quite notably in the early days of English punk, when Jamie Reid's photo-collage for the Sex Pistols captured the defiant challenge punk rock posed to class and authority. Tragically unable to recapture the *joie de vivre* of the early days of SI, Debord took his own life in December 1994, shortly after completing a documentary film on his work.

Five years after Debord's suicide, events would prove that the spirit he had championed still survives. On December 5, 1999, the front page of the *New York Times* featured a photograph that would have cheered him up. Taken by Jimi Lott of the *Seattle Times*, it showed Mr. and Mrs. Santa Claus being escorted home by four riot police-men, the latter wearing Ninja-turtle combat boots and padded breastplates. The violent protests against the World Trade Organization in Seattle had so disrupted holiday shop-ping, explained the caption, that the Yuletide pair had to be put under police protec-tion.

As one flipped through the newspaper, one quickly realized that the former Saint Nicholas (a historical figure incidentally recast in 1931 by Coca-Cola as the beloved red and white icon we now identify with Christmas shopping), was not the only consumer icon that needed police protection. Riot troops had been posted in front of all retail stores in downtown Seattle—guarding Starbucks, Banana Republic, Coach, Gap, and Gucci, just to name a few. The entrance of Niketown in particular looked like the set of *Star Wars*, with hooded figures in black armor standing at atten-tion, their four-foot bludgeons poised to strike.

It looked like the police were confronting rowdy crowds not to protect civil liberties and political institutions—but to protect global brands. Though one didn't have to be a trend forecaster to feel that brand backlash was coming ("My wish for the New Year was to get through meetings without someone mentioning branding," joked renowned Web page editorial designer Jessica Helfand shortly after), most of us never expected it would be so sudden, so graphic or so ready-for-prime-time-television. The revolution will not be televised, sang Gil Scott-Heron in 1974. Wishful thinking, indeed. The anti-consumerism, anti-brand revolution, complete with demonstrators smashing store windows, was on the eleven o'clock news. Replays showing over and over the same scenes were aired every ten minutes, as if to "brand" the violent images in the mind of viewers.

Kalle Lasn, editor of *Adbusters* magazine in Vancouver and famous for advocat-ing what he calls "culture jamming," was one of the few people who weren't surprised by the Seattle uproar. In fact, the December 1999 issue of his magazine had an article predicting that the WTO conference would be "a historic confrontation between civil society and corporate rule." His book, *Culture Jam: The Uncooling of America*, had just been released. *Time* magazine had praised him for taking arms against our three-thou-sand-marketing-message-a-day society. Still, he wasn't prepared for what he saw when he went to Seattle to observe the riots.

"It was like a festival," he says. "Except for a few people confronting cops, demonstrators were laid-back, happy, having fun. There was a lot of street theater, spon-taneous happenings, and cheerful pranks being played." It had a Situationist ambiance, for sure. But then, unexpectedly, Lasn got his first whiff of tear gas. "I'll never forget that smell," he says. "Nor will I forget the savage look on the faces of the policemen. They really didn't get it."

But who gets it? Why are the global brands a threat to our very existence—a threat so real it galvanized 30,000 people to take to the streets? "There were more than one hundred different groups," tells Lasn. "Environmentalists, students, anarchists, but also musty old socialists, Christians tired of the violence on TV, critics of genetic engineering, and card-carrying union members—every single one of them worried about some unofficial global government body enforcing an elite corporate agenda."

During the WTO riots, my friends in the design community were in a state of complete denial. No one talked about what was happening in Seattle. Heck, we were still nursing our Las Vegas hangover following the "hedonomic" AIGA (American Institute of Graphic Arts) conference held two months earlier. There had been practically no references then to the social or environmental responsibility of designers, let alone their role in "supporting, or implicitly endorsing, a mental environment so saturated with commercial messages that it is changing the very way citizen-consumers speak, think, feel, respond and interact," to quote the language of First Things First 2000, the *Adbusters* manifesto signed by thirty-three prominent designers worldwide. In fact, when AIGA president Michael Bierut, in his closing statement in Las Vegas, had made a passing reference to this controversial call for moderation in marketing, some people in the audience had booed his comments.

But, as luck would have it, that same week—for the fifth anniversary of Debord's death—I had given my graphic design students at the School of Visual Arts a series of *dérive* exercises directly inspired by my own SI experience and studies. First they had to draw a map of all their travel, wanderings and whereabouts in New York City during the last three months, plotting on paper their perception of time-space in the Big Apple. Their map, I told them, was supposed to be an "aid to reverie," a tool for "annexing their private space into the public sphere." Then, they had to explore and draw the Beaux-Arts colonnade at the Manhattan Bridge anchorage, with the idea that urbanism was in fact "the organization of silence."

Though the discussions, laughter, confessions and astute comments generated by my students as we reviewed their serendipitous maps and awkward sketches reaffirmed my faith in design and art education, I am not sure they *really* got it. How could they? Unlike my instructor in Paris forty years ago, I couldn't ask my M.F.A. students to spend a whole semester observing the sidewalk. My education at the government-sponsored Beaux-Arts school of architecture had been free, whereas, in contrast, theirs was expensive. To pay for their hefty tuition, my students had gone into debt, worked overtime or impoverished themselves. I was keenly aware that I couldn't squander their money—they were consumers of a knowledge I was trying to share with them. As a result, my class had to be a spectacle of sorts—not the powerful and lasting experience gained by the subversion of spectacle.

ON FTF
Loretta Staples

The recent multiple publishings of the First Things First Manifesto 2000 came as no surprise to me. We're now at the turn of the millennium, and the heady days of "graphic agitation" that preceded it have drawn to a close. Through the typographic radicalism of the mid-1980s through the 1990s, graphic design professionals got it all out of their systems. On top of it, the digital revolution that technically sustained all that agitation saw us through unprecedented shifts as the democratization of design wrested graphic control out of our (professional) hands. The end isn't just near. It's upon us. (Witness Rudy VanderLans's goodbye-ish declaration in *Emigre* 49 that "there are no significant debates happening in graphic design today.")

Sobriety and reflection seem in order.

Despite the earnest, well-intentioned re-declaration of the manifesto—an attempt to kick-start design into the new millennium—I remain skeptical. A significant portion of the design profession proves, day in and day out, its inability to engage complex critical topics—an inability most clearly conveyed in the lack of self-critique that characterizes design magazines, conferences, professional organizations and annual awards through which it publicizes and sustains itself (not to mention omnipresent corporate sponsorship). This describes the discursive space of design, the institutional delimiters that define our profession.

Yes, "there are pursuits more worthy of our problem-solving skills [than advertising and marketing]." Yes, "unprecedented environmental, social and cultural crises demand our attention." Yes, "many cultural interventions, social marketing campaigns, books, magazines, exhibitions, educational tools, television programs, films, charitable causes and other information design projects urgently require our expertise and help." Or do they?

Recently, I was reading a progressive political magazine, *Z*, and couldn't help but notice how "badly" designed it was—a desktop-published venture. But as soon as I caught myself recoiling (albeit slightly) from its appearance, I recognized how irrelevant professional graphic design was to *Z*'s identity, and to its editors and audience. As a designer I tried to envision how I might remake the magazine, but all my imaginings recast the publication in a crisp light completely antithetical to the spirit of the publication. This experience illuminated the limitations of my own initial response and the predictability of graphic conventions. Maybe *Z* is just fine as it is.

Could it be that increasingly graphic design is less the solution and more the

Originally published in *Emigre*, no. 52 (Fall 1999).

problem? This is the squeamish possibility professional graphic designers are loathe to confront, because in so doing, the profession risks undoing itself. This is the threat posed by any rigorous discursive critique. And graphic designers are as seduced as their clients and publics into believing design's mythological status (after all, we made the myth; it's called "self-promotion"). If graphic design is to begin re-situating itself as a cultural practice, this is where the conversation needs to begin: right at home. How inextricably linked is professional design to corporate agendas? Is anything besides optical pyrotechnics (read: "eye candy") at work within the award-winning designs we've all learned to love over this past decade? Does graphic design simply propagate the lingua franca of modern-day "production values," or is it (are we) capable of constituting more complex messages and meanings?

To begin grappling with these difficult questions is the real challenge. Designers tend to respond by "personalizing" their work (as an "expressive" counter-position to the neutral anonymity of "information"). But as far as I can tell, this just results in the next round of "radical" design, or even worse, bad "art."

I take issue with VanderLans's claim that there's "nothing that you can really sink your teeth into." There's a lot. But is the profession up to it? I'm wary. Design's cultural location precludes the vantage points that would afford insight. Those who've glimpsed through these peepholes are going elsewhere, if they haven't already, seeking new opportunities for visual critique and radical cultural practice. I suspect these renegades have always been around, but most designers are too busy patting themselves (and each other) on the back to notice critical alternatives. Designers need to stop talking to themselves. When design is able to recognize itself as "other," it will begin to come to terms with its own limitations and the opportunities that reside elsewhere.

An example: I didn't notice any response from the graphic design community to Thomas Frank's review of *Perverse Optimist* (see page 251), a compendium of Kalman's work. While I'm as much a fan as anyone, Frank's incisive review succinctly pointed out the limitations inherent in Kalman's critical position as a designer. Beneath the clever sophistication is a stunning naïveté: "What Kalman overlooks is that it is not simply a fluke that a 'radical' like him has become one of the most sought-after architects of the corporate façade . . . That business allows 'radicals' to do its graphic design is not the inexplicable exception, the 'crack in the wall' that Kalman believes to be such an opportunity for disruption; it is the rule." The design community has always been too busy idolizing Kalman to subject his work to serious critique. It took a cultural critic to point out the ironies. (I guess designers don't read *Artforum*, much less *Z*.)

In closing, I call on the manifesto's signers (and all its adherents) to take a close, hard look at the cultural location of your own practice. If you're serious about your claims, take apart everything you even thought you knew about what you're doing. Set out in uncharted territory. But if you do, if you really do, something tells me you'll no longer recognize what you're doing as design. Because that will no longer be what it is. For this new work, as a new kind of practice, will need a new name.

And we don't know what to call it yet.

CULTURE
AGENTS

Ⅰn the late Eighties Rudy VanderLans referred to graphic design as a "cultural force." At the time it seemed absurd that a service profession catering to the needs of clients could exert real influence on a broader culture, but VanderLans was simply repeating what progressive designers from the early twentieth century onward had asserted about their role as communicators influencing all facets of society. Proclamations espousing "Good Design Is Good Business" and "Good Design Is Good Citizenship" had been floating around for decades, but when the "cultural force" motto was coined (in a promotional advertisement for *Emigre* magazine) the modernist concept of design as savior of the world from evil had long been overtaken by an upswing of interest in style and fashion. And yet VanderLans was ahead of the curve. Graphic design and culture were indeed intersecting in a variety of significant ways, not the least of which was a unique relationship to the computer and digital revolutions that spawned the World Wide Web. Graphic designers had been thrust into the forefront of new media with pronounced impact on the consumer culture that availed itself of these new modes of communication.

Graphic design had indeed become a cultural agent, but not always for what might be considered *good* (a decidedly slippery and subjective measure that for the past two decades has pitted so-called socially responsible against socially apathetic designers). Critics argue that while it is a force, graphic design is also the tool of marketers and promoters that have tapped into hip codes as a way to entice and allure consumers into brand loyalties resulting in unnecessary expenditures that perpetuate wasteful indulgences. Of course, not all designers engage in such activity, but the very essence of graphic design is to fuel the excesses of consumer society.

The raging debates of the mid-Nineties through the present have centered on responsible practices and what that entails. As Max Bruinsma asks in his essay "Culture Agents" (page 57), can the same designer who produced cigarette billboards create an anti-smoking campaign? Or can designers work for large corporations and still retain the integrity necessary to be independent citizens? These grandiose questions about ethics and morals have had more gravity in a world where design is increasingly part of the problem *and* the solution of how much is too much coercion given our natural penchant to consume. As argued in essays in this provocative section, design is an agent that sparks desire, but must this be written off entirely as negative? Can there be coexistence between ideals of the heart and reality in the marketplace? Will graphic design continue to be a cultural force or a cultural farce?

Steven Heller

WHY JOHNNY CAN'T DISSENT
Thomas Frank

"The public be damned! I work for my stockholders." —William H. Vanderbilt, 1879
"Break the rules. Stand apart. Keep your head. Go with your heart."
—TV commercial for Vanderbilt perfume, 1994

Capitalism is changing, obviously and drastically, but our ideas about capitalism—about what's wrong with American life and about how the figures responsible are to be confronted—haven't changed much in thirty years. Call it, for convenience, the "countercultural idea." It holds that the paramount ailment of our society is conformity, a malady that has variously been described as over-organization, bureaucracy, homogeneity, hierarchy, logocentrism, technocracy, the Combine, the Apollonian. We all know what it is and what it does. It transforms humanity into "organization man," into "the man in they gray flannel suit." It is "Moloch whose mind is pure machinery," the "incomprehensible prison" that consumes "brains and imagination." It is artifice, starched shirts, tailfins, carefully mowed lawns and always, always the consciousness of impending nuclear destruction. It is a stiff, militaristic order that seeks to suppress instinct, to forbid sex and pleasure, to deny basic human impulses and individuality, to enforce through a rigid uniformity a meaningless plastic consumerism.

As this half of the countercultural idea originated during the 1950s, it is appropriate that the evils of conformity are most conveniently summarized with images of 1950s suburban correctness. You know, that land of sedate music, sexual repression, deference to authority, red-scares, and smiling white people standing politely in line to go to church. Constantly appearing as a symbol of arch-backwardness in advertising and movies, it is an image we find easy to evoke.

The ways in which this system are to be resisted are equally well understood and agreed upon. The Establishment demands homogeneity; we revolt by embracing diverse, individual lifestyles. It demands self-denial and rigid adherence to convention; we revolt through immediate gratification, instinct uninhibited, and liberation of the

Originally published in *Emigre*, no. 49 (Winter 1999). © 1995 The Baffler. Used with permission of the publisher (*www.thebaffler.com*).

libido and the appetites. Few have put it more bluntly than Jerry Rubin did in 1970. "Amerika says: 'Don't!' The yippies say: 'Do it!'" The countercultural idea is hostile to any law and every establishment. "Whenever we see a rule, we must break it," Rubin continued. "Only by breaking rules do we discover who we are." Above all, rebellion consists of a sort of Nietzschean antinomianism, an automatic questioning of rules, a rejection of whatever social prescriptions we've happened to inherit. Just Do It is the whole of the law.

The patron saints of the countercultural idea are, of course, the Beats, whose frenzied style and merry alienation still maintain a powerful grip on the American imagination. Even forty years after the publication of *On the Road*, the works of Kerouac, Ginsberg, and Burroughs remain the *sine qua non* of dissidence, the model for aspiring poets, rock stars, or indeed anyone who feels vaguely artistic or alienated. That frenzied sensibility of pure experience, life on the edge, immediate gratification, and total freedom from moral restraint which the Beats first propounded back in those heady days when suddenly everyone could have their own TV and powerful V-8, has stuck with us through all the intervening years and become something of a permanent American style. Go to any poetry reading and you can see a string of junior Kerouacs go through the routine, upsetting cultural hierarchies by pushing themselves to the limit, straining for that gorgeous moment of original vice when Allen Ginsberg first read "Howl" in 1955 and the patriarchs of our fantasies recoiled in shock. The Gap may have since claimed Ginsberg and *USA Today* may run feature stories about the brilliance of the beloved Kerouac, but the rebel race continues today regardless, with ever-heightening shit-references calculated to scare Jesse Helms, talk about sex and smack that is supposed to bring the electricity of real life, and ever-more determined defiance of the repressive rules and mores of the American 1950s— rules and mores which by now we know only from movies.

But one hardly has to go to a poetry reading to see the countercultural idea acted out. Its frenzied ecstasies have long since become an official aesthetic of consumer society, a monotheme of mass as well as adversarial culture. Turn on the TV and there it is instantly: the unending drama of consumer unbound and in search of an ever-heightened good time, the inescapable rock 'n' roll soundtrack, dreadlocks and ponytails bounding into Taco Bells, a drunken, swinging-camera epiphany of tennis shoes, outlaw soda pops, and mind-bending dandruff shampoos. Corporate America, it turns out, no longer speaks in the voice of oppressive order that it did when Ginsberg moaned in 1956 that *Time* magazine was

> always telling me about responsibility.
> Businessmen are serious. Movie producers are serious.
> Everybody's serious but me.

Nobody wants you to think they're serious today, least of all Time/Warner. On the contrary: the culture trust is now our leader in the Ginsbergian search for kicks upon kicks. Corporate America is not an oppressor but a sponsor of fun, provider of lifestyle accoutrements, facilitator of carnival, our slang-speaking partner in the quest for that ever-more apocalyptic orgasm. The countercultural idea has become capitalist ortho-doxy, its hunger for transgression upon transgression now perfectly suited to an eco-nomic-cultural regime that runs on ever-faster cyclings of the new; its taste for self-fulfillment and its intolerance for the confines of tradition now permitting vast lat-itude in consuming practices and lifestyle experimentation.

Consumerism is no longer about "conformity" but about "difference." Advertising teaches us not in the ways of puritanical self-denial (a bizarre notion on the face of it), but in orgiastic, never-ending self-fulfillment. It counsels not rigid adherence to the tastes of the herd but vigilant and constantly-updated individualism. We consume not to fit in, but to prove, on the surface at least, that we are rock 'n' roll rebels, each one of us as rule-breaking and hierarchy-defying as our heroes of the 60s, who now pitch cars, shoes, and beer. This imperative of endless difference is today the genius at the heart of American capitalism, an eternal fleeing from "sameness" that satiates our thirst for the New with such achievements of civilization as the infinite brands of iden-tical cola, the myriad colors and irrepressible variety of the cigarette rack at 7-11.

As existential rebellion has become a more or less official style of Information Age capitalism, so has the countercultural notion of a static, repressive Establishment grown hopelessly obsolete. However the basic impulses of the countercultural idea may have disturbed a nation lost in Cold War darkness, they are today in fundamental agree-ment with the basic tenets of Information Age business theory. So close are they, in fact, that it has become difficult to understand the countercultural idea as anything more than the self-justifying ideology of the new bourgeoisie that has arisen since the 1960s, the cultural means by which this group has proven itself ever so much better skilled than its slow-moving, security-minded forebears at adapting to the accelerated, always-changing consumerism of today. The anointed cultural opponents of capitalism are now capital-ism's ideologues.

The two come together in perfect synchronization in a figure like Camille Paglia, whose ravings are grounded in the absolutely non-controversial ideas of the golden Sixties. According to Paglia, American business is still exactly what it was believed to have been in that beloved decade, that is, "puritanical and desensualized." Its great opponents are, of course, liberated figures like "the beatniks," Bob Dylan, and the Beatles. Culture is, quite simply, a binary battle between the repressive Apollonian order of cap-italism and the Dionysian impulses of the counterculture. Rebellion makes no sense without repression; we must remain forever convinced of capitalism's fundamental hos-tility to pleasure in order to consume capitalism's rebel products as avidly as we do. It comes as little surprise when, after criticizing the "Apollonian capitalist machine" (in her book, *Vamps & Tramps*), Paglia applauds American mass culture (in *Utne Reader*), the pre-eminent product of that "capitalist machine," as a "third great eruption" of a Dionysian "paganism." For her, as for most other designated dissidents, there is no contradiction between replaying the standard critique of capitalist conformity and repressiveness and then endorsing its rebel products—for Paglia the car culture and Madonna—as the obvi-ous solution: the Culture Trust offers both Establishment and Resistance in one con-venient package. The only question that remains is why Paglia has not yet landed an endorsement contract from a soda pop or automobile manufacturer.

Other legendary exponents of the countercultural idea have been more fortunate— William S. Burroughs, for example, who appears in a television spot for the Nike corporation. But so openly does the commercial flaunt the confluence of capital and counterculture that it has brought considerable criticism down on the head of the aging beat. Writing in the *Village Voice*, Leslie Savan marvels at the contradiction between Burroughs's writings and the faceless corporate entity for which he is now pushing product. "Now the realization that *nothing* threatens the system has freed advertising to exploit even the most marginal elements of society," Savan observes. "In fact, being hip is no longer quite enough—better the pitchman be 'underground.'" Meanwhile Burroughs's manager insists, as all future Cultural Studies treatments of the ad will no doubt also insist, that Burroughs's presence actually makes the commercial "deeply subversive"—"I hate to repeat the usual mantra, but you know, homosexual drug addict, manslaughter, accidental homicide." But Savan wonders whether, in fact, it is Burroughs who has been assimilated by corporate America. "The problem comes," she writes, "in how easily any idea, deed, or image can become part of the sponsored world."

The most startling revelation to emerge from the Burroughs/Nike partnership is not that corporate America has overwhelmed its cultural foes or that Burroughs can somehow remain "subversive" through it all, but the complete lack of dissonance between the two sides. Of course Burroughs is not "subversive," but neither has he "sold out": His ravings are no longer appreciably different from the official folklore of American capitalism. What's changed is not Burroughs, but business itself. As expertly as Burroughs once bayoneted American proprieties, as stridently as he once proclaimed himself beyond the laws of man and God, he is today a respected ideologue of the Information Age, occupying roughly the position in the pantheon of corporate-cultural thought once reserved strictly for Notre Dame football coaches and positive-thinking Methodist ministers. His inspirational writings are boardroom favorites, his dark nihilistic burpings the happy homilies of the new corporate faith.

For with the assumption of power by Drucker's and Reich's new class has come an entirely new ideology of business, a way of justifying and exercising power that has little to do with the "conformity" and the "establishment" so vilified by the countercultural idea. The management theorists and "leadership" charlatans of the Information Age don't waste their time prattling about hierarchy and regulation, but about disorder, chaos, and the meaninglessness of convention. With its reorganization around information, capitalism has developed a new mythology, a sort of corporate antinomianism according to which the breaking of rules and the elimination of rigid corporate structure have become the central article of faith for millions of aspiring executives.

Dropping *Naked Lunch* and picking up *Thriving on Chaos*, the ground-breaking 1987 management text by Tom Peters, the most popular business writer of the past decade, one finds more philosophical similarities than one would expect from two manifestos of, respectively, dissident culture and business culture. If anything, Peters's celebration of disorder is, by virtue of its hard statistics, bleaker and more nightmarish than

Burroughs's. For this popular lecturer on such once-blithe topics as competitiveness and pop psychology there is nothing, absolutely nothing, that is certain. His world is one in which the corporate wisdom of the past is meaningless, established customs are ridiculous, and "rules" are some sort of curse, a remnant of the foolish 50s that exist to be defied, not obeyed. We live in what Peters calls "A World Turned Upside Down," in which whirl is king and in order to survive, businesses must eventually embrace Peters's universal solution: "Revolution!" "To meet the demands of the fast-changing competitive scene," he counsels, "we must simply learn to love change as much as we have hated it in the past." He advises businessmen to become Robespierres of routine, to demand of their underlings, "'What have you changed lately?,' 'How fast are you changing?,' and 'Are you pursuing bold enough change goals?'" "Revolution," of course, means for Peters the same thing it did to Burroughs and Ginsberg, Presley and the Stones in their heyday: breaking rules, pissing off the suits, shocking the bean-counters: "Actively and publicly hail defiance of the rules, many of which you doubtless labored mightily to construct in the first place." Peters even suggests that his readers implement this hostility to logocentrism in a carnivalesque celebration, drinking beer out in "the woods" and destroying "all the forms and rules and discontinued reports" and, "if you've got real nerve," a photocopier as well.

Today corporate antinomianism is the emphatic message of nearly every new business text, continually escalating the corporate insurrection begun by Peters. Capitalism, at least as it is envisioned by the best-selling management handbooks, is no longer about enforcing Order, but destroying it. "Revolution," once the totemic catchphrase of the counterculture, has become the totemic catchphrase of boomer-as-capitalist. The Information Age businessman holds inherited ideas and traditional practices not in reverence, but in high suspicion. Even reason itself is now found to be an enemy of true competitiveness, an out-of-date faculty to be scrupulously avoided by conscientious managers. A 1990 book by Charles Handy entitled *The Age of Unreason* agrees with Peters that we inhabit a time in which "there can be no certainty" and suggests that readers engage in full-fledged epistemological revolution. "Thinking Upside Down," using new ways of "learning which can . . . be seen as disrespectful if not downright rebellious," methods of approaching problems that have "never been popular with the upholders of continuity and of the status quo." Three years later the authors of *Reengineering the Corporation* ("a Manifesto for Business Revolution," as its subtitle declares) are ready to push this doctrine even further. Not only should we be suspicious of traditional practices, but we should cast out virtually everything learned over the past two centuries!

> Business reengineering means putting aside much of the received wisdom of two hundred years of industrial management. It means forgetting how work was done in the age of the mass market and deciding how it can best be done now. In business reengineering, old job titles, and old organizational arrangements—departments, divisions, groups, and so on—cease to matter. They are artifacts of another age.

As countercultural rebellion becomes corporate ideology, even the beloved Buddhism of the Beats wins a place on the executive bookshelf. In *The Leader as Martial Artist* (1993), Arnold Mindell, "Ph.D.," advises men of commerce in the ways of the Tao, mastery of which he likens, of course, to surfing. For Mindell's Zen businessman, as for the followers of Tom Peters, the world is a wildly chaotic place of opportunity, navigable only to an enlightened "leader" who can discern the "time-spirits" at work behind the scenes. In terms Peters himself might use were he a more meditative sort of inspirational professional, Mindell explains that "the wise facilitator" doesn't seek to prevent the inevitable and random clashes between "conflicting field spirits," but to anticipate such bouts of disorder and profit thereby.

Contemporary corporate fantasy imagines a world of ceaseless, turbulent change, of centers that ecstatically fail to hold, of joyous extinction for the craven gray-flannel creature of the past. Businessmen today decorate the walls of their offices not with portraits of President Eisenhower and emblems of suburban order, but with images of extreme athletic daring, with sayings about "diversity" and "empowerment" and "thinking outside the box." They theorize their world not in the bar car of the commuter train, but in weepful corporate retreats at which they beat their tom-toms and envision themselves as part of the great avant-garde tradition of edge-livers, risk-takers, and ass-kickers. Their world is a place not of sublimation and conformity, but of "leadership" and bold talk about defying the herd. And there is nothing this new enlightened species of businessman despises more than "rules" and "reason." The prominent culture-warriors of the right may believe that the counterculture was capitalism's undoing, but the antinomian businessmen know better. "One of the t-shirt slogans of the sixties read, 'Question authority,'" the authors of *Reengineering the Corporation* write. "Process owners might buy their reengineering team members the nineties quote: 'Question assumptions.'"

The new businessman quite naturally gravitates to the slogans and sensibility of the rebel 60s to express his understanding of the new Information World. He is led in what one magazine calls, "the business revolution" by the office-park subversives it hails as "business activists," "change agents," and "corporate radicals." He speaks to his comrades through commercials like the recent one for "Warp," a type of IBM computer operating system, in which an electric guitar soundtrack and psychedelic video effects surround hip executives with earrings and hairdos who are visibly stunned by the product's gnarly 'tude (It's a "totally cool way to run your computer," read the product's print ads). He understands the world through *Fast Company*, a successful new magazine whose editors take their inspiration from Hunter S. Thompson and whose stories describe such things as a "dis-organization" that inhabits an "anti-office" where "all vestiges of hierarchy have disappeared" or a computer scientist who is also "a rabble rouser, an agent provocateur, a product of the 1960s who never lost his activist fire or democratic values." He is what sociologists Paul Leinberger and Bruce Tucker have called "The New Individualist," the new and improved manager whose arty worldview and creative hip derive directly from his formative 60s days. The one thing this new executive is definitely *not* is Organization Man, the hyper-rational counter of beans, attender of church, and wearer of stiff hats.

In television commercials, through which the new American businessman presents his visions and self-understanding to the public, perpetual revolution and the gospel of rule-breaking are the orthodoxy of the day. You only need to watch for a few minutes before you see one of these slogans and understand the grip of antinomianism over the corporate mind:

> Sometimes You Gotta Break the Rules (Burger King)
>
> If You Don't Like the Rules, Change Them (WXRT-FM)
>
> The Rules Have Changed (Dodge)
>
> The Art of Changing (Swatch)
>
> There's no one way to do it. (Levi's)
>
> This is different. Different is good. (Arby's)
>
> Just Different from the Rest (Special Export beer)
>
> The Line Has Been Crossed: The Revolutionary New Supra (Toyota)
>
> Resist the Usual (The slogan of both Clash Clear Malt and Young & Rubicam—maybe they'll sue each other!)
>
> Innovate Don't Imitate (Hugo Boss)
>
> Chart Your Own Course (Navigator Cologne)
>
> It separates you from the crowd (Vision Cologne)

In most, the commercial message is driven home with the vanguard iconography of the rebel: screaming guitars, whirling cameras, and startled old timers who, we predict, will become an increasingly indispensable prop as consumers require ever-greater assurances that, Yes! You *are* a rebel! Just look at how offended they are!

The problem with cultural dissent in America isn't that it's been co-opted, absorbed, or ripped off. Of course it's been all these things. But the reason it has proven so hopelessly susceptible to such assaults is the same as the reason it has become so harmless in the first place, so toothless even before Mr. Geffen's boys discover it angsting away in some bar in Lawrence, Kansas: it is no longer any different from the official culture it's supposed to be subverting. The basic impulses of the countercultural idea, as descended from the holy Beats, are about as threatening to the new breed of antinomian businessmen as Anthony Robbins, selling success & how to achieve it on a late-night infomercial.

Our businessmen imagine themselves rebels, and our rebels sound more and more like ideologists of business. Henry Rollins, for example, the maker of loutish, overbearing music and composer of high-school grade poetry, straddles both worlds unproblematically. Rollins's writing and lyrics strike all the standard alienated literary poses: he rails against over-civilization and yearns to "disconnect." He veers back and forth between vague threats towards "weak" people who "bring me down" and blustery declarations of his weightlifting ability and physical prowess. As a result he ruled for several years as the preeminent darling of *Details* magazine, a periodical handbook for the young executive on the rise where rebellion has achieved a perfect synthesis with corporate ideology. In 1992 *Details* named Rollins a "rock 'n' roll samurai," an "emblem . . . of a new masculinity" whose "enlightened honesty" is "a way of being that seems to flesh out many of the ideas expressed in contemporary culture and fashion." In 1994, the magazine consummated its relationship with Rollins by naming him "Man of the Year," printing a fawning story about his muscular worldview and decorating its cover with a photo in which Rollins displays his tattoos and rubs his chin in a thoughtful manner.

Details found Rollins to be such an appropriate role model for the struggling young businessman not only because of his music-product, but because of his excellent "self-styled identity," which the magazine describes in terms normally reserved for the breast-beating and soul-searching variety of motivational seminars. Although he derives it from the quality-maximizing wisdom of the East rather than the unfashionable doctrines of Calvin, Rollins's rebel posture is identical to that fabled ethic of the small capitalist whose regimen of positive thinking and hard work will one day pay off. *Details* describes one of Rollins's songs, quite seriously, as "a self-motivational superforce, an anthem of empowerment," teaching lessons that any aspiring middle-manager must internalize. Elsewhere Iggy Pop, that great chronicler of the ambitionless life, praises Rollins as a "high achiever" who "wants to go somewhere." Rollins himself even seems to invite such an interpretation. His recent spoken-word account of touring with Black Flag, delivered in an unrelenting two-hour drill-instructor staccato, begins with the timeless bourgeois story of opportunity taken, of young Henry leaving the security of a "straight job," enlisting with a group of visionaries who were "the hardest working people I have ever seen," and learning "what hard work is all about." In the liner notes he speaks proudly of his Deming-esque dedication to quality, of how his bandmates "Delivered under pressure at incredible odds." When describing his relationship with his parents for the readers of *Details*, Rollins quickly cuts to the critical matter, the results that such dedication has brought: "Mom, Dad, I outgross both of you put together," a happy observation he repeats in his interview with the *New York Times Magazine*.

Despite the extreme hostility of punk rockers with which Rollins had to contend all through the 1980s, it is he who has been chosen by the commercial media as the godfather of rock 'n' roll revolt. It is not difficult to see why. For Rollins the punk rock decade was but a lengthy seminar on leadership skills, thriving on chaos, and total quality management. Rollins's much-celebrated anger is indistinguishable from the anger of the frustrated junior executive who finds obstacles on the way to the top. His discipline and determination are the automatic catechism of any small entrepreneur who's just finished brainwashing himself with the latest leadership and positive-thinking tracts; his poetry is the inspired verse of *21 Days to Unlimited Power* or *Let's Get Results, Not Excuses*. Henry Rollins is no more a threat to established power in America than was Dale Carnegie. And yet Rollins as king of the rebels—peerless and ultimate—is the message hammered home wherever photos of his growling visage appears. If you're unhappy with your lot, the Culture Trust tells us with each new tale of Rollins, if you feel you must rebel, take your cue from the most disgruntled guy of all: lift weights! work hard! meditate in your backyard! root out the weaknesses deep down inside yourself! But whatever you do, *don't* think about who controls power or how it is wielded.

• • •

The structure and thinking of American business have changed enormously in the years since our popular conceptions of its problems and abuses were formulated. In the meantime the mad frothings and jolly apolitical revolt of Beat, despite their vast popularity and insurgent air, have become powerless against a new regime that, one suspects, few of Beat's present-day admirers and practitioners feel any need to study or understand. Today that beautiful countercultural idea, endorsed now by everyone from the surviving Beats to shampoo manufacturers, is more the official doctrine of corporate America than it is a program of resistance. What we understand as "dissent" does not subvert, does not challenge, does not even question the cultural faiths of Western business. What David Rieff wrote of the revolutionary pretensions of multiculturalism is equally true of the countercultural idea: "The more one reads in academic multiculturalist journals and in business publications, and the more one contrasts the speeches of CEOs and the speeches of noted multiculturalist academics, the more one is struck by the similarities in the way they view the world." What's happened is not co-optation or appropriation, but a simple and direct confluence of interest.

The people who staff the Combine aren't like Nurse Ratched. They aren't Frank Burns, they aren't the Church Lady, they aren't Dean Wormer from *Animal House*, they aren't those repressed old folks in the commercials who want to ban Tropicana Fruit Twisters. They're hipper than you can ever hope to be because *hip is their official ideology*, and they're always going to be there at the poetry reading to encourage your "rebellion" with a hearty "right on, man!" before you even know they're in the auditorium. You can't outrun them, or even stay ahead of them for very long: it's their racetrack, and that's them waiting at the finish line to congratulate you on how *outrageous* your new style is, on how you *shocked* those really stuffy prudes out in the heartland.

CULTURE AGENTS
Max Bruinsma

Back in that mythical year of rebellion, 1968, a German student leader in Paris named Rudy Dutschke developed an idea that sounded blasphemous to his French counterparts, the young revolutionaries who were about to storm the next Bastille. Dutschke argued that trying to seize the strongholds of bourgeois power by

This is an expanded version of an article originally published in *Adbusters*, no. 37 (September/October 2001).

force would amount to romantic heroism of the most ineffective kind. Instead, he proposed a rather less sexy strategy: go in, behave—and take over. He called it "the long march through the institutions."

Dutschke's idea of slowly infiltrating the centers of power and engendering change from within had a fatal flaw: it didn't take into account an age-old reflex of youthful activism—they want the world, and they want it *now*. To work patiently in the lair of the enemy until you've reached the point where you can stand tall and say, "We're going to make some changes around here," is a tough act to follow. Even today, when youth often seems a prerequisite for power, it is hard to withstand the lure of the status quo once you are a part of it.

On the other hand, there has probably been no time in history when Dutschke's strategy could be employed more successfully. Today's institutions are hardly the buttressed retreats of the powerful they once were. And power itself has been considerably democratized, by the joint forces of flattening social hierarchies and the empowering effects of the media. The average individual in Western society has more tools, more platforms and more opportunity to fight for what he thinks is right than the Paris revolutionaries could have ever dreamed of. Everybody can have their fifteen minutes of fame now. The question has become: how to use them? And why?

Design is an essential factor in answering this question. A famous Paris '68 slogan was, "*l'Imagination au pouvoir!*" It was a slap in the face of those who tried to keep things as they were, unquestioned. Design played a pivotal role in the Paris uprising that year, not only in getting the message across that things *could* be different, but, more importantly, getting people to read it with a broad smile of recognition, which any marketeer will confirm is the first stage of action. The power of imagination has since proven to be immense—and totally unattached to ideology. Some of the Paris activists' poster designs and slogans can compete with the best art direction and copy writing ever— "Under the Pavement, the Beach!"—but the design lessons implicit in activism have been embraced most effectively by that old stooge of Big Capital, advertising. And not just since 1968. With only slight exaggeration, one can hold that any innovation in mass propaganda has started with the powers that be slashing the opposition and taking over their PR approach. The techniques of mass communication are as "value-free" as elementary math. What counts is the reason for using them: is it to sedate consumers or to activate citizens?

This distinction cannot be made so clearly anymore. What if Benetton proves to be a serious factor in raising AIDS awareness? What if Greenpeace starts selling branded pullovers through a worldwide network of franchises? Well, then those who think that commercialism and good causes are incompatibly opposed have a problem. Which they do.

I'm convinced that one can do both: earn a good living by working for companies that are not obviously out to poison the world (although they may have their tacky sides), and at the same time work with those whose critical view on the bigger picture you share. Although it is hard to imagine that an anti-tobacco billboard could be made by the same designer who creates Marlboro ads, allegiance and critique are not incompatible—*should* not be incompatible. The idea that one should be completely and utterly faithful to those who pay you strikes me as rather medieval. As does the idea of total and utter opposition to anything that doesn't comply with your own standards. The absolute antithesis between an ideologically purist periphery and the corrupted centers of power seems to me to be as obsolete as that between Utopia and Babylon. They both have become suburbs of the global village, with a lot of traffic between them.

One great potential of the mediated society, with its open access to the infrastructures of mass communication, is that if you care enough, you can make a difference right in the center of the discourse. Although you may not be in a position to forge radical change *now*, you could be part of the public debate and help change the perspective. Showing the other side of issues that are being hijacked by single-interest lobby groups and compensating for simplistic views on complex problems, are activities for which graphic designers are very well placed. As communicators in a world which hinges on communication, they share a large part of the responsibility for the quality of the public debate.

Culturally speaking, in spite of the growing forces of corporate convergence and globalization, the world has become a network of peripheries. These peripheries may be called lifestyles, subcultures, pressure organizations, lobby groups, themed communities, special interests, activists or what have you, but regardless of their tag, they interlink, communicate, interact and overlap. Linking these peripheries with each other and with what remains of the centers of cultural identity and power is a design commission of the greatest importance. In my view, it's a commission that is central to any design activity—it is here that designers actively become cultural agents.

Maybe this is the designers' version of the "long march through the institutions": designers *can* make a huge difference, not just because they know how to make things look appealing—although that helps—but more importantly because they are, or ought to be, experts in imaginative communication and in structuring messages to be understood by a broad audience. Since design has become not just a problem-solving tool but a visual language, designers are in a perfect position to channel critical notions and alternative views into even the most prosaic commissions. When working from this mentality, designers could take the imagination to the next level, activating a critical sensibility instead of merely triggering buying impulses. This view on design will not accept that design's visual language be used as a "hidden persuader" (Vance Packard, 1957). Quite the contrary: it aims at being openly provocative, directed at a critical and visually literate audience.

Commercial culture today pays lip service to an increasingly critical public, adopting slogans like, "Sometimes you gotta break the rules" (Burger King), "Innovate don't imitate" (Hugo Boss), or, "Be an original" (Chesterfield cigarettes). In his exemplary article on advertising as "the whispering intruder" (*Eye*, no. 29, Autumn 1998), Rick Poynor pointed out that "this rhetoric, exhilarating as it might sound, is nonsense—there is nothing remotely radical about upholding the status quo, however stylishly you do it—it is part of a larger tendency, particularly in American advertising, to claim for the consumer the language and 'attitude' of uncompromising rebellion."

When "rebellion" becomes a lifestyle option promoted by major commodity brands, it's time to regain some of the territory lost to advertising and hark back to the lessons of Paris '68. True, they were designers of their own messages. They had not yet begun the "long march." But quite a few of them, in Paris and elsewhere, have subsequently shown that commercial success and social responsibility are not incompatible. Their design mentality is a *modus operandi* that judges form in terms of content, and sees content in terms of action. Since the core of design, for any medium, is to connect information with actions by readers or users in a social and cultural context, it follows that designers should be aware of their ethical and social responsibilities. From this mindset the world of communication is regarded not as the abstract result of information theory, nor as a neutral field of "problem-solving" expertise, but as a very real environment in which real people interact on the basis of real needs and real information. Beyond formal virtuosity, the designer has a responsibility, as Dutch designer Jan van Toorn put it in the 1970s, to "visualize the origins and manipulative character of a message"—a necessity that grows all the more urgent as the information society shifts towards an information deluge. This mentality of engagement with the contexts of design, and with the people and causes which it serves, can be the basis for engendering change in a society and culture which are *not yet* perfect.

Even if a studio's main work is "mainstream," a periphery of experimental and communitarian work can still be central to its development and innovation. Imagine that every design studio donated a small percentage of its time and resources to "the public cause," however they perceive it—this single act would help take back some of the public domain that is now so dominated by advertising in its blandest form. It could give an effective quality impulse to the public debate on matters that are now discussed mainly along the distant edges of power. Design can be a potent tool to channel these peripheries back to the center of the civil discourse of democracy, the *agora*, the marketplace of ideas and opinions which is the public domain. That, ultimately, is what responsible designers, as cultural agents, should aim at: keeping the eyes and minds of their fellow citizens wide open.

THE CASE FOR BRANDS

by the editors of the Economist

Far from being instruments of oppression, they make firms accountable to consumers

Imagine a world without brands. It existed once, and still exists, more or less, in the world's poorest places. No raucous advertising, no ugly billboards, no McDonald's. Yet, given a chance and a bit of money, people flee this Eden. They seek out Budweiser instead of their local tipple, ditch nameless shirts for Gap, prefer Marlboros to homegrown smokes. What should one conclude? That people are pawns in the hands of giant companies with huge advertising budgets and global reach? Or that brands bring something that people think is better than what they had before?

The pawn theory is argued, forcefully if not always coherently, by Naomi Klein, author of *No Logo*, a book that has become a bible of the anti-globalization movement. Her thesis is that brands have come to represent "a fascist state where we all salute the logo and have little opportunity for criticism because our newspapers, television stations, Internet servers, streets, and retail spaces are all controlled by multinational corporate interests." The ubiquity and power of brand advertising curtails choice, she claims; produced cheaply in third-world sweatshops, branded goods displace local alternatives and force a gray homogeneity on the world.

Brands have thus become stalking horses for international capitalism. Outside the United States, they are now symbols of American's corporate power, since most of the world's best-known brands are American. Around them accrete all the worries about environmental damage, human-rights abuses, and sweated labor that anti-globalists like to put on their placards. No wonder brands seem bad.

PRODUCT POWER OR PEOPLE POWER

Yet this is a wholly misleading account of the nature of brands. They began as a form not of exploitation, but of consumer protection. In pre-industrial days, people knew exactly what went into their meat pies and which butchers were trustworthy; once they moved to cities, they no longer did. A brand provided a guarantee of reliability and quality. Its owner had a powerful incentive to ensure that each pie was as good as the previous one, because that would persuade people to come back for more.

Originally published in the *Economist*, 8 September 2001. © 2001 The Economist Newspaper Group, Inc. (*www.economist.com*). Reprinted with permission. Further reproduction prohibited.

Just as the distance created a need for brands in the nineteenth century, so in the age of globalization and the Internet it reinforces their value. A book-buyer might not entrust a company based in Seattle with his credit card number had experience not taught him to trust the Amazon brand; an American might not accept a bottle of French water were it not for the name of Evian. Because consumer trust is the basis of all brand values, companies that own the brands have an immense incentive to work to retain that trust.

Indeed, the dependence of successful brands on trust and consistent quality suggests that consumers need more of them. In poor countries, the arrival of foreign brands points to an increase in competition from which consumers gain. Anybody in Britain old enough to remember the hideous Wimpy, a travesty of a hamburger, must recall the arrival of McDonald's with gratitude. Public services live in a No Logo world: attempts at government branding arouse derision. That is because brands have value only where consumers have choice, which rarely exists in public services. The absence of brands in the public sector reflects a world like that of the old Soviet Union, in which consumer choice has little role.

Brands are the tools with which companies seek to build and retain customer loyalty. Because that often requires expensive advertising and good marketing, a strong brand can raise both prices and barriers to entry. But not to insuperable levels: brands fade as tastes change (Nescafé has fallen, while Starbucks has risen); the vagaries of fashion can rebuild a brand that once seemed moribund (think of cars like the Mini or Beetle); and quality of service still counts (hence the rise of Amazon). Many brands have been around for more than a century, but the past two decades have seen many more displaced by new global names, such as Microsoft and Nokia.

Now a change is taking place in the role of brands. Increasingly, customers pay more for a brand because it seems to represent a way of life or a set of ideas. Companies exploit people's emotional needs as well as their desires to consume. Hence Nike's "just-do-it" attempt to persuade runners that it is selling personal achievement, or Coca-Cola's relentless effort to associate its fizzy drink with carefree fun. Companies deliberately concoct a story around their service or product, trying to turn a run-of-the-mill purchase (think of Häagen-Dazs ice cream) into something more thrilling.

This peddling of superior lifestyles is something that irritates many consumers. They disapprove of the vapid notion that spending more on a soft drink or ice cream can bring happiness or social cachet. Fair enough: and yet people in every age and culture have always hunted for ways to acquire social cachet. For medieval European grandees, it was the details of dress, and sumptuary laws sought to stamp out imitations by the lower orders; now the poorest African country has its clothing markets where second-hand designer labels command a premium over pre-worn No Logo.

The flip side of the power and importance of a brand is its growing vulnerability. Because it is so valuable to a company, a brand must be cosseted, sustained and protected. A failed advertising campaign, a drop-off in quality or a hint of scandal can all quickly send customers fleeing. Indeed, protesters, including Ms. Klein's anti-globalization supporters, can use the power of the brand against companies by drumming up

evidence of workers ill-treated or rivers polluted. Thanks, ironically enough, to globalization, they can do this all round the world. The more companies promote the value
of their brands, the more they will need to seem ethically robust and environmentally
pure. Whether protesters will actually succeed in advancing the interests of those they
claim to champion is another question. The fact remains that brands give them far more
power over companies than they would otherwise have. Companies may grumble about
that, but it is hard to see why the enemies of brand "fascism" are complaining.

TRUTH IN ADVERTISING
Naomi Klein

The young blonde girl has a bar code tattooed on her forehead as if she were a box of corn flakes. The indignant words "I am NOT a piece of your inventory" appear beside her. And in the corner: "www.zeroknowlege.com."

When I first saw this print ad, I figured it was just another dot.com trying to
do the reverse-marketing thing: isn't it terrible the way kids are preyed upon by marketers? Listen, we feel your pain. Now let us tell you about a great new way to buy
toothpaste online. . . .

What I didn't know at the time was that Zero Knowledge sells encryption software for the Internet that allows users to surf and make purchases without having their
every move "data mined" by market researchers. This isn't another "Image Is Nothing,
Thirst Is Everything" Sprite campaign; Zero Knowledge really is selling a product that
protects kids from predatory marketing, just like the ad claims. In other words, this company was doing something very strange indeed: in a marketscape filled with cognitive
dissonance, double talk and outright lies, it was telling the truth. The possibility hadn't
even occurred to me.

If I seem cynical, it's because I have spent far too much time studying corporate branding campaigns and their complicated relationship with the truth. I'm not talking about whether Tide really gets your clothes whiter but another, more problematic
kind of advertising truth. Over the past fifteen years, most successful brand-driven companies have attempted to cut through the clutter of consumer culture by forging deeper,
more lasting relationships with their customers. They have done this, for the most part,
by developing sophisticated "brand identities," a process which, for lack of a better
description, is about identifying the inner truth of a corporation.

Originally published in *AIGA Journal of Graphic Design* Vol. 18, no. 2 (2000).

In many ways, the branding process mimics the rituals of spiritual or religious quests for truth and enlightenment. To identify their company's brand identity, executives and brand managers sequester themselves in retreats as they probe the deepest meanings of Unilever or Cisco Systems. They emerge from their Socratic sweat lodges clutching profound truths about human aspirations and ideals. We have heard from Nike, for instance, that it is not a shoe company but an organization whose mission is to communicate notions of transcendence. We have heard from Starbucks that it isn't about coffee, but community and "the third place"; we have heard from Microsoft that it is not a software company but a possibilities company, that IBM sells not computers, but "solutions." Martha Stewart is not a home decorator or a caterer but an ideology about old-time family nurturing and doing it yourself. Polaroid's inner brand is joy, not to be confused with the Gap, which isn't selling clothing but unrestrained exuberance.

After their inner truths have been revealed, these companies then produce extraordinarily elegant brand image campaigns to express their new identities. This is a very involved process. First, it requires constant transfusions of fresh meaning: new political ideas, new music, new ideas about community, new historical figures to mine. Next, it requires new pieces of cultural real estate to play host to the campaigns: branded lifestyle magazines, sponsored concerts and art exhibitions, interactive superstores, billboards so large they swallow entire buildings.

Dwarfed by these ambitious branding projects, it becomes difficult for mere mortals to compete with their own expressions of meaning, which is precisely why, increasingly, it is brands—not intellectuals or activists or religious leaders—that are the principle truth-tellers of our corporate age. They are the ones speaking loudest about meaning, helping us to look with awe and wonder at the world, even if what we are looking at, ultimately, are branded sneakers, lattes and laptop computers.

Quite understandably, the people behind these campaigns have come to think of themselves as cultural philosophers, spiritual guides, artists, even political leaders. For instance, Benetton, rather than using its ads to extol the virtues of its clothing, opted instead to communicate what Oliviero Toscani believed to be fundamental truths about the injustice of capital punishment. According to the company's communication policy, "Benetton believes that it is important for companies to take a stance in the real world instead of using their advertising budget to perpetuate the myth that they can make consumers happy through the mere purchase of their product."

It seems like a noble goal, yet Benetton's political branding campaigns implicitly promise customers a happiness of another sort—not just beauty, status or style, the traditional claims fashion companies make, but virtue and engagement. And that's where the problems arise, because this claim is simply not true. Benetton's clothing has nothing to do with AIDS or war or the lives of prisoners on death row, and by using these issues in sweater advertisements, Benetton is inserting a layer of distance and mediation—represented by the Benetton name itself—between consumers and these important issues. Put another way, Benetton's political campaigns aren't about truth *in* advertising, but truth *instead* of advertising, the transformation of truth itself into a marketing product.

Though less dramatically, this experience is present in almost all ambitious brand-meaning projects. There is a fundamental dichotomy between the promise embedded in brand meaning campaigns—of community, of transcendence, of pure joy—and the usually banal experience of consumption. Quite simply, branding doesn't deliver. We don't find community at Starbucks, a global commons through Cisco or transcendence through Nike, just as we don't find political engagement through Benetton.

Because enlightenment is permanently out of stock at the mall, as brand managers seek to deepen their quest for truth and meaning, they necessarily sever ties with the products and services they are actually selling, thereby fostering even more cognitive dissonance. The brand has evolved, as Tibor Kalman put it, from a mark of quality on the product to a "stylistic badge of courage" on the consumer. And because these badges, no matter how beautiful, no matter how filled with brilliant insight, have been divorced from the products they represent, the entire corporate branding industry is rapidly poisoning our relationship with the very idea of truth.

It shouldn't be at all surprising that this process is breeding a kind of anti-brand backlash. As marketing becomes more ambitious, and brand identities more meaning-filled, companies such as Nike, Starbucks, Wal-Mart and Microsoft are increasingly finding themselves the target of activist campaigns slamming them for everything from alleged sweatshop abuses to predatory business practices. More and more, activists, connected to one another on the Internet, are taking the claims that corporations make in their marketing campaigns and measuring them against their real-world corporate practices, with often devastating results. Commenting on the phenomenon, Scott Bedbury, a former brand manager for both Nike and Starbucks, describes the Internet as "a truth serum" for brands, actively helping consumers to expose the hypocrisy behind even the most successful branding campaigns.

This rise of anti-brand activism is a direct response to the dichotomy between the powerful claims brands place on truth and meaning, and the reality of what consumer products deliver and how they are manufactured. The branding economy is a series of broken promises, of unfulfilled desires. It feeds off of all that is truthful in our culture and then ritualistically betrays those truths by using them not for self-knowledge or social change, but as props.

SUSTAINABLE CONSUMERISM
Chris Riley

I'm an advertising guy.
    I wanted to make that clear as we engage in this conversation about sustainability. Advertising is intrinsic to consumerism and, as you all know, consumerism is about creating desire.

Now, I am very happy in this environment. I like advertising. I enjoy helping create it and I enjoy being associated with strong businesses that are growing. Strong businesses are important. I grew up in Manchester, England in the Seventies. Let me tell you, you learn a lot about the importance of strong businesses when they are in short supply. So I come at this question of "sustainability" from that place. I am not an "environmentalist" in the classic sense. I have not dedicated my life to protecting our environment, though I have huge respect for those who have.

One of the big inventions of consumerism is the "brand." You all intuitively know what I mean when I talk about brand. Yet there are as many different perspectives on what brands are as there are brand owners. It may help if I share with you the way I think about brands. I think of brands as business ideas that have achieved cultural influence. Big brands influence culture in a big way, small brands in a small way.

What interests me about this perspective is that it hinges on two huge ideas. The first is that a brand is a "business idea" and the second is the notion of cultural influence.

Let's talk first about a business idea. There has been a lot of work done on this subject. On the one hand you can focus on the business "model." The business model is all about the way a business creates wealth. For the last few years, many young technology entrepreneurs have been presenting their business models to venture capitalists for investment. The VC looks at their presentation and asks two questions: is this a good business model that will generate a return on my investment, and is this person likely to do it for me? The business model is about capitalism. It is about Return on Investment (ROI). It is about the Commodity. In one of its most refined forms, the business model's effectiveness hinges on the financial value ascribed to relationships. This is the way capitalism renders everything as a commodity, to be bought and sold. For example, the value of AOL exists within the relationships created by the service. These relationships are then exploited to create wealth.

The problem with this way of thinking about business is that is under-represents the social and cultural role of business. When Time/Warner merged with AOL,

---

Originally published in *Emigre*, no. 59 (Summer 2001). Originally delivered as a presentation at the Metropolis Design Conference in San Francisco, February 2001.

what kind of business would be created as a consequence? Is AOL's commodity, its relationships with people, like my daughter at her iMac in her bedroom, to be traded as, well, just any other stuff? I understand that the contents of an oil field, for example, are an easy commodity to understand, or the value of owning land, or the ability to make a fine automobile, or . . . but wait. Things are looking harder as I go through that list.

In the film *Wall Street*, we are introduced to Gordon Gecko—remember "lunch is for wimps"? The film reveals the way business commoditizes everything within a capitalist system. The futures of the workers' lives are in the hands of traders who care little and understand less about them. The young adventurer ends up in a limo with a beautiful woman who informs him that he has earned a reward from Gecko—her. The film uncovers the ugly truth of pure capitalism: the human experience is simply another commodity to be traded for financial gain.

It need not be so. In fact, other work in the field of business analysis suggests that a pure focus on the capital aspects of business is a deeply flawed way of thinking about how business works and how businesses can succeed in the long run. Some early pioneers of consumer businesses seemed to understand this: Ford, Kohler, Cadbury and Lever, to name a few. In their world, business was an integral part of society. The role of the business was not only to generate wealth for the business owner, but to create opportunity for all who engaged in the business transaction, from the entry-level employee to the most distant customer. Business is a practice, not an entity. It is entirely the product of relationships. As capital became more and more powerful, primarily as technology enabled businesses to scale to the global level, so the human relationship factors that underpin business were eroded. This is where we find ourselves today.

The emergence of corporatism as the dominant ethic of business analysis is recent and will be transient. As Kees van der Heijden has pointed out in his book *Scenario: The Art of Strategic Conversation*, "We define structural profit potential as an attribute of a system capable of creating value for customers in a unique way that others find difficult to emulate." In other words, profit is an outcome, not a sole reason, for business. Many who have started small businesses or are part of family enterprises understand this deeply. Those who have lived through harsh times in Flint, Michigan or Liverpool, England are also aware of this simple, human truth.

What seems to be happening as we enter the next phase of our economic evolution is that many of these chickens are coming home to roost. Businesses that focused solely on maximizing financial ROI seem to have become disconnected from their customers, their employees and their shareholders. This powerful alliance—with many individuals participating in all three experiences—can be credited with driving a fundamental change in the environment for business in the twenty-first century.

I wonder why?

Information technology had stimulated the creation of a culture of knowledge and it is sweeping the world. In the culture of knowledge everything seems knowable, but also everyone wants to know. From the vicarious experience of survival to a basic understanding of the capitalist system and its attendant marketing habits, people feel smart and informed. And guess what? They are.

The world of marketing and the world of brands have been rocked by these changes. Nothing seems to work quite as it did. Which brings me to that idea of "cultural influence." It turns out that the degree to which businesses engaged with their public, creating relationships that either sustained, evolved or eroded value, was linked less to their ability to create powerful business models and more to their ability to create valuable *relationships*. This is news to many in the M.B.A.–riddled world of U.S. consumer marketing, but it is an unquestioned fact of life in Asia and Europe. Here's what happened.

As marketing mechanized the process of relationship management, the consumer got less emotional value out of the relationship. If money is a symbol of the value of a relationship, they simply reduced the amount of money they were willing to pay for the relationship they had with amoral marketing companies. These companies are not bad, but they are sort of culturally autistic. By remaining unable to engage with consumers as human beings with rich cultural lives and complex social environments, businesses were unable to communicate. Thus, they tended to scream and become abusive the more they craved and needed consumer attention. We see the results of cultural autism on our screens every day: persistently aggravating advertising sending manifestly corrupt messages into our homes.

But in the culture of knowledge the consumer knows. And is rebelling. Recent research that I have been involved in at Wieden & Kennedy has begun to highlight what is going on. We were interested in the evolving relationship between the consumer and big business. We had already come to the view that the brand was a surrogate for the business idea and that if we were to evolve and grow the brands we worked on, we needed to understand more deeply what they symbolized and how people were relating to them.

As part of one study, I was in Tokyo talking to a producer of Japanese hip-hop records about the idea of being "modern." I mention this because in some ways the transcendent themes of the modern experience were there to be witnessed within that conversation. He was twenty-six. I was forty-two. He was from Tokyo. I was from Manchester. Yet we were both intimately aware of and engaged with the work of Ian Anderson and The Designers Republic. When I asked him (through our excellent translator, who had herself lived in Kensington, London, only three blocks from my old home) how he perceived the idea of the modern and where he saw culture evolving, he said: "To a more mental place." He went on to discuss in depth the fact that products have narratives as well as benefits. We know everything about these products. The whole story. From the vantage point of someone born in 1975, business had to engage with the whole truth of consumerism. That involved two important and related realities: firstly, that non-sustainable consumption would destroy everything we have and could have, and secondly that the consumer experience was deeper and richer than is ever acknowledged by mainstream marketing.

As we at Wieden & Kennedy travel the world and talk to people for all types of reasons, these themes emerge. Big Business is not perceived to be a *de facto* problem: it is the lack of imagination, creativity and responsibility within the idea of corporate business that sucks. Brands are seen as manifestations, as surrogates, for the business people who create them. The consumer wants—no, demands—a relationship with those people.

From Brazil, a young media entrepreneur asks, "I just have one question: Who are you?"

And who can answer that simple question? The emergence of a culture of knowledge that is global in scale, due to the attendant networking that now defines communication and social interaction, has brought the real issues facing our Post–Industrial Age culture to the fore. Brands can no longer survive on a diet of artificial benefit creation (remember the Tense, Nervous Headache?) or the assumption that somehow we are dysfunctional and need to be "fixed." We, the individuals who consume, whose money oils the wheels of corporate capitalism, are not broken. We don't need to be fixed. We, to paraphrase an old Subaru ad I was involved in, don't need to use what we consume to increase our standing with our neighbors. We can relate to the size and shape of our bodies in a way that helps us enjoy the life, liberty and pursuit of happiness promised in our Constitution. We do not need products to be symbols of empowerment; we *have* power. We do not aspire to manufactured dreams that reduce our capacity to feel individual. In short, nearly every branding tactic of the past will fail in the future.

Because the nature of transaction between consumers and businesses has moved on.

The cultural role of brands is to respond to the spirit of the times. In the early 1930s, when Coke employed Norman Rockwell, the company transcended its role as a purveyor of refreshment and became deeply embedded in the emerging identity of American consumerism. These values were to sweep the world: optimism, faith in the possibility of harmonious diversity and egalitarianism. In an era when students were being shot at Kent State and carpet bombing was destroying the lives of hundreds of thousands of people on the South East Asian peninsula, Coke tried to "teach the world to sing . . . in perfect harmony." Like it or hate it, it was an attempt to project more than the benefit of refreshment. Its power lay in the confidence with which it voiced a perspective.

If we were to respond today, we would respond to the culture of corporate repulsion. By which I mean this: the transcendent themes of new consumers emerge from their experience as the progeny of the Consumer Age. They have known little else. They have engaged with and then experienced the emotional hollowness of the consumer promise, that what you buy dictates how well you feel. They still felt bad when things didn't go right. They have learned through experience that promises are shallow and that there must be an ulterior motive for everything. Some would say that they are cynical. But I do not believe that they are. I believe that they are aware.

As they view the world they are aware of how it is all linked. They did media studies in elementary school; they watched *Sesame Street* and learned about ecology from *Fern Gully*. What seems to be the case is that they have a different narrative than previous generations of consumers. Their narrative embraces their position within a complex and interlinked world. As millions of the young swap banalities yet create networks of relationships on AOL Instant Messenger, they understand only too well the power of causality: that what you do has an effect, somewhere.

They are translating that experience to their life as consumers. In fact, they are rethinking the way they consume. Rather than becoming trapped within the manufactured aspirations of the mass market, they are seeking to create experiences that connect them in a meaningful way to ideas and ideals that are worth something. They take control over their futures by taking control over their expectations. And, talking of futures, they are very concerned about the legacy of wanton excessive consumerism as practiced by the previous generation. In their view, they have inherited the consequences of consumption for consumption's sake with scant regard for the long-term future of either themselves or their children. Or, to put it another way, with scant regard for meaningful human relationships and responsibilities.

Surveys such as those of the Yankelovich Research Company have directed our attention for years to the evolution of a fresh perspective on consumption among the young. Well, it seems to be here, and if you are in any doubt you only need to look at the fortunes of the Fortune 500 and the near total collapse of the great marketing brands as they surrendered to the ultimate commoditzing business: Wal-Mart. What happened to Kellogg, McDonald's, P&G, Coke, Oldsmobile and a host of others is that they ceased to maintain and develop a dynamic business idea that intersected with the values of their customers. The brand is the manifestation of that relationship, as I have said, its surrogate. Van der Heijden would refer to this as a squandering of two things: distinctive competencies and a dynamic relationship with customers. Over time, the values of our consumers evolve and competitors emulate our core competencies, delivering them for less cost and reducing distinctiveness.

There are two distinct developments, one in the realm of competencies and one in the realm of consumer evolution, that threaten established brand owners who fail to create a dynamic model for brand and business development.

First, we need to acknowledge that the single-pointed pursuit of capital growth has thwarted attempts at creating a sustainable model of consumerism. Technology has been evolving at a hair-raising rate but business models have not. Detroit and the oil industry remain locked in a death grip grounded in the idea of exploitation for enrichment. The consequence: a pathetic response to increasing anxiety regarding all forms of pollution and near indifference to the issue of gradually disappearing resources. The automobile industry has been the bellwether of all consumerism but seems intent on donating that leadership to other categories that more effectively respond to the spirit of this age.

At a time when technology is delivering the means to reduce the impact of the car on our environment, Detroit is marketing machines that speak to the command and control exploitation culture of the past. The Lincoln Navigator, the Chevrolet Suburban. This is 1970s technology, but more important, this is 1970s culture. It is about dominance, power, exploitation, and it is deeply masculine, or rather a kind of warped version of masculinity that finds an echo in the corruption of sport at the hands of capitalism: the NFL, the NBA. This is how the new consumer sees the old brands.

Secondly, we need to accept that things are different now. The world in which our children have developed has taught them much. We have taught them much. They are individuals existing in complex cultural systems. They have transcended vague notions of monocultural national values and the politics of supremacy. They do not trust us. Their version of leadership is not command and control, it is not J.F.K., L.B.J., Churchill, Thatcher or Reagan. If the Clinton presidency taught us anything, it was surely this: leadership is about acknowledging uncertainty rather than manufacturing certainty. We are all flawed, and it is how we respond to that fact that defines our future. This sensibility is endemic among new consumers. The Cluetrain Manifesto reflected this as its authors indicated a way forward: markets are conversations. Absolutely, and so are brands. The question is, what do we want to discuss?

The answer is kind of everything.

At the top of the list is the identity question and the values consumers wish to be associated with as they engage in transactions with companies. Deeply embedded in this question lies their relationship with a world they feel increasingly connected to and in a small way responsible for. They no longer accept the cultural autism of corporate brands. They want a conversation about where we are together. What we are doing and how can we do it better? They want to enjoy the benefits of a healthy economy (don't we all?) without the guilt of screwing it up for everyone else. How can you enjoy your smart new shoes if you know there are unhappy people living in dangerous conditions so that you can have them? This was never part of the promise but it was always part of the reality. Now that reality is visible and the new consumer is aware and engaged. This means we have to be also.

The sustainability question is intrinsic to the identity question. In a culture that has rejected exploitation, has confronted inequity, and is striving for a utopian ideal of life, liberty and happiness, sustainability has huge cultural value. Within the semantics of the word is the resolution of a paradox: it is about keeping what we have, not losing it.

This means everything.

When you talk to new consumers, the idea of impact, or the idea of sustainability, is right at the front of their minds. It is in lock step with a variety of other humanitarian issues. It may be part of a mystical or spiritual value system. It may be part of a reality check and related to their immediate urban environment. It may simply be part of their general awareness of the world in which they live. Whatever the reason, it is there. It is part of their response to the disappointment of mass consumerism, particularly the mass consumerism created and fueled by the growth of television.

> While our cars may be shiny, and our stocks may be booming, there is another story to be told. There is an emptiness inside, a void in the soul of America. The TV functions as a conduit for the lowest common denominator of public dialogue. Whether it be Regis Philbin or *Beverly Hills 90210*, the world

learns about America by the cotton candy that we call "Must See TV." And it works. Only 25% of teenagers between the ages of 13–17 can name the city where the US Constitution was written, but a full 75% know that you can find the zip code 90210 in Beverly Hills, California. [Adam Werbach, *The Thin Green Line*]

I quote Adam Werbach because he is a particularly eloquent representative of the new consumer generation. Passionately committed to the Environmental Movement, he was the youngest-ever president of the Sierra Club (at age 26) and now propels his agenda through a video production company and Web site called "The Thin Green Line." As a media sophisticate, he understands the relationship between the issues of environmentalism and what he would consider to be the insidious actions of mass marketers in concealing the truth of consumption from the consumer. Of equal importance is the connection he draws between the feeling of loss that exists within our mass consumer culture and the explosion of environmental concerns. This connection is the critical link between the future and history of brands.

Consumerism's great contribution to Maslow's hierarchy is desire. In many cases branded goods are promoted as a means of self-actualization. The notion is that, fully empowered by access to the right stuff, an individual can get a grip on his or her own reality and project a kind of instant individuation, a personality that is both unique and yet belongs to a larger group. The trick is always, as we know, for the brand to influence the idea of the group to which people aspire. And people seem to like this.

It turns out that buying stuff because it satisfies desire is okay. In fact, it is rather pleasing. There are many people in the world today who would love the opportunity to get stuff because they want it rather than be restricted to only satisfying their needs. And before we run off in an apoplectic rage about the sinfulness of desire, I am afraid to tell you that it is a basic human truth. We want as well as need. The experience of desire is nice! We love it! In my view, the crisis of consumerism is not that it creates desire, but that it fails to satiate. Most critiques of consumerism and the advertising industry it created seem to focus on how bad creating desire is rather than asking if we can create desire for, well, something else.

This turns out to be on the minds of the new consumers: I want to want, but I want to want what will actually satisfy me.

So imagine if we, as the creative fuel of an evolving consumerism, were to shift the focus of desire from something we can never satiate to something we can. To me that is the essence of the new consumerism. It has all the thrill of the old, but this time it actually delivers.

This is where we can begin a serious conversation about sustainable consumerism. This is when we can look brand owners in the eye and talk honestly and openly about the challenges they face. The ability to create great stuff is not necessarily correlated to the ability to create great relationships. Within relationships that thrive, all parties are able to enjoy the experience. The brand owner who ignores the consumer-values part of the equation fails to acknowledge the human dimension to the relationship. As we proceed into a consumer world within which many different versions of the same stuff offer marginal differentiation for the consumer, we will become ever more reliant on the quality of the relationships we create. While the Internet utopians of rationality argue that information technology will reduce everything to price value based comparisons, the consumer is mourning the loss of human contact. The loss of valuable relationship. Just look at the mourning ritual of the recently bereaved Oldsmobile franchise.

In a recent speech to a conference hosted by *Metropolis* magazine, I put up the following slide: "The modern consumer adds environmental impact to the perceived cost of consumption and is attracted to companies who acknowledge their responsibility by embracing incremental improvements in environmental impact."

This observation was grounded in conversations we had with consumers in the research I have been involved in at Wieden & Kennedy. Here is what seems to be going on: the sustainability question has become a flash point for the anxiety that permeates the relationship people feel they have with business. The continuing lack of interest expressed through brands by business in this question is seen as symptomatic of the corporatization of the consumer experience. The profit motive is seen to have trumped basic human decency. Carl Pope, of the Sierra Club, once told me that the environment was the issue that almost guaranteed a young voter turnout. It has become a focus of their fear that they will lead meaningless lives in servitude to massive businesses whose sole concern is shareholder value. It signals the threat they feel: that they have little control over their lives and that business cannot be trusted.

The upshot of this is that "sustainability" has become their issue. The new consumer owns the new consumption, and their values will dictate which brands succeed and how. There is no barrier being put up by the consumer to the idea of sustainable consumption.

I was discussing these issues with a designer called Alex Gajowskyj. Alex had designed the "world shoe" for Nike. The idea was to create a product with minimal waste, designed for manufacture and usable by the people who made it. In a deep way, the project reflects the response a good company like Nike has when confronted by this issue. Nike has started to move towards sustainable consumption as it acknowledges the feelings of both its consumers and its employees. Alex's experiment was a central part of this evolution. In his words, this is what they learned:

> Tradition, natural opposition to change, and a reliance upon "tried and trusted"
> business practice represent the biggest obstacles for any business seeking global
> growth. [Alex Gajowskyj, Shoe Designer]

In other words, if the consumer is not the barrier, then the business is. Part of the dynamic evolution of distinctive competencies, to use Kees van der Heijden's idea, is to evolve away from the traditions and practices that hinder the ability of the business to engage fully with the consumer.

Evolving consumer values demand that modern brands rethink the transactions they rely on for consumer attention. This is why brand owners need to care about the sustainability question. It is a cultural phenomenon as well as a real issue. If brands are to respond to the spirit of the times, they need to respond to this most crucial element of contemporary culture. Furthermore, they need to acknowledge that, as a symbol, it is also a symptom of a deeper dysfunctionality between brands in general and the consumer. The relationship between consumer and mass brands has decayed to such a point that the days of premium-priced high-margin branded products seem to exist only in our fantasy world. We need to change that; people want more! But now they want more from us as people rather than more of our stuff.

Here is a comment by Clive Whitcher, who oversees Strategic Planning for Saatchi & Saatchi on their Toyota business:

> Prius buyers are ecstatic about the car and what it says about Toyota. Toyota's their hero for finally doing something tangible about the environment—one guy came to a group with a collage featuring evergreen springs and a rose stuck to (recycled) paper! The love is akin to what people felt in the '70s when Toyota was their savior—saving them from bad gas mileage when prices went up and there were lines at the gas station and of course from bad domestic quality and ridiculous domestic "downsized" compacts. [Clive Whitcher, Saatchi & Saatchi]

The movement has started. There are companies, like Nike and Toyota, that are responding to their consumers' deeply felt issues. But on a broader scale my question is: Where are the designers? Where are the ad guys? How can we develop skills and practices that respond to this evolution? How will we determine the effectiveness of what we do when the entire industry is trapped in an unevolved capitalist paradigm? How can clients trust that the advice they are being given responds to the reality of consumer culture when that advice remains locked in process-based thinking from the 1970s? It is time to challenge these traditions, as Gajowskyj has stated. We have in our midst the most well-informed talent in the history of our young industry. Coupled with mind-expanding technology that helps us learn and execute ideas better and faster than ever before, we have no excuse to fail the people we create our work for, both clients and consumers.

Sustainability is just that: it is about sustaining, providing nourishment, keeping going. Brand owners who nourish their consumers with meaningful ideas and representation, designers and advertising people who take a similar approach and help their clients keep going, will recognize that consumerism is, like everything else in our world, about evolution. In this case, evolution away from the self-destructive impulse of mass commoditization and towards a sustainable consumerism that satiates our desires for strong relationships grounded in our common humanity.

DON'T LET THE BUGGERS
GRIND YOU DOWN!
Ken Garland

Do you think large corporations should be allowed to splash the insignia of their Corporate ID over your country and my country and everyone else's country, without restraint? Of course you don't. However much you agree with freedom of choice, however much you object to censorship, however much you resent the straitjacket of mindless planning control that stifles originality and diversity, you surely believe that there must be some sort of limit to the public display of signs. Any one of us, confronted by some vast advertising billboard obscuring our view of a much loved and otherwise unspoiled landscape, would feel a surge of resentment at such an insensitive affront. Whether we would take it upon ourselves to do anything about it is another matter; but at least we share our strong disapproval and contribute to the climate of opinion on these matters.

Occasionally you hear that public pressure has had an effect on a particularly crass intrusion, and the offending party has been shamed or compelled into removing their sign. But as often as not those objecting are regarded as prudes, do-gooders, nosey-parkers, busy-bodies, snoopers, bigots—interesting, isn't it, how many pejorative terms may be summoned in order to denigrate the objectors?—are made to feel that the sin of censoriousness is greater than the sin of erecting a billboard just a bit bigger than some people might think appropriate; after all, it's only a matter of opinion, isn't it?

When it comes to the siting of signs and billboards in the urban environment we are in confusing territory. Certainly, there is a place for them: like most people I welcome the cheerful vulgarity of Piccadilly Circus; and on returning to New York, it's essential to make a beeline at the earliest opportunity for the high-voltage, neon-charged boost of Time Square's sign fest. But replicas of Times Square or Piccadilly Circus in the centers of every city in North America, and Europe, and Asia, and Africa, and so on? Certainly not, I hear you cry; there's a time and place for everything; we must be sensitive to the diversity and distinctiveness of our environments, be they the big city or small town; we are all conservationists now, de-da, de-da, de-da. . . .

Oh yes? And what about the ubiquitous signage of the multinationals, the Cokes and the Pepsis, the Holiday Inns and the Marriotts, the McDonald's and the BurgerKings? Where's the sensitivity, where's the respect for the diversity and distinctiveness of the environment? These marauding multis bang up their relentless, outsize Idents all over your town and my town and anyone's town, and their care for the envi-

---

Originally published in *AIGA Journal of Graphic Design* Vol 15, no. 1 (1997).

ronment is zilch. Never mind what they *say* (for of course, they have bevies of honey-tongued PR wordsmiths working around the clock on this one): look at what they *do*. From a rogues' gallery stretching from Central Europe to Central Asia, from the Yucatan to the Yukon, from Hong Kong to Hamburg, I'll offer you just two exhibits.

First, Gaspé in the Province of Québec, Canada: on the sacred spot where the great French explorer, Jacques Cartier, first set foot on mainland Canada and claimed it for King Louis in 1534, standing proudly against the matchless scenery of the Gaspé Peninsula, is the largest and most gruesome McDonald's sign I've ever seen. This isn't just vandalism, it's downright desecration.

Second, from Chittagong in Bangladesh, South Asia: in a country which is largely a flat, alluvial plain terminating in the huge delta at the confluence of the Ganges and Brahmaputra Rivers, Coke and Pepsi have chosen to play out their most bitter battle for the taste buds of the most crowded, most poverty-stricken country in the world by carving out slices of their pathetically few and pathetically small hills, alongside the main road through the city, as sites for their monstrous signs. This is repeated dozens of times throughout Bangladesh. Who the hell do these people think they are, with their hill-chopping feuds?

So how are the flagrant abuses typified by these examples to be countered? Not, I swear, by appealing to the better natures of the abusers; they'll go on whacking up elephantine horrors as long as we let them, in the name of free competition in the market place and all the rest of the cynical, hypocritical persiflage they can muster so effectively in the twinkling of an eye. No, it's the voters, the townspeople, the representatives of the abused environments who have to screw the buggers down. In spite of their vast power, they don't yet have it all their own way. Let me wave a little wand of hope from the direction of Whistler, British Columbia.

At almost the farthest point in the country from Gaspé, this holiday resort has ruthlessly controlled the multis who want to trade within its city limits. For those who think the likes of McDonald's and Holiday Inn cannot be curbed in their rampant quest for having the largest signs in town, I offer them these two testimonials to good town planning. It doesn't make me like their god-awful logos any better, but at least they're boiled down to an inoffensive scale and we can live with them.

If Whistler can do it, so can any other community. And as for us designers, why don't we boycott the abusers until they get the right message, instead of aiding and abetting them? If we don't, we should be thoroughly ashamed of ourselves. Whose side are we on?

SAVING ADVERTISING
Jelly Helm

Fifteen minutes before I met James Brown for the first time, I was sitting in the hotel room of his manager, Roosevelt Royce Johnson, at the Fairmont Hotel in San Francisco. My partner Stacy and I were planning to feature Mr. Brown in a commercial for Nike, and Roosevelt had invited us to his room to discuss Mr. Brown's marketing potential. Incense burned in the room, the maid was making the bed and Roosevelt had brought in stage-sized speakers so he could play us James Brown's latest single, coincidentally called "Just Do It," which he recommended we use for the soundtrack of the TV spot. That didn't seem very likely, because although the song title was the same as Nike's tagline, it had a slightly different meaning. The lyrics, as I remember them, went "Just do it, do it, do it, do it . . . all night long."

Roosevelt told us about Mr. Brown's other marketing ventures, including two signature fragrances for men and women. The perfume was called "Try Me." The cologne was called "I Smell Good."

We went downstairs, briefly met Mr. Brown and joined the police-escorted motorcade towards the convention center. We arrived at the back door, and in a scene reminiscent of the nightclub entrance in *Goodfellas*, we snaked our way through the bowels of the building towards the dressing room. Lining the sides of the hallway, shoulder to shoulder, were all the convention center employees, in uniform, standing at attention and saying, one by one, "Good evening Mr. Brown," "Hello Mr. Brown."

After a blistering show, we returned backstage to present the storyboards to Mr. Brown. It's dangerous meeting legends—they can only disappoint—but an hour and a half with James Brown revealed an intense, warm, sincere, intelligent man. I was already floating before he remarked to me, "You have a broadcasting voice. You ever done any broadcasting?"

No, not really.

"Radio? Disk jockey? MC?"

No, I said again, increasingly embarrassed.

Stacy interrupted: "He sang in a rock band."

James slapped his hand on the table, pointed at me and erupted, "I knew it! You got the FEELING!"

Advertising can be such a fun business.

I love the people. Some of the smartest, funniest, kindest, most creative, most

Originally published in *Emigre*, no. 53 (Winter 2000).

alive people I know I've met through advertising. Five of the people in my wedding party were people I met in the business. Including the woman in the white dress.

Advertising is rewarding in its ability to let you express yourself. Something about the act of creating something and then sharing it with the world. Industrial designer Victor Papanek compared it to the feeling of building and then flying a kite. I remember the first ad that I created that actually ran. It was an in-house ad for the college newspaper. I stopped at each newsstand and looked at paper after paper to see that my idea was really running in the newspaper.

Advertising is a bit of a paradox. While it is a wonderfully fruitful and stimulating and rewarding way to make a living, it is also increasingly criticized. While thousands of people find our work entertaining, a growing number find it disturbing. In a 1999 Gallup poll, advertising ranked forty-third of forty-five professions based on ethics and honesty. *Adbusters* is a thriving, if niche, magazine that sets out to "galvanize resistance against those who would . . . diminish our lives." Articles critical of advertising are cropping up more frequently in mainstream magazines such as *National Public Radio*, *Harper's* and *Newsweek*.

Why do people criticize us? Are we allowed to ask that question?

I had thirteen years of Catholic education so I know a little bit about unacceptable questions. In fourth grade we studied Adam and Eve and their two sons, Cain and Abel. "Where did Cain and Abel find girlfriends?" This, I discovered, was an unacceptable question. And when the questions were allowed, the answers often weren't very satisfying. In a discussion about the afterlife in sophomore Scripture class, I asked whether Jews and Protestants who lived good lives could enter heaven. Father didn't have to search long for the answer. "In heaven, God has a beautiful mansion. God sits in the living room with the Catholics gathered around his feet. Jews sit on the porch." We can do a better job asking ourselves tough questions and attempting honest answers.

As we stare into the new millennium, it is important that we look with a critical eye at what we do, its effects on the world and how we can do our job better. For the next few pages, let's say there are no unacceptable questions and try our best to examine the issues with an open mind. (I might add that after school I encountered more than a few Catholics who were very willing to entertain tough questions. Doubt, as one priest friend of mine told me, either exposes false gods or strengthens one's faith.)

So why is advertising increasingly criticized? One reason, I'm convinced, is because there's so much of it. Of course there are more magazine, outdoor, TV and radio ads than ever, but the latest category is "guerrilla media," also known as "ambient advertising," or as a friend of mine calls it, "vandalism."

As an ad person, putting a "got milk?" sticker on bananas seemed creative, but when I brought one of those bananas home last week, it felt intrusive, which of course was what it was meant to be. Do any of us really want advertising on our food? The *Wall Street Journal* recently reported Pizza Hut's failed plan to project their logo on the moon with lasers. They were dissuaded not by common sense or good taste, but because it was technically impossible. It's all part of a trend where more and more public space is becoming privatized.

Between the stickered bananas and the ads over the urinals and on the floor of our supermarkets, we're exposed to three thousand commercial messages a day. That's one every fifteen seconds, assuming we sleep for eight hours, and I'd guess right now there's someone figuring out how to get to us while our eyes are closed. Advertising is a $450 billion business. That's just media advertising. When you throw in packaging, point of purchase and direct mail, it's closer to a trillion. A trillion dollars. This blitzkrieg of advertising is relatively new.

Much of advertising's growth—it's grown eightfold since 1935—came in reaction to America's new techniques of mass production, which required mass consumption.

In 1959, retailing analyst Victor Lebow wrote in the *Journal of Retailing*: "Our enormously productive economy . . . demands that we make consumption our way of life, that we convert the buying and use of goods into rituals, that we seek our spiritual satisfaction, our ego satisfaction, in consumption. We need things consumed, burned up, worn out, replaced, and discarded at an ever increasing rate." And so, advertising evolved from being a relatively passive source of information to a persuasive tool for manufacturing desire. This may be getting closer to the reason advertising is criticized: the role we play in helping to create a consumer economy.

Since 1950, Americans have consumed as much as all of the world's peoples who have ever lived. Our economy depends on it. Two-thirds of our gross domestic product is consumer-driven. We have helped create a world of abundance that has been very good for a lot of people. Not just everyone in our business. Virtually everyone in our country, and every industrial country, has reaped rewards from our consumer economy. According to the 1998 U.N. Human Development Report: "More people are better fed and housed than ever before. Living standards have risen to enable hundreds of millions to enjoy housing with hot water and cold, warmth and electricity, transport to and from work—with time for leisure and sports, vacations and activities beyond anything imagined at the start of the century." Unfortunately, this describes only a small part of the world. And the disparities are deep.

The fifth of all the people in the wealthiest industrial nations—United States, Canada, Europe, Australia and Japan—account for 86 percent of total private consumption expenditures. The middle three-fifths account for 12.7 percent of the spending. The bottom fifth account for 1.3 percent.

The richest fifth consume 58 percent of the world's energy, 65 percent of the electricity, 87 percent of the cars, 74 percent of the telephones, 46 percent of the meat and 84 percent of the paper. In each of these areas, the share of the bottom fifth is in single digits. Some immediately see a problem there. The disparity is too wide to be equitable. It's not fair.

But suppose you look at this in another way. Suppose you see this pizza not as finite but as a snapshot, a step along the way towards a superabundant world. One day, can't everyone have the TVs, cell phones, SUVs, videogames and mega-malls that we have?

Simply put, no.

To understand why, we have to look at the idea of sustainability. In a sustainable system, consuming doesn't deplete or permanently damage resources. Thirty years ago the environmentalists told us the problem would be that we'd run out of oil, or nonrenewable resources. Good news. We haven't. The bad news is that the way we consume hurts the world in two other ways. First, we're overusing renewable resources. Things like water, fish and wood. We're using them faster than the earth is able to regenerate them. We're cutting down trees too fast; we're overgrazing too much land; we're overfishing. Second, we're overextending the earth's sink capacity. The earth has a natural ability to absorb waste, as long as we don't push it to do more than it can handle. Consuming as much as we do creates an enormous amount of stuff, gas and solid waste.

What about recycling?

Recycling is a good idea, and it makes us more aware of the issue of waste, but it doesn't touch the problem. Most of the waste comes from the manufacturing, packaging and distribution of what we use—things beyond our control. Per capita waste has increased three-fold since 1980.

Basically, it won't work to keep going the way we're going. We can't sustain it. If everyone consumed the way Americans do, we would need four more earths to support it. We've reached our limit.

Many of the people working on this dilemma, scientists and sustainability experts, have arrived at a common solution. If we compare their solution to where we are headed as an industry, it may hold the answer to why we're targeted by critics.

The *overconsumers* are the 20 percent of the people living in industrial countries. They're the ones consuming at a rate that cannot be sustained.

The *sustainers* are the middle 60 percent. They have electricity, clean water, adequate food. They have fewer cars and depend more on public transportation. They're not deprived. And their style of living does not threaten the earth.

The *excluded* are the bottom 20 percent. They have very limited and in some case no access to clean water, safe food, shelter and health care. Because of their dependency on the land, they also deplete resources in an effort to survive. So, surprisingly, their style of living also threatens the earth.

In order to create a sustainable system, the bottom 1.1 billion people must increase their consumption levels, the middle 3.3 billion must continue down the same road, and the top 1.1 billion need to consume in more appropriate, responsible ways.

In fact, if we look at where our industry is heading, we're ignoring the *excluded*, encouraging the *sustainers* to join the *overconsumers*, while pushing the *overconsumers* to an entirely new stratum: *super-duper-overconsumers*.

Despite being keenly aware that we live on a finite planet, with a limited amount of resources, we continue to perpetuate a world-view of continuous, unlimited and ever-expanding consumption. We continue to encourage runaway spending, in direct opposition to the sort of action recommended to get us out of the mess we're in.

That's how ecologists and scientists are looking at it. Let's look at advertising from a sociologist's view.

Advertising apparently works. We're spending more than ever. Yet somehow we're not keeping up. The social demands of spending rise faster than our income. A Roper Center poll revealed that the amount of annual income required so that you can "fulfill your dreams" doubled between 1987 to 1994. Luxuries have become "necessities."

As my wife and I build a home together, we've discovered that there are standard items that we're almost expected to own, the required trappings of being a young American couple: an answering machine, a cordless phone, at least one television, cable TV, a VCR, a stereo, cassette player and CD player, a microwave, dishwasher, washer and drier, air conditioning, two cars. Owning these things would have made you the talk of the neighborhood barely a generation ago. Now you stand out by not having them.

Trying to keep up has its costs. Credit card debt is at the highest ever, doubling from 1990 to 1996. Household savings are at the lowest point ever, one-fourth of what they were fifteen years ago. Do you know how many households making more than $100,000 say they can't afford everything they really need? 27 percent.

How much is advertising responsible for this?

To answer, it may help to examine the way advertising works—the process that goes on in the mind of a person targeted by our ads.

Advertising's goal, of course, is to make you want something. To create desire. That begins by making you unhappy with what you currently have, or don't have. Advertising widens the gap between what you have and what you want. Wanting to buy something, then, is a response to the feelings of dissatisfaction, envy and craving. A perpetual state of conflict.

It's on these emotions that a world economy and a dominant philosophy have been built, encouraging the act of spending to increase personal happiness, well-being and, ultimately, one's identity. These aren't controversial ideas. They're merely a description of the process.

When I use the word advertising, I don't mean any individual ad. A particular ad can be entertaining or funny or touching or boring. We need to look beyond the emotional reaction created by a specific ad and look at the combined effect of the thousands we see. Advertising's influence comes from the common theme underlying every ad, repeated thousands of times, day after day after day: *Buying things will make you happy*.

When you build a system on a foundation of desire, dissatisfaction, envy and inadequacy, people buy things, yes, but it's no surprise that it happens at the expense of some damage to the psyche.

The dangers of materialism is one of the few topics virtually every world religion agrees on. Which tells me we should pay attention. It only takes two world religions to agree to keep me from eating pork. And if materialism's not bad enough, we are increasingly telling people that their non-material needs may be fulfilled through consumption.

Increasingly, account planning involves using anthropologists' tools to determine deep human longings—freedom, belonging, fulfillment, power, love—and showing how our clients' products can fulfill those needs.

In a speech to the American Association of Advertising in April 1999, the chairman of the agency conglomerate Interpublic Group admitted that, "The people who sell you sport utility vehicles are selling you the means to go anywhere you like. You're almost certainly not going to go there. But you are going to feel pretty powerful. They're putting you in the Power Business, the Feel Good Business."

To claim that a particular brand of SUV will make you more powerful is not exactly a lie, but as essayist Jonathan Dee wrote, it's "a kind of truthlessness." In perpetuating that truthlessness, in telling people *it's not who you are, it's what you own*, advertising distorts something essential about ourselves, something invisible, but possibly the most important aspect of our humanity.

Ecologic unsustainability, social instability, materialism, spiritual damage. Wow. What do we have to say about this?

My first response, when confronted with the effects of overconsumption and my involvement as someone in advertising, was utter denial. I never in my life intended to widen the inequality gap or misuse natural resources or create a world hooked on junk. Furthermore, I've never even met a person who has! We are good people. None of us, as far as I can tell, intended for this to happen. I just wanted to meet James Brown! How did it get so out of hand?

When cars first came out, people thought of them as clean transportation, because horse manure didn't come out of the tail pipe. But the auto business quickly learned that they weren't as clean as they originally thought. Advertising's not as clean as we originally thought.

I disagree with the critics who think that people in advertising are creeps. My research, conducted with hundreds of people, tells me that people in advertising are thoughtful, intelligent, idealistic, compassionate, creative. In short, all the traits necessary to do the right thing. Unfortunately, we are often paralyzed because though we recognize some of the shortcomings of our business, we don't know where to start.

A good place to begin is by confronting the fact that some of the consequences of what we do as an industry don't always line up with what we believe as individuals, and see what we can do about it.

Someone must be thinking: "You're not criticizing advertising, you're criticizing capitalism. We're the tail of the dog. Advertising is simply a tool of corporations."

It is true that we cannot expect a revolutionary change in advertising without a revolutionary change in business. This has already begun.

Ray Anderson is the CEO of Interface, a $1 billion carpet company that's part of one of the earth's dirtiest industries. By its own count, Interface produces over 10,000 tons of solid waste, 600 million gallons of polluted water and 62,000 tons of carbon dioxide every year.

Recently Anderson had an unlikely address for his shareholders: "I am a plunderer of the earth. Someday people like me may be put in jail." Interface, with the help of an environmental consultancy from Sweden called The Natural Step, is one of a number of corporations taking major steps to retool itself towards conducting business in a sustainable way.

One of Interface's neater ideas: leasing carpet instead of selling it. It allows them to control the recycling so that the carpet doesn't end up in a landfill. As Anderson said,

"Business and industry have to change or we will take the Earth down with us. This is the next industrial revolution."

This brings up a critical question: *Must we wait for our clients to take the lead? Is there room in our partnership with business to play more than an ethically neutral role? Must we have a blind dedication to growing our client's business, regardless of the outcome? If our clients are leading us down a path that is not socially or ecologically sustainable, or that is harmful to human nature, do we resist, and how?*

I don't think any of us like the idea of being ethically neutral. Every industry has an ethical code, a line not to be crossed, no matter the cost. Economist and philosopher John Ruskin called this line the "due occasion," when it is a person's duty to die rather than go against a principle critical to his or her profession. What are those due occasions? Ruskin said, "[For] the soldier, rather than leave his post in battle. The physician, rather than leave his post in plague. The lawyer, rather than sanction injustice."

What is our due occasion as advertisers?

One man took a stab at identifying it. He ran an ad agency in New York. In one of the last statements he ever made, in the preface to a book he never finished, Bill said:

> You and I can no longer isolate our lives. We must practice our skills on behalf
> of society. We must not just believe in what we sell, we must sell what we
> believe in.

Bernbach's words are deceivingly simple.

"Believe in" is more complicated than whether we personally like a product. A product must be evaluated as to how it affects the entire community. Even beyond choosing products we believe in, can we continue to promote reckless spending given the evidence of how it affects the health of people and the planet?

It seems to me, knowing as much as we do, we can't go back to our cubicles and merely argue about concepts. It's like rearranging deck chairs on the Titanic. In light of what we know, debating meaningless issues such as the merits of East Coast versus West Coast advertising has gone from irrelevant to absurd. There's nothing wrong with improving creativity and debating techniques, but it must be done within a wider context. What is most important to us? That we make our work more entertaining? Or that we make it more equitable? That we start another creative revolution? Or are we in need of a different sort of revolution?

We have made amazing strides in creativity, technique and economic growth, but how satisfying are these advances if we ignore or explain away the consequences of our work? Wouldn't we find deeper joy in celebrating our creativity if it existed within a broader context? Don't we want to say, "I feel good about my job," not because we have fun or because we work on cool commercials, but because our profession contributes to human growth and is good for the health of the community?

It's unrealistic to think advertising will start a revolution. Advertising isn't meant to set social policy. But advertising is very effective at listening and reacting to public will. And the public seems to be catching on to the costs of our extreme patterns of overconsumption.

In a 1995 Merck Family Poll, 82 percent of Americans agreed that "most of us buy and consume far more than we need. It's wasteful." In the summary of the poll's findings, the report's authors state: "People of all backgrounds share certain fundamental concerns about the values they see driving society. They believe materialism, greed and selfishness increasingly dominate American life, crowding out a more meaningful set of values centered on family, responsibility and community."

I don't need a poll to tell me this. Because I know, when it comes down to it, that the road of reckless materialism is unsatisfying to the human spirit. The world is waking up. Maybe because of the millennium, change seems easy to embrace right now. How will we respond?

Change is easy for us. We can change in an instant. Unlike the changes Ray Anderson made at his carpet company, we don't have factories to re-tool or technologies to improve or components to reinvent. We only have to change in our minds, and once we do, we've changed for real.

What sort of change do we need?

It's time to revise our industry's code of ethics. In 1924 we identified our principles and wrote them up as the AAAA Standards of Practice. We must rejuvenate and reclarify those standards given what we now know about the state of the world and our relationship to it. The code asserts, among other things, an obligation to the public and a dedication to expressing the truth. "The truth" is tough to pin down, but it certainly cannot include promoting ideas or products that are harmful to the health of the planet or society at large.

I believe we all agree on this in principle; it's just a question of defining what it means.

For example, many agencies already take stands against tobacco, because it is easy to see the link between tobacco and the ill health of the community. The link between other products and the ill health of the world is often less obvious.

The 1998 United Nations Human Development Report on Consumption helped clarify that link: "Consumption clearly contributes to human development when it enlarges the capabilities and enriches the lives of people without adversely affecting the well-being of others, when it is as fair to future generations as it is to the present ones, when it respects the carrying capacities of the planet, and when it encourages lively, creative individuals and communities."

With that as a guide, I propose three clarifications, restatements, of our industry principles. The first:

1. PROMOTE ONLY THOSE GOODS AND SERVICES
THAT BENEFIT HUMAN DEVELOPMENT

As I said, I believe we all agree with this in principle. None of us would promote cigarettes for babies or a home security system that uses landmines. But it's never that black and white. How do we determine something that seems so subjective? To a certain degree, it will always be subjective, but there are questions we can ask:

- How is the product made? Does it responsibly use natural resources? Does manufacturing it create unnecessary waste or pollution? What are its health, safety and environmental impacts?
- Is it produced equitably? Are the people on the assembly line empowered or exploited?
- Is it distributed fairly? Does it benefit one group disproportionately?
- Does it contribute to the growth of communities? Does it help us meet our needs? Does it make people more creative, strengthen them, bring them together? Or does it isolate and separate people?

As we change our priorities from short-term to long-term gains and carefully scrutinize our clients, customers have demonstrated they're willing to meet us halfway.

Whether it's the increasing consumer support of fairly-traded coffee, which insures that small coffee producers are not exploited, or the recent student movement protesting sweatshop manufacturing of college apparel, which the *New York Times* called "the biggest wave of campus activism since the anti-apartheid movement in the 1980s," people are beginning to understand the inter-relatedness of their buying and consuming decisions and the rest of the planet, and demonstrating that they are willing to make the right choice.

The second principle is also a re-clarification of our industry's commitment to the truth.

2. REFRAIN FROM PROMOTING RECKLESS, IRRESPONSIBLE, COMPETITIVE CONSUMPTION

Advertising as a force to create false needs is a relatively recent phenomenon, tracing back to less than a century ago. Is it possible for advertising, while remaining creative and effective, to return to its original purpose of informing and educating?

If we are committed to the truth, we must ask ourselves, is it truthful to promise that material goods will fulfill deep, human, non-material needs? Is it truthful to market high-cost status goods to the urban poor? Is it truthful, knowing what we do about the effects of consumerism, to continue to promote it as a viable lifestyle?

Can we sell without doing these things? It depends on which aspects of human nature we choose to speak to with our work. Do we encourage greed? Do we speak to people as individualists pursuing maximum personal gain to the exclusion of others, or as members of a community, a person whose choices affect a larger group of people?

My third proposal concerns the way we market to a demographic group that represents over $200 billion of spending power. Children.

Our industry has had impressive results at marketing to kids. I recently heard a planner tell the story of researching the target audience for a lollipop commercial. The target was kids aged five to twelve, but her research had shown that there are sharp divisions within that group. Five- and six-year-olds like bright, bold colors and busy things to look at. Seven- to nine-year-olds like funny sounding words they can repeat. Bobbley-wobbley. Toodley-woodley. Ten- to twelve-year-olds like seeing adults in foolish situations, because it makes them feel smarter and more in control.

She showed us the commercial based on her findings and it unsurprisingly featured a bumbling, clumsy adult on a busy, colorful set, talking about the lollipop using funny sounding words like bobbley-wobbley and toodley-woodley. And, she reported, kids bought up those lollipops by the handful.

Armed with such sophisticated tools, the battle for kids' dollars is relatively one-sided.

According to an article in *American Demographics* entitled "Born to Shop," children as young as three ask for brand names. Six-month-old babies recognize corporate logos and spokesmen.

Psychologists tell us that to a child, all information is educational. They simply cannot distinguish between advertising and other types of information. And so it is impossible to "target" them without being, by definition, manipulative.

Commercializing the experience of childhood has deep consequences. Ninety-three percent of teenage girls say shopping is their favorite activity. As a society, we shake our heads and complain about how materialistic kids are, yet we refuse to see the connection between their values and our military-scaled marketing to them.

While some believe the answer is media training for kids, I believe that the blame-the-victim approach puts responsibility on children instead of where it belongs, on us.

In civil society, we must put the welfare of children ahead of economic benefit. We must follow the lead of countries such as Sweden, Denmark, Norway and the province of Quebec and . . .

3. BAN ALL BROADCAST ADVERTISING TO CHILDREN UNDER 12

Whether we will take such a radical step depends on whether we believe this group holds more value as consumers or as children. This is an ambitious call-to-action. Maybe it's unrealistic to expect that we would change a system that, at least in the short run, benefits us. But I'd like to think that all of us would rather participate in a system that is healthy and fair. I'd like to think that we have the capability to understand that our ultimate well-being is tied to the community's well-being, and that exploitative relationships that may initially benefit us will eventually cost us, either through a damaged planet, a damaged social structure or a damaged soul.

But how many people reading this have the power to implement such a dramatic plan in an agency? Some of us do. But most of the people able to make such changes probably stopped reading a long time ago. "He's nuts. He doesn't understand

Originally published in *Emigre*, no. 52 (Fall 1999).

reality. He doesn't understand the way life works." I wouldn't blame them. In their shoes, I'd probably think the same things. They're too invested to risk making any dramatic changes.

But on the other hand, you might be feeling bothered by some of the things I've written—they might be things you've thought yourself—and you might be feeling a bit powerless to do anything. You might find yourself a week from now, taking a shower, drinking a cup of coffee, and some of these ideas are still nagging at you. I would pay attention. I would pay attention, because as my friend Ken said, that is a gift. The gift of hearing. It is the first gift you will have to put to use if you want to affect any change.

Real change will not come swooping in with the adoption of an oath, it will come gradually, as one by one we become aware of these issues and question our individual roles.

Your second gift landed you your job. Your creativity, your intelligence, your ability to look at problems in unusual ways. No one else is in the position to make as much difference on these issues as you are. Not social workers, not teachers, not priests. No one else has the creativity, the energy and the opportunity that you have.

As a person with the gift of creativity, confronting these sorts of issues is your heritage.

According to anthropologists, in primitive cultures and ancient tribes it was the creative people, the men and women who saw visions and could create artistic objects, who served as the conscience of the community. They were the priests and shamans. Your genes are practically commanding you to do something!

Where to begin? Look into these issues for yourself. Read the U.N. Human Development Report on Consumption. Look into the work being done by places like the Center for a New American Dream (*www.newdream.org*) and the Positive Futures Network (*www.futurenet.org*). Talk about these things at work. Have a conversation with your boss. Talk with your friends. Start a discussion group.

These issues are often bewildering. But the good news is that we don't have to have a complete answer. We just need to have a desire to earnestly pursue these issues, to seek a complete understanding of our work and its effects on the world. If we shine a light on what we do, I am confident that truth and our best instincts will combine to help us take the right steps.

As social activist and educator Howard Zinn said, "If we do act, in however small a way, we don't have to wait for some grand utopian future. The future is an infinite succession of presents, and to live now as we think human beings should live, in defiance of all that is bad around us, is itself a marvelous victory."

SAVING JELLY
Michael Rock

If there was any worry that our vast design-industry stockpiles of political naïveté were dwindling, one need look no further than *Emigre* for reassurance of their inexhaustible abundance. The recent feature article, "Saving Advertising" (*Emigre*, no. 53), coupled with the continuing responses to First Things First Manifesto 2000 stand as testimony to the ascendancy of over-simplification and the decline of nuance.

It is remarkable that design and advertising workers are so conflicted about the value of their work, so intent on the radical reformation of the professions they practice. Perhaps that deep dissatisfaction is a byproduct of an education system that promises more than the industry can deliver. Perhaps that anxiety is the lingering effect of a variety of modern ideologies that suggested that designers were either artists, free of the chains of commerce, or agents of progressive social engineering. Whatever the root cause, the worrisome aspect is that we don't seem to be developing any useful theory to lead us through this maze. As a result we continue to get the lite-radicalism *Emigre* has popularized.

"Saving Advertising" starts out earnestly enough, but in place of insights into the dilemmas facing advertising designers, author Jelly Helm regurgitates well-worn pieties and planet-saving programs, skillfully avoiding any original ideas. Its only after four pages of incisive insight—such as "I disagree with the critics who think that people in advertising are creeps"—that Helm unveils the shattering conclusion of his research (set off in italics for emphasis): "the reason advertising is criticized [may be] *the role we play in helping create a consumer economy.*"

My god, stop the presses! Where has Helm been for the last two-hundred-plus years of critical discourse? Since Dr. Johnson first muttered, "Promise, large promise, is the soul of an advertisement," library shelves have groaned under the weight of analysis from writers as diverse as Carlyle, Huxley, Russell, Barthes and Williams, all clamoring to excoriate the ad-men of their time. Helm seems blissfully unaware of such precedent. His senses of wonder and injury are palpable.

Helm follows his stunning revelation with a radical methodology for spiritual resuscitation that can be summed up as follows: (1) Promote good things; (2) Don't promote bad things; (3) And for god's sake, protect the innocent children. But by the time he actually works his theory down to the level of individual action—the true test for any of these sanctimonious programs—all he can come up with is: "Talk about these things at work. Have a conversation with your boss. Talk with your friends. Start a discussion group."

Originally published in *Emigre*, no. 54 (Spring 2000).

While I rest easier knowing there are discussion groups breaking out in ad agencies worldwide, I am left with the sinking feeling that Helm's prescriptions won't get us very far. Helm inhabits a blissfully simple world. There's a bubble labeled *Capital*, a bubble labeled *Consumers*, a bubble labeled *Advertising* and clean, straight arrows connect them in orderly systems. There is no free will on planet Helm, no critical perception, no ambiguity. Consumers, especially angelic children, sit transfixed in front of televisions taking orders from the great advertising gods (of which, until his recent enlightenment, Helm was one.)

The point that seems to elude Helm is that it is impossible to separate good advertising from evil advertising. Changing the content of an advertisement may save the soul of the individual art director but will not change the function of advertising or its operational language. Helm tries to have it both ways; he wants to make advertising nicer without upsetting its profitability or the centrality of its role in consumer culture. But Helm's vision of nice advertising is a façade, the theoretical equivalent of tossing the tapestry over the dunghill.

Antonio Gramsci argued that the ideology of a dominant culture is incorporated in all discourse contained within in it, including the discourse of resistance. Taken in this light, Helm's stand against *bad* advertising makes two inferences: (1) Advertising can be sanitized; and (2) Advertising actually has the power he reports it to have, that it is an overwhelming force that must be checked. But rather than deconstruct the power underlying the advertising industry, Helmian resistance simply builds the myths that advertising agencies want to build anyhow, i.e., it is both ethical and omnipotent. (Can you imagine agency heads around the world are crying out, "Please Jelly, don't tell them all how powerful and effective we are!")

In addition, for all Helm prances around capitalism and consumption, he is silent on the issue of privately owned and controlled mass media. Yet commercial mass media and advertising are inseparable as *audience* is the product advertisers buy from media outlets like television networks, newspapers and magazines. Ad campaigns are called campaigns for a reason: they are pitched political battles in a war for the hearts and minds of *consumers*—which is the current name for what we used to call *citizens*. And let's not forget, it's the multiplication of the media and the huge growth in media outlets—funded by advertising dollars applied to gain access to all those ripe markets—that creates the spiraling demand for all us graphic and advertising designers on both sides of the editorial-advertising divide.

All public speech is inherently political precisely because it is persuasive and designed to shape consciousness. That after all is the point of a *mass* media. At the moment I live in a city (Rome) full of art and architecture, most of which was crafted to market hardcore Catholic ideology. (The Vatican may have originated the cross-platform branding campaign.) The fact that it is persuasive doesn't necessarily condemn it. Advertising has a much more complex and integrated role in society than a simple equation of good versus evil. Like any language it is a highly articulate and developed social construct. And contrary to popular mythology, advertising is not an omnipotent force.

Advertising will always reflect all the contradictions already embedded in our culture. We have been willing to live with advertising to gain the advantages of an expansive mass media. But as a form of public speech, it is unreasonable to expect that advertising wouldn't be as diverse, and as often disagreeable, as public speech itself.

Ultimately, money power and persuasion are inextricably linked. The only way to effectively transform advertising is to propose significant changes in the economic structure that supports it—for instance public funding of election campaigns. Without dramatic economic restructuring, plans like Helm's amount to nothing more than that program in New York City that funded cardboard murals of curtains and plants to be placed in the windows of abandoned buildings.

The real problem—and it's a problem that plagues contemporary discourse—is the lack of definition of a recognizable enemy. Antonio Negri and Michael Hardt put it clearly: "The identification of the enemy . . . is no small task given exploitation tends no longer to have a specific place and that we are immersed in a system of power so deep and complex that we can no longer determine specific difference or measure. We suffer exploitation, alienation, and command as enemies, but we do not know where to locate the production of oppression." We want to lash out at something, we just can't figure out what.

Helm ends his plaint with the winsome question: "How many people reading this have the power to implement such a dramatic plan in an agency? Some of us do." Sorry to burst your bubble, but actually you don't. And neither do a handful of sanctimonious designers passing manifestos from successful studios and insular academic offices to *enlightened* agencies. You may personally decide to live a pious life, and organize discussion groups, but that will not change the functional capabilities of the medium you attempt to manipulate, and from which you simultaneously benefit.

My problem with all this piety peddling, and this includes First Things First, is that this hand-wringing just won't produce results. Let's try an experiment. In every instance of these arguments, substitute the word *speech* for *advertising*. No one goes around claiming that everyone who speaks should only speak about good things. And no one blames language itself for the existence of hate speech, slurs, obscenity or insults. No one argues we should reform language because people use it to do bad things. (Well actually some do, but that's a different story.) Simple plans to make everyone start acting nice will never work. Imagine if all writers took a pledge to be meaningful or thoughtful or kind? Can you imagine a world where people only said nice things?

Obviously I can't.

READING AT THE BREAKFAST TABLE
Natalia Ilyin

In a 1902 Quaker Oats ad, a buxom Gibson girl delicately holds a mask away from herself with ironic distain. The mask bears the face of an old woman. The copy reads: "Quaker Oats makes your blood tingle; nerves strong and active; muscles powerful. It makes flesh rather than fat, but enough fat for reserve force. It builds children up symmetrically into brainy and robust men and women. You can work on Quaker Oats, it stays by you."

If the truth be told, I long for a faithful cereal. A cereal with those 1902 Quaker Oats attributes could become very special to me. Think of it: a cereal that makes one's blood tingle yet stays by one for the long haul. Goodbye, costly birth control methods. Hello, fiber.

Yes, I want my cereal to build flesh rather than fat. And I think I speak for everyone over forty when I say that I desire nothing more than to hold the mask of my incipient crone-hood away from me ironically, and to bask in recovered days of symmetrical and brainy youth.

I like this ad from 1902. I like laughing at it. But I might as well laugh directly at myself, for almost one hundred years later, I am still believing the messages on cereal boxes.

After twenty years of poststructuralist yammering, I imagine that you have heard a rumor or two around the halls that the myths of our particular culture are not bound in big books. They are not hand-lettered into the hefty parchment of, say, a *Neibelungenlied* or a *Voluspa*. No, we like to tell our stories on TV, on billboards, Web sites, on T-shirts and in movies. We use every substrate available to tell the stories that keep our commercial juggernaut juggering along. And we print some of our most virulent myths on the flimsy cardboard of cereal boxes.

First thing in the morning, bleary-eyed and caffeine-starved, many of us begin our day by reading a cereal box. And with our average breakfast serving of thirty-one grams of cereal with a half-cup of skim milk, we take in messages about whom we should emulate and what we should want and how we should live our lives.

Now, before I get started, I just want to remind you that Roland Barthes, the author of the great introduction-to-taking-apart-contemporary-symbolic-images book *Mythologies*, was run down by a bakery truck. The forces of rampant consumerism got him in the end. So it is with much trepidation and soft soles that I tread on the sensitive toes of the multinational conglomerates that make possible our daily thirty-one

Originally published in *AIGA Journal of Graphic Design* Vol. 17, no. 3 (1999).

grams of grain product. I fear being chased around by a General Mills sixteen-wheeler in a deserted Costco parking lot. Nevertheless, let's get started.

I have four cereal boxes in front of me: Special K, Smart Start, Cap'n Crunch, and Honey Bunches of Oats. They are all, strangely, of similar caloric and nutritional value, which surprised me, for I firmly believed that Special K (110 calories per 31 grams) would be quite a bit less caloric than Cap'n Crunch (110 calories per 27 grams). The only real thing that's different about them, aside from taste and texture, is their packaging.

First, Special K. Many were the teenage days that I began a new makeover-shapeover with a large bowl of Special K in skim milk. It was considered the slim breakfast, the controlled breakfast of the 1970s.

Yes, the familiar, rounded, 9-inch-high *K* still dominates the box. That *K* is a vestigial remain of the original Mr. Kellogg's signature, printed on every box of his corn flakes in the early 1900s to reassure the customer that he stood behind every box. (This signing smacks of the patriarchal, but we will let it pass in order to concentrate on that big *K*.)

In the beginning, W. K. Kellogg's small red signature stood for quality and assurance. So a huge red *K* means a huge amount of quality, a huge amount of assurance. For the moment we will ignore the redness of the 9" *K*. The color of red lipstick, blood and sexual excitement will not subliminally tempt us. And neither will the appealing rounded ascender of grand proportion—must I draw you a Freudian picture here? The implicit sexual-fulfillment routine we shall leave for another time.

The joining of the top and bottom of the *K* resembles the narrow female waist, long a genetic marker of fecundity. When women go through menopause, they generally lose their waistline. A small waist was the perfect image for Special K when it was a cereal that championed the trim female figure. But the times, they have a-changed. And we can tell, by image and subject matter, that the marketing group at Special K is under fire.

The current box was designed by a committee of nervous people. Special K is the midst of a personality crisis.

No longer, public opinion tells its branding group, can a cereal be marketed on the basis of its effect upon the female shape alone. That would be sexist. That would be wrong. So they've decided to use images that relate to health on top of their images that relate to beauty.

The crux of Special K's identity crisis is spelled out in the red headline on the back of the box: "Look good on your own terms . . . one step at a time." When you figure out what that nonsensical command means, please drop me a postcard.

These days, a picture of nine purple-clad people galloping toward a cure for breast cancer lies right over that psychosexual, small-waisted *K*. A pink banner (binding the feet of the *K*) proclaims the slogan, "Help Support Strong Women," in an attractive femmy reverse drop-shadowed italic. And below, in a no-nonsense sans serif, we read the ultimate mixed message: "See back panel for what YOU CAN do to HELP. NET WT. 12 OZ. (340g)."

Now. Why is some marketer telling me to look on the back panel of a cereal box that sports a sunrise on the upper left and "11 ESSENTIAL VITAMINS & MINER-ALS/FAT FREE!" on the upper right—why is this marketer telling me to bring my "Box Tops for the Cure" to a race against breast cancer? It is a fine thing, the Komen Race for the Cure. But why is Special K proclaiming:

> Take the following steps and you will be on your way to looking and feeling great!
> 1. Take Time for Yourself—Rest, exercise, get fresh air and wear a smile. Be sure to practice monthly breast self-exams and regularly schedule a mammogram . . .
> 2. Be Strong—Every day give your body the essential nutrients found in Kellogg's Special K.
> 3. Get Involved—The Komen Race for the Cure is for Everybody.

Because it sells cereal, that's why. Eat this cereal, says the package implicitly, follow these steps, and you will look great and not get breast cancer. The marketers are tapping in to something, for this is the story we like to tell ourselves. We like to think we can control the disease with boxtops, and eat Special K, and be safe. If you get the disease, well—you must have forgotten to wear a smile one day, so it's your fault.

What a uniquely American split! Define your fate, get out there and be an individual. But follow our rules, and do traditionally female, socially responsible acts like nurturing the sick. If you do good by your fellow woman you will be rewarded with health. And Special K is there by your side, egging you on. Faithful, like 1902 Quaker Oats.

Next in my lineup of cereals is Smart Start, also a Kellogg's cereal. Like Special K, it is a healthy, do-the-right-thing cereal. But it is not a cereal suffering from ambivalence. Every image is singing the same tune on this box. The box itself is a slim column, made of a thick cardboard with a luxurious layer of gloss coating. The words "Smart Start" are spelled out in a letter-spaced contemporary slab face that looks like something Tobias Frere-Jones might have designed in high school.

The cereal and its soothing milk drips off a soothing spoon that floats in the air in front of a soothing retro milk jug screened back in a soothing blue hue. (The fact that the cereal itself looks like shed insect casings must have been something for the design team to overcome.) Most interesting is the small red logo-dot in the lower left-hand corner. Upon close observance, this very dot now contains two Ss, (one assumes for Smart Start, not Schutzstassel) and above said dot is the slogan "Carpe Diem—Seize the Day."

It's an aggressive box, printed in black and red (along with that soothing cloud-like blue). It's the kind of box that knows what's good for you. It is a box you might buy if you were thirty-one, just married, working in Human Resources at Banana Republic, and just starting to get an inkling that your dreams and your life are different things.

The back of the box is a veritable amalgam of commands. A 72 pt. "Seize The Day" banner headline is followed by:

Wake up before the sun and chase it down! Make every moment count. Live
life to the edge of all possibility. Rise above the obstacles in life and focus on
the positive. Discover a new place, new activity, new people . . . just discover.
Volunteer at a shelter, a hospital, a school, etc. . . . Dare to be adventurous. Set
goals, challenge yourself and achieve them. Do it for yourself. Be your own
person.

It's enough to deplete your supplies of folic acid. Because of that slabby face I
asked myself if the cereal was being marketed to men or women. But when have men
ever needed to be told to "set goals, challenge yourself and achieve them?" When was
the last time you had to tell a man, "Do it for yourself. Be your own person." These are
the rules hammered into men's heads from the time they can toddle. Women, on the
other hand, feel that if they could just memorize all these maxims and live life to the
edge of all possibility they wouldn't be popping Xanax while separating their lights from
their darks.

Cereal marketers know that most clinically depressed people are women. On
the side of the box, the Kellogg's Smart Start Journal is available for two boxtops. It sports
a lovely tree on its cover, branching through a field of yellow blooms and a multi-hued
morning sky. Now, if I happen to see a guy on the subway clutching a journal with a
field of yellow blooms, I'll let you know. Women are the target of this marketing campaign.

Smart Start promotes our American myth of Horatio Alger. If you just work
hard enough, wake up before the sun, make every moment count, rise above this and
focus on that, you will not just start the day but seize it—you will rise above your present situation and live a better life. We Westerners just love this kind of thinking. It is a
little like the postmodern idea of the novel—that idea was to throw the responsibility
of making meaning onto the shoulders of the reader. The Smart Start plan is to throw
the responsibility for a good life onto the sloped shoulders of the cereal eater. Personal
striving, Americans like to think, can overcome all obstacles. That's because we've never
been invaded by a foreign power. But I digress.

Special K was worrying itself sick over looking good versus healthy eating.
Smart Start puts its marketing money on zest and vigor. But weight, looks, diet and zest
for life mean little to the marketers that package our next two cereals. Let's start with
Cap'n Crunch, the most interesting of all the packages.

The box is bright red, a color that stimulates the salivary glands because of its
primal association with raw meat. Upon that red background are printed three different images of men. This is a cereal marketed to little boys.

In the upper left-hand corner is a small portrait of the Quaker. His stern navy
hat, stock tie and white wig put one in mind of a benign Jehovah. He is not smiling,
but he is not frowning. He wears an expression at once avuncular and pleasant: he is the
Good Father. Carl Jung would have said that the Quaker personifies "Logos," our intuitive conception of masculine consciousness, which we believe is characterized by "discrimination, judgment and insight."

The package itself is dominated by the delighted face of Cap'n Crunch, a character who shares the benign characteristics of The Good Father—similar hat, similar white hair. He is a cartoon Captain Kangaroo—an accessible father figure. A semiotician would say that Cap'n Crunch relies on his socially stable signifiers (his captain's hat and epaulettes) to remind his young viewers of his maturity and value, while his expression is that of a gleeful child, creating a relationship between himself and the viewer. He shows emotion, invites inclusion, has the capacity to relate—he is an intuitive conception of feminine consciousness. He is the personification of "Eros," the opposite of the Quaker.

An ad for Disney's *Tarzan* takes up the lower left corner of the box. Tarzan is crouched and muscular. Leaning on his knuckles, he betrays his ape upbringing. Behind him is his ape mother. Here we have the Hero in his battle for deliverance from the Mother. All of these male stereotypes are fantasy—substitutes for reality that allow the child to entrench himself behind them against life. "Perhaps," said Jung once, "these eternal images are what men mean by fate."

But back to cereal. Here we have the last box. Honey Bunches of Oats. It is not telling me about health, weight, what I should value in life or what men are. It is the only cereal that mentions the flavor of what is in the box. In fact, it builds its entire case upon flavor. A Post cereal, it is "Breakfast Made Right" and features a big blue ribbon on the front and testimonials of flavor on the back. This is a box designed to offer inclusion. We here at the Post Cereal Company like this one the best. Come along and join the gang of happy cereal eaters.

The type is a mix of mock handwriting, the ink is warm amber punctuated with calming blue. "Just munch it! Just crunch it!" states the type on the back of the box. "I love the nutty cinnamon-y taste!" says Rich from Human Resources. And Sue from Research volunteers that "Joe in Finance told me how much he loved it . . . now I can't stop eating it!"

Instead of being exhorted to hold the line, have the thin waist, run for the Cure, and seize the day, suddenly we are being told how much everybody loves something, and how we can love it, too. This is a box designed to appeal to the Girlfriend Response, and has the same effect on women that the chatty sales gals on QVC do. "We're all just enthusiastic girlfriends here—so go get that Visa card, and let's have some fun!"

The box pulls off the most obvious of all manipulation devices. By running type around all four edges, the designer gets you to mix up the contents (necessary because of the addition of almond slivers) before you open it. And yet somehow I didn't mind. I was relieved that no one was telling me that I should seize anything. Of all these cereals, it is the only one I opened, and now only a few flakes remain. I think I feel my blood tingling. This could be the faithful cereal I have been searching for, the one that stays by me for the long haul. With all this energy, perhaps I should tune in to QVC and order some holiday items.

MANIFESTOS

Manifestos, statements of purpose, and calls to arms are time-honored means of launching oppositional movements and staking individual positions. F. T. Marinetti's first Futurist Manifesto of 1909 opened the floodgates with his boisterous, fire-and-brimstone attack on Italy's political and cultural status quo. The Italian Futurist movement, which he founded, was built on the tenuous foundation of manifestos as were many other radical groups and schools. But the "art" of manifesto writing, which had a renaissance in the late Fifties and Sixties, atrophied in the Seventies and mid-Eighties around the same time that radical political ideas took a back seat to the comfort of bourgeois lifestyle. But by the late Eighties the juices again began to boil and new ideas surfaced. In graphic design culture this was apparent within certain design academies and among progressive designers. The individual call-to-arms was a means to establish a beachhead in a war against convention.

Tibor Kalman was the most prodigious and vociferous of the manifesto-ists, but his were not like the self-serious screeds that had preceded him. While certainly resolute, he combined sarcasm and anger into an ironically authoritative stance against professional glitz, corporate-inspired mediocrity and commercial hucksterism. His manifestos warned against excess and pleaded for social relevance yet were cut with humorous indignation. Even when unrealistic, Kalman's bravado touched chords among those who read and heard him. His unambiguous "Fuck Committees" manifesto was a battle cry against the bane of professional practice as well as a sly parody of radicalism itself. One always knew what side he was on, but never knew from where he was coming.

During the Nineties, and in large part owing to Kalman, manifestos became rather common. A few designers with axes to grind could grind away on the pages of design magazines, from *I.D.* to *Eye*. Some of these borrowed the manifesto style to caricature them. Still others were heartfelt expressions intended to make statements that would rally followers. The manifestos selected herein, from the sincerity of Bruce Mau to the skepticism of the students at Central St. Martins College of Art and Design, cover that spectrum in its entirety.

Steven Heller

ME, THE UNDERSIGNED
Jessica Helfand

What is it about the manifesto that stirs us so? Defined as "a public declaration of principles or intentions,"[1] manifesti have been penned for centuries to decry injustice or to define truth, to denounce authority or to restore faith— even to rethink purpose and reassess value. In practice, the modern manifesto seems mostly to combine idealistic wish lists with idiosyncratic value judgments: buried somewhere in there is a kind of implicit kernel of protest, but what exactly do these manifesti protest *against*, the reader wonders? Such solemn proclamations of opinion—sheer moral outrage masquerading as factual observations—have their modern roots in early twentieth-century art movements whose advocates managed to wax poetic while at the same time rallying their troops for revolt. There was the Cubist Manifesto ("The time has come for us to be the masters," wrote Guillaume Apollinaire in 1913), and five years later, the Dada Manifesto ("Every man must shout," wrote Tristan Tzara. "There is great destructive, negative work to be done."). André Breton "hurled formal warnings to society" in his impassioned 1925 Surrealist Manifesto, while Filippo Tommaso Marinetti dubbed his own 1913 Futurist Manifesto "incendiary" as he preached a celebration of danger (glorify war!), a renunciation of classicism (destroy the museums!) and a radical redefinition of beauty that scorned women, endorsed aggression and embraced artistic freedom at all costs.[2] To read Marinetti now, nearly one hundred years later and outside the turbulent political climate in which he was originally intended to be read, is to understand fervor as a basic operating principle—and arguably, to consider some of the more fatuous promises of the digital age in an entirely new light.[3]

The tempestuous era framing the pronouncements of early modernist doctrine is, of course, long gone. In its wake, postmodernists seem to have comparatively dispassionate views: they simply refuse to take anything very seriously. ("While modernism thrived on multiple manifesti," explains the *New York Times* cultural critic Edward Rothstein, "postmodernism's manifesto might be that no manifesto is possible.") So how to explain its sudden return? Art movements aside and fascist tendencies notwithstanding, the manifesto, in its purest incarnation, is still largely considered a powerful purveyor of ideology; by conjecture, it is also a provocative social stimulant for self-appointed

Originally published in *Eye*, no. 38 (Winter 2000).

activists. Activism itself can be a potent motive for putting pen to paper, and it is likely that the modern-day activist's tactical advantage lies in mastering the art of such pointedly dogmatic prose. It is precisely this imperiousness, this preachiness, that sets it apart from everything else we read: from the Cluetrain Manifesto ("Hyperlinks subvert hierarchy"), to David Gelernter's Second Coming Manifesto ("Computing will be transformed"), to Bruce Mau's Incomplete Manifesto for Growth ("Ask stupid questions"), to the First Things First Manifesto ("We propose a reversal of priorities),[4] to the Dogma Manifesto ("We propose a vow of chastity"), to the New Puritans Manifesto ("We believe in grammatical purity"), to the U.N. 2000 Peace Manifesto ("Respect all life"), to the Unabomber Manifesto (just under thirty-five thousand words about why we *shouldn't* respect life and, well, enough said).

Actually, not nearly enough said. There are hundreds, even thousands of manifesti in general circulation, and it would not be an overstatement to suggest that the great majority of these are eminently forgettable, unabashedly self-aggrandizing or just plain tiresome in their pandering attempts to define What Is Important: consider, for example, the Simplicity Manifesto ("Simplicity is power!") or the Internet Manifesto ("No information shall be censored!"). There are manifesti written to oppose pretty much anything: like the Squash the TV Bugs Manifesto, which vociferously rejects the overuse of what its advocates call "Obnoxicons" (the faux blind-embossed, semi-transparent network identification logos that reside in the corners of TV screens). There are even manifesti written to oppose manifesti, such as the Anti-Manifesto ("What's the matter with kids today?"[5]) and the Anti-Anti Manifesto ("The First Amendment isn't an excuse for ignorance").

Conversely, it is the rare but delightful manifesto that combines original insights with welcome doses of irony: I am thinking here of P. J. O'Rourke's Clinton-bashing Liberty Manifesto ("There is only one basic human right: the right to do as you damn well please"), or Karrie Jacobs's modernist-bashing Fruitbowl Manifesto ("Perfection is intimidating. You have to be on your best behavior to live with it"). To be fair (and historically accurate), manifesti on topics of universally acknowledged importance—civil jurisprudence and nuclear disarmament, for example—have been written in the interests of reducing confusion, consolidating opinion or securing widespread consensus. Documents such as these are not only initially relevant, but also accumulate added value over time. (A good example is the Bertrand Russell and Albert Einstein 1955 Manifesto that laid the foundations for the modern peace movement.)

In general, though, the philosophical tenets upon which so many modern manifesti lay their claims often seem inflated, invented or simply self-serving. And what better medium to promote such exploits than the World Wide Web? As a publishing platform, it is uniquely positioned to both display and distribute the gospel according to anybody-who-wants-to-volunteer-an-opinion. The Web is a maelstrom of rampant self-expression, a First Amendment free-for-all. (On the up side, networked culture is also devoid of such interpersonal perils as oppression, hierarchy, domination and exclusivity. It is socially non-sectarian: an anti-proletariat.) This "reading" of the Internet as a kind of natural habitat for self-publishing is precisely what encourages so much impassioned writing. In truth, and beyond its claims of efficiency and progress, the Web's facility for networked data exchange supports a kind of hopelessly reciprocal social infrastructure that has become an unusually fertile breeding ground for the manifesto. Funny that the social equalities presumed possible on the Web have themselves spawned such didacticism—with its overtones of moral superiority, its artistic idealism, its philosophical imperatives. And it is precisely this kind of didacticism—the world according to me, me, me—that has, in a sense, become the Web's *lingua franca*.

At the core of this not insignificant cultural paradigm shift lies the Internet itself, a broad and still largely undefined social platform that levels the playing field to such an extent that we no longer know where we stand—or what, more importantly, we stand *for*. Enter the manifesto: preaching to the converted, the non-converted, whoever will listen. Bearing in mind the limited attention span of the general public, the typical contemporary manifesto is pithy, abbreviated and strident in tone, a staccato series of ex-cathedra statements and, it is hoped, quote-worthy sound bites. Here is the basic formula, as I see it: Take an idea. Break it down into its component parts. (Write short sentences: think *doctrinaire*.) Add paragraph breaks. Bullets. Numbers. Now add Lots! Of! Punctuation! Assume everyone on the planet will agree with you and proceed to express yourself with the much-anticipated collective enthusiasm of the madding crowds. Upload keywords. And post! If you are feeling unsure about any of this, get a few friends together and coerce them into adding their names to your list of lofty ideals: "We, the undersigned" means if your ship goes down, you are not the only one onboard.

With this in mind, it seems somehow appropriate that I take a stab at writing my own manifesto. Surprising as it may seem to my loyal readers, I have no particular political ideology or aesthetic bias or subversive agenda to proclaim, no prevailing morality to preach or aggrieved practices to denounce. There are no signatories to this manifesto—or, as a very wise friend of mine is fond of saying, "my views do not represent anyone but me."

My manifesto is a rant. It is intended to debunk the exalted claims of wannabe philosophers and soapbox proselytizers, to critique the posturing and the pretense, the lofty promises, the loose-cannon platitudes. My manifesto applauds original thinking and admonishes cheap shots. It supports the intrinsic merits of personality and it skewers the implausible motives of "personalization." It commends modernism, where appropriate, and critiques marketing, where not. It tries to acknowledge the authentic (what's progress?), to identify the artificial (what's plagiarism?) and to illuminate the difference between the two. Its goal is to cut through the clutter and rebuke the rhetoric, to reconsider some of the ideas that really matter—at least to me.

Then again, my views do not represent anyone but me.

MANIFESTO™

1. Information architecture is not architecture.
2. Empowerment is not the same as entitlement.
3. Personalization is not the same as personality.

4. Convergence remains more successful in concept than in execution.

5. The proliferation of mysterious acronyms is inversely proportionate to the number of original ideas in the world.

6. The installed base of couches still overshadows the number of personal computers in general circulation.

7. Less is a chore.

8. The killer app never killed anybody.

9. Faster is not the same as better.

10. Space is not the final frontier.

ANNOTATIONS TO THE MANIFESTO

1. In the early 1990s, Clement Mok took the stage at a New York AIGA business conference and, with great fanfare, proposed the term "information architect" as a more accurate title for what most graphic designers—especially those engaged in new and complex media—do for a living. My view then was the same as now: as long as we are choosing new titles, I would like to change mine to "brain surgeon." Much as we would prefer to think otherwise, design, unlike architecture (and for that matter, brain surgery) remains an industry in which one need not—indeed, cannot—be certified to practice. Architecture is architecture, information be damned. What we design, as novel and revolutionary as it might seem at the time of our designing it, is still just design. Simply stated: graphic design is probably not going to kill you if it falls on your head.

2. In a talk several years ago at the Cato Institute (a non-partisan public policy research foundation in Washington, D.C.), author and sometime political pundit P. J. O'Rourke remarked: "Freedom is not empowerment. Empowerment is what the Serbs have in Bosnia." Freedom of expression (an issue of some consequence to manifesto-writers) is a constitutional right, but in extreme cases—the Unabomber Manifesto, for example—free expression becomes forcible terrorism and the consequences are lethal. At the same time, the relationship between the autonomies such "freedoms" can provide through technology (long-distance learning, for example) contribute to a sense of exalted personal entitlement: if anybody can get a Harvard degree online, then why not me? (If anybody can get a Harvard degree online, then what is to become of Harvard?) It is easy to see how quickly (and inappropriately) empowerment contributes to our sense of entitlement: but while both share a certain quality of warped fetishism (one is fed by illusions of digitally enhanced grandeur; the other, by distorted perceptions of privilege), they are *not* interchangeable.

3. The advent of customized everything may well contribute to the entitlement-versus-empowerment debate but is of particular concern to issues of privacy. "Personality" is what makes you special. "Personalization" telegraphs the illusion that you are special: yet to enable technologies to customize your profile is to expose your identity, streamline your personality and ultimately jeopardize the very privacy that is your most inalienable right. "Personality" is to "unique" what "personalization" is to "univer-

sal." "Personalization" means you have submitted information that enables you to be tracked: it is a front for surveillance that lets you be repackaged as a "you" that is a distributable demographic statistic. Personally, I am waiting for someone to offer customizable encryption software that lets me be *me*. The Electronic Privacy Information Center claims to offer an array of tools that protect such privacies through e-mail—from "snoop-proof" mail applications to virtual paper shredders. For more on the status of privacy policies, and the availability of these resources, see: *www.epic.org/privacy/tools.html*.

4. Though it promises the kind of seamless integration we have imagined since the dawn of the Industrial Revolution, convergence remains largely a myth. The phrase "out of the box" (the wireless dream of convergent hopefuls) is equally problematic. Yet what remains critical—and largely unresolved—are the economic imperatives that drive not only the manufacture of our digital devices, but more importantly, their inevitable consumption. Beyond the perils of monopolization (as seen, for instance, in the protracted, two-year, well-publicized antitrust suit against Microsoft) there are compelling arguments for the enduring value of "healthy" competition. For more on the relationship between convergence and stagnation, see: *www.convergence.org/info/faq.html*.

5. In the days of Marx and Marinetti, manifesti were passionately scripted: adorned with flowery or extreme language, punctuated with inflammatory suggestion, filled with mixed metaphor and near-hallucinogenic word pictures. By contrast, today's offerings are skimpy and forcibly restrained—even brusque. To what do we owe this seismic shift in style? Is terse language a consequence of modernist reduction, streamlined sentences mirroring the formal economy of, say, synthetic plastics? Are punchy, bulleted "tips" more likely to seize a reader's attention, given the likelihood that he or she is already under attack by a veritable deluge of information? Contemporary manifesto-speak has supplanted lyrical prose with generic jargon: we think we sound smarter when we abbreviate with such concocted acronyms, but in reality, the opposite is more likely to be true: in the entire lexicon of universally-accepted new media jargon, the acronym is the most annoying component. Beyond "eyeballs" and "drill-downs," beyond "action items" and "affinity groups" and "data mining" lie a conspiracy of enigmatic abbreviations, of "KPI(s)" and "CSF(s)" (key performance indicators and critical success factors); "users" (read people) are evaluated for their "LMS" (lifestyle management services) and "mindshare" (read products) analyzed for their "UBV" (unique brand value). All of these "HRS" (human resource strategies) are, of course, intended to maximize saturation opportunities for BRANDING—a concept that, to me, instantly conjures up images of cattle being torched on the belly by a very hot iron.

6. According to a report published in 2000 by the Annenberg Public Policy Center, low-income families (defined as those with an income of less than $30,000 per year) are much less likely to have computers, or Internet access, or newspaper subscriptions compared with their middle income ($30,000–$75,000 per year) and high income (over $75,000 per year) counterparts. Of all the media surveyed, children spend the most time with television, over two hours per day (147 minutes). They spend the least time per day on the Internet (fourteen minutes per day).

7. I remain firmly convinced that good designers are good editors. This means

having not only the instinct, but a willingness to commit that instinct—a sense of conviction—to articulate why one choice is preferable to another. Editing, like much of the
reductivist thinking that characterizes classic design education, suggests a kind of basic
working methodology that not only shapes formal decisions, but also informs conceptual ones. It is a pretty simple equation: just say *no*. And yet, in this age of more-better-
faster, never before has something so simple been so hard to communicate. In the area
of online publishing, this is an especially precarious issue: just because you can do or say
or publish or design something, must you? Is less better? Not necessarily. But it certainly
seems harder to come by. The plea for a pared-down ideal, however, is not unique to
the design disciplines: similar core values are proposed, for example, in the Dogma
Manifesto, published "in the hope of rescuing world cinema from decadent bourgeois
individualism" by Danish filmmakers Lars von Trier and Thomas Vinterberg in 1995. To
qualify for the Dogma "seal of approval" a film must comply to Dogma's "vow of
chastity," which includes using only available light and sound, avoiding false conventions
(such as props) and eliminating all traces of directorial personality—including the director's credit. Inspired by such dreamily idealistic notions of formal restraint, British novelists Nicholas Blincoe and Matt Thorne founded the New Puritans earlier this year:
their ten-point Manifesto embraces an allegedly "puritan" code of writing, defined by
pledges to "shun poetry," "avoid elaborate punctuation," and (my personal favorite)
"eschew flashbacks."

8. In my own experience, the common denominator uniting nearly every new
business pitch I have witnessed over the past decade lies in the misguided notion that a
single idea is capable of revolutionizing anything, let alone the Internet. More troubling
still than this is the expectation that revolution can be achieved through, um, *software*.
Though I willingly acknowledge the unparalleled global progress in interpersonal
telecommunications systems (consider the advances in mobile computing, for instance),
I do not accept the notion that there is one person, or advancement, or piece of soft-
or hardware, in or out of the box, that will fundamentally alter (let alone "kill") the
Internet.

9. The legacy of the clickable button is a study in misinterpretation. Buttons,
when they do not slip through buttonholes as ways of fastening our clothing, are little
more than miniature mechanisms for managing power: we switch them on or off, adjust
their settings from low to high, push them in elevators to travel up and down. In the
interests of spatial economy, buttons tend to be small, scaled to the circumference of an
adult fingertip. They are not gender specific and have few if any cultural associations
beyond their generic and increasingly iconic value as emblems of point-and-click persuasion. Buttons tend to be square or elliptical, and are frequently embellished with
needlessly elaborate drop-shadows and "enhanced" with rollover responsiveness so that
they do really pointless things like FLASH or BLINK to let users know they have been
activated. Sadly, buttons, the unfortunate product of the last ten years of digital evolution, are as ubiquitous as they are utilitarian. At their best, perhaps, they are invisible.

And yet buttons have come to represent the idealized speed—instantaneity,
even—with which we characterize modern life. The misnomer here lies in the fact that

although modern conveniences simplify certain activities, life's essential complications endure. Consider the telephone: does speed-dialing do anything to cut through the misery that is voicemail? Is button-pushing ever used to advance one's interminable wait on hold? Still, we persist in the assumption that faster is what happens when we push buttons, and that faster is better—failing to recognize, as James Glieck observes in his insightful book (appropriately enough, entitled *Faster*) that "neither technology nor efficiency can acquire more time for you, because time is not a thing you have lost . . . it is what you live in."

10. Last year, the U.S. Congress passed the Commercial Space Act, legalizing the privatization of manned space flight. The same dream of wide open spaces that sent Columbus to the New World will soon send every dot.com entrepreneur to the moon in his very own customized space shuttle. Though it may be hard to imagine that the space age may indeed by dawning, it is harder, still, to accept the reality that civilian interplanetary travel is a buyer's market. My view: once the moon has become a tourist attraction, it is a pretty safe bet to assume that its frontier credibility will be a thing of the past.

Notes
1. *The American Heritage Dictionary of the English Language,* 3rd ed. (Boston: Houghton Mifflin Company, 1996).
2. Marinetti's impassioned prose offers a comparatively radical analysis of the plethora of bad Web sites in daily evidence. He writes: "A repugnant mixture is concocted from monotonous sensations and the idiotic religious emotion of listeners buddhistically drunk with repeating for the nth time their more or less snobbish or second-hand ecstasy."
3. Equally incendiary, Karl Marx and Frederick Engels's classic 1848 *Communist Manifesto* vilifies capitalism and sings the plight of the working man. It also predates Breton and Marinetti by a full half-century.
4. For the complete text and signatories, plus coverage of the media response to this update of Ken Garland's original 1964 Manifesto by the same title, see *www.adbuster.org/campaigns/first*.
5. Given the freedom, would we dance in the streets? Or destroy them? For more on the zine Anti-Manifesto (Safe, Effective and Free!), see the following Web site: *www.zyworld.com/10584832.fc/anti-manifesto.htm*.

AN INCOMPLETE MANIFESTO FOR GROWTH
Bruce Mau

1. ALLOW EVENTS TO CHANGE YOU.

You have to be willing to grow. Growth is different from something that happens to you. You produce it. You live it. The prerequisites for growth: the openness to experience events and the willingness to be changed by them.

Originally published in *Life Style* by Bruce Mau (New York and London: Phaidon Press, 2000).

2. FORGET ABOUT GOOD.

Good is an unknown quantity. Good is what we all agree on. Growth is not necessarily good. Growth is an exploration of unlit recesses that may or may not yield to our research. As long as you stick to good you'll never have real growth.

3. PROCESS IS MORE IMPORTANT THAN OUTCOME.

When the outcome drives the process we will only ever go to where we've already been. If process drives outcome we may not know where we're going, but we will know we want to be there.

4. LOVE YOUR EXPERIMENTS (AS YOU WOULD AN UGLY CHILD).

Joy is the engine of growth. Exploit the liberty in casting your work as beautiful experiments, iterations, attempts, trials and errors. Take the long view and allow yourself the fun of failure every day.

5. GO DEEP.

The deeper you go the more likely you will discover something of value.

6. CAPTURE ACCIDENTS.

The wrong answer is the right answer in search of a different question. Collect wrong answers as part of the process. Ask different questions.

7. STUDY.

A studio is a place of study. Use the necessity of production as an excuse to study. Everyone will benefit.

8. DRIFT.

Allow yourself to wander aimlessly. Explore adjacencies. Lack judgment. Postpone criticism.

9. BEGIN ANYWHERE.

John Cage tells us that not knowing where to begin is a common form of paralysis. His advice: begin anywhere.

10. EVERYONE IS A LEADER.

Growth happens. Whenever it does, allow it to emerge. Learn to follow when it makes sense. Let anyone lead.

11. HARVEST IDEAS. EDIT APPLICATIONS.

Ideas need a dynamic, fluid, generous environment to sustain life. Applications, on the other hand, benefit from critical rigor. Produce a high ratio of ideas to applications.

12. KEEP MOVING.

The market and its operations have a tendency to reinforce success. Resist it. Allow failure and migration to be a part of your practice.

13. SLOW DOWN.

Desynchronize from standard time frames and surprising opportunities may present themselves.

14. DON'T BE COOL.

Cool is conservative fear dressed in black. Free yourself from limits of this sort.

15. ASK STUPID QUESTIONS.

Growth is fueled by desire and innocence. Assess the answer, not the question. Imagine learning throughout your life at the rate of an infant.

16. COLLABORATE.

The space between people working together is filled with conflict, friction, strife, exhilaration, delight and vast creative potential.

17.

Intentionally left blank. Allow space for the ideas you haven't had yet, and for the ideas of others.

18. STAY UP LATE.

Strange things happen when you've gone too far, been up too long, worked too hard, and you're separated from the rest of the world.

19. WORK THE METAPHOR.

Every object has the capacity to stand for something other than what is apparent. Work on what it stands for.

20. BE CAREFUL TO TAKE RISKS.

Time is genetic. Today is the child of yesterday and parent of tomorrow. The work you produce today will create your future.

21. REPEAT YOURSELF.

If you like it, do it again. If you don't like it, do it again.

22. MAKE YOUR OWN TOOLS.

Hybridize your tools in order to build unique things. Even simple tools that are your own can yield entirely new avenues of exploration. Remember, tools can amplify our capacities, so even a small tool can make a big difference.

23. STAND ON SOMEONE'S SHOULDERS.

You can travel farther carried on the accomplishments of those who came before you. And the view is so much better.

24. AVOID SOFTWARE.

The problem with software is that everyone has it.

25. DON'T CLEAN YOUR DESK.

You might find something in the morning that you can't see tonight.

26. DON'T ENTER AWARDS COMPETITIONS.

Just don't. It's not good for you.

27. READ ONLY LEFT-HAND PAGES.

Marshall McLuhan did this. By decreasing the amount of information, we leave room for what he called our "noodle."

28. MAKE NEW WORDS. EXPAND THE LEXICON.

The new conditions demand a new way of thinking. The thinking demands new forms of expression. The expression generates new conditions.

29. THINK WITH YOUR MIND. FORGET TECHNOLOGY.

Creativity is not device-dependent.

30. ORGANIZATION = LIBERTY.

Real innovation in design, or any other field, happens in context. That context is usually some form of cooperatively managed enterprise. Frank Gehry, for instance, is only able to realize Bilbao because his studio can deliver it on budget. The myth of a split between "creatives" and "suits" is what Leonard Cohen calls a "charming artifact of the past."

31. DON'T BORROW MONEY.

Once again, Frank Gehry's advice. By maintaining financial control, we maintain creative control. It's not exactly rocket science, but it's surprising how hard it is to maintain this discipline, and how many have failed.

32. LISTEN CAREFULLY.

Every collaborator who enters our orbit brings with him or her a world more strange and complex than any we could ever hope to imagine. By listening to the details and the subtlety of their needs, desires, or ambitions, we fold their world into our own. Neither party will ever be the same.

33. TAKE FIELD TRIPS.

The bandwidth of the world is greater than that of your TV set, or the Internet, or even a totally immersive, interactive, dynamically rendered, object-oriented, real-time, computer graphic-simulated environment.

34. MAKE MISTAKES FASTER.

This isn't my idea—I borrowed it. I think it belongs to Andy Grove.

35. IMITATE.

Don't be shy about it. Try to get as close as you can. You'll never get all the way, and the separation might be truly remarkable. We have only to look to Richard Hamilton and his version of Marcel Duchamp's large glass to see how rich, discredited and underused imitation is as a technique.

36. SCAT.

When you forget the words, do what Ella did: make up something else . . . not words.

37. BREAK IT, STRETCH IT, BEND IT, CRUSH IT, FOLD IT.

38. EXPLORE THE OTHER EDGE.

Great liberty exists when we avoid trying to run with the technological pack. We can't find the leading edge because it's trampled underfoot. Try using old-tech equipment made obsolete by an economic cycle but still rich with potential.

39. COFFEE BREAKS, CAB RIDES, GREEN ROOMS . . .

Real growth often happens outside of where we intend it to, in the interstitial space— what Dr. Seuss calls "the waiting place." Hans Ulrich Obrist once organized a science and art conference with all the infrastructure of a conference—the parties, chats, lunches, airport arrivals—but with no actual conference. Apparently it was hugely successful and spawned many ongoing collaborations.

40. AVOID FIELDS. JUMP FENCES.

Disciplinary boundaries and regulatory regimes are attempts to control the wilding of creative life. They are often understandable efforts to order what are manifold, complex, evolutionary processes. Our job is to jump the fences and cross the fields.

41. LAUGH.

People visiting the studio often comment on how much we laugh. Since I've become aware of this, I use it as a barometer of how completely we are expressing ourselves.

42. REMEMBER.

Growth is only possible as a product of history. Without memory, innovation is merely novelty. History gives growth a direction. But a memory is never perfect. Every memory is a degraded or composite image of a previous moment or event. That's what makes us aware of its quality as a past and not a present. It means that every memory is new, a partial construct different from its sources, and, as such, a potential for growth itself.

43. POWER TO THE PEOPLE.

Play can only happen when people feel they have control over their lives. We can't be free agents if we're not free.

FUCK COMMITTEES (I BELIEVE IN LUNATICS)
Tibor Kalman

It's about the struggle between individuals with jagged passion in their work and today's faceless corporate committees, which claim to understand the needs of the mass audience, and are removing the idiosyncrasies, polishing the jags, creating a thought-free, passion-free, cultural mush that will not be hated nor loved by anyone. By now, virtually all media, architecture, product and graphic design have been freed from ideas, individual passion, and have been relegated to a role of corporate servitude, carrying out corporate strategies and increasing stock prices. Creative people are now working for the bottom line.

Magazine editors have lost their editorial independence and work for committees of publishers (who work for committees of advertisers). TV scripts are vetted by producers, advertisers, lawyers, research specialists, layers and layers of paid executives who determine whether the scripts are dumb enough to amuse what they call the "lowest common denominator." Film studios put films in front of focus groups to determine whether an ending will please target audiences. All cars look the same. Architectural decisions are made by accountants. Ads are stupid. Theater is dead.

Corporations have become the sole arbiters of cultural ideas and taste in America.

Our culture is corporate culture.

Culture used to be the opposite of commerce, not a fast track to "content"-derived riches. Not so long ago captains of industry (no angels in the way they acquired wealth) thought that part of their responsibility was to use their millions to support culture. Carnegie built libraries, Rockefeller built art museums, Ford created his global

Originally published in *Tibor Kalman: Perverse Optimist*, edited by Peter Hall and Michael Bierut (London: Booth-Clibborn Editions, 1998).

foundation. What do we now get from our billionaires? Gates? Or Eisner? Or Redstone? Sales pitches. Junk mail. Meanwhile, creative people have their work reduced to "content" or "intellectual property." Magazines and films become "delivery systems" for product messages.

But to be fair, the above is only 99 percent true.

I offer a modest solution: find the cracks in the wall. There are a very few lunatic entrepreneurs who will understand that culture and design are not about fatter wallets, but about creating a future. They will understand that wealth is a means, not an end. Under other circumstances they may have turned out to be like you, creative lunatics. Believe me, they're there, and when you find them, treat them well and use their money to change to world.

THE VOW OF CHASTITY
First-Year Students at Central St. Martins College of Art and Design, London

AUTHOR'S NOTE—First Year design brief: Monday 26 February–9 March 2001. Set by John Morgan at Central St. Martins, London. These design rules had the expressed goal of countering "certain tendencies" in graphic design at St. Martins. Each first-year student had to sign up and swear to submit to the rules for the duration of the project. They were produced with tongue in cheek and in direct reference to the Dogma95 "Vow of Chastity" for filmmaking by Lars von Trier and Thomas Vinterberg.

I swear to submit (for the period of this project) to the following set of rules drawn up and confirmed by DOGMA 2001:

1. CONTENT MATTERS: DESIGN NOTHING THAT IS NOT WORTH READING.

The job should speak for itself (if it doesn't, the designer hasn't learned to listen). Books showing pictures of other designers' work must not be referred to (unless as part of a critical study).

From *Dot Dot Dot,* no. 3 (Summer 2001).

2. IMAGES MUST NOT BE USED UNLESS
THEY REFER DIRECTLY TO THE TEXT.

(Illustrations must be positioned where they are referred to in the text; foot- or side-notes must be positioned on same page as the text they refer to.)

3. THE BOOK MUST BE HAND-HELD
(AND DESIGNED FROM THE INSIDE OUT).

"Coffee-table books" are not acceptable.

4. THE FIRST TEXT COLOR SHALL BE BLACK;
THE SECOND COLOR RED.

Special colors, varnish and lamination are not acceptable.

5. PHOTOSHOP/ILLUSTRATOR FILTERS ARE FORBIDDEN

6. THE DESIGN MUST NOT CONTAIN SUPERFICIAL ELEMENTS.

(Maximize the data-ink ratio, no chart junk.)

7. TEMPORAL AND GEOGRAPHICAL ALIENATION ARE FORBIDDEN.

(That is to say that the design takes place here and now. No pastiche.)

8. GENRE DESIGN IS NOT ACCEPTABLE.

(No "smile in the mind." Leave graphic wit to comedians. No thoughtless application of style.)

9. FORMATS MUST NOT BE "A" SIZES.
PAPER MUST BE CHLORINE-FREE.

It must be off-white.

10. THE DESIGNER MUST NOT BE CREDITED
(UNLESS ALL OTHER WORKERS ARE ALSO CREDITED).

Designing and making is collective work.

Furthermore, I swear as a designer to refrain from personal taste! I am no longer an artist. I swear to refrain from creating a "work," as I regard the instant as more important than the whole. My supreme goal is to force the truth out of my characters and settings. I swear to do so by all the means available and at the cost of any good taste and any aesthetic considerations.

Thus I make my VOW OF CHASTITY.

Signature: _____

Name: _____

St. Martins, London, Monday 26 February 2001
The first-year students on behalf of DOGMA 2001
(John Morgan)

CRITICAL
LANGUAGES

It was nearly twenty years ago that Massimo Vignelli took the podium at the first symposium on graphic design history, "Coming of Age" at the Rochester Institute of Technology. "Other professions, like architecture, to name one, are really sustained and forwarded by criticism," he said in 1983. "If you open a graphics magazine from the last thirty years, there never seems to be a page of criticism, just attractive little biographies and that is it. Do you think we can go on without criticism? Without criticism we will never have a profession." Twenty years later, thoughtful writers on design are still trying to figure out exactly what graphic design criticism is, or what it should be.

In February 2001, several hundred critics, historians, educators, students and practitioners met in New York at the American Institute of Graphic Arts's first conference on design history and criticism, "Looking Closer," to address the question anew. It is not an easy one. At the center of it all is the elusive nature of graphic design itself. More often that not, graphic design is ephemeral, resisting the scrutiny that an architecture critic can employ when focusing on something as public and substantial as a building. It is usually not something that is consumed by the public as a thing in and of itself, so the consumer service that restaurant and movie critics provide is not required. And, despite the rise of tropes like "The Designer as Author," most graphic design is about someone else's message, which makes literary criticism a questionable model.

Yet the past two decades have seen each of these models tested, retested, combined and superceded. Graphic design has been analyzed as an example of pop culture, like a rock song. It has provided fodder for theoretical academic criticism, refracted through the specialized lenses of Marxism, feminism, deconstructivism and more. In perhaps the most convincing evidence of its maturity as a field, it has even become a source for parody and satire. No one answer is final, but the quest goes on. The writers in this section focus not just on writing critically about graphic design but on writing critically about graphic design criticism. Can we go on without criticism? Obviously not. Now if only we could figure out what it is.

Michael Bierut

THE TIME FOR BEING AGAINST

Rick Poynor

While I was thinking about this talk, I received an e-mail from a designer I know. In the subject line, at the top of the message, it said: "The time for being against is over." When I read the message itself, I discovered that this did have something to do with its content, although only in a roundabout way. The writer was concerned not to be seen by his colleagues as an activist, in the mold of *Adbusters*, or some similar group. As it happens, I had never suggested he was anything of the kind, but this slightly awkward but memorable phrase—"the time for being against is over"— seems to crystallize many aspects of society and culture as we experience them today.

For the fact is that, among our own group, designers—and especially young designers—this appears to be a fairly general view. The phrase is taken from a book called *The World Must Change: Graphic Design and Idealism*. It's a quote from a Dutch design student: "I do not want to separate. I have no interest in being against. I want to include. The time for being against is over." Not long ago, a design historian of my acquaintance, a clever young woman with a Ph.D., said something very similar to me: "You can't be against everything all the time." I used to teach at the Royal College of Art and this issue of not being against things—the consensual feeling that we have somehow reached a point of *rapprochement* or healing or wholeness—came up all the time. To be against things was to be negative, and what's the point of that? You can't change anything by being "against things"—the world is what it is—so all that negative energy is just going to boomerang back on you in the end. By being against things, especially when most people agree that the time for being against things is over, you will only make yourself unhappy.

The whole issue came to a head for me when I sat in on a project with an environmental theme, organized by one of the other Royal College of Art tutors. He gave a spellbinding performance, unleashing a scintillating stream of facts, statistics and examples of earlier environmentally based art and communication projects. He outlined the issues and constructed a cogent and provocative set of arguments. The students—about forty of them, all studying at masters level, young adults in their mid-twenties—sat there

Originally a lecture presented at "Looking Closer: AIGA Conference on Design History and Criticism" in New York City, February 2001. © 2001 Rick Poynor.

like a bunch of sullen, unresponsive kids, offering only a few occasional, usually sarcastic remarks. Here was someone who was very definitely against things, but this display of a fiercely engaged, critical intelligence seemed to make this group uneasy. It's not even that they argued against his point of view. Why should they? What a waste of energy, and for that matter, how uncool! The time for being against things is over.

If this is anything like the dominant view—at least among educated young people—then these do not appear to be very propitious times for any kind of criticism, let alone design criticism. Because, as I have always understood the term, to be critical involves not taking things for granted, being skeptical, questioning what's there, exposing limitations, taking issue, advancing a contrary view, puncturing myths. On occasion, of course, the critic will take the role of supporter and advocate. He or she will seek to persuade us that some idea or thing is deserving of our full attention and merits a closer look. The critic will act as interpreter and explain some seemingly arcane aspect of culture that many or most of us don't yet grasp and are perhaps inclined to resist. But this process of supportive elucidation will always imply its opposite: that there are objects and projects that are not worthy of our attention, that are problematic, flawed and sometimes possibly even pernicious. Any would-be critic who practices only the role of supporter and advocate, who never finds fault, sees nothing to contest, is not really a critic at all.

While it's hugely encouraging for anyone who continues to think criticism matters that a conference like this should take place—it's almost unthinkable, at the present time, that a British design organization would mount such an event—design criticism continues to survive in, at best, a precarious state of health. How could it be otherwise? To exist at all, criticism depends on two things: a range of suitable outlets and a body of people—the critics—to supply the criticism. We don't have enough of either. If criticism is struggling in a wider cultural sense, if proprietors of mainstream media believe it is simply not required by most ordinary readers and viewers, and readers and viewers show every sign of endorsing this judgment (because the time for being against is over), then it would be very optimistic indeed to expect specialist trade publications aimed at practicing graphic designers to lead the critical fight-back. On the contrary, as a very young discipline, graphic design criticism needs to learn by "looking closer" at critical practice in neighboring areas. Fortunately, the critical mentality is so deeply entrenched that it still thrives in pockets elsewhere, and there are even signs of a possible renewal.

I'll return to this later, but first I'm aware that I need to state my own position more clearly to supply the context for these remarks. The term I have sometimes used for the practice I would like to engage in is "critical journalism." I have occasionally described myself as a "critic," for reasons of expediency, but "critic" is a pretty strange passport description, and I really just see myself as a writer with a lasting, fairly serious commitment to design and visual culture. I engage in different ways with material that interests me, depending on the forum and audience. I certainly hope there's always some strand of critical awareness in anything I publish—I might be wrong about that, of course—but the writing undeniably slides up and down a scale between relatively impersonal journalism at one end (though I'm not interested in doing this kind of writing) and criticism, in some notionally purer, much more personal and perhaps more academic sense at the other. Most of the time it will be strategically located somewhere near the middle of this scale—hence my use of the term "critical journalism." It's an attempt to combine journalism's engagement with the moment and its communicative techniques with criticism's fundamental requirement for a worked-out, coherent, fully conscious critical position: a way of looking at, and understanding, the world, or some aspects of it, anyway.

But to explain this fully, I need to go a little further because the kind of writing I now do, in this particular field, comes directly from my experiences as a reader going back many years. I've always read criticism and I've always read critical journalism. Much of my education and sense of the world has come from undirected, personal reading across a range of cultural fields—literature, music, social history, film, photography, fine art and other subjects. I'm sure most of you could say the same. I have always been engaged by writing that seemed to assume the existence of readers like me: people who just happened to have an interest in a subject, whatever it might be—the postwar novel, Kurt Schwitters's collages, New German Cinema, the French Nouvelle Vague—because they took meaning and pleasure from it and believed it to be important. This writing wasn't directed exclusively or even perhaps largely towards an audience of academic peers and students, even if the academy was often its point of origin. It wanted to discover a broader audience. It was aimed outwards at any intelligent, literate, thinking individuals, from any background, with the curiosity to undertake their own personal researches and see what they could find out.

There's a nice term for the kind of writer who chooses to occupy this cultural position, to think in public and address the broadest possible readership—it's "public intellectual." One hundred years ago such a position would have been taken for granted. Intellectual discourse was a public activity accessible to any educated citizen. Fifty years ago it was still perfectly viable. Think of figures like the architectural writer Lewis Mumford, the psychologists Bruno Bettelheim and Erich Fromm, the art critic Clement Greenberg. A few months ago, the New York publisher Basic Books organized a debate on "The Future of the Public Intellectual"—you can read an adapted version on the *Nation's* Web site. Four of the six panelists were academics—among them Herbert Gans, professor of sociology at Columbia University, and Stephen Carter, professor of law at Yale. The other two were critical journalists: the British writer Christopher Hitchens and Steven Johnson, co-founder of *Feed* magazine on the Web—more on him a bit later. Today, the public intellectual is often thought to be an endangered species. Public intellectuals were sustained by an audience of learned readers that has dwindled hugely since the 1960s, even if it hasn't entirely gone.

Do graphic designers form any significant part of that remaining core of readers with a commitment to ideas and the independent life of the mind, expressed through the act of reading? Are they, in other words, really interested in criticism? And, conversely, are those with a commitment to ideas the slightest bit interested in graphic design? These are daunting questions, when framed in those terms, as I think you'll probably agree.

Let's stick to designers for the moment. For as long as I have been writing about graphic design, I have heard it repeated like a mantra—by designers themselves and, more worryingly, even by one or two design writers—that designers as a professional group, as a type of person, "don't read." Not that they don't read history, or philosophy, or literature. But that they don't read, period. Not even the undemanding lifestyle magazines they like to "graze" to catch up on the latest styles and trends. As someone who has voluntarily chosen to write about this material, and could have done something else instead, I suppose that makes me a pretty extreme form of masochist. Why go on with it? First, because I don't really believe it. I suspect that the designer who pronounces blithely that "designers don't read" is often just talking about himself (it usually is a "him," too). I know too many designers who do read and care about writing to accept the generalization, even if it holds true for the majority. Second, because it struck me quite early on, as someone then writing about architecture, art and three-dimensional design, as well as graphics, that graphic design was a genuinely fascinating area of study. In art or architecture, it sometimes feels as though all that remains is to add footnotes and corrections to the huge corpus of criticism, theory and history that already fills the libraries. Graphic design, by comparison, was still relatively unknown, uncharted territory. There was work to be done. There was the excitement of discovery and getting to things first—a huge motivation for any writer, whether engaged in journalism or criticism.

The other thing that struck me—and this is where these points connect up—is that, given the relatively open, unprofessionalized status of graphic design writing, as well as the nature of its potential audience, it ought to be possible to find a way of writing about the subject that corresponded with my own preferences as a reader. My models here, in many ways, were the music press, as it was in the late 1970s and early 1980s, and the serious film press, as it is even now. Both of these areas had hugely knowledgeable, talented, independent writers, who earned a living from their enthusiasms by writing critical journalism for a broad, smart, demanding readership that might include academics, but was open to anybody who shared the writers' perspectives, passions and tastes.

I hesitate to give too many examples because, in my case, they are necessarily mainly British. I'm thinking of the kind of writing you might have found in the music paper *New Musical Express* during the punk and post-punk years, or the film magazine *Sight and Sound* at any point in the last four decades. The sort of prose produced, in America, by a music writer like Greil Marcus or film writers like Jim Hoberman and Amy Taubin (both of whom write for *Sight and Sound*). Books like Ian MacDonald's extraordinary, meticulous, track-by-track study of the Beatles, *Revolution in the Head*, which teases a revolution in sensibility from the song-writing process. Or Jon Savage's *England's Dreaming*, which sees British society refracted through punk rock. Or David Thomson's brilliant *Biographical Dictionary of Film*, one of the truly essential film books, lovingly crafted and periodically updated by a master essayist who has much to teach any would-be critic operating in *any* cultural discipline. These writers are both hip and scholarly, generous but rigorous, and they make the reader feel that their subject truly matters. It always seemed to me that graphic design, as a ubiquitous form of popular culture, could be written about in much the same way and that this was the strategy, if one could pull it off, that would be most effective in winning readers.

And here we return to the nub of the problem. For who, indeed, *are* the readers? Well, as we all know, in the main they are people involved in design—the ones who can be bothered to read, that is. Design has many beautifully produced, highly professional publications, but, by and large, they are not read by non-designers, nor do they expect to be. That's rather strange, though, if design really does have the cultural importance and meaning that we constantly tell ourselves that it has. It's like a music press read only by musicians, or a film press read only by filmmakers. Film and music publications *are* read by professionals, but the whole point of these magazines is that they address a broad, general readership. Design magazines, however, are mostly trade publications, and you wouldn't expect ordinary members of the public to read *Hotel and Catering Weekly* or *Liquid Plastics Review*. Yet, to judge by the look of them, design magazines aspire to be very much more than this: they are lavish, confident, magnificently visual. You can even buy them on certain newsstands. They win press awards. The problem is that no matter how good some of these publications are, the fact that they address and serve a professional audience of designers must inherently limit their ability to criticize their subject matter. I'm generalizing, of course, because I do think some are much more genuinely critical than others, but still there are certain lines that are rarely if ever crossed.

Yet, at the same time, as anyone who's tried it well knows, finding outlets for graphic design writing outside its dedicated press—outlets which could, in theory, allow much greater freedom to be critical—is always a struggle. Earlier this month, Jessica Helfand, a designer who also writes regularly, published a big piece about Milton Glaser in the *Los Angeles Times*, based on a review of his book *Art Is Work*. It was a rare and notable exception. I recently wrote a longish essay about graphic authorship for one of the British Sunday papers. Amazingly, they ran it on the cover of the culture section, but it was touch and go for a while. There were real concerns behind the scenes, among some of the editors, that it was "too specialist," even though I had done everything I could to "open up" the subject for the general reader, and it was pegged, opportunistically, on the publication of Bruce Mau's heavily promoted book, *Life Style*, and several appearances by him in London in the course of the following week. I automatically included a brief explanation of graphic design near the start of the piece, and I notice that Jessica did exactly the same thing. Imagine a review of a novel that felt obliged to begin with an explanation of "fiction," or a feature about art that felt it was necessary to explain the mysterious craft of "painting." Graphic design may be everywhere, but for commissioning editors, it would still seem to be largely invisible—and a little bit odd. Let me read you the headline and intro to my article:

> Is it art? Is it photography? No, actually, it's graphic design.
> Rick Poynor reports on how the quiet, selfless people who used to organize
> the pictures and words became authors themselves.

I hasten to add that these words were written by the editors, not by me. What this shows, with depressing clarity, is that any discussion of graphic design in the mainstream media must almost always start by zeroing the clock. It has to assume that the general reader has never heard of this arcane activity, pursued by a secret order of modest, self-effacing hermits dedicated to a vow of silence, even if by now most worldly, educated, broadsheet-reading people will have noticed that the world is looking pretty slick these days and someone must be responsible. Why, they may even have a graphic designer in the family! Articles like this are one-offs, and I'm sure it will be exactly the same next time. It's encouraging to see the significance of graphic design acknowledged at all, but I can't say I find it especially satisfying to produce this kind of article, because the level of sophistication possible, when writing for an audience of designers, is often considerably higher.

Three-dimensional design fares much better in mainstream media for a very predictable reason. Often there is something to go out and buy, a gadget or a chair, or there's a new look you could try at home. This kind of consumer journalism rarely rises to the level of cultural criticism. One could also argue that the relentless focus on design as stylish consumerism is fundamentally damaging to public and, for that matter, professional conceptions of designing, but at least design is routinely acknowledged as having a role in culture. We have to start somewhere. With graphic design, however, there is rarely a commodity as such, unless it's a design book—as with Glaser and Mau—but design books are reviewed in only the most exceptional cases. There is no unceasing flow of new product, as with music, films or novels, and consequently no obvious need for a weekly consumer guide in a newspaper or glossy magazine's culture pages, advising us where best to spend our cash. Graphic design is not, in most cases, a thing-in-itself—it's a formal property, a rhetorical dimension, a communicative tissue of something else. It may be an essential component, and the object may not properly exist without it, but its contribution is still usually just taken for granted, played down or overlooked by reviewers and critics whose expertise lies elsewhere. In truth, these days I don't believe that graphic design should be separated out in most cases. By doing that, we end up with the kind of distorted, self-aggrandizing view so often seen in the design press, where design is the be-all-and-end-all—at least in its own eyes—and is often considered almost independently from the project and purpose it serves. I should add that one obvious exception to this is graphic authorship, where the content of a project, as well as the form, is determined by the designer. Here, if the trend continues, and there are commodities for sale, or experiences to be had (perhaps in the form of an exhibition), review coverage may in time become a more regular feature in the press.

So where does all of this leave us? It leaves us in a distinctly paradoxical position, with a subject matter that we all agree plays an essential role in everyday life and culture, yet which lacks regular, direct outlets for critical public discussion. A subject that ought to engage ordinary people—its end-users—and quite possibly does engage them, but one that remains shadowy and mysterious, a shaping force in the contemporary world without any apparent cause.

I'm sure you don't want to hear about my long dark nights of the soul, so I'll pass quickly over the number of times I have wondered whether I was deluding myself about design's importance, and have come very close to conceding that it really is a subject of very little interest—unless you are a designer—and a crazy way for any halfway serious writer to spend his or her time. I wish I could offer you a rousing, multi-point program with lots of emphatic "musts" in it—"graphic design writing *must* do this, it *must* do that"—but the process of finding a way to write about this subject is much more tentative and exploratory than that. The only way to discover how to do it, or whether it can be done at all, is to try it. A few years ago, when the need for design criticism was a regular theme, one or two people started complaining—often in the pages of *Emigre*—about the inadequacies of design journalism, and on many points they were absolutely right. But where are they now? What have they written and where did it appear? I don't see their bylines much, or even at all.

In the early 1990s, most of the best writing on graphic design came from designers. A few emerging designer-critics were very productive and visible for a while, but I suspect that the point came when they had to choose: writing or design? Understandably, they chose design. Yet, if someone really wants to be a writer, if that's his primary ambition, then that is what he has to do for much—perhaps most—of the time. Write! Take a look at the standard in neighboring disciplines. There are brilliant people out there in the writing world and they are not kidding around. What you quickly learn, if you try to live by freelance writing, is that you are engaged in a constant process of trial and error and continuous negotiation to find spaces to write in the way that you want. That's the challenge and the fun. Those spaces won't be just handed to you because you mean well. You have to prove yourself by writing, then build by degrees on the space you have gained. The goal is to propose or be given assignments that allow you the freedom to do what you want as a writer, while satisfying the legitimate requirements of the publications for which you work. I hope it's clear from this that I am certainly not saying that design writing must necessarily be limited or bound by the "rules" of the marketplace. My own experience has shown me that design writers potentially have rather more room for maneuver than many of them—and their academic critics—sometimes imagine.

This brings us back to the question of developing a critical position. This is absolutely crucial to any discussion of criticism and I hope it's something we'll be exploring in the course of the day. Everyone has opinions and preferences—"everyone's a critic," in that limited sense—but while infusing journalism with a lively dose of personal opinion might make for entertaining writing (or not), this cannot be classed as serious criticism. I don't believe that a writer, operating regularly in mainstream media, can declare her position in an overt way, as a separate, sign-posted statement, every time she puts her fingers to the keyboard. An article for a magazine or newspaper is not an academic essay, and many articles are quite short—1,000 words, 1,500 words—but over time, if a writer has a critical position, it will be implicit in everything she does, and regular readers, coming to new pieces by her, will bring this understanding with them.

An example: Earlier, I mentioned the British music and pop culture writer Jon Savage. I've been reading his pieces for years and have a clear sense from his writing of who he is, what he stands for, what he values, what he believes. I can see his weaknesses too, but the crucial thing, for me as a reader, is that his vision of the world has depth and makes sense—that it adds something to my own understanding when I read him. I trust his judgment and this is the essence of the compact between reader and critic. Another example: Many of you will have read Judith Williamson's book *Decoding Advertisements*. For ten years, in the 1980s, Williamson worked as a film critic for several magazines, including the British political and cultural weekly *New Statesman*. Her film essays and reviews, collected in the book *Deadline at Dawn*, are models of incisive, provocative, enlightening critical journalism—film writing that really is a form of cultural criticism, not mere reviewing. Williamson always does her job. She captures the films she reviews with great particularity, but she goes much further than that, effortlessly sifting them as evidence for tidal shifts and movements and patterns forming in the society that created them. She relates her experience of the screen to her experience of the world.

Unfortunately, in mainstream print media that kind of intellectually ambitious, highly engaged writing about popular culture is now increasingly rare. Savage and Williamson are both writers whose political convictions are obvious—Savage is a gay socialist and Williamson is a feminist and Marxist. They have struggled with recent changes in the media agenda and have retreated, to an extent. These days there are many talented prose stylists able to divert and amuse us, but not many able to supply a deeper critical view. Too much writing now seems to serve what the American cultural critic Thomas Frank, in his new book *One Market Under God*, calls "market populism." This writing accepts a market-determined consensus. It doesn't question and it certainly doesn't attack. It embraces current economic and political reality as inevitable, a manifestly reasonable state of affairs, requiring no criticism or dissent: the time for being against is over, after all. Looking at design writing in the design press, as it's currently practiced in this same marketplace, much the same conclusion holds true. Most of it plays safe.

In recent years, I've been thinking a lot about my own critical position. I don't see how you can do this kind of writing regularly, for any length of time, without considering these issues. Why *are* you writing? What, ultimately, is the point? I believe I have always had a position of some kind, but that doesn't mean it has necessarily been unambiguous, clear or sufficiently developed. To some extent, like many people, I felt bound by the circumstances I was in. I have always been a writer, but for a while I was an editor, too. Those can be tricky roles to reconcile. An editor needs to be more open, more eclectic, more inclusive than a writer—not that I'm suggesting a writer should be narrow. Nevertheless, if I had let my obsessions and core concerns as a writer dominate my role as an editor, the result would have been a much narrower publication.

For a long time, I was preoccupied with questions of value and this was one concern that did apply equally to editing and writing. I was first drawn to design, as a non-designer, because I noticed how intensely I responded to it, how much it meant to me as a viewer and user, and I wanted to know why. My engagement with the experimental design of the late 1980s and early 1990s was prompted by a sense of excitement at its aesthetic and communicational possibilities, and also by its coded, sub-cultural dimension. Moreover, at that stage, these design approaches were still controversial, so the role of writer-as-advocate seemed worthwhile, particularly in Europe where design criticism was less developed than in the United States. But the very success of these new design approaches by the mid-1990s, their global use as style by business and advertising, and the uncritical collusion of some designers in this process, obliged me to re-examine this earlier commitment. Of course, I was well aware of the market's tendency to recuperate and commodify even the most radical interventions and strategies. Art critics had long ago declared the artistic avant-garde to be dead for this reason, and the same fate had befallen one countercultural uprising after another. I knew all this, but I had never witnessed the phenomenon close-up, as some kind of participant, and in the early days, the take-up of these design approaches as fashionable style didn't seem very likely, however obvious it might look in retrospect.

These days, what I find most pressing, as a writer, is how design functions in society and what we imagine it is for. This is something that should in theory concern everyone, but for the discussion to be meaningful, we have to find ways to talk about design outside the self-interested enclave of the design business itself. Despite the various problems I have highlighted, I am optimistic. The Web now presents enormous possibilities for all kinds of criticism. The Web site *Arts & Letters Daily*, started by Denis Dutton, an academic, is a brilliant idea, providing links to excellent writing all over the Web. It often gets more than 20,000 visitors a day. It's extremely well edited. For instance, it picked up the *Los Angeles Times* article on Glaser by Jessica Helfand, as well as one on Glaser in the *Boston Globe*. Dutton argues that for diverse points of view and open, robust criticism, things have never been better than they are today. Speaking as one of his regular readers, I'm starting to think he might be right. *Arts & Letters Daily* makes a vast amount of material easily available that one would not otherwise be likely to see.

Steven Johnson, co-founder of *Feed*, the Web-based magazine, takes a similar view. Speaking at the "Future of the Public Intellectual" forum—which I discovered through *Arts & Letters Daily*—he said: "There's been a great renaissance in the last five years of the kind of free-floating intellectual that had long been rumored to be on his or her last legs. It's a group shaped by ideas that have come out of the academy but is not limited to that . . . a lively new form of public intellectualism that is not academic in tone."

If this is true, these are ideal conditions for the kind of free-ranging, critical reading I was talking about earlier. They are also, of course, ideal conditions for the free-ranging critic. Johnson talks about the ways that writers, using a dynamically updated homepage, linked to the Web-based publications they write for, will be able to achieve a level of engagement and interaction with readers that has never been possible in the past, although it has often been conjectured.

In the mid-1990s, it was almost impossible to challenge the commercial uses of design. At that point, there was no larger public discussion to inform and sustain such a specialized critique. Dissenting voices were marginalized, barely heard in the media and seen as hopelessly old-fashioned in many people's eyes. We were still, at that stage, in the history-has-ended, ideology-is-over phase of post–Berlin Wall economic triumphalism. The techno-libertarians were having a field day and their relentless message—how con-venient for big business—was always: "Let the market decide!" By the end of the decade, though, it was clear that many people shared a growing unease at the absence of any strong, visible opposition to the swaggering might of global big business as it smoothly muddled its own interests with ours, as though they were by definition necessarily the same. First Things First 2000 launched in several countries in August 1999, was an attempt by a group of design people to test the water, to try out one or two supposedly passé ideas about design priorities, and see whether anyone agreed. Many were apparently infuriated, but the text has received an international groundswell of support. The protests on the streets of Seattle at the end of 1999 confirmed the scale of disenchantment with global capitalism in the most spectacular fashion. It was a watershed event. Naomi Klein's book *No Logo* needs no introduction from me, but I can report that the public response in Britain to an argument about branding that probably could not have been made five years ago has been nothing less than phenomenal. *No Logo* has provided a vital litmus test for the changing mood, and other cultural critics are also contributing exhaustively researched, intellectually challenging, book-length polemics. I have already mentioned Thomas Frank's *One Market Under God*. In Britain, an environmental writer called George Monbiot, author of *Captive State: The Corporate Takeover of Britain*, is another consistently compelling, passionate, argumentative voice.

So, we propose to talk here today about design criticism. For me, these writers demonstrate in the most vivid and inspirational way possible what criticism really means. With considerable guts, they are puncturing some of our most powerful and persuasive contemporary myths—myths sustained in part by design—and taking issue with immense corporate and governmental opponents. Any of them could easily opt for something much less demanding, yet they are determined to speak out and say what they think. They refuse to accept the complacent, lazy, foolish and solipsistic notion that "the time for being against is over." (And, let's face it, that day won't arrive until we're all sitting around on fluffy clouds congratulating ourselves for having arrived in heaven.) The problem for design is that it almost dares not open its eyes to what is really going on, to its own complicity, and to its manifest failure to face up to its own responsibilities and argue convincingly that design might be anything other than a servant of commercial interests. Start pulling the knot with any determination and the whole arrangement might begin to unravel. No, there's too much at stake. Better to pretend design's few critics are "naïve" or "elitist" or some other piffle, do your best to ignore them, carry on regardless, and perhaps it will blow over soon.

For anyone with the stomach to be a critic, there is certainly no shortage of targets, causes, issues or places to start.

THEORY IS A GOOD IDEA
Matt Soar

AN INSULAR PROFESSION

It has been said many, many times that graphic designers don't read. And yet, as this latest offering in the successful *Looking Closer* series attests, such an assertion is clearly wrong. Or is it? Perhaps these books are being bought and read by *non-designers*. Perhaps—*finally*—other people are taking an active interest in this otherwise insular profession.

So who might *they* be? And what if *they* bone up on the history and culture of this business *so* well that *we* designers can no longer speak with unchallenged authority about what has always belonged to us? Perhaps, as a protective measure, we should develop a special language that is so complex and arcane, no one else will be able to play? After all, doctors have done it. So have engineers and lawyers. (Harold Innis, the rather less celebrated Canadian contemporary of Marshall McLuhan, even had a term for it. He called them "monopolies of knowledge.")

In fact, designers do have a language all their own. Just stop someone in the street and try engaging them in a conversation about kerning, or point size, or white space. To get a better idea how this might feel to Johnny Pedestrian, sit yourself down in front of the TV and carefully watch an episode of the show *ER*. Here's what I saw when I tried it: a mother looks on in horror and awe as the busy doctors fuss over her critically ill young son. The woman—and by extension me, the viewer—is drawn in by the dazzling jargon of the doctors and nurses, while simultaneously being rendered helpless and frustrated by it. "Intubate!" *Intubate?* As she pleads with the medical staff for some inkling of what is actually being done to her boy's body, one doctor condescends to translate this deliciously opaque jargon into ordinary language, even as he works.

In this situation, at least, we are in awe of the doctors; and why wouldn't we be? After all, they're *saving lives*! The point I want to make in this short essay, however, is that, in this culture, all complex language is not treated equally. Indeed, the most striking contrast of all is probably to be found in the comparison of hard or applied sciences (brain surgeons; rocket scientists) and relatively "soft" sciences, like sociology, media studies and communication, and even the humanities (including the study of literature, history and religion). Indeed, the most virulent strains of anti-intellectualism in America are centered on the kind of academics who don't use calculators or wear lab coats: the tweedy brigade that dares to make claims about *our* dear world (as opposed to the world of lab rats and dying people—since they don't really count) without showing us the

Originally a lecture presented at "Looking Closer: AIGA Conference on Design History and Criticism" in New York City, February 2001.

numbers to back it up. And if they do have numbers, it always seems to be for things we already know about, *thank you very much*, like television violence or advertising.

One such tweedy guy, the eminent British scholar Terry Eagleton, has argued that "Hostility to theory usually means an opposition to other people's theories and an oblivion of one's own" (quoted in Walker and Chaplin's *Visual Culture: An Introduction*).[1] Excuse me? Let's play that back again: "Hostility to theory usually means an opposition to other people's theories and an oblivion of one's own." Wow. How much clearer could that be? We *all* have theories! But some of us don't know it! I'll add my tweedy two cents: we, as designers, had better figure out what *our* theories are before someone else beats us to it.

Here's a too-brief example: Tibor Kalman, bless him, used to make a big fuss about how designers should start being *bad* (i.e., misbehave in the interest of a higher ethical *good*). The implicit theory here is that if only ten thousand designers would finally agree to stand up and say "Okay, enough's enough, from now on we're gonna be *bad*," the world would begin to change. *My* theory says that's admirable but unrealistic. It's called the theory of ideology, and it holds that, regardless of personal wishes, there are subtle forces at work in the world that serve to maintain the status quo: not written laws exactly, but compelling *ideas*—the unwritten rules of life in this particular capitalist democracy of ours, at this particular time in history, including the ubiquitous yet slippery notion we call "common sense."

Designers pride themselves on clarity of vision: when presented with a jumble of ideas, we more or less *re*present them visually in an organized and—if we want to win an award—*engaging* manner. That said, if we really want to understand ourselves and our place in the world, we have to be prepared to routinely run this equation in reverse, too: we have to be willing to seek complexity where simple answers seem to suffice. Let's return for a moment to the idea of common sense. What could be simpler? Well, lots of things. After all, "common sense" has, in the past, led us to believe that it's perfectly sensible to burn witches, that the Earth is of course flat, and that imprisoning men who fall in love with other men is best for everybody.

The Italian theorist Antonio Gramsci developed an extensive argument about the tyranny of common sense. And quite understandably: it was the "common sense" of Mussolini's fascisti that sent Gramsci to die in jail with the declaration, "We must stop this brain from thinking for twenty years." Fortunately for many of us he managed to keep thinking and writing from his cell, protecting his thoughts using a specialist language. (For example, he referred to Marxism as the "Philosophy of Praxis," which proved to be sufficient to get his work past his censors.)

In the inhospitable atmosphere of Thatcherite Britain, where, as Andrew Howard recently noted in an important article in *Eye* magazine, there was apparently "no such thing as society,"[2] the group of intellectuals responsible for the earliest genesis of cultural studies had to, as their unofficial mantra, "keep it complex." To be fair, however, Stuart Hall—a seminal figure in this field—always saw cultural studies as a two-pronged approach: being both "at the very forefront of intellectual theoretical work" *and* recognizing "the responsibility of transmitting those ideas . . . to" everyone else.[3] (If cultural studies can be criticized, it is for the repeated omission of this second obligation by a few of its practitioners.)

In some senses what I am saying here is not new. Designers and design writers have been chewing this stuff over for some time. For example: Andrew Blauvelt's editorial essays in *Visible Language*; Rick Poynor and Michael Rock in *Eye*, and Tibor Kalman, Abbott Miller and Karrie Jacobs in *Looking Closer*.[4] Academics, too, remain hard at work: John Walker and Sarah Chaplin, in their 1997 text *Visual Culture: An Introduction*, actually have a chapter called "Coping with Theory"; there's also a great essay on the history and uses of jargon in Marjorie Garber's latest book *Academic Instincts*; see also the works of Michael Bérubé, Edward Said, Terry Eagleton, Gerald Graff and Umberto Eco.[5] So—not all academics are resistant to being understood, nor are all designers necessarily resistant to theory.

DESIGNERS AND THEORY

I think one of the main reasons designers are rightfully suspicious of other people's theories is the science of signs, better known as semiotics, or semiology. As the joke goes, "semiology" is another way of saying "half an -ology"—and we could be forgiven for concluding as much, given its *apparently* half-assed premises. As one expert observer said recently: the "semiological literature has remained elusive to most people. The main reason for this is fairly simple: its advocates have written in a style that ranges from the obscure to the incomprehensible."[6]

I'm certainly not going to defend or damn semiology right here, suffice it to say that, like love, I think it's better to have experienced it and given up on it than never to have been there at all. I *do* think that, at least in design circles, it has inadvertently served to lend credence to the stereotype of intellectual endeavor as self-serving nonsense. At least one of the reasons why designers have really seemed to get their fingers burned by theory in general is that semiology was never conceived as a tool for design. To me, that's a little like trying to use a telescope to bake a cake.

NOT JUST TWEEDY: NUTTY, TOO

I think it's important to understand that only occasionally do new ideas generated in the academy make their way into the media—and thence into the popular realm. Unfortunately, as with its attitude to most things, the media tend to focus on the outlandish, since business-as-usual is not news. Indeed, as the philosopher Jacques Derrida has pointed out: "The one thing that is unacceptable these days—on TV, on the radio, or in the papers—is intellectuals taking their time, or wasting other people's time. . . . Time is what media professionals must not waste—theirs or ours."[7] For example, according to the media, at least, the latest fad to sweep universities and colleges across the land is the study of whiteness.

While I would not want to characterize the *New York Times* as a bastion of anti-intellectualism, a recent article about the study of whiteness in their *color* magazine (of all places) did raise my suspicions. The headline read "Getting Credit for Being White." What's interesting here is that, although the article itself presents a *fairly* even-handed exploration of some of the most ambitious thinkers in this area, the headline clearly betrays a distinct hostility—framing the topic not as an extension of existing concerns over the dynamics of racial inequality, but as a disingenuous bid for tweedy legitimacy. (Marjorie Garber, in her 2001 volume *Academic Instincts*, has recently referred to journalism such as this as "aren't they silly?" articles.)

Compare this with the poster I designed for an on-campus presentation by another one of the leading thinkers on the same subject. Richard Dyer has been writing about whiteness, not since yesterday lunchtime, but for around a decade. His lecture was called "Whites Are Nothing," to emphasize the invisibility of whiteness as a racial category. Sure, the title's equally provocative, if not more so, but here at least the obligatory pun is absolutely appropriate (nothing = invisible). And here's the difference: the implicit target in Dyer's case is the subject matter itself, *not* the practitioners; the message, *not* the messengers.

This is a just a fleeting example, but it serves to suggest that media representations of people who think for a living can often be wantonly misleading and, at their worst, *ad hominem*. As Todd Gitlin has recently commented: "Everyday life, supersaturated with images and jingles, makes intellectual life look hopelessly sluggish, burdensome, difficult. In a video-game world, the play of intellect—the search for validity, the willingness to entertain many hypotheses, the respect for difficulty, the resistance to hasty conclusions—has the look of retardation."[8]

WHY I STUDY GRAPHIC DESIGN

Now to a subject closer to all our hearts: Graphic design is very well positioned to become a conspicuous cultural force in the coming years. Indeed, there is now an awareness among many designers and design writers that it is on the verge of becoming more than merely one among many anonymous cultural industries. Its cultural—and now political—import is, I think, undeniable.

This is amply illustrated by comparing two mailers I recently received, one from the AIGA, advertising the 2001 annual conference, titled "Voice." Over an image of the now-infamous butterfly ballot are the words "Design Counts." And surely it does: the conference, originally to be held in Washington, D.C., in September, included in its schedule political lobbying efforts on behalf of the profession. Compare this with a poster that arrived through my mail slot from the Art Directors Club a few days later. Folding it open revealed the following legend: "Imagine a World Without . . . Art Direction." *Art direction?* If the design profession is beginning to raise its sights, to recognize its own importance in the world as the AIGA mailer suggests, it appears (at least based on the ADC poster) that our first cousins in the advertising business are utterly content to continue gazing at their beautifully art-directed navels.

The same scenario played itself out yet again just recently: even while the AIGA was working hard to reschedule "Voice" after the attacks of September 11, the ADC, right on cue, delivered its latest call for entries: a poster showing a close-up of a man, shot from behind, with his pants around his ankles, having just finished using the toilet prominently featured to his right. New York—*the world*—goes through epoch-making political convulsions, and the ADC (headquarters: Manhattan) charges on blindly with bathroom humor to burn.

What excites me about graphic design in particular, then, is that its range of potential commitments, be they cultural or political, is far broader. I'm thrilled that the profession itself is reaching a stage in its growth where it can recognize and seize its own moment. My plea is that designers, design writers and students of design (I include myself in all these categories) remain alert to the mind-dampening force of anti-intellectualism, make every effort possible to continue making inroads into other people's theories, and find out more about our own. We must send out firm roots that will help to situate design in relation to those "foreign" theories, for all that it might do to enhance our understanding of what we do and our place in the world. Further, I hope that people coming up through college into design practice will eat up whatever theory they can get their hands on with all the healthy skepticism they can muster. As the cultural critic Stuart Hall has noted, "The only theory worth having is that which you have to fight off, not that which you speak with profound fluency."[9]

It is clear to me that we need to cultivate a healthy regard for theory—any and all theory—to evaluate it on its own terms, take what we need and remember that if graphic design is really going to mature, it needs theory not merely as a design tool, but as a way to make it truly significant and consequential in the decades to come. Right now the alternative is to see designers' generally liberal-to-progressive tendencies swallowed up—along with everyone else's—in yet another "Great Moving Right Show" (to use a memorable phrase of Hall's); a worrisome shift, wrapped as it is in the garb of national unity, shopping for freedom and the insidious conflation of activism and terrorism as equally un-American activities. In other words, as "common sense."

Notes
1. John Walker and Sarah Chaplin, *Visual Culture: An Introduction* (Manchester/New York: Manchester University Press/St. Martin's, 1997), p. 51.
2. Andrew Howard, "There Is Such a Thing as Society," in *Looking Closer 2: Critical Writings on Graphic Design*, ed. Michael Bierut, William Drenttel, Steven Heller and DK Holland (New York: Allworth Press, 1997), p. 195–200. Originally published in *Eye*, no. 13 (Summer 1994).
3. Stuart Hall, "Cultural Studies and Its Theoretical Legacies," in *Stuart Hall: Critical Dialogues in Cultural Studies*, ed. Stuart Hall, David Morley and Kuan-Hsing Chen (London: Routledge, 1996), p. 268.
4. Blauvelt, "Disciplinary Bodies: The Resistance to Theory and the Cut of the Critic," *Visible Language* 28, no. 3 (1994): 196–202; Blauvelt, "New Perspectives: Critical Histories of Graphic Design," editorial essays appearing in *Visible Language* 28, no. 3–4 (1994), and 29, no. 1 (1995); Poyner and Rock, "What Is This Thing Called Graphic Design Criticism?" *Eye* 16 (Spring 1995): 56–59; Kalman, Miller and Jacobs, "Good History/Bad History," in *Looking Closer: Critical Writings on Graphic Design*, ed. Michael Bierut, William Drenttel, Steven Heller and DK Holland (New York: Allworth Press, 1994), 25–33.
5. Walker and Chaplin, *Visual Culture: An Introduction*; Marjorie Garber, *Academic Instincts* (Princeton: Princeton University Press, 2001); Michael Bérubé, *Public Access: Literary Theory and American Cultural Politics* (London: Verso, 1994); Edward Said, *Representations of the Intellectual* (New York: Pantheon, 1994); Terry Eagleton, *The Significance of Theory* (Oxford: Blackwell, 1990); Gerard Graff, "Academic Writing and Uses of Bad Publicity," *South Atlantic Quarterly* 91, no.1 (1992): 5–17; Umberto Eco, *Travels in Hyperreality* (New York: Harcourt Brace Jovanovich, 1986).

6. Justin Lewis, *The Ideological Octopus: An Exploration of Television and Its Audience* (London: Routledge, 1991), p. 25.

7. Jacques Derrida, "The Deconstruction of Actuality," *Radical Philosophy* 68 (Autumn 1994): 30.

8. Todd Gitlin, "The Fenaissance of Anti-Intellectualism," *Chronicle of Higher Education*, 8 December 2000, B7–B9.

9. Hall, p. 265–266.

THAT WAS THEN, AND THIS IS NOW: BUT WHAT IS NEXT?
Lorraine Wild

The following essay is based on the transcript of a talk that I gave at "101: The Future of Design Education in the Context of Computer-Based Media," a symposium organized by Louis Sandhaus and presented at the Jan van Eyck Akademie in Maastrict, the Netherlands, in November of 1995. It is highly speculative, and reading it now, I think that some of the conditions that I describe have already shifted, but that is the nature of the speed of change that confronts us. I was simply trying to capture and describe the moment that we educators and practitioners are in right now. (You blink, and it has changed.) I wish to thank the Jan van Eyck Akademie for giving me the assignment and the time to collect and record my thoughts.

I'm standing here not as an authority on multimedia or design education, but from the position of working inside of design education for twelve years, and connecting it with my own experience as a student from the mid-70s through the early 80s. That, and the context of my experiences at CalArts, and my ongoing experiences as a design practitioner in Los Angeles, has had an impact on the way that I see the future of work in design. I can't pretend that what I say will apply to all graphic design educators and practitioners everywhere. But in the United States, Los Angeles is usually regarded as the place where both good and bad things happen first, because Californians are crazy and will try anything. Yet, usually, what happens there ends up happening everywhere else, sooner or later. So today I'm just speaking from my own experiences, but on the other hand, all I can say is: *you'd better watch out.*

I'd like to start by describing some recent observations that have affected my thoughts about what's going on in the profession that we are educating designers to enter.

Originally published in *Emigre*, no. 39 (Summer 1996).

THE BIGGER PICTURE

Recently the *Los Angeles Times* featured an article about one of the many invisible wars of rivalry between the metropolitan areas of San Francisco and Los Angeles, over which one would achieve economic domination in the new field of multimedia.[1] The gist of the article was that northern California held the lead in hardware (as in technology) development and financing, and that southern California held the lead in software (as in content) and its financing, and that it was not clear which area would end up drawing the most benefit from the phenomenal growth attached to the new technologies. But what caught my eye was that the state tax rolls already had hundreds of businesses registered as multimedia developers. A few years ago, Nicholas Negroponte of M.I.T.'s Media Lab predicted that the movie industry would be "the smokestack industry of the 90s,"[2] and the report in the *Los Angeles Times* reinforced this idea, claiming that the infrastructure dedicated to telling stories could contend, economically, with the infrastructure for delivering the stories. In fact, what the article summarized was the interweaving of Silicon Valley and Hollywood into a blended economy, and that Siliwood was already regarded as a source of economic regeneration in California.

This is the environment that ten or so undergraduates and six or so graduate students from CalArts will walk into this May, and on into the future . . .

HIGH ANXIETY

In October of 1995, the American Institute of Graphic Arts held its biennial national conference in a hotel in Seattle. Previous conferences have consisted of lectures by various graphic design world heavyweights of their latest work, or presentations by large-scale clients. Other issues are covered, such as history, professional practices, ethics and design education, but generally, AIGA conferences in the past have functioned as professional love-fests, where the main goal was the (at least temporary) glorification of graphic designers by graphic designers. But a new, more serious generation leads the AIGA now, and the 1995 conference was advertised with the following text: "We all know that design is going through a period of unprecedented change. Is the profession you care about passionately on the verge of a renaissance—or extinction? Is the business world finally beginning to appreciate the value of what you do? Or is public access to technology going to put us all out of business?"

The Seattle conference was different. First of all, there were no general presentations by graphic designers of their current visual work, and none of the speakers who addressed the topic of the future of the profession used any current work by other graphic designers to illustrate their notions of where the future was leading. In other words, there was a real disconnection between the work that graphic designers specifically produce now—good, bad or ugly—and the preoccupation with the larger question of what we might be doing in the future.

One of the most important presentations of the conference was a dialogue on the main stage between Bill Drenttel, partner of Drenttel, Doyle & Partners, a very successful design consultancy in New York, and Nancye Green, partner of Donovan and Green, an equally successful New York design office. They did not show any examples of their work, but spent forty minutes discussing how absolutely confusing and challenging it was to be running a large design consultancy in 1995. The conditions that they described so persuasively could be characterized as follows:

- The problems that clients were bringing them had become exponentially more complex, in part because of the range of possible media that presented themselves as possible solutions;
- Audiences themselves were more complex, split into micromarkets or scattered globally;
- They were being asked to address these complex audiences; yet, paradoxically, the multimedia audience had to be seen as a large group of audiences of one;
- Earlier models for staffing and managing and organizing a design practice didn't seem appropriate to these challenges, which meant that designers were now faced with the challenge of organizing teams, often including expertise from outside of graphic design, to adequately cope with their clients' projects;
- Research was hard to define and hard to bill for;
- Despite the delight in producing images, designers had to recognize that making visual things was now only one way of working in design;
- A lack of credibility was so pervasive as a cultural phenomenon that trying to create genuine communication through a haze of excess marketing was making life more difficult for everybody;
- And finally, the constant pressure of time continued to mitigate against the leisurely solving of any of these problems.

I thought that Drenttel's and Green's presentation was a defining moment in contemporary American graphic design, although whether or not it was recognized as such by a large percentage of the audience in Seattle is debatable. Possibly, it made many of the designers in the audience very uncomfortable because it was such a definitive, intelligently expressed description of not knowing. Neither Drenttel nor Green delivered their message hopelessly, but by setting aside the seductive images of their accomplished work in favor of confronting the massive uncertainties of practice as it is experienced daily, it was perhaps the most painfully honest presentation that the graphic design profession had seen in a while. (Certainly just as honest a moment as when the audience, who obviously wanted to celebrate their embrace of technology, their plucky willingness to accept change no matter where it brought them, applauded wildly as a designer at Adobe Systems showed some video footage of herself destroying a Macintosh computer with a sledgehammer.)[4]

Anyway, memories of Seattle were still fresh when I encountered this statement by Michael Rock of the current Yale design faculty in a recent issue of the *AIGA Journal*: "That contemporary design education has been thrown into a state of confusion both aggravates and reflects a pervasive professional confusion. It is inherently impractical to fully prepare students to work in a field that has so little sense of its immediate future or professional position."[5]

This statement took me aback; it's quite extreme! Yet all the evidence of a severe realignment in design practice has been piling up. For two years now I have witnessed a steady acceleration of change—an expansion of the range of technical possibilities, which affects the nature of what designers aspire to do, and what they fear being denied if their skills somehow fail to fit the potential of the new media. These possibilities have been anticipated for years, since the computer started being integrated into graphic design as a production tool. It was so easy to say, "Oh, it's just another tool" (or, more compellingly, "It's just a really fast idiot") as long as it was simply being used to replicate earlier manual tasks. But now, new media expand the problem of communication to encompass dimensions of time, sound, motion—and, suddenly, the graphic in graphic design seems constrained or parochial. The two-dimensional expertise of the graphic designer appears to be a professional liability rather than a ticket to greater participation in the communication of the future. And the new media tools open up the possibility for communication to a radically expanded number of people, challenging the fragile claims to authority that designers have worked so hard to establish. As Michael Rock stated, the inter-relationship between practice and education cannot be circumvented or denied. To build a future in the face of these challenges to the definition of graphic design practice, I think we have to look with somewhat of a cold eye at the source or sources of our current paradigms of education and practice that come from the past.

WAY BACK IN THE 80S

In 1983, I was asked by the Society of Typographic Arts (now the ACD) to write an essay on the ideal design education.[6] At the time, I was teaching at the University of Houston in Texas in both the architecture and the graphic design departments. I had graduated from Yale University the year before, and while I was there, buried under the burden of completing my master's degree thesis, I found myself envying the quality of the general education that the younger undergraduates were receiving. There were limitations on the amount of specialization that any bachelor's degree student could take— and instead of holding them back, it seemed to enable them to communicate their ideas and intentions with the rest of the world.

Of course the arguments exist that an elite institution like Yale is merely a finishing school for privileged students already destined for leadership positions in society, but like a lot of other American institutions, Yale had diversified their student population from the late 60s on through the admittance of women and an increased percentage of minorities. The undergraduate student body did not fit the cliché of the old Ivy League, and still the education was impressive. The alumni newsletter chronicling an endless list of accomplishment in all fields seems to indicate that the educators at that university were doing something right.

So what was it? After looking at it really closely, and after going on to teach at a state university that had incorporated more specialized job training in lieu of traditional academic development under the rubric of a more pluralistic and pragmatic definition of an undergraduate curriculum, I could see that it was the Yale tradition of endless writing and reading, requirements across a general field of subjects, and most importantly, a constant stress on intellectual inquiry and curiosity that sustained graduates far beyond their years on the campus. It seemed clear to me then (and that's what I ended up writing about in 1983) that the best thing an undergraduate design education could do would be to embrace that serious commitment to cultural generalism, because designers needed to be literate and intellectually flexible if they were going to be able to communicate with any meaning, energy or authority in their society and culture.

I should add right away that this spirit of inquiry was notably missing from my own graduate education in the very same university. In 1980 the master's degree program at Yale was one of the last bastions of late modernist design rigidity, enforced with discipline; all rules and mannerisms combined to produce an exterior façade of professionalism, no questions asked. I will always remember when a visiting tutor asked us graduate students to describe what it was that was important to us as designers. Everyone responded mechanically with clichés about problem-solving and communication, when in fact, methodologies of communication had never been discussed; we were really most anxious to complete our typography problems in the blandly abstracted Swiss style that our faculty deemed correct.

It was true that this style, which passed for well-thought-out graphic design at Yale and other design departments in the late 70s and early 80s, was also the style of corporate America. If you mastered it, you were guaranteed employment in any one of a score of offices on the eastern seaboard. Though it was certainly never articulated as such, the intellectual preparation of students as communicators has become secondary to a sort of vocational education limited to the production needs of the profession, or at least what the profession thought that it needed, in the short term.

EVEN BEFORE THE 80S

But a hallmark of modernist design education in the United States has been its see-sawing relationship to the field of practice. There was no academically sanctioned design education in the United States before the arrival of various European designers associated with the avant-garde, like Moholy-Nagy, who brought the New Bauhaus to Chicago (independent for a brief while, eventually finding a home at the Illinois Institute of Technology), or Gyorgy Kepes at M.I.T., or Joseph Albers, first at Black Mountain College and then at Yale. The world of these educators a mere sixty years ago began the development of a professional design pedagogy in the United States, connecting education with the modernist promise of social and cultural amelioration through practice.

I feel queasy about the series of broad generalizations I am about to make in an attempt to summarize the evolution of this modernist ideal in the United States, because I don't want to make it seem simplistic, but for the sake of brevity, please bear with me:[7] The big shift in design teaching that was brought by this first generation of émigrés to the United States was a move away from the constant production of visual novelty, or restyling as a commercial art. They also expanded design activity from aesthetics to encompass a conceptual operation, where design projects and problems in two or three dimensions were generated by an internal analysis, without preconceived notions of solutions, from inside the problem to outside the surface. Form would follow function, which was understood in graphic design as meaning. This new idea brought about an explosion of creativity to a field that had not been noted for a great deal of conceptual innovation. But this new approach was also accompanied by a very strong aesthetic of its own, which we are all familiar with, and which over time tended to shift from being a visual signifier for the conceptual basis of the project to becoming a stand-in for substance itself.

And the way that happened in the United States has something to do with the struggles of the first generation of designers who worked hard at promulgating the modernist project in the commercial-professional context of the United States after 1945, and who fought for recognition in that context. They found that a most efficient way to connect to their clients as consultants was to tie their own identity as artists and individual creators, or stars, to the work that they produced. Like movie stars or famous artists (figures more easily understood by commercial and popular culture), their work was increasingly championed on the basis of personal authorship (even if the work was actually the product of a thirty-person office), rather than for its merits. This is not to say that there weren't plenty of meritorious projects; they just weren't sold or understood on that basis: not only by clients, but by the design profession itself.

By the time I was in design school in the mid-70s, the phrase "the star system," describing the process of getting known for one's work on the basis of receiving awards, and building one's reputation and personal identity on that, was openly acknowledged by students with more than a bit of cynicism (and a bit of jealousy, especially during the 80s when even minor league stars were making so much money).

This had its effect on design education, obviously. Since work that succeeded was presented as the result of individual genius, and since modernism could not be discussed as a style with conventions because it was alleged to be free of them and continued to be confused as a signifier for truth, graphic design curricula increasingly moved from the problems of truly conceptual practice to the induction into the modernist style, combined with the development of the personal ability to will one's work into correct and persuasive shape. There was a blip of time in the early 1970s in which this did not happen (and I will get to that interesting moment shortly), but otherwise the trajectory of design from a conceptual activity to a kind of compromised personal artistry in the service of commerce has been quite direct.

A MAJOR DIGRESSION

The events that interrupted this trajectory, other than the blip that I have just mentioned, were the onset of semiotic theory, cultural criticism, postmodernism and, to a certain extent, graphic design history as consciousness-raising in graphic design education. The influence of these theories (even when mistranslated or misunderstood by graphic designers) brought new life into a field that was in serious danger of terminal trivialization. Patterns in the production and consumption of public imagery began to be discussed, and the natural assumptions of the profession began to be understood as constructions.

Simultaneously, the number of graphic design students kept increasing. The number of designers kept increasing. Different kinds of people, such as women, gays and minorities of all types, began to shift the profile of the profession. Students and teachers reading theory started questioning the basis for the values and hierarchy inside and outside of the profession. And around the same time that designers started perusing Derrida, these pale gray machines that made awkward looking typography were multiplying in their offices.

THINGS TO COME

To return to the blip of the early 1970s, which prefigured all of this, in a truncated way. In the United States, the crisis of the late 1960s—which circled around opposition to the Vietnam War, the ongoing fights for civil rights and women's rights, the onset of assassinations and urban upheaval—had shaken the faith of so many people in the institutions around them. In graphic design, it was already evident that the attenuated rationalism of modernism was the style of the military-industrial-corporate machine. Looking for alternatives, young designers looked to the roots of early modernism, with its commitment to constant activist revolution, to reinvigorate their own efforts. An obsession with taking control of systems rather than being controlled by them became critical, and understanding systems became more important than aesthetics, momentarily. Buckminster Fuller, Marshall McLuhan, the *Whole Earth Catalog* (with its wry subtitle, "a catalog of tools") and the guerrilla TV collective Ant Farm were on many aspiring designers' reading lists, and it was assumed that both the tool of the future and the medium of the future was . . . video. Those back-breaking porta-paks engendered dreams of a medium that would shake its audience out of complacency, restore spontaneity and democracy to the media, and turn passive spectators into active citizens. Video would provide an out to designers frustrated by the limitations and control of predetermined form.

This was the same period when a fascination with problem-solving methodologies—brainstorming and all sorts of other analytical techniques—were also being explored as a way to short-circuit the easy assumptions of formalism. The politics of the time encouraged the spontaneous, ad-hoc and collective natures of these explorations.

On the aesthetic side, the influences of Andy Warhol and Robert Venturi helped reinvent the way designers saw the pop culture environment that formed the context of their work. Hitting thirty, the singular aesthetic of abstracted modernism was not to be trusted, and the stiff cultural hierarchy between high and low was beginning to crack. Though the modernist style was not fully abandoned at this point, graphic design teaching and practice was briefly energized by this moment of hippie modernism, where the conceptual problem was once again in the foreground. Designers dreamt of a utopia of connection to the community through the peaceful use of technology.

But . . . the porta-paks were too heavy, no one had time for real-time video, and the dreams of revolution attached to local access cable TV fell out of favor when truly large scale cable companies offering round-the-clock presentations of old sitcoms clarified the situation that such access, in video or cable TV, was still inexorably one-way; passive, not the gateway to revolution.

By and large, graphic designers were not to pay attention to the role of technology in their futures until the pale gray boxes were completely ubiquitous. What was initially disguised as the distress over the Macintosh as a generator of typography (or a creator of instant graphic designers) has proved to be a much larger anxiety over the effect of the new media on the current conception of the design profession itself, and whether the constructs that have governed practice and education up to this point are even going to survive the full implications of the technology.

TOO MUCH TO LEARN

When designers first began to notice that the use of the computer demanded that they now had to resume responsibility for details of production, there was immediate consternation that the trade-off for increased aesthetic control, and the constantly disappointed promise of increased productivity, had been to re-mire the designer in a practically premodern publishing operation, where editing, designing, printing and distribution could be collapsed into a simpler, less capital-intensive operation, full of potential. But merely mastering the technology seemed to overshadow the ability to pause and notice where the work could go. Educators and practitioners were distracted by the whole new bag of necessary skills that greatly impacted craft: the ever-expanding number of software programs to master, added on top of all the older mandated skills and techniques.

Intentionally or not (in fact, despite the best of intentions), the problems of mastering digital technology for print production tended to crowd out what little time was given over to the conceptual development of design in most curricula. Of course, talented teachers have always managed to insert conceptual development into the process of skill acquisition, and in fact that is what has prevented the teaching of design from being completely subsumed into this technological shift.

But basically, for the last few years design educators have been faced with the conundrum best expressed by the classic Texan phrase, "trying to stuff twenty pounds of manure into a ten-pound bag." Or as Meredith David and Andrew Blauvelt stated more elegantly: "The synthesizing potential of the digital realm rejoins many previously discrete tasks, suggesting not only the problem of increased knowledge and skill, but also the potential for designers to entertain notions of authorship and entrepreneurial independence. Such demands for greater skill and knowledge will not be thought of as the burden and sole responsibility of the designer . . . instead, experience and knowledge will be gained through work and communication with others outside our discipline while activities such as 'creation,' 'production,' and 'distribution' become more fully integrated."[8]

How are graphic designers, at least as we currently prepare them, going to be able to go beyond the entertaining of notions of authorship and entrepreneurial independence into substantive participation in the production of this new media? Where will they gain the skills to collaborate with those who know what they don't? These questions tug at me as I see CalArts graduates go out into the world with the intention and ability to work in new media. Though there are tons of job opportunities for those students, it is not self-evident to the world out there that the skills of a graphic designer are critical to the success of new media projects. I also see the way that opportunities to work in multimedia come to practicing designers. Often, designers are approached with projects that have already been strategized, which may need a visual retooling after the fact. This doesn't contradict the already established model of the print designer providing the visual interface between the client and the intended audience. But it obviously frustrates the entire promise of new media to break down the barriers between form and content (not to mention the old conceptualism that insisted on an idea behind the image); what use is it if graphic design is segregated to the application of form?

The new media have begun to reverse the processes that have led to the specialization of graphic design out of a field of general design practice. This threatens to tip our professional definition upside down. The contemporary identity of the graphic designer was only constructed after printing and typesetting technologies isolated the activity of planning and form-giving from both the development of content and the actual production of printed matter. Modernist practice evolved from that industrial separation, and the intensified personalization of conventional design activity in recent years can be seen as a continuation of those processes in the extreme. The identity of graphic design is constantly reified by its own pedagogies, practices, professional awards, journalism and even history, which, until now, focused on the visual presentation of printed matter. Whereas the problems and projects that constituted graphic design seemed so stable, multimedia brings additional dimensions of difficulty and complexity that are only peripherally related to graphic design practice as it is commonly understood. Suddenly, interactivity and the design of interfaces, the connection between information and users, demands thought in terms that range from the industrial understanding of human factors to the theatrical culture of entertainment. A visual sensibility is a valuable thing to have, but it is only one sensibility; a good sense of timing and sound are now really important as well.

And ideas of what might be done with the new media are the most important of all. While designers worry about their own qualifications or competency to make this work, anyone can get their hands on the technology; one project, and you, too, can be a multimedia developer. Hovering over all of this is the problem that there actually are different levels of skills (in understanding principles of programming, for instance) that affect the quality of work in ways that many designers just beginning to experiment with Director can barely understand.

In her essay "The Pleasure of Text(ure)," Jessica Helfand, an American graphic

designer who works in multimedia, asked the question: ". . . so who designs these products? . . . game designers, software designers, interface designers, production designers,
programming designers, and occasionally, even graphic designers. In most multimedia
settings, the 'designer' is the person with the vision, not necessarily the person who is
'visual.' The designer can be the author, publisher, producer, or even the programmer . . .
because multimedia production is driven by forces that, though creative in intent, are
not primarily visual in nature, the role of designers in the medium still remains to be
invented . . ."[9] Helfand cautions that, "though its production is by necessity team-driven,
multimedia is best served when the underlying vision is a singular one. It is in authorship, not the authoring tools, that such work becomes possible."[10]

    That several producers or publishers of CD-ROM projects or interactive pro-
grams don't acknowledge the need for graphic design as a district part of their development is often lamented by graphic designers as proof of yet more design philistinism.
A more likely reason for this resistance might be that in new media, the connection
between content and its presentation is so tight that there is barely any conceptual space
in which to see a separate need for development of the visual independent from the verbal. When that is combined with our general Western rationalistic distrust of the surface
and a certain resistance to truly acknowledging the power of visual presentation—or
style—(by both the philistines and the design purists), you get what we have now: a lot
of stuff being designed without designers!

    Another disjuncture between the new media and graphic design as we know it
is that the process of large group or team projects in multimedia has less to do with the
division of labor in print production, and is much more akin to collaborative enterprises,
such as theatrical production, TV production or movie-making in the entertainment
industry. And in those enterprises, the identity and independence of individuals responsible for the visual presentation, such as cinematographers, film and video editors, production designers, art directors, property masters and costume and set designers, are
secondary in both the hierarchy of the production and in the point of view of the audience to the vision or authorship of the director (and perhaps the screenwriters). While
the accomplishments of the visual collaborators may not be highly celebrated and com-
pensated, the ability to launch current and future projects rests with the authors—the
directors and screenwriters. A current danger to the independence and fragile claim on
authorship currently enjoyed by graphic designers is the inability to understand how to
translate their own value or power into the team production of most new media, since
authorship in terms of production is not granted to those who only give the project its
visual form.

EXPANDING THE FIELD

While specialization in graphic design accelerated during the last decade, many design
educators have been pointing out the need for students of design to have strong general educations (like the ones I had observed undergraduates receiving at Yale) to enable
them to be culturally and socially literate in the context in which they will be work-

ing. At the same time, we have also wanted to produce students who had enough specialized training to enable them, if not to master their crafts, to at least be employable once they graduated. The balance between generalization and specialization was thrown out of whack by the overwhelming problems of digital competence, and the (largely unstated) conviction that to master the new tools was the most critical thing a student could do. This was reinforced by a profession that immediately began to hire graduates based on their knowledge of programs, mostly to lift the burden of technical competency from the busy professionals running their offices. The short-term focus seemed to be entirely on production.

In the United States, this same generation of younger designers who could not afford to dismiss new technology as mere aberration were also the designers who were struggling, because of their exposure to and interest in critical theory, to make work that in one way or another tried to deal with issues of meaning and communication brought on by the new technology. For this they were rewarded with an attitude of complete disdain from the older, authoritarian stars, who could only read their work as the result of mindless fooling around with computers, and an affront to the modernist tradition (which in this case was not tradition at all, but really a demand for obedience and deference to the past).

And while a great deal of time was spent specializing, mastering the programs, an aesthetic evolved that was a hybrid between the theoretical and critical analyses of design that the students were being exposed to, and an embrace of certain visual signifiers of the technology that was enabling the production of print itself. A good example of this is the explosion of interest in font design that started in the late 80s, as the exploration of digital capability opened up this once arcane craft to the experimentation of many. At the same time, a certain destabilized, postmodern interpretation of function also allowed for a reconsideration of appropriateness as a design value for letter design, which completely re-energized font design and made it an interesting design problem once again. Oddly enough, this has become the subject that enabled a great deal of generalist discussion and debate on the future uses of design.

But this is all still within the construct of the craft we know, not within the expanded field that looms ahead of us. It appears that we have to completely rethink the problem of design curricula, and the balance between the conceptual work and form-giving. If we look closely at what computers can do now, we see that they have distinct qualities that differentiate them from the characteristics of the printed media. In his article "Computers, Networks, and Education," Alan Kay (of Apple and M.I.T.) lists their salient qualities as: "interactivity, transmutability (ability to deliver information in a variety of formats), the ability to show information in many perspectives (verbal and visual, still and moving, solid and transparent, etc.); the ability of computers to build models or simulations that allow one to 'test' conflicting theories or ideas; the ability to tailor the digital media to the interest or proclivity of the user, and finally, the ability of the user to create enlarged archives, libraries, databases."[11]

Kay goes on to describe these qualities as essential to the process of teaching and informing the public: "To make contexts visible, make them objects of discourse and make them explicitly reshapable and inventable are strong aspirations very much in harmony with the pressing needs and on-rushing changes of our own time. It is the duty of a well-conceived environment for learning to be contentious and disturbing. . . ."[12]

This is very reminiscent of the old call for the educational initiative in design education to return to conceptual models, grounded in strong generalist backgrounds that foster inquiry, and to create engines to propel work into the future, attached to a utopian dream of a direct engagement with the future.

One could continue to teach graphic design as a viable sub-specialty of design practice (even one that was entirely dedicated to print!) and still get an education that would prepare one to work in an expanded field of media. But to do so, the conceptual aspects of communicating in an environment where the nature of information and the way it is received and understood by its audience must be assumed to be in a state of constant flux. This would more accurately identify graphic design as a specialty within a wider definition of design as a conceptual operation. It would also necessitate an understanding of the capabilities (and weaknesses) of specific formats, and an honest assessment of the strengths and weaknesses of various conceptual approaches to various media. But the inherent weakness of graphic design as a discipline for understanding the wider operations of new media is its insistence on isolating the visual translation as the final product of the designer, and a concentration on the final product as the ultimate gauge of the expertise of the designer. (But of course this is not a simple duality; to suggest that there is more to it than the visual is not to deny the critical presence of the visual.)

If you return to the issue of authorship in multimedia, it is clear that priorities in education have to shift away from the focus on perfection of craft. Beyond training the eye to see, technique is an unstable thing. Actually, one of the peculiarities of design education at this moment is the fact that many students possess greater technique on the computer than their teachers, anyway. What teachers can lead students to is a greater understanding of methods of research, of questioning, of learning how to learn that we all need to internalize, more than ever. And there are other things that must be added to the education of designers to enable them to participate as something other than visual packagers as well:

- Writing as a means of conceptual and expressive development;
- Techniques of verbal expression, rhetoric, narrative and story-telling (the engineering underneath verbal communication;
- The grammar of film, particularly the syntax of editing, cross-cutting and sequencing in time to create narrative;
- Sound;
- The grammar and psychology of games, which function as narrative structures as surely as storytelling or film;
- Techniques of visual rhetoric, syntax and semantics, using examples from the high art to popular culture, including advertising;
- The awareness and critique of communicative systems as artificial constructs;

- Understanding the social, cultural and functional possibilities within the realms of real and simulated space, the public and the private;
- Collaboration; knowing what you don't know, looking at models of other team-produced design (advertising, filmmaking, architecture) that involve negotiation and accommodation, complex technical processes and the negotiation of consensus.[13] This, needless to say, flies in the face of the designers' fantasy of artistic autonomy. Also needed in the new design education are:
- A history that expands to include a social and cultural development of media;
- And perhaps in contradiction to the last few points, a more serious consideration of fantasy, surrealism, game playing, pranks, simulation, bricolage and other forms of marginal subversion to map out the spaces in between, the entrepreneurial possibilities as a source of stimulation and creativity in approaching new media with a free hand.

DESIGN REDEFINED?

In "Cyberidaho: The Reality of What's Not," Peter Anders speculates that we will soon see "a new breed of professional, a cyberspace architect who designs . . . scenarios. The talents of the cyberspace architect will be akin to those of traditional architects, film directors, novelists, generals, coaches, playwrights, video game engineers. The job of the cyberspace designer will be to make the experience seem real."[14] A somewhat more abstract description appears in Richard Coyne and Adrian Snodgrass's article "Problem Setting within Prevalent Metaphors of Design": ". . . by changing the dominant metaphors it is possible to redefine problems in more readily addressed terms. So in switching from the metaphor of design as information processing we may, for example, characterize design as a process of enablement within a community of expertise. . . . the required solution may not be a technological one. . . . What are the means of collaboration? . . . The practitioner does not come to a situation with fixed, predefined problem statements, but undertakes investigation and engages in dialogue through which appropriate metaphors emerge."[15]

There is not much in either of these descriptions that fits in with the conventional job description for graphic designer. I have no doubt that graphic design will continue to be produced, but whether or not graphic designers as we now know them will continue to propagate is really what's in question. (Is the historical definition of the graphic designer too tied to a specific technology and ideology to expand beyond it?) And as speculative as both the future job descriptions that I've just cited sound, I think they represent conditions or ways of working that already exist, but which still confuse because they coexist with the older models—which is what I think Drenttel and Green were trying to describe last fall in Seattle.

I recently watched a friend apply, and get in, to film school. She had to supply an essay describing her intentions; samples of writing and scripts; and samples of photographs, sketchbooks and videotapes. As I watched her going through this process, I found myself wondering: now how is this different from design?

I only want to add a point about the aesthetics, actually, because I have gone on now for some time with this generalist's reverie, an idea of radically broadening what might make up the training of a designer, and I don't want to leave you with the mistaken impression that there is nothing interesting left to do in visual design, or that there aren't real things to be made in the world. There are so many interesting problems: What combinations of word, image and form will communicate in the not exclusively linear environment of new media? The improvisation of comedy, the intuitiveness of jazz, the branching narratives of hypertext, the cross-cutting of TV, the density of advertising, the sampling of pop music, the endless windows within windows of software itself?[16] These are all stylistic elements of a new syntax that we've already seen but have only begun to take seriously now that we actually have a technology that can utilize them.

In the last few years, a way that young graphic designers resisted the Juggernaut of professionalism and the expansion of social control through the mass media was to subject the public language of design to a deconstructed, critical reading, which led so many to deny the ability to use that public language at all. But a frustration with that impasse has finally led some of those same critics to understand that the representation (or selling) of style, and the way that people use style are actually two different things. As designers, we are beginning to understand the multiple strategies that open up if we "embrace style as a functional language."[17] The logjam over the preoccupation with specific form may yield a more interesting dialogue on the subject of the variety of visual languages made possible in this moment of expansion.

THE TRAIN HAS LEFT THE STATION

While the challenges to graphic design and design education posed by new media carry such great potential for the renewal of design, we cannot pretend that this technological phenomena has been designed, or is waiting, just for us. New media will go ahead without our participation, which for many designers may be okay. The price of participation may actually be the end of graphic design as we know it, and the price of separation will probably be the maintenance of the low profile of graphic design in the public consciousness. The risk carried by the generalization of design education dedicated to new media may be the exaggeration of a split between academia looking to the future, and practitioners still preoccupied with skill and techniques and the very real short-term pressures of running their businesses. Will the practitioners be able to connect the problems that they are obviously experiencing—articulated in so many ways in Seattle—with a new definition of who they are looking for to join them in creating their work? Will the educators be able to develop these generalists who somehow must manage to specialize, too? Can it possibly be done in four-plus-two years of graphic design training? Can we stand this almost generational split that the ascendancy of the new media is forcing upon both sides of the profession?

Who this new media will serve, who will have access and control—these are even bigger questions that transcend our individual efforts. That is why you find media news coverage on page one, or the front of the business page of the newspaper, not in the cultural reportage. But while these questions go unanswered, a culture is in the process of being created. The American literary critic Larry McCaffery predicts that, "Cultural renewal will result when we have not only met the challenge of coexisting with the beast of technology driven change, but have also learned how to dance with it."[18] The dance has no rules: some of the music seems awfully familiar, but design educators and practitioners must be willing to stumble all over themselves in this murky but most entertaining moment.

Notes

1. Amy Harman, "Multimedia is a New L.A.–S.F. Grudge Match: Will the Recently Hatched Industry Nest in Northern or Southern California?" *Los Angeles Times*, 1 October 1994: A-1; and "Hollywood and Technology: Welcome to Siliwood: Will the Convergence of the Creative and Technical Lead to a Jobs Revolution?" Los Angeles Times, 12 September 1995: J-4.
2. Stewart Brand, *The Media Lab: Inventing the Future at MIT* (New York: Penguin, 1987), p. 5.
3. Advertisement, *AIGA Journal of Graphic Design* 13, (1995).
4. Luanne Seymour Cohen, "High Anxiety," (Seattle AIGA Conference, October 1995).
5. Michael Rock, "Introduction," *AIGA Journal of Graphic Design* 13, no. 1 (1995): 12.
6. "More Than a Few Questions About Graphic Design Education," *Design Journal* 1, no. 2: 8–10.
7. Lorraine Wild, "Europeans in America," in *Graphic Design in America: A Visual Language History*, ed. Mildred Friedman (Minneapolis: Walker Art Center, 1989), pp. 152–69.
8. Meredith Davis and Andrew Blauvelt, "Building Bridges: A Research Agenda for Education and Practice," *AIGA Journal* 13, no. 1 (1995).
9. Jessica Helfand, *Six Essays on Design and New Media* (New York: William Drenttel, 1995), pp. 26–27.
10. Helfand, *Six Essays*, p. 33.
11. Alan Kay, "Computer, Networks, and Education," *Scientific American Special Issue on Computers* (1994).
12. Kay, "Computer, Networks, and Education."
13. "In architecture, there are not only creative and technical processes, but a social one as well. You have to negotiate conflicts, you have to identify where the areas of consensus are, and so on. So, educationally, you have to provide people with the skills to operate in the social arena, whether it's big software projects, architecture, certainly film and media" [William Mitchell, interviewed in "The ID Multimedia Forum," *I.D.* 41, no. 2 (March/April 1994): 42].
14. Peter Anders, "Cyberidaho: The Reality of What's Not," *Design Book Review* (Winter 1993): 20.
15. Richard Coyne and Adrian Snodgrass, "Problem Solving Within Prevalent Metaphors of Design," *Design Issues* 11, no. 2 (Summer 1995): 33.
16. See Larry McCaffery, "Avant-Pop: Still Life After Yesterday's Crash," in *After Yesterday's Crash: The Avant-Pop Anthology* (New York: Penguin, 1995), pp. xxii–xxiii.
17. Andrew Blauvelt, "Under the Surface of Style," *Eye*, no. 18 (Autumn 1995): 64–71.
18. Larry McCaffery, "Avant-Pop: Still Life After Yesterday's Crash" (paraphrase), in *After Yesterday's Crash: The Avant-Pop Anthology* (New York: Penguin, 1995), p. xvii.

WHAT HAPPENS WHEN THE EDGES DISSOLVE?
Loretta Staples

The focus of today's visual landscape is the *indistinction* between things. In print and on screen, edges dissolve to create a virtually seamless panorama, privileging continuity and ambiguity above legibility. Ten years ago this would have been regarded as a visual assault; today it seems perfectly natural. The blur is the emblem of design in the 1990s.

The blur epitomizes the dissolution of the visual formalisms that have dominated twentieth-century design. Nothing better exemplifies the increasing dominance of photographic properties in all areas of visual design. Nothing better showcases the pervasive influence of digital tools, in particular Adobe Photoshop. And no other visual attribute better characterizes the ambiguity of our identities within a highly mediated culture.

When Neville Brody produced a typeface in 1991, he called it Blur. He was in good company—a band of the same name emerged in the British music scene at roughly that time, and soon afterwards an eclectic art and culture magazine called *Blur* was launched in the United States. Seemingly overnight, twirls, whirls and blurs appeared in the work of designers within and outside the academy. It was clear that extravagant visual effects were replacing the structural sureties of the past.

Until the mid-1980s it seemed that the classic devices of alignment—margins, columns and grids—would persist forever as the basis of design teaching and practice. These were measurable, discernible tools for organizing information within the page, which through their steadfast presence afforded typographic freedom. Today the computer together with the intellectual strands of postmodernism (semiotics foremost among them) challenge the way information is presented and even reading itself. And if reading is challenged, it follows that the letters which constitute much of what is read are also called into question.

Letters are still an important factor in contemporary design, but in the virtuality of cyberspace, poised delicately in phosphor, they are considerably more ephemeral than in the past. The new computer-generated environment has had a more profound impact on design than most designers—pragmatically preoccupied with the treats and inconveniences of incipient technologies—care to acknowledge. (The effects of the desktop publishing revolution are still being felt.) This is a space where narratives can be undone by the discontinuities of hypertext, where letters can exist one moment as flat and two-dimensional and in the next as rounded forms seen as if in flight. This is a space

---

Originally published in *Eye*, no. 18 (Autumn 1995).

where the ease of manipulation of the medium threatens the message, where "user-friendliness" overrides the authority of the author, where "readers" are given free rein to hop, skip and jump through an intangible environment.

While designers involved with the technical parameters of computers explore the complexities of interface design, those who work with print are more concerned with aesthetics. The ephemerality of text on screen has migrated back to the page, as software applications such as Fontographer and Photoshop have allowed designers to make and unmake typefaces through myriad manipulations—"filters," as Adobe Photoshop calls them. Text and images can now be twirled, posterized, displaced, sharpened, extruded, diffused and, of course, blurred. But not just blurred—Photoshop provides five blur filters.

Such effects have, of course, been available previously in photography, but they made little impact on graphic design. Before the digital revolution, the need for specialized photographic equipment and training meant that photography was a distinct subset of design practice and education. Today, digital tools and production techniques have made photomanipulation available to the masses and have extended the completion of the photographic process: a photograph is no longer in its definitive form on film in the camera or even on the print—the process ends tentatively at the last "Save" within Photoshop. Blurring in photographically based graphic design used to communicate something about speed or focus. But today's blurred objects are not moving particularly quickly, nor do they serve to draw attention to a foreground element. Nowadays, blurring is used to create a particular ambience—a space within which one object is scarcely differentiated from the next.

Video photography, popularized by MTV from 1981, has made its mark on effect-driven graphic design, which has had to respond to public demand for newness and variety. The proliferation of video imagery has also affected expectations of aspects of image quality, including the cropping, editing and texture of pictures and the relationship between camera angle and scene. As if striving for the fast pacing of television and the graininess of the television monitor's low resolution, print design began to incorporate video imagery and texture. Once again the computer provided the means, this time to capture video frames for further manipulation in Photoshop. So whereas once the conventions of print were represented on television, now the conventions of television are represented in print. Both are combined in "multimedia" or on the computer, which is the tool used to produce most of the images that are found on both.

Along with the blurring of the relationships between media and between original and replica comes a blurring of the professional boundaries between designers within different media. The computer has leveled the field, leaving designers in each sector to scramble for ownership of part of the turf. Increasingly, this turf is the multimedia marketplace.

Digital technology has rendered the design process at once more accessible and more elusive. As hardware and software packages continue to drop in price, more novices enter the arena as practicing designers while some of those schooled in earlier techniques and aesthetics continue to apply old principles—inappropriately at times—to new problems. When designing their first CD-ROM titles, graphic designers tend to reproduce the page on screen while video producers strive for the effects of film and television. Both struggle with interface design, a practice which has more in common with industrial design.

How are we to respond when technology allows illegibility to become an acceptable norm? Pessimists talk about the collapse of common sense as an elite design class foists stylistic decadence on a naïve public. Optimists hail the liberation of the reader from the authority of the writer and view the new visual landscape as inherently participatory. Whether we celebrate or despair, it is clear that the techniques of digital image-making have combined with the aesthetics of deconstruction to create a malleable visual landscape modulated by the "production values" of mass media and made ubiquitous by the exponential increase in computer processing power over the last decade.

We are living in a time of profound ambiguity, at once liberating and unsettling. The physical and institutional boundaries through which we have traditionally defined ourselves and against which we have rebelled—whether political, sexual or cultural—are in flux. We are not sure who we are or who we want to be, and there is no moral imperative to spur us towards a decision. What are we to do when we no longer recognize the culprit? And why bother, when the next upheaval, whether an act of political terrorism or of plastic surgery, can speedily reinvent us?

In this boundary-free world, we can never be sure of where responsibility lies. The chain of causality includes real and virtual acts, some of which can be reversed by a simple "Undo" command, others which are indelible. The interplay between the two and our efforts to disentangle them lead to confusion. The quickened pace afforded by technology has slowed our reactions—mesmerized, we can scarcely formulate our response to what we see before the ground shifts, reframing us in yet another context.

Whether blurring is about the promise of infinite possibilities or the decadence of digitally enhanced leisure, it epitomizes the world we live in today—transmutable, mediated, ambiguous. As we reflect on the turn of yet another century, the blur raises the question: what exactly did we see, anyway?

THE TROUBLE WITH TYPE
Rudy VanderLans

"In every typeface there is, irrespective of its purpose, a more or less independent aesthetic value of form, which in turn also has its own direct expressivity." —Karl Gerstner[1]

In the article "Decay and Renewal in Typeface Markets," published in *Emigre*, no. 42, Alan Marshall addresses the age-old complaint of people in the type industry that piracy will ultimately kill the industry. Marshall counters by stating that, "Type markets are conditioned by a complex set of economic factors whose force lies in their ability to evolve in the light of social and cultural changes."

Being a relative newcomer in this industry, I can't help but notice that this "evolution" is marked by an increasing lack of respect for the artistic product itself. With the passing of each of the giants of type manufacturing, a new company takes its place selling mostly derivative typefaces, spending fewer dollars on the development of original designs and more dollars on marketing and selling fonts. With a few exceptions, the bulk of the new or surviving foundries and distributors have only one goal: to sell as much type as cheaply as possible without concern for the quality, use, conservation or development of typefaces. Despite his own accounts on the demise of such influential companies as Monotype and ATF, Marshall, throughout the article, remains steadfast and writes, "Total industrial chaos seems just about as unlikely as the threatened collapse of the quality typeface market." He points out, like others before him, that type is really only half the story and that how type is used is what really counts. One solution to type piracy and the preservation of quality type is through education. Educate users about type, and crummy rip-off versions will simply disappear.

While there is much merit in this solution, it is difficult to ignore that the type companies that *did* educate, such as ATF and Monotype, are the ones that have fallen by the wayside or are struggling to survive. Few type companies today invest in the education of type usage and the heritage of type design the way that Monotype or ATF did in the first half of the twentieth century. Compare the Image Club catalog with, let's say, the *ATF Type Specimen* book, or Agfa's printed materials with the *Monotype Recorder*, and you'd have to be blind not to see the obvious difference in quality, both visually and in terms of content. Where are the Stanley Morisons, the Beatrice Wardes, the Jan van Krimpens, the Frederick Goudys and the Morris Fuller Bentons of today?

Perhaps this is simply a transitional period, and perhaps Marshall is right and

Originally published in *Emigre*, no. 43 (Summer 1997).

ultimately the cream rises to the top. Currently, however, things look rather bleak. One reason why we see ever more companies selling cheap derivatives by the CD load and fewer companies genuinely involved in the design of new typefaces is that the United States, one of the largest typeface markets in the world, continues to deny copyright protection to typeface designs. While there are other methods to protect typeface designs, none is as effective as copyright. Patent protection, for instance, is limited both in terms of time and territory, since it is granted for only fourteen years and it is not universally accepted by other countries, as is copyright protection.

The idea behind a copyright is to provide protection to encourage the development of new and innovative work, ultimately for the benefit of society. Without this protection, there is less incentive for individuals or companies to create new work, as it can be copied by anyone the moment it is made public. While copyright protection does not automatically stamp out piracy or infringement, it does give artists the opportunity for legal recourse in the event their work is copied without permission. In the absence of proper protection methods and with copying extremely easy with today's digital technology, companies investing in quality type will continue to disappear, and with them the heritage of five centuries of typeface development. These losses will definitely not benefit anybody.

Typeface piracy has always existed, but it is obvious that with each new technology the act of copying has become easier and that copies have become increasingly indistinguishable from originals. Today it requires literally no expertise of any kind to make a perfect copy of a typeface. Without proper protection, typefaces have become easy targets for opportunists eager to bank on the public's desire for typefaces.

The United States is one of the few, if not only, industrialized nations in the world that does not extend copyright protection to typeface designs. The reason for this comes from the old copyright doctrine that typefaces, like most industrial designs, are considered to be utilitarian and that they exhibit insufficient original authorship. In general, such articles are not copyrightable, unless they contain artistic features capable of existing separately and independently of the overall utilitarian shape. Furthermore, the courts that have upheld the Copyright Office's decision regarding typefaces have also expressed other concerns. By granting copyright protection to typefaces, the court has argued, the freedom of the press might be impeded. But typeface designers do not seek to claim ownership of the alphabet; they seek protection for the various *expressions* of the alphabet. Designers recognize that as an idea, the alphabet should remain unprotectable, since it is part of the public domain. Typeface designs, on the other hand, are the expressions of that idea. And as expressions of an idea, they constitute original works of authorship.

The Copyright Office's decision to bar all typeface designs from copyright protection intrigues me for two reasons. First, it goes to the very core of what a typeface is, a debate that has occupied many pages in *Emigre*. Second, this argument cuts to the very center of our livelihood: the design, manufacture and distribution of original typeface design. The Copyright Office's decision, which dates back to 1978, is outdated. The typeface industry has changed significantly since this decision. The postmodern and deconstructivist theories that circulated throughout art schools in the Eighties and Nineties had a profound influence on the design of typefaces and typography, ultimately freeing them from the restraints of functionality. Coupled with new methods of creating type facilitated by the personal computer, a renaissance in typeface design has taken place that has no precedence in its five-hundred-year history. This fact has been duly noted by curator Ellen Lupton who, in the recent show *Mixing Messages: Graphic Design in Contemporary Culture*, at the Smithsonian's Cooper-Hewitt Museum, gave singular attention to typeface design, and reflected upon font production as "a new form of underground publishing."[2]

In today's image-conscious information era, type is taking up an increasingly prominent role in giving shape to the world around us. As such, typeface design is now regularly discussed in the mainstream press, is shown in major museums, is the topic of countless anthologies, annuals, how-to and other design books. Typeface design was even the topic of a recent television program on MSNBC's *The Site*. Writer Neil Feineman, quoted in an article about typeface design in the *Los Angeles Times*, reflects upon this recent phenomenon. "Quirky type and page design," he says, "have come to be harnessed simply for their trendiness, not because they blend to create meaning."[3] While trendiness is a description not all type designers like, Feineman's statement does underline how typefaces have moved from being simple carriers of linguistic meaning to expressions of entire trends. Or, as design critic Michael Rock puts it, typefaces "document and codify the 'current,' generating the artifacts that will serve to frame our own generation."[4] It is this particular quality of secondary meaning and expressivity that has earned the new crop of fonts such high acclaim and exposure, and demonstrates that there is ample original authorship in typeface design.

THE BEAUTY OF TYPE

There are at least two separate aspects to a typeface. First, there is the utilitarian-alphabetic aspect, which allows it to create linguistic meaning when letters are combined into words and words into sentences, etc. The other is the artistic aspect, the different type designs that express the alphabet visually in myriad ways. It is the latter that makes type so desirable because type users recognize the value of differentiation that a particular typeface design brings to their message. This is why they pick one typeface over another with such determination.

Obviously, type is functional as well, but not intrinsically so. First, the individual letters have to be arranged so that they make sense. Context is everything. Once this is accomplished, a typeface can make the spoken word and ideas visible, but it can do so in many different ways. In that respect, a typeface functions much like a photograph or a painting. Just as you can represent a tree differently by photographing or painting it in a variety of styles, so you can represent a text differently by setting it in a number of type styles and sizes.

There are many typefaces that have artistic features that far outweigh their ability to communicate linguistic messages. In fact, there are typefaces that have artistic features that diminish and sometimes render the linguistic utility of the typeface completely useless, making it "illegible." Take the initial caps used in illuminated manuscripts, for instance. While they were considered to be the visual expression of the word of God, much of the verbal meaning was derived from the context in which they were used. It is not the individual letters that are functional. The utility of a typeface also heavily depends upon the intention of the user. Arrange letters arbitrarily and no linguistic meaning is generated, yet the visual, artistic qualities of the typeface remain and can easily be incorporated into all kinds of visuals.

This raises some obvious questions; if a typeface is considered illegible, is it still a typeface? And where exactly does one draw the line between legible and illegible, or, for that matter, between typeface and picture? Take, for instance, the letters created by the artist William Wegman, which are made up of his dogs laid out on the ground to form letter shapes. Are they pictures of dogs, or pictures of alphabetic characters? Is this a typeface, or is this a photographic illustration? Probably all of the above, but what makes them so original is their distinct visual features, not their alphabetic utility.

Regardless of the level of artistic authorship in a typeface, the fact remains that a typeface has a certain level of utility, which is exactly why it is considered unprotectable. What is problematic with this assessment is that *all* things visual have some level of utility; yet photographs, illustrations and most other visual expressions are usually granted the copyright protection that is denied to typefaces. What is the intention of the photographer when he or she takes a picture, and what is the intention of the painter when he or she sets out to do a painting, and the illustrator when doing an illustration? Isn't that communication, too? Aren't we asked to "read" a photograph much like we read a text? Take the photograph's "utility" as a container of meaning away and what is left? The illustrations in an airline safely guidelines booklet, too, function much like letters. By arranging the separate pictures in a particular order they create meaning—how to jump out of a plane, how to put on an oxygen mask, etc. Or, take a series of panels in a comic strip. Don't these pictures also function much like type? Take the utility of these images away or rearrange the pictures, and little is left. Yet somehow such illustrations seem to be considered by the Copyright Office to be without utilitarian function and are fully copyrightable, as are photographs, paintings and almost any other kind of visual art.

This exception of excluding typeface designs from copyright protection becomes particularly problematic in relation to typefaces that are pictorial. Regardless of William Wegman's status as a world-renowned artist whose dogs are the subject and object of thousands of pieces of visual art, the moment they were laid down on the floor to create letters, according to the Copyright Office's ruling, they lost their status as dogs and became utilitarian objects whose shapes were in the public domain.

Similarly, it would be interesting to hear Disney, a company that rigorously protects its intellectual property rights, argue against anyone taking Mickey Mouse and manipulating him into a twenty-six-letter alphabet. Of course, Wegman and Disney would make the argument that the parts that make up the letters, the photographs of the dogs and drawings of Mickey Mouse, are themselves copyrighted and trademarked icons. But what are most letters but shapes made up of various parts similarly copy-rightable? There are typefaces that are made up out of tree parts; some are made out of intricate geometric shapes. BitPull, an electronic typeface designed by the Dutch type laboratory LettError, literally pulls together bits of images of any shape to form letters. I can create copyrightable art by combining any abstract or non-abstract element into infinite variations unless I arrange them such that they become recognizable as letters, at which point they fall in the public domain. An odd idea, don't you think?

The alphabet is a system, but it's an idea that exists without a single fixed expression. It materializes only after the letters have been fully rendered. This can be done in infinite ways, with each interpretation representing an original work of authorship containing significant expressive and artistic qualities. Typefaces, as I've pointed out, can even exist separately and independently of their utility. These are all characteristics that make most forms of art qualify for copyright protection. Therefore, to exclude all typeface designs across the board from copyright protection, simply because of their utilitarian aspect, seems arbitrary, particularly in light of the fact that most forms of art contain utilitarian functions. To exclude typefaces simply because it would be difficult to discern between what some perceive to be the existence of many look-alikes is also moot, since this problem is not unique to typeface design. Thousands of records, books, paintings and illustrations are produced each year, and each person has the opportunity to register his or her work with the Copyright Office. In case of a dispute, it becomes the court's decision to determine who may claim the work. Typeface designs, on the other hand, are simply not considered worthy.

If there is a positive side to the growing number of companies selling knockoff typefaces by the thousands, it must be that it indicates that the public has an insatiable appetite for type. While it might seem that the pirates are fulfilling a yeoman's job feeding the masses with inexpensive typefaces, it must not be forgotten that the fonts they sell are usually copied from others. Without copyright protection, however, little incentive exists for the companies and individuals who actually produce these typefaces to continue to invest in the development of new typefaces or the adaptation of existing typefaces to emerging technologies. Instead, we will be left with dozens of companies selling knockoff fonts, run by individuals who feel it is within their legal right to copy any typeface the minute it comes out. None has an interest in typefaces beyond their profitability, which is obvious by the complete absence of product source information. While their CDs often boast the inclusion of award-winning "designer" fonts, we are usually left guessing who these designers are. No design methods are discussed, and no references are ever made as to the source material of the typeface designs. While they might brag that we all stand on the shoulders of giants, they never disclose who these giants are, since historical references are never mentioned. Thus, the anonymity of both typeface origin and designers is perpetuated, and little by little, with each supersaver release, the heritage of typeface design is erased.

Typeface design is a living and breathing art form which, as Paul Elliman points out, imbues its model with attributes that "convey the dynamics of history, anthropology, linguistics, political science, sociology, economics, and so on."[5] It is a sad fact that we allow the people who are the least interested in typeface design, the knockoff companies who are tripping all over themselves to release poor quality derivatives, to benefit the most from it. I guess those typefaces, too, tell us something about our culture, but it's hardly something to be proud of. I would like to believe that Alan Marshall is right, and that the type industry and quality typefaces will survive. Copyright protection would greatly serve this ideal, but it's something that needs to actively be pursued. This article is one of my contributions to a much larger effort by type aficionados from around the world who are determined to win copyright protection for typeface design in the United States.

Notes
1. Karl Gerstner, *Compendium for Literates* (Cambridge: MIT Press, 1974).
2. Ellen Lupton, *Mixing Messages: Graphic Design in Contemporary Culture* (New York: Cooper-Hewitt National Design Museum and Princeton Architectural Press, 1996).
3. Irene Lacher, "The Difficult Type," *Los Angeles Times*, 28 June 1993.
4. Michael Rock, "Typefaces Are Rich with the Gesture and Spirit of Their Own Era," *I.D.* (May/June 1992).
5. Paul Elliman, "Reading Typography Writing Language," *Fuse 10: Freeform* (Summer 1994).

IS IT BETTER TO REVIVE THAN TO DECEIVE? DESIGN AND COMPLICITY: HERBERT BAYER'S SILENT LEGACY

Sol Sender

In this essay, I will be looking at "Deutschland Ausstellung," a booklet that was published in 1936 to coincide with an exhibition of the same name. "Deutschland Ausstellung" used the occasion of the 1936 Berlin Olympics to present Germany and its people to an international audience. Clearly a piece of Nazi propaganda, it placed smiling faces and a glorious history alongside the Nazi swastika. The booklet presented a Germany proud of its history, its culture and its movement to build a strong and modern nation. This was three years after Jews had been expelled from the Civil Service, two years after they had been removed from the Artists Guilds and one year after they had been stripped of their German citizenship. What may not be generally known is that "Deutschland Ausstellung" was designed by Herbert Bayer, renowned Bauhaus master typographer and celebrated European émigré who helped bring modernism to the United States.

Originally published in AIGA/Chicago's *Inform* Vol. 13, no. 1 (2000).

Noticeably absent from any of Bayer's monographs, this piece may well shatter any perception of him as a rescued European artist fleeing from tyranny. It may also undermine our desire to see the Bauhaus as simply an oasis of moral and artistic integrity in a rapidly devolving Germany. At the very least, the booklet reveals that erasure has been a strategy in the construction of Herbert Bayer's legacy.

I will not argue that the existence of this booklet should remove Bayer from the pantheon of foundation figures in modern design. I will, however, argue that it necessitates a reassessment of the evolution of modern design and its various relationships to twentieth-century European politics. This is not a work that is best pushed aside when looking at the totality of Bayer's achievements and the lessons of his visual style. Rather, it may be that one profound lesson that Bayer's career offers to contemporary designers lies in the very problem of his work for the Nazis.

STRIPPING CONTEXT FROM CONTENT

Contemporary writing about graphic design is often characterized by an inability to engage fully with the complex history from which modern design practice emerges. Too often this writing tends towards the history of form-making, or provides a shallow romanticization of design heroes. When such tendencies result in a failure to address the spectacle and crimes of fascism in 1930s Germany, we are left with a critical void which demands engagement.

The Holocaust, in particular, is a historical event of such significance that it has demanded intense investigation and an exploration into human behavior. It is of critical importance in any analysis of the cultural and artistic production that precipitates its occurrence. "Deutschland Ausstellung" is one such production. Though it has been pictured and briefly mentioned in a number of important essays and books of the past fifteen years, in each instance the authors have failed to sufficiently address the meaning or crisis of Bayer's willingness to lend his skills to articulate the Nazi movement. I find such failures shocking. Such a failure, after all, perpetuates Bayer's legacy of denial about his work. My criticisms of these instances are an attempt to break that resounding silence, and to assert the relevance of complicity in the troubling evolution of modern design.

As much as we might like to think otherwise, the rise of fascism did not mean the end of the modern movement in European design. Tension, compromise and complicity are, unfortunately, concepts that are as politically and aesthetically significant as utopia, resistance, exile and emigration. We cannot understand the full complexity of modern design without confronting both sides of the moral, political and aesthetic transformations wrought by World War II.

In the opening pages of Ellen Lupton's and J. Abbott Miller's seminal work on design and theory—*Design Writing Research*—a stunning montage from "Deutschland Ausstellung" is pictured. In this montage a mass of people swell forward, Nazi flags in the foreground. On the right, three Nazi archetypes are presented. They are the worker, the peasant and the soldier. On the left is a swastika medal, its presence branding an otherwise typical modernist montage. Finally, a book-like shield, centered at the bottom of the spread, frames the typography. Though not large enough to be legible in Lupton and Miller's reproduction, it reads: "The Fuhrer speaks and millions listen to him. The working people, the peasantry and the regained right of self-defense are the supports of National Socialist Germany."

Surprisingly, there is no mention or discussion of the booklet in Lupton's and Miller's subsequent essay, which is titled "Deconstruction and Graphic Design." It would seem that only the formal qualities of the piece are of interest to them. The book-like shield which frames Bayer's typography is used as an example of a book-within-a-book formal device that Miller and Lupton employ in the design of their own essay. We are left with only the caption to reveal the troubling complexity of Bayer's work.[1] The proximity of the essay on deconstruction, however, may shed light on Lupton's and Miller's surprising lack of commentary.

Deconstruction escapes the politics of modernism in its intense and sometimes obsessive analysis of the structures of language and meaning. For all the creative experimentation and intellectual exploration that deconstruction has inspired (particularly at Cranbrook in the 1980s), it has also accompanied a troubling blindness to the tragically straightforward content that history often delivers. Here, that dynamic is made evident. Lupton's and Miller's interest in the formal qualities of Bayer's piece—and only its formal qualities (at least in this instance)—serves as an uncomfortable reminder of Bayer's own response to being confronted with the booklet later in his career:

> "When asked . . . about his contribution to this project for the Nazis, Bayer's only comment was, 'this is an interesting booklet insofar as it was done exclusively with photography and photomontage, and was printed in a duotone technique.'"[2]

Bayer's comment seems to reflect an inability or unwillingness to take responsibility for his actions, express public remorse or attempt to explain the conditions which precipitated his propaganda work for the Nazis. Christopher Burke, in his book on Paul Renner, describes how "Bayer later painted out all those elements [in his work] that made explicit Nazi references."[3] Perhaps Bayer was horrified by his own complicity, or perhaps he felt that it was better for his career and historical legacy to conceal and erase that work, given what the world, by then, knew about the Nazis and the Holocaust. Regardless of his motives, for us to ignore his complicity and silence forecloses on the potential for an ongoing relationship between graphic design and politics. We are left with an aesthetic legacy that bespeaks an unconscious allegiance with an incomplete history, rather than the creative and often overtly political vision of the avant-garde that precedes and informs Bayer's work.

THE EVOLUTION OF AN AESTHETIC

In Benjamin Buchloh's essay, "From Faktura to Factography," we find a more complete history, with wider historical and political concerns. Here is one of the rare pieces of art historical research that successfully tracks the intensity of the relationship between the aesthetic practices of modern design and the politics of early to mid-century Europe—particularly in the Soviet Union. Buchloh seems well aware of the troubling evolution of Rodchenko's and El Lissitzky's careers and how they reflect the tragedy of the "great utopia's" shift to totalitarianism. But by the time he gets to Bayer, he seems unable to trace an equally complex dynamic in the problem of "Deutschland Ausstellung." In his essay, he includes a picture of the same "Deutschland Ausstellung" spread which Lupton and Miller reproduced. He uses it to illustrate how the aesthetics of montage shifted, from the revolutionary propaganda of the Soviet Union, through fascist Italy and Nazi Germany, until finally—in the person of Bayer's emigration to the United States—it is transformed into a tool of the "ideological apparatus of the culture industry of Western capitalism."[4]

At stake, for Buchloh, is not Bayer's complicity, but the devolution of the art of montage at the hands of totalitarian and then capitalist propaganda interests. Bayer's engagement with capitalism seems as damning as his engagement with fascism. Clearly, this cannot be the case. Despite the very real issues associated with the United States' own propaganda campaigns, they cannot be compared with the crisis of Bayer's designs for Nazi Germany and the silence that has followed—a silence which has defined the very boundaries of his legacy.

Truthfully, Buchloh's essay is not about graphic design. It is about "art." And in it, there is an implication that graphic design is a tragedy that befell art. In such a configuration, the client (Nazi Germany) is the villain and the designer (Bayer) is the fool. The resulting argument insults Bayer but lets him off the hook. Ultimately, it diminishes the significance of graphic design and its historical relationship to the avant-garde. It also ignores some crucial developments in the relationship between art and politics, a relationship, which here informs the designer-client configuration. Clearly, that relationship is at the root of the problem with Bayer.

In his essay, "Out of Austria: Herbert Bayer," Rolf Sachsse argues that Bayer was psychologically attached to the rewards of working for a client, and was unable to ever "get to a point of figural creation without outward stimulation."[5] For Sachsse, Bayer's aesthetic explorations seemed attached to "an anticipatory obedience, an eager anticipation of the wishes of his clients, whoever they might be."[6] Perhaps this quality of Bayer's work is characteristic of the larger problem of complicity. In Germany, a social system, a network of propaganda and a bureaucratic process combined to create the context for acts of unimaginable horror, while protecting collaborators and perpetrators, on every level, from facing the implications of their "work." Bayer's connection to this network of evil is, according to Sachsse, born of an emotional need that Bayer finds fulfilled in the otherness of the client. But Sachsse's insight into Bayer's psychological character is just that. He doesn't extend his argument into an analysis of politics and the evolution of modern design. He doesn't see the significance of this designer-client configuration as a problematic foundation for the practice of modern design, nor does he discuss graphic design as a significant development in the aesthetic practices of modernism. But it is. The evolution of the designer-client relationship is extremely troubling in the climate of the totalitarianism of the 1930s, but if we are to learn from it, we must also see it as paradigmatic. It permanently scars the aesthetics of modernism and our understanding of its application to the practice of graphic design.

If we were to presume a historical evolution of modern design, beginning in 1917 and ending with the present, there would be certain defining moments. One of those moments needs to be 1936 Germany. It was a moment that should be remembered for the existence of a relationship between a designer, Herbert Bayer, and a client, National Socialism. What has survived of that moment? What can we learn from it now? For today's designers, the question of Bayer's complicity may provoke a concern with how our design work could inadvertently result in the success of a group, idea or product which may ultimately prove dangerous, wrong or evil. In the case of Bayer, to simply question his public consciousness (how much did he know?) avoids the larger question of responsibility for ignorant or unconscious acts of political consequence. How much do we know about our clients? How much do we care to know? How much does, or should, that knowledge affect the fundamental quality and success of our work? For design historians, the problem of complicity in Nazi Germany may be of as much significance as the idea of utopia in the early years of the Soviet Union. Unlike those years in the U.S.S.R., it was the denial of the relationship between art and politics that laid the foundation for the complicit acts of some of Germany's finest modern designers, architects and filmmakers. Be it the extreme of Leni Riefenstahl's *Triumph of the Will* or the troubling ambiguities of Mies van der Rohe's interaction with the Nazis, each is characterized by an insistence on the separation between aesthetics and political ideology. The depoliticization of design in the 1930s, as well as an extremely dubious understanding of neutrality in WWII, may well inform the emergence of a neutral Swiss style in the 1950s, as well as our current debates about the roles and responsibilities of the designer in the production of culture. It may be that design is inherently political insofar as it is a sophisticated mode of visual and verbal communication. It may be that the politics of design is an essential component of a more complex and engaging mode of design practice and historical examination. One thing is certain: to be political is to take action when circumstances demand it and to take a stand when one needs to be taken— something of which Herbert Bayer seemed wholly incapable. May we begin to learn from his failures as much as we have learned from his successes.

POSTSCRIPT

After writing this essay, I discovered a passage in Arthur Cohen's 1984 monograph on Bayer. In it, Bayer has described to Cohen, his Jewish biographer, how he had been forced by the Nazis to include the stunning swastika montage at the last moment. Furthermore, he claimed that it was exactly these kinds of events that led him to leave Germany, if nothing else for the safety of his Jewish wife and Jewish daughter. I have since wondered whether these "facts" necessitate a rewrite of my essay and a reconsideration of Bayer's complicity. I have decided that they don't. I remain skeptical of Bayer's motives. Not only was Cohen Jewish—he was a prominent thinker and writer on Jewish

culture. If Bayer was, as Sachsse claims, psychologically attached to the rewards of working for a client, who's to say that he was not also psychologically attached to the rewards
of working with his biographer? Furthermore, Bayer's statement belies a presumption
that it was only that one montage (pictured by Lupton, Miller, and Buchloh) that makes
"Deutschland Ausstellung" such a troubling piece. In fact, the entire piece propagates
German culture and nationalism at a time when horrible crimes were being committed on a national scale. As Jeremy Ainsley recently put it in his excellent analysis of Bayer:

> The catalog . . . shows, page by page, that it was an important popular mani-
> festation of national and, at times, racist propaganda, in which central concepts
> of National Socialist ideology were used as organizing principles.[7]

The Jewish identity of Bayer's first wife and daughter makes clear that the manifestation of that racism in National Socialist Germany was not only pervasive and ubiquitous, but something which turned friend against friend, family against family, and a
nation against itself. Could a man want to save his daughter while doing work that perpetuated the machinery of her potential destruction? In 1930s Germany, yes. And that
tragedy is something that Bayer could never face, explain, or, seemingly, understand.

Notes
1. It reads: "Brochure, designed by Herbert Bayer, 1934. Republished in Gebrauchsgraphik, April 1936. The Nazi
   publication uses the structure of a book-within-a-book. The shield-like book appears against backgrounds
   depicting the 'folk' masses and Germany's natural and industrial resources" [Ellen Lupton and J. Abbott Miller,
   Design Writing Research (New York: Kiosk, 1996), p. 2]. Interestingly, Lupton and Miller's citation is the only one
   that dates the booklet from 1934.
2. Benjamin Buchloh quoting Christopher Phillips in Benjamin Buchloh, "From Faktura to Factography," in *The
   Contest of Meaning*, ed. Richard Bolton (Cambridge, Mass.: M.I.T. Press, 1989), p. 77.
3. Christopher Burke, *Paul Renner: The Art of Typography* (New York: Princeton Architectural Press, 1998), p. 148,
   footnote 5.
4. Buchloh, "From Faktura to Factography," p. 76.
5. Rolf Sachsse, "Out of Austria: Herbert Bayer," *Camera Austria International* 46 (1994), p. 10.
6. Sachsse, "Out of Austria," p. 9.
7. Jeremy Ainsley, *Graphic Design in Germany: 1890–1945* (Berkeley and Los Angeles: University of California
   Press, 2000), p. 206.

DE STIJL, NEW MEDIA, AND
THE LESSONS OF GEOMETRY
Jessica Helfand

In his collected essays, *Architecture and Disjunction*, Bernard Tschumi argues that frames as architectural elements derive their meaning through juxtaposition. "They establish memory," he writes, "of the preceding frame, of the course of events." This idea that a structural element can serve a graphically direct yet intensely personal need is a compelling notion indeed, and recalls the ambitions of earlier twentieth-century visionaries who sought to embrace social order and spiritual harmony through simple, formal means: this is perhaps most true of the de Stijl group, an informal confederation of artists, architects and designers working in Holland between 1917 and 1931. Strangely, however, while the lessons of modernism in general—and de Stijl in particular—have found their way into contemporary design education and practice, the invaluable formal principles upon which this thinking was based remain virtually absent in the design of new media.

In 1915 and 1916, theosophist M. H. J. Shoenmaekers published *The New Image of the World* and *Principles of Plastic Mathematics*. Suggesting that reality might best be expressed as a series of opposing forces—a formal polarity of horizontal and vertical axes and a juxtaposition of primary colors—the author posited a new image of the world, expressed with "a controllable precision, a conscious penetration of reality and exact beauty." In an age in which we are bombarded with frequent, dense and often contradictory messages about what it is we are saying, meaning and making, this statement is refreshingly straightforward. Read literally, it also provides an inspirational way of deconstructing the complex role design plays in our increasingly digital culture. Most important, perhaps to the designer lamenting the intractable restrictions of today's technological climate, the formal language of de Stijl—and its celebration of the purity of the X-Y axis—is inspiration indeed.

As the primary theoretical influence behind the de Stijl movement, Shoenmaekers's thinking paralleled the evolution of a reductive visual vocabulary that embraced ideals at once utilitarian and utopian: with this vocabulary, artists such as Piet Mondrian and Theo van Doesberg produced work that, in its spare elegance, has had a lasting effect on twentieth-century aesthetics. Thought to be radical at the time of their initial publication, today these ideas are surprisingly relevant, as they—and the work they influenced—suggest a deceptively simple way to think about the formal, temporal and cultural phenomena that collectively define new media. In an effort to resolve the rela-

Originally published in *Eye*, no. 24 (Spring 1997).

tionships between structural form and transient content, between cyclical time and infinite space, and between a message transmitted and a message received, the propositions of de Stijl suggest an ideal paradigm with which to evaluate the role and effectiveness of design in an electronic age.

To practitioners of de Stijl, the reduction of pure form was considered a symbolic translation of complex cultural ideals. While it possessed no notable political cause *per se*—unlike Malevich and the Russian Constructivists, or Marinetti and the Italian Futurists—it argued for a kind of convergent thinking that links it unequivocally to the culture of new media. The goals of elevating society, of bridging the gap between the collective and the individual, and of gesturing to a kind of utopian ideal were expressed enthusiastically in the work, as well as in the writing of position papers, exhibition catalogs, commercial publications and other forms of propaganda. These manifestos are evocative reminders of de Stijl ideology: in their evangelism and rhetoric, they bear a strong resemblance to much of the propaganda espoused by contemporary new media culture. Unlike contemporary media, however, the visual evidence of de Stijl thinking was both surprisingly simple and enormously sophisticated. Perhaps for this reason, it was also quite beautiful. In the wake of such triumphant breakthroughs in the distillation of human thought, why have we veered so far from the lessons of modernism?

Today, as designers struggle to define better ways of representing ideas in two-, three-, and four-dimensional space, Shoenmaekers's ideas, dating from more than a century ago, offer us a way to better understand and clarify these questions. To begin with, the question of "controllable precision" suggests a standard for designers struggling to rationalize their role in the convergent morass of telecommunications commonly known as "new media." Here, the very value of design is in question: as interpersonal exchanges coexist and multiply in a landscape laden with sophisticated electronic options, one might argue that the function of design is marginalized—if not rendered entirely obsolete—or that the role of the designer itself is imperiled. We have perhaps unwittingly ceded control: to our computers, to our audience, to the demands of a new and increasingly global economy. But the opportunity to define—even celebrate—precision lies at the heart of what we can and should do. This elevates and objectifies our role, and redefines our mission as architects of a new visual order.

"Controllable precision" is of course impossible in an environment characterized by such random and perpetual change. What is possible, however, is to think about design as a system of limitations, and to consider the role of the designer as one who articulates that system. Establishing a grid, understanding the permutations of a template as a flexible armature within which information can be delivered, is a good example of the graphical application of such a system, in print as well as on the screen. With the ongoing advances in browser technologies (such as frames, borderless frames, tables and so forth), a more resolved formal articulation of space is now possible on the screen, making "controllable precision" an eminently achievable goal.

This system—the establishment of the template, its formal attributes, and its compositional potential for iterative recombination—is not only the principal function of design in online media, but its greatest contribution. Conversely, what happens between the frames is not: the indulgent, memory-intensive aesthetic that evidences itself on many proprietary Web sites only serves to demonstrate how technical complexity short-circuits "good" design. With error prompts preempting any opportunity for theatrical or visual impact, the mood is irrevocably broken, an enduring reminder that a shield of intrusive technology lies between you and your screen. This is the "interface" at its worst: simply stated, this is what happens when design gets in the way.

Alternatively, the simplicity that characterizes de Stijl thinking—and the order that can be traced in Dutch painting as far back as the seventeenth century—suggests a better model for organizing space and achieving visually engaging and functionally successful solutions. In his own work, van Doesberg identified this purist reduction as an attempt to "expel the narrative." In this view, the designer is the director rather than the actor, and design is less about experience and more about framing the experience. The success of this proposition rests largely in rethinking ways of articulating space, and suggests that we reconsider the screen as a kind of picture palace. To challenge the picture plane is to radically adjust our thinking about what a screen is, what a computer is, and what role design plays in the mix. Central to this is a formal appreciation of modernism and a fundamental understanding of its *lingua franca*: geometry.

This appeal to modernism, however, has been virtually overlooked in these early days of new media design. Today, the prevailing aesthetic leans away from realism, opting instead for a primitive sampling of poorly rendered, often cartoon-like illustrations masquerading as familiar, habitable spaces. Worse still, with the advent of Virtual Reality Modeling Language (VRML), what was objectionable in 2D now becomes horrifying in 3- and 4D. Here, Schoenmaekers's notion of "penetrating reality" suggests an intriguing alternative to such tiresome examples of forced and phony simulacra. The opportunity to reconstruct reality rejects the overused models and metaphors that currently exist—the faux street scene, the mock desktop—in favor of a simplified and inherently more flexible visual vocabulary—one based on simple geometric form.

The suggestion that geometry can address the human condition lies at the core of classic architectural discourse and is everywhere present in the ideology and practice of de Stijl. Described as "neoplastic," architecture in this period favored a kind of elementary constructivism evidenced in anti-decorative, asymmetrical and colorful explorations of spatial displacement. Such experiments—the famous red, blue and yellow Rietveldt chair (1918), for example—indicated the extent to which simple form could explode with new and provocative possibility. Mondrian's *Broadway Boogie Woogie* (1926) was an attempt to codify the dynamic pulse of the city through the restrained use of horizontal and vertical lines, the expression of two opposing forces. It is no coincidence that this work gestured to the space beyond the limits of the canvas: indeed, the desire to embrace infinite space was in no small way influenced by Einstein's theory of relativity, which had been published several years earlier.

Like the de Stijl artists, we can identify with the imposed rectilinear parameters circumscribing our work, as we struggle to define the opportunities for creative expression on screen. We can share their pointed fascination with infinite space as we explore the limitless real estate options introduced by the phenomenon of cyberspace. But unlike them, our work today has yet to reveal itself as inspired, informed by their legacy, their thinking, the empirical evidence of their prolific labors. In the end, as reality itself is called into question by the notion of virtual space and the users (read audiences) who dwell there, "beauty" (not to mention "exact beauty") is indeed in the eye of the beholder. This is of course the true goal of interactivity: designers often struggle in particular with the intangible temporal component implicit in these new media, where experience is meant to be customized and mutable. How can design address consistency—of place, of identity, of need—and still speak to the perpetual changes that characterize the transient nature of these phenomena? Of great relevance to new media, de Stijl practitioners concerned themselves with resolving the relationship between the static and the dynamic. Their interest in challenging the formal interplay of geometric elements suggests that the orchestration of components can simultaneously gesture to the fixed and to the flexible, to the precision as well as to the elusiveness of "exact beauty." In this view, the same reductive visual vocabulary cannot only support such seemingly conflicting ideals (static/kinetic, variable/constant, universal/unique), but can perhaps begin to suggest more innovative solutions for structuring new systems, mapping new spaces, and reaching new audiences along the way.

THE CRITICAL "LANGUAGES"
OF GRAPHIC DESIGN
Johanna Drucker

This paper addresses the history of attitudes towards criticism in design within nineteenth- and twentieth-century intellectual contexts and looks to the contemporary condition of design in electronic formats and platforms as a way of asking the question, "How are we to conceptualize what is *graphic* about graphic design?" This question is a subset of the larger inquiry that begs illumination, even in the early twenty-first century—how to establish a foundation for graphesis, or visual representation as a field of knowledge? And what are the critical and theoretical approaches appropriate to it?

Theoretical and critical approaches to graphic design rely heavily—and paradoxically—upon analogies between visual forms and language. The phrase "languages of design" inscribes that analogy in such familiar terms that the assumptions underlying it

Originally a lecture presented at "Looking Closer: AIGA Conference on Design History and Criticism" in New York City, February 2001.

almost disappear. The paradox results from the fact that the fundamental *visuality* of graphic design is sacrificed when its specificity is subsumed within a critical framework premised on concepts of language.

The censored form of an 1898 poster by French artist Alfred Choubrac makes this paradox apparent. When informed that his can-can dancer was apparently displaying too much of her lace underclothing for so public an image, rather than redraw the image, Choubrac reworked the poster with a banner over the offending portion that proclaimed, "This part of the image is banned." A text thus stands in for that segment of the image that is not to be viewed. Read another way, this statement makes clear that the function of text is not only to cover what can't be seen, but that in doing so, text covers and conceals visual form. What is always rhetorically the case in critical writing about design is here demonstrated graphically. Critical writing substitutes language for image, basically swapping out text for visual elements in exactly the manner Choubrac's redrawn image made explicit. The special case of the censored poster is in fact a demonstration of the general case of critical language in its relation to images.

Much graphic design criticism not only attempts to use language for discussion of visual form, but also pushes the use of linguistic analogies. In so doing, it engages in a sleight of discourse, substituting not only a word for an image, but a linguistic premise for a visual one. Graphesis, the idea that knowledge can be represented in visual form as a distinct mode of symbolic communication with its own rules and systems, is always at a disadvantage because criticism functions most effectively and familiarly in language. These analogies between "languages" of visual communication and language as a system of verbal communication have repeatedly reinforced the perception that this is a useful, logical and even truthful way to understand graphic design from a critical perspective. But is it?

The phrase "the language of graphic design" is part of a very specific history of approaches to graphic form. It conjures associations of systematic principles ordering visual elements with maximum effectiveness and streamlined elegance. This is classic twentieth-century modernism, the international style of mid-century, in which the lucid presentation of visual material was organized to seem like the natural order of communication. Exemplary—even emblematic—of such work is the well-known 1950 publication, *Sweet's Catalogue Design Progress* by Ladislav Sutnar and K. Lönberg-Holm. The striking project that forms the center of this piece is their graphic redesign of the *Techron* catalogue. Through an integration of content analysis and graphic presentation, their work epitomizes this rational sensibility and its communicative efficacy. Starting with a catch-all, randomly sequenced arrangement of time-pieces, text and jumbled page layout designed half a century earlier, Sutnar and Lönberg-Holm developed an approach to design that was systematic and generalizable rather than project specific. Though they linked their concept of systematicity to an image of traffic and information flow, the more fundamental idea of ordered rules functioning as a "grammar" of design underlies their text.

The use of the analogy between language and visual forms in graphic design, or in discussions of pattern and visual art, has precedents in the nineteenth century (earlier in architecture). This analogy is suggested by the title of the monumental volume by

Owen Jones published in 1856, *The Grammar of Ornament*, another significant landmark in the field of design history. The use of this analogy between language and visual forms in graphic design participates in broader attempts to formalize and systematize areas of human knowledge and their representation. Such efforts are the product of nineteenth-century attempts to rationalize areas of humanistic inquiry, aligning them with the perception that scientific knowledge has greater truth value and thus greater cultural authority than humanistic disciplines whose methodologies are largely descriptive and subjective, qualifiable rather than quantifiable. Scientific thought provided models for rational order as a governing principle of the natural world. The cultural authority that attends to such disambiguating methods continues to predominate in our contemporary culture. Though the elusive dream of a systematic approach to graphic design, grounded in principles that function according to an analogy with language, now bears a nostalgic stigma, the primacy of language has been reinforced by another type of authority, that of formal languages in digital technology.

In the twentieth century the concept of the "languages of design" and its parallel formation, "theories of visual communication," became a commonplace notion that circulated widely through the profession and its training ground in curricula and textbooks for the graphic designer. The approach had many assumptions in common with those of modernism in the visual arts, in particular, a drive to articulate a set of universals that would always hold true within formal, visual expressions. The attempt at creation of a rigorous visual system, such as that developed in the Bauhaus curriculum through the work of, among others, the influential figure Josef Albers, was an almost unquestioned desideratum of the design world in its moves towards definition and professionalization. The systematic approach was premised on the belief that a formal system of rules for effective design could transcend historical circumstance. The principles of formal relations were conceived to be absolutes, governing visual elements in a scheme that had parallels in the project of formalization of natural languages in many fields. The influence of analytic philosophy, mathematics and formal logic in the early decades of the twentieth century established a foundation for asserting the benefits of formal methodologies for the *production* of works of visual art and graphic design as well as for the critical analysis of visual art. After mid-century, these principles bore mature fruit in the visual form, organizing principles and international influence of Swiss design, on the work of Josef Müller-Brockman, Anton Stankowski, Paul Rand and legions of others.

These systematic approaches and their basis in formalist methodologies, as well as their attendant ideological baggage, came under attack in the 1970s. Feminist theory, cultural studies, the principles of deconstructionist criticism and post-structuralist analyses called attention to the complicity between claims to universal truth-values within objective-seeming formal systems and the institutionalization of power relations in social and cultural institutions. Perversely, in this same decade, the effect of semiotics on many humanistic fields—including graphic design—was to conceive of every available artifact (visual, aural, material, etc.) as a "text." The overwhelming projection of the linguistic paradigm onto every area of symbolic discourse went forward at the same time as deconstructionist attacks were aimed at the "logocentric" premises of Western philosophy.

By the 1980s, erosion of such predominant models was in part effected through the capabilities of new technology. Digital media encourages an easy blurring of the boundaries of image and text through production methods that are radically different from those of more traditional or conventional production methods grounded in hot type, mechanical and darkroom photography, and photomechanical methods of production. The emergence of an aesthetic of "illegibility"—the famously unreadable work of designers like David Carson or P. Scott Makela in the late 1980s and early 1990s—seems an utterly consistent expression of a moment in which the authority of language is undermined through theoretical attacks on logocentrism that coincide with the exuberant exploitation of the hybrid capabilities of digital media. The celebration of simulacral modes coincided with the simultaneous erosion of the legibility and credibility of language in an apparent undercutting of its critical authority. But critical approaches within the context of Cranbrook and the McCoys, for example, or Lorraine Wild before and after her move to Cal Arts, and the important work of Ellen Lupton and J. Abbott Miller relied heavily on semiotic and linguistic theory in their attempts to grapple with the problems of visual graphic form. Meanwhile, lurking in the wings was a yet another incarnation of the persistent trope of formal systematicity—now in the form of the mathematical underpinnings of digital media. If natural language, with all its flawed idiosyncrasy, had been held up for generations as the model of potentially systematic representation of thought within human expression, then formal language, logic-based, computational and unambiguous, would present the most extreme version of this promise. But is it a promise fulfilled? Would we wish it to be?

There are unexamined premises within this inquiry that require another backtrack through the historiography of graphic design history before they can be addressed, one that looks at the connections between the stylistic rhetorics within design discourse and the critical rhetorics that establish criteria of their success. Cultural authority resides within that set of connections—between the rhetorical expectations of design and the terms on which it is assessed. The cultural authority that attends to design in our current moment is grounded in very specific values, familiarized to the point of invisibility. The process of defamiliarizing these premises puts them into relation with a longer, historical perspective—in which this is merely one moment in the history of graphic design and its critical discourses.

A very brief, almost telegraphic overview of earlier moments in design history will have to serve to invoke these various points within the modern history of graphic design before concluding with a return glance at the opening questions about the critical frameworks that address the graphic character of design.

Manuals for the printing trade served as the sole repository of written information about design up until the late nineteenth century. Precious little self-conscious discussion of design found its way into these publications, which were meant to provide technical instruction to the production staff in a print shop. The emphasis in such texts was on efficiency, and suggestions to create sketches or mock-ups on paper in advance of actual setting of type were supported largely by an argument that such preparation could spare the compositor the time and effort of resetting. Considerations such as spacing, choice of display or body type, were dictated almost entirely by availability. The structure of public notices, title pages and book and page layouts proceeded according to classical rules of proportion, largely absorbed as habit and convention rather than as articulated precepts. Publications like *The Inland Printer* introduced aesthetic considerations chiefly on the grounds of efficiency and communicative efficacy. Semantically driven hierarchy, which would appear to be commonsense, nonetheless took time to come to the fore as a design consideration. Little or no design "discourse" was to be found even reading between the lines of these instrumentally oriented manuals. The field remained as flat, as literal in its approach, as the relation of relief surface to paper in the transfer of ink.

While pragmatism dominated the trade publications, a concept of aesthetic design emerged slowly within the world of book and poster activity that synthesized principles from such major movements as Impressionism and post-Impressionism in France and the Arts and Crafts movement in Scotland, England and the United States, as these intersected with work in commercial venues. Graphic design and book production, particularly fine print work, are quite different zones of activity. But attention to the qualities of composition, organization and formal features of presentation in practice and in its discussion found considerable support in the precepts of late-nineteenth-century aestheticism. The influence of Thomas Cobden-Sanderson on William Morris and in turn on Will Bradley were not without impact in the broader commercial field. The rhetoric of such productions was pitched against the numbing effects of industrialization, the components of hand-made or crafted form, though often put at the service of mass-produced items (print publications, shoes, light bulbs, soap and so on), suggested aesthetics were an alternative to industrial mechanization. But aesthetics was and would continue to be a secondary consideration in the advertising realm where the link between communication and marketing was paramount. No trade manual or codification of the design profession would have been likely to pose its production as an opposition to the forces of mass-produced commercial activity. Likewise, aesthetes isolated their ideas from mass-market concerns. Walter Crane's *Line and Form*, for instance, made no reference to "communication" in the commercial sense, focusing instead on concepts closer to the principles of classical architecture such as proportion, or to the musical analogies dear to the sensibility of nineteenth-century symbolism and its aesthetic precepts. Thus the sinewy organic lines, elegant earth-toned colors and finely drawn images that show up in the work of the Beggarstaffs, on the pages of *Ver Sacrum*, or in the advertising imagery of Lucien Bernhard have a common root in the visual order according to which the natural world is set apart for distinction from the industrial underpinnings on which such productions operate and whose interests they actually serve.

In the early twentieth century the evangelical tone of reform movements and socially progressive campaigns produced a righteous promotional approach to consumer culture. A work like *Jesus was an Ad-Man*, its title meant un-ironically, exhibits the curious combination of faith and capitalist zeal as a foundation for advertising rhetoric.

Increased capacities for production brought about a need for increased consumption, and the creation of artificial (or at least, enhanced) desire found itself in lockstep with the development of scientific methods for advertising design. Graphic design received a boost from the world of commercial advertising that differentiated it from the craft of book production and from the aesthetic attention lavished on artist-drawn posters. The American advertising professional, no longer an "artist," focused on sales in the name of moral "uplift" while design rode a wave of production and prosperity cycles in the 1910s and 1920s. Civic and moral virtue went hand in hand with hard work and honest consumption in this rhetoric. And the graphic style that accompanied such ideals was declamatory and directly promotional.

While American design stressed marketing, with organization and legibility, brand name recognition and standardization as its hallmarks, Soviet and European designers established some of the first systematic curricula for the teaching of graphic design. With the establishment of the Bauhaus, as well as parallel institutions within the newly formed Soviet Union, a shift occurred that had major implications for the design profession as we know it today. Drawing on the radical use of abstract forms in visual art that had been one of the signature elements of the avant-garde, Herbert Bayer, Lazar El Lissitzky, Joost Schmidt and their counterparts in the Soviet context, developed a concept of design grounded in principles of visual order and systematic precepts. The explosion and then taming of avant-garde innovation, coinciding as it did with a self-conscious search for "languages" of abstraction in visual fine art, created the first rationalized foundation for design as a discourse with its own rules. Building on such works as Kandinsky's *Point and Line to Plane*, educator-designers such as Georgy Kepes and Laszlo Moholy-Nagy created manuals that outlined organized principles of communication. Pragmatism and moralizing ceded to clean efficiency and systematic organization. These formal "languages" of design would dominate the graphic field and its critical self-conception throughout the rest of the twentieth century. The emphasis on formal properties within such systematic discussions allowed them to lay claim to an ahistorical universality while establishing a stylistic basis for the modernism that linked avant-garde abstraction to corporate identity systems.

American design in the 1930s, still fraught with moral and reform sensibilities, engaged another set of concerns that would last through the Depression years, World War II, and into the 1950s—an emphasis on normative imagery in vignettes and scenarios of family and civic life. By embedding products within illustrations or photographs that communicated a narrative of everyday dependability for the average and, increasingly, upwardly mobile American family, advertisers knit the public and private spheres of business and domestic life into a finely wrought fabric whose pattern justified spending on the basis of hygiene, independence, security and style. Design publications specialized along lines that reflected segments of a market—outdoor advertising, print campaigns and, eventually, television spots. Public service campaigns, such as the famous series of posters for Rural Electrification produced by Lester Beall, had much in common with those of their European and Soviet counterparts in the field of propaganda campaigns. Exceptions to this abound, of course, and the highly stylized and elegant work of designers like McKnight Kauffer or Adolphe Cassandre borrowed heavily on the fine art traditions of modernism to promote goods and services in quotidian as well as luxury markets. As a profession, graphic design came into its own, intent upon aesthetic validation as well as integrity, and the two reinforced each other's legitimacy.

The hiatus in normal activity caused by the Second World War, accompanied as it was by a massive intensification of production in all sectors, left a legacy of infrastructure and affluence. Propaganda, recruitment, war bond campaigns and other graphics associated with the war gave way in peacetime to an unprecedented level of professionalism in graphic design. The full-blown development of an international style, associated with Swiss design, matured in the 1950s, carrying in its abstract and geometric minimal codes all the signs of a neutral aesthetic. Organization, legibility, elegance—these were all characteristics of a "cool" modernism, with its unfussy sans-serif typography, its semantically neutral-seeming forms with templates and grids conspicuously grounded in rational aesthetics. Design took on the aura of a profession closer to architecture and engineering than drawing and painting. The rhetoric that came to the fore in this period became the stock in trade of design schools and organizations. The predominance of a publication like *Graphis*, the awarding of prizes in professional arenas, the integration of corporate and cultural sensibilities—all sustained an integrated approach to systematic design style, unremittingly self-serious, important as an aspect of the international, "one-dimensional" (to use Herbert Marcuse's apt contemporary term) culture it served.

The 1960s self-consciousness introduced a critical reflection into the design world. Cuteness, playfulness, an awareness of the "pop" function of advertising art and of its impact twisted the solid international style rhetoric on its edge. Though the grinding out of textbooks for "communications" programs continued (and to some significant extent, still does) to use the rhetoric of "visual language" as a dominant, if unexamined, motif, the practice of design shifted gears through the introduction of a certain clever irony. Taking the system less than seriously, the work of designers like Quentin Fiore (in his work with Marshall McLuhan) or prominent and very successful firms such as Doyle, Dane and Bernbach, demonstrated the viability of undercutting the systematic "language" of design with quips, quotes and asides with a nod to a knowing audience. The incorporation of this audience, an admission of complicity with the consumer-viewer, broke the purely formal frame that had been a premise of visual organization throughout the earlier decades of the twentieth century. The acknowledged "textuality" of visual images came under semiotic investigation in the 1960s as well, with the critical contributions of Roland Barthes, as well as McLuhan, so that a critical case for "reading" images took its place beside the use of "languages of design" as the basis of production.

The other legacy of the 1960s was a political counterculture, alternative and aggressive, and focused on control of symbolic systems as a crucial site of strategic intervention into mainstream venues. The consumerism of the 1970s, somewhat chastened by contrast to 1960s exuberance (and Vietnam-era affluence), was in continual dialogue with the identity politics issues raised by the Civil Rights and Women's movements. Semiotics became increasingly popular as a way of decoding the ideology of style, and the concepts of structuralism informed design and visual art through their connection to academic critical theory. The cost-effective, bottom-line graphics of the 1970s, with their rather bland corporate identity campaigns and somewhat diluted international style sensibility, began to show the influence of photographic systems for typesetting. Though desktop publishing didn't prevail until the mid-1980s generations of Macintosh computers made equipment widely available and economically accessible, the automation of aspects of book production, distribution, management and conceptualization reoriented the industry towards an information systems approach to design and away from graphic display or its aesthetics. The proto-deconstructionist impulses of Neville Brody, for instance, fueled design's self-conscious self-examination from within even as the edge of the digital technology began to appear on the horizon of the aesthetic field.

As cultural studies forged one active area of 1980s design discourse, pushing concerns about identity, AIDS, activism and subcultures to the fore, another powerful force undercut the old formal paradigms of graphic design in the name of deconstruction. By demonstrating the alignment between hegemonic forces and an international style, critics of design revealed the complicity between modern design and systems of power whose repressive agendas could not be wished away. Even as firms like Chermayeff and Geisman might push their "daring" and "innovative" facility to create logo designs and elaborate corporate identity systems, the street graphics industry worked to promote AIDS awareness through direct, smart, campaigns aimed at communication and self-empowerment. The development of a cult of illegibility within various sub-cultural environments, such as *Ray Gun*, and the archly self-conscious, always inventive and re-inventive publication *Emigre*, exhibited a clear desire to "diss" the established tenets of graphic design. Design theory became a trendy field of study, and the semiotic disease broke out among the students and faculty of major institutions. Theory proved to be a hungry beast, and a rapid succession of intellectual frameworks was required to keep its insatiable cravings at bay. The effect of such work on graphic design was more academic than practical, with a sub-industry of critical writing and languages working feverishly to deconstruct the logocentric premises of symbolic practices while at the same time aggressively promoting the need for critico-theoretical discourse. Why? Graphic design seemed disadvantaged without some kind of scaffolding to support its productions. There was a sense that the profession no longer simply needed organizations and awards for fine, slick, clever or successful campaigns, but needed a metalanguage of self-conscious critique in order to decode its complicity and contradictions as another among many simulacral artifacts in contemporary life. April Greiman, the McCoys, Cranbrook, CalArts and other nodal points of critical activity epitomized the complex factors of postmodern design in its first theoretical and practical formations.

The rise of the celebrity designer in the 1990s, coinciding with a major boom cycle in American consumer industries fueled, at least in the public imagination, by the dot.com phenomenon, deposed the critical languages focused on "display" and simulation with a new vocabulary of interactivity and interface. Illegible, provocative work by David Carson promoted him to star status while writing about his work created new expectations at the intersection of style, celebrity and design. The aesthetic of digital manipulation became riddled with the hybrid, morphing manipulations that eroded all boundaries between media of input. Specificity of tool and media—pen, pencil, brush, paint, stroke or water-based pigment—no longer held. Nor did the age-old distinction between text and image. Medium-enforced but more deeply distinguished in aesthetics, philosophy and other systems of belief, this distinction had enabled a phrase like "languages of design" to resonate with meaning generations earlier—when language held the upper hand in appearing systematizable, stable and ordered according to rules of grammar. Syntax and semantics, formal and meaning-based registers, seemed to exist as a paradigmatic condition of language, extractable as a system of principles that might be usefully applied to visual elements in graphic design. Such premises were hard to sustain in a moment when the fungible character of all data leveled their identity in a digital environment. Enacted stylistically by Carson and others as an exercise in illegible form, this elision of categories at the level of display produced other anxieties about the need or possibility of ever communicating effectively in a noise-filled environment.

Theory-speak also created tensions of its own, alienating professionals from their academic counterparts, inventing a critical elite and seeming to elevate obscurantism to the level of insight. Too bad, since what was lost in this debate was what was at stake in a politics of public discourse—one that might have at least introduced some level of discomfort into the engines of complicity that were driving the publicity machine of celebrity orientation so relentlessly into the design field. Theory, after all, did have the tools to reveal very basic aspects of the design field and the designer's condition. Whose interests were being served? How was the most "naturalized" imagery culturally loaded? And how were surface rhetorics concealing or enabling values other than those they appeared to espouse? What are the ideological underpinnings of any particular discursive formation? How are they to be named? How are they put into operation? How are we complicit with them? These are crucial aspects of any representational activity (which, by definition, is ALL of human activity). But in a mad rush to professionalize theory as an aspect of design curricula, these basic issues seemed—at least momentarily—to be lost.

To that end, the current condition of graphic design deserves its moment of attention here at the end. For the critical languages that encode new observations and prescriptions for the role of the designer within electronic media also has its tropes and metaphors, as well as concealing certain agendas under yet another naturalizing set of terms. Only now these are the terms of informatics. No longer interested merely in finding rules for predictable effects in relations of visual elements, the theory of design practice will now necessarily grapple with such issues as content analysis, information architecture and the design of interactive processes such as navigation. Dynamic data sets, files that have real-time parameters in them, multi-authored and browser-specific environments—these all introduce variables that cannot be controlled in the same way that type on a page or layout in a page sequence can. And after all, even that simpler- seeming task turned out to elude the disciplinary legislation of a set of "rules"—even if fundamental parameters for legible and pleasing aesthetics were generalizable into principles. Design, like any other form of human expression, turns out to partake of universals only to the extent that any historical moment of its manifestation is part of a larger pattern of symbolic communication. The specificity of any expression is precisely proportional to its capacity to serve as an index to that set of conditions that participate in its production—and to which it returns its meaning as effect. Any universal "language" will always stop just short of where real communication begins—in difference, deviation and distinction.

In summary: the analogy between language and visual form became a commonplace in twentieth-century criticism and design curricula. The term comes into common currency in visual art and graphic design in the early decades of the twentieth century—most specifically within the context of those now-historic efforts to establish systematic premises for the use and understanding of visible forms. Such concepts have their precedents, within earlier attempts to perceive, or create, systematic structures within architectural, visual or decorative forms. And they have their glorious triumphant moments in twentieth-century activity, when a rhetoric of scientificity permeated all manner of humanistic and aesthetic disciplines—all of which aspired to the condition of authority that had come to attend the natural, physical sciences in that era. Highest on the truth chain, such disciplines appeared to reveal transcendent, rather than contingent, facts. Visual artists took up inquiries that mimicked those of their contemporaries in the lab, struggling to research the laws that might govern composition according to an inviolable and absolute set of design principles. Later, these principles became a garden variety of terms and approaches to design, not necessarily incorrect, but oddly quaint-seeming to our contemporary sensibility—as court decorum, though adorable in small doses, hardly suffices for our daily communications or behaviors. Such extremes of formalism had in them a utopian aspiration that has not only been abandoned, but whose precepts no longer seem either necessary or desirable as goals—the establishment of absolute terms for successful design. Such activity had been a manifestation of rationalized aesthetics, of a "logic" that did not see itself as a rhetoric, but as an articulatable system of fixed parameters of graphic production.

And now? A whole new world of possibilities, in the simplest creative sense, but also, a change of heart and a change of technological possibility. The meta-data metalanguage of design—program and display, code and data, the relation of style sheets and xml-tagged artifacts, of DTDs and mark-up—borrows heavily from the world of computer science. Computational methods, grounded in formal logic and its constraints, carry their own ideological baggage. The cultural authority that attends to such methods is weighted heavily by the validation accorded to scientific discourses, and their supposed foundation on quantifiable and therefore unambiguous (read, "truthful") grounds. Natural language, once subject to the rational regimes of a science-oriented linguistics, has been replaced in the critical hierarchy with formal languages and their logic-based orientation. Should the old trope of the "languages" of design be revived now, it would require a whole new set of caveats and cautions—lest we fall into an even more absolute-seeming trap with yet another layer of authority attendant upon it.

The critical languages that have accompanied the development of graphic design as a field will, no doubt, continue to refine themselves in concert with the development of new tasks and structures, new stylistic manifestations and their underpinnings. What is "graphic" about graphic design continues to need elucidation—as the evolution of whole new realms of information visualization and visual interfaces to the management and organization of information are integrated into our functions of daily life in entertainment, business and education. The denaturalization of these as truth-functions will require the same critical attention as did those earlier forms of display—and we ignore the visual characteristics by which these forms communicate only at the peril of a profound ignorance and blindness—since it is through their visuality that they communicate. This paper has examined the search for a set of systematic precepts as a foundation for an aesthetic of display, but it has barely touched on the question of the way this concept both benefited and constrained the exploration of visuality. Perhaps now, as greater fluency develops in the broad population for visual symbol-making and manipulation, an era in which a significant fluency for grasping the bases of meaning in production in graphic design will emerge.[1]

Note

1. The interested reader is referred to the work of Estelle Jussim, Neil Harris, Michelle Bogart, Victor Margolin, Herbert Spencer, Mike Mills, Roland Marchand, Maud Lavin, Ellen Lupton, Lorraine Wilde, Anne Burdick, Dan Friedman, Jessica Helfand and Steven Heller, as well as issues of *Emigre*, previous *Looking Closer* volumes, and other publications of Allworth Press for further reading.

STATE
OF THE
ARTS

Graphic design is a way to make a statement. But it is—and always has been—also a way to make a living. Asked to define the first principal of architecture, H. H. Richardson was said to have replied, "Get the job." It was not long ago that graphic designers were commercial artists. Even today, most of the twenty thousand members of the American Institute of Graphic Arts (not to mention the two hundred thousand or more that the AIGA suspects is out there working in the profession one way or another) consider their profession to be, first and foremost, *work*. And by definition, most graphic designers do this work in a world defined by getting the job and doing the job, by clients, budgets and deadlines, and, of course, by the uneasy tension between making a statement and making a living.

Whether pursuing their professional goals with an eye towards advancing the dignity of each human being (see Richard Buchanan) or simply "greasing the wheels of capitalism with style and taste" (see Mr. Keedy), most graphic designers do not work in isolated garrets or ivory towers. Yet the everyday working life of the graphic designer has gone largely unexamined. Forget for a moment about the daunting challenges presented by rampant globalization. What, instead, are the dozens of tiny compromises that each designer must make every day? Surround it with as much theory and criticism as you like, but in the end graphic design is made by people and for people. Who are they? How do they interact when the doors are closed? We develop our own specialized language to describe what we do, how we do it and why someone else should pay for it. But what premises lie behind an oft-repeated (but seldom questioned) mantra like "design is problem-solving?" And, if the answer to all arguments is that it's all about the work, what is this stuff we're making, anyway? Where does it go, how does it function, and what do people make of it once they're finally confronted with it?

Today, designers are examining the implications of every stage of the design process, and the critical decisions that surround the practice of graphic design. In this section, writers look closer at the work we do, the way we do, and the reasons we should bother at all.

Michael Bierut

GRAPHIC DESIGN AND THE NEXT BIG THING
Rudy VanderLans

A few months back Louise Sandhaus contacted me to see if I was interested in creating an issue of *Emigre* that would document "101: The Future of Design Education in the Context of Computer-Based Media," a symposium she had organized at the Jan van Eyck Academy in Holland. The symposium explored questions about what future graphic designers are being educated for and what the role of the designer will be. To encourage me to publish this information, Louise assured me that people were probably chomping at the bit for *Emigre* to introduce this material in some intelligent and interesting way.

While ambivalent about the value of such crystal ball events, what intrigued me about this request was how *Emigre* continues to be regarded as the place there where the "Next Big Thing," for lack of a better term, is not only regularly covered but also expected to be covered. The many disgruntled letters about our recent shift in editorial policy away from such popular phenomena underline this fact.

This "feeding the trout," as one letter writer put it, the act of somehow keeping our readers abreast of trends, is an impossible task. Having been privy to the making of one trend in no way prepares one to recognize the harbingers of the next. I'm unsure whether this is because the Next Big Thing is simply a product of hindsight, or because it is human nature to regard groundbreaking work as the final solution, nullifying the possibility of the next Next Big Thing. The latter is particularly tempting to believe when you've had your moment in the sun while riding the Next Big Thing wave, but piques the younger generations who are eager to have their own experiences of experimentation and discovery.

Still, if you think about it, after hundreds of years of formal, typographic experimentation on the page, you would assume that we must at some point have exhausted the possibilities. Someone will come around, though, and disprove this, I'm sure. Tibor Kalman thinks otherwise when he states in *Eye* that "People haven't started fucking with the printed page in a serious way yet . . ."[1] Picturing what has passed before us, however, I cannot for the life of me think of what it could be that hasn't already been done. Actually, one could argue we reached that saturation point quite some time ago. Anything

Originally published in *Emigre*, no. 39 (Summer 1996).

in print that appears new today can be considered a variation on age-old themes. Purely from a formal point of view, that Layered Thing was fairly well explored by Piet Swart and Wolfgang Weingart. That Anti-Mastery Thing was pretty well exhausted by Fluxus and Punk, that Reconstructivist Thing was long ago mastered by just about everybody from Apollinaire to Edward Fella and that Illegible Thing was difficult to top after Victor Moscoso and Wes Wilson were done battling over who could make the reader more cross-eyed. The only significant contribution introduced to graphic design in the last ten years or so, as Laurie Haycock Makela once pointed out, might have less to do with anything visual than with how design is produced and who it is produced by.

While the idea of the Next Big Thing is ludicrous to some, it's obvious that many hunger for it. Having documented, for a while at least, one such Next Big Thing, our magazine continues to receive inquiries from journalists and critics alike curious what the next Next Big Thing might be and where to find all the young energetic designers doing "crazy new things." You can smell the desperation—with the absence of the Next Big Thing, what do they write about?

But let's imagine for a second that there will be no Next Big Thing in design. At least not for a while. Nothing to catch the attention of the design press, to sweep all the design awards, to receive all the lecture invitations, to function as a source of inspiration and discussion for all. Here's an idea to fill that void; we can try our hand at judging design by its content, by the ideas and messages that it attempts to communicate. Imagine design competitions picking winners based solely on the value of what they communicate, instead of how they communicate. The moral, ethical and political biases of the judges would come to the fore, for sure, but no more or less than the formal biases of judges who rule competitions now. Design would be discussed only as it affects the message. For instance, a submission could be considered of great public value but would not win an award simply because the design, although formally stunning, obscured the message. What would the design annuals look like then?

Of course it will never happen, because designers are visual types who have a tendency to either obsessively reduce or overly complicate the ideas of their clients, often without much concern for what is actually communicated. It is not that designers are insensitive or disinterested in the social and cultural functions of the messages they give form to; it's just that they don't always see the necessity (or have the opportunity) to integrate their personal ideologies into their professional work. They enjoy giving form to ideas. If designers were made of ideas, they'd be their own clients.

The World Wide Web is often hailed as the Next Big Thing in graphic design, but it's a problematic environment for graphic designers. One problem is that it has limited graphic possibilities. The coarse resolution of the computer screen, the inability to fix layouts and typefaces and the overpowering presence of the browser's interface all restrict the designer's ability to impart a specific visual character to a Web site. These also restrict the designers' ability to leave their signature imprint, which is even more problematic, since for many designers this is the single most important asset of how they market themselves. With the absence of the stylistic choices usually available in print, many designers will refrain from getting involved, while others, by hook or by crook, will try and bend the medium to fit their personal preferences for typographic expression and style. That's why so many Web sites look like what designers do in print but applied to the screen.

If there were ever an opportunity for graphic design to be more involved with content, the World Wide Web is it. With the computer functioning as the great visual equalizer, content instead of form is what ultimately may come to differentiate and qualify Web sites. However, according to my own assessment regarding the value placed on content within graphic design, judging a Web site on the strength of its content will not soon gain popularity, at least not within the narrow world of graphic design. Unless, of course, you expand the notion of what graphic design is. Which brings me back to the future of graphic design.

Whether or not designers will be able to make the transition from print to screen, and whether or not the technology will ever deliver on the promise of seamless multimedia for everybody, remains to be seen. But as we ponder the question of how graphic designers will cope with the seemingly inevitable changes ahead, we should not lose sight of what we're trying to accomplish. The purpose of what we do as designers will remain fairly basic: to communicate as effectively as we can those messages and ideas that we most care about. Having the option to do this differently and with more pomp and circumstance than before raises interesting questions not just regarding "how" but also "why."

Writer Paul Robert's observation that "The irony of the information revolution is that consumers neither like nor expect long, densely written tests on their computer screens"[2] suggests a radical shift in people's reading habits. This shift has long been contemplated by designers and critics alike concerned with how to best address the reading habits of future generations raised on MTV and video games in an era of increasing information overload. This is problematic, however, since I can't help but wonder why, as graphic designers, we should concern ourselves with pleasing readers suffering from short attention spans. How are we certain hat by catering to their diminishing interest in linear reading and by relying on the power of images and sound bites as an alternative, we actually increase such notions as comprehension and cognition?

As a result of my own interest and experiments regarding how to best aid the reader, I've become increasingly unconvinced about the power of images to tell stories and the value of open-ended narratives. Knowing where to apply such means is crucial.

When viewing Elliott Earls's entertaining CD, *Throwing Apples at the Sun,* I enjoy the fact that I, the reader, can construct my own meaning from the seemingly disparate elements of image, sound and text. It is the very purpose of this project. When reading an essay, on the other hand, I crave for knowing what the author means so that I can learn and respond and ask specific questions if necessary.

When Louise Sandhaus, in *Emigre 36,* practices what she preaches and designs her essay "Click" in a manner that aspires to the nonlinear, multilevel environment of the World Wide Web or CD-ROMs, the result is a dynamic orchestration of text and images that subverts the conventional make-up of the page. Whether it functions as intended depends on who you ask. As a designer I'm drawn in by the curious visual presentation, but as a reader I'm unsure about sequence and often lose the thread of the writing due to the many distractions and options vying for my attention—not unlike when I'm surfing the World Wide Web or scanning a CD-ROM.

In *Emigre* 37 both designer Stephen Farrell and writer Steve Tomasula make eloquent arguments to support the notion of using animated texts and images to subserve reading and enrich meaning. Theoretically it holds water, and I want to believe they are right because their work is so shockingly beautiful. But when I try to actually read their short story "TOC," the experience is not as smooth as I had hoped. The story is laid out with distinct visual gestures, but I'm unclear how to read them or what the authors mean. I'm uncertain how to fill in the gaps or make the connections. Is it my fault, as a reader, that I don't understand? Or is it the authors'? Or does it matter at all?

In *Emigre* we have published many such theories and experiments, but their applicability in the real world, besides functioning as the Next Big Thing, has proved to be limited. This is exemplified by designers such as Katherine McCoy, Jeffery Keedy, Ellen Lupton and J. Abbott Miller, who are often presented as the key protagonists and apologists for the new theories that have inspired recent design trends, but who in reality create designs that apply only to a minimal degree the theories that so outrage the critics.

Shooting holes in the new theories, of course, is easy, since they are usually general in scope and allow for different levels of interpretation, depending on the job at hand. McCoy et al. demonstrate time and again that they are extremely skillful at implementing their theories. There are few books out on the market that more brilliantly combine text and image and in the process truly aid reading and extend meaning, than the books created by these designers. And the books look far more traditional than the theories that inspired them.

Instead of nipping the theories in the bud, the critics should try their hand at how these ideas trickle down to the mainstream and are applied indiscriminately and irresponsibly. The opening essay in David Carson's book *The End of Print* would be a good place to start. To justify his typographic aerobics on the page, Carson often refers to the changing reading habits of the audience and borrows from the theory that if you engage the readers and make them work at decoding the text, they will better remember what they read. Granted, it did take me quite a bit of work to figure out that the sentences in the essay needed to be read from bottom to top. But what I end up remembering about the essay is not so much what I read, but how difficult it was to read it at all. This type of work, as Andrew Blauvelt suggests, has less to do with redefining the notion of readability or literacy than with creating product differentiation and establishing the personal style of the designer.

But if designers have a tendency to apply their signature styles willy-nilly to whatever commissions come down the pike, design critics often tend to paint with a rather broad brush to establish their holier-than-thou agendas regarding the social responsibility of the designer, the public good, fellow readers and other such stuff. The new theories, as some critics claim, have no interest in such noble causes. However, when voicing their objections regarding the new theories and the work it has spawned, the critics conveniently steer clear of addressing specific designs, and instead use bodies of work such as Rick Poynor's anthology *Typography Now: The Next Wave*. These anthologies present anything but a unified collection of work or theory. They consist, for the most part, of posters, covers and other commercial, experimental and student projects especially short on text, big on image and particularly suited for reproduction in small format. Here too, besides functioning as the Next Big Thing (as the book's title claims), the work can hardly be considered as serious research addressing the needs of future communication modes. But for the critics, who rarely judge designs within their specific context, they serve perfectly in pointing out all that is wrong with today's empty, self-centered designerism. This is usually followed by bizarre acts of overextension leading to conclusions that the new theories are not concerned with society's more mundane yet invaluable means of communication such as novels, educational texts, timetables, instructional manuals, application forms, etc.

If the new theories are not much concerned with these, it is because they acknowledge that the old theory provides most of the answers for these applications. What the new theories are concerned with is that the old theory does not properly address the new media and the multiplicitous environments and audiences that graphic design now both serves and is comprised of. Which brings me back to the Next Big Thing.

If the new theories have generated disappointing results concerning conventional print design, then the old theory has shown little ability to adapt to the new environments of electronic publishing. For instance, if legibility is a social concern, why then have our most respected typographers largely ignored issues of typographic excellence on the computer screen? As we're entering the information age, which will most likely play itself out on low resolution monitors, you can either ignore what is going on around you and then later complain about the irresponsible behavior of today's designer and the general downfall of literacy and all that, or you can help provide a solution. For the graphic adventurers among us, this probably means having to abandon certain personal expressive preferences, and for our most learned typographers, it might mean adapting sophisticated typographic traditions to fit the still primitive world of electronic publishing. Somehow this combined knowledge must be able to generate a visual language capable of being both legible and engaging.

The following might seem paradoxical, because at *Emigre,* for the short term at least, as we're trying to deal with the new technologies that surround us, we see more use for the teachings of the young Jan Tschichold than the writings of, let's say, Frances Butler. While we're being primed for sensory overload, the reality of electronic publishing still consists of system crashes, tedious downloading problems, links gone dead, incompatibility and the many stylistic restrictions described earlier. The simplicity and social concerns of Tschichold's ideals, that "communication must appear in the briefest, simplest, most urgent form,"[3] as outlined in the text *Elementare Typographie*, are far more practical than the multilevel, interactive, hypertextual and audiovisual forms of communication that, according to Butler, will better match the "fluid, additive, nonsyntactic, and above all, extremely sophisticated thought process that are the natural birthright of all humans."[4]

Notes

1. Tibor Kalman, interviewed by Moira Cullen in *Eye*, no. 20 (Spring 1996): 16.
2. Paul Roberts, "Virtual Grub Street," *Harper's* (June 1996): 71.
3. Published in *Typographische Mitteilungen*, no. 10 (1925): 198, 200.
4. Frances Butler, "Retarded Arts: The Failure of Fine Arts Education," *AIGA Journal of Graphic Design*, no. 30 (1995): 30.

TELLING THE TRUTH?

Milton Glaser

I went to Las Vegas for the first time to participate in the AIGA conference. I was booked at the Venetian—a hotel whose vast vistas of painted, cloud-filled skies had required the skills of more mural painters than existed in Venice during the entire fifteenth century.

On my first day at the hotel, I noticed a sign that said "Grand Canal." I asked the concierge at the reception desk where it was. "One fight up," she said. The earth reeled beneath my feet. A canal one flight up; what a concept.

The canal was, in fact, upstairs, complete with gondola and gondolier who would cheerfully take you around a bend to the Piazza San Marco. Later that same day, the hotel's plumbing broke down, and suddenly the entire ground floor began to smell like Venice on a warm day. I actually found myself wondering whether the hotel had planned it. Is there such a thing as virtual smell?

On the Dallas leg of the flight from Las Vegas after the AIGA conference, the hostess entered the aisle with a vigorously steaming tray of hot towels. I noticed that a wine glass filled with water was the source of the steam.

"What is that?" I asked the hostess, pointing to the glass.

"Dry ice and water," she replied.

"Is that for drama?" I asked.

"Yes," she replied.

Even to a dormant mind, a trip to Las Vegas inevitably raises the question, "What is real?" and, by inference, "What is truth?" It actually provided the subtext for the conference itself, notably in Kurt Anderson's talk on whether real is better than fake and Denise Caruso's concern about whom to trust on the Net.

Obviously, the question of "What is the truth?" is one of humankind's most persistent questions, but it seems ever more insistent at this moment than at any other time.

Originally published in *AIGA Journal of Graphic Design* Vol. 18, no. 2 (2000).

What can it mean when a freezing glass of dry ice is used to simulate a streaming towel on a plane trip? Can this modest deception benefit either the airline or the passengers? Where was the decision made to do it? In the boardroom? In the advertising agency? On the flight itself? Does the airline believe that the drama of the steaming towels will suggest a policy of concerned service? What happens to the customer in the last row of the plane when he is handed a cold towel while the tray above his head is steaming madly? Does he doubt his own nervous system? What makes me uncomfortable with all of this? Why do I believe that harm is being done? All of which leads us in a convoluted way to the question of professional ethics.

"How can we tell the truth?" can be thought of as two separate questions. The first part asks why we believe what we believe; the second, where ethical questions begin, involves our responsibility to others.

One must start with the presumption that telling the truth is important for human survival, but at this moment of relativism and virtuality, I'm not sure how many would agree on what truth is or how important it is in our private and professional lives.

But we must begin somewhere. The question becomes a professional one, because as designers or *communicators* (the preferred current description), we are constantly informing the public, transmitting information and affecting the beliefs and values of others. Should telling the truth be a fundamental requirement of this role? Is there a difference between telling the truth to your wife and family and telling the truth to a general public? What is that difference?

As a profession that defines itself by effectively persuading others, it's impossible to consider our work outside the context of advertising, an activity that is so fundamental to our economy and so pervasively influential that it may have informed our idea of what truth is, more than any other single thing.

We drown in the sea of relentless persuasion that we help create as well as receive. There are now ads under our feet in supermarkets. I opened a fortune cookie the other night and found that an advertisement for an e-commerce company had replaced my fortune (I am not kidding). And some months ago, we were informed that the pauses in Rush Limbaugh's talk show had been electronically eliminated to gain six more advertising messages per hour. All of these messages intend to sell rather than inform, and tend to distend or modify the truth in ways that we can no longer see. Our brains and sense of truth cannot be unaffected by this onslaught.

For years I have struggled with the question of whether designers, by virtue of their positions as communicators, should have more ethical responsibility than the average good citizen. Perhaps a better question would be "Should they have less?"

WHO NEEDS ETHICS
Tim Rich

I confess. I too have sold my soul. My copy book is not clean. In the past, I have taken the devil's dollar and written an article about design for a magazine sponsored by a tobacco company. If they called me tomorrow, I'd probably write for them again. They didn't edit my words and they paid on time. That may put me firmly in the realms of the Antichrist on some people's scale of ethics, or I may appear saintly next to another's client list of weapons dealers, nuclear power stations, and torture equipment manufacturers. That's the problem with ethical considerations—they're so subjective. The question is always, "Where do I draw the line?" or, in the case of designers and illustrators, "Just who will I draw the line for?"

I know exactly whom I wouldn't write for, but when I ask designers if they have a similar view, most look at me in surprise and mumble something like "anyone without a checkbook and pen," or, if they're feeling particularly recession-beaten, "we've got enough problems getting any new clients at all let alone being ethically sensitive about the whole thing, thank you very much." Yet in their "private lives" these same people are usually politically informed and environmentally aware, select their newspapers with ideological precision and probably tip more than 20 percent. Why is it that so many designers simply leave those personal thoughts and opinions behind when they walk through the studio door?

The question is particularly pertinent for designers who run their own business; they are, after all, making the final decisions about how the business operates and whom they work for. I would wager that most consultancies don't have any set rules about whom they will and won't design for. I would also wager that even fewer would be happy to discuss such an issue with their employees. And I don't blame them for ignoring the issue, because debating the "cleanliness" of a potential client could be a nightmarish experience. Let's take an example. Pharmaceuticals research company X approaches you to design its next annual report. The budget's generous, the creative brief invites something fresh and innovative, and the client team appears to be sane. So, how do you go about auditing the ethics of the company's approach to animal research, labor relations, or the environment? It would take an investigative journalist months to compile a printable critique. How can a design company spare the time or the money involved in such an audit?

One alternative would be to give the client an "ethical questionnaire." They could react badly to questions such as, "Do your outflow pipes kill wildlife in nearby

Originally published in *Print* Vol. 50, no. 3 (May/June 1996).

rivers or estuaries?" or, "What is your view on current labor law for junior lab technicians?" But, you never know, they may be delighted to share their embarrassing secrets with you. Perhaps the best you can do is pay for some recent press clippings about the company and place a few telephone calls to friends or acquaintances who know something about the pharmaceuticals industry. Well, in my experience, very few design companies would even go to those lengths. The most common approach is to cross your fingers and smile hopefully. Of course, you risk getting a shock when the copywriter delivers 1,500 elegantly sculpted words on how Company X is the world leader in testing poisons on live animals for the military.

There are times when you don't need to snoop into the private drawers of a potential client to know that what they do offends you. If you're a radical vegan separatist, you would probably not make a new business call to the local abattoir. But even if a new client is okay with you, how do you know whether they are acceptable to your employees? What would you do if designer Y—the only person in the studio with time for more work—refuses to work on client Z's corporate identity project because he objects to Z's activities?

It raises interesting questions about how highly you value your employees. Most design consultancies are not democracies. The owners call the shots, the employees follow orders. But if the designer objecting to a client happens to be the brightest star in the firmament of design, it's unlikely to be in the owners' interest to fire him. Some employers might take a tougher stance. A director of a British design company recently stated in public: "If we were asked to do a brochure for a nuclear power company, for example, and a designer told me they did not approve of nuclear power, I would tell them that it was not the view of the company so they therefore must work in a professional manner and do the job."

To my knowledge, such confrontations are rare. That's partly because many designer-employees in the commercial sphere have lost sight of what it is they produce. To them, a client is a client is a client. They're given a brief by a bored account executive, they spend hours at the Mac tweaking type, they go Photoshopping for a while, and at some point it all goes off to the great repro house in the sky. They've lost sight of the effect of what they do. The process of designing has taken over from an appreciation of what they have created. When the annual report or stationery or poster returns from the printer, it is pored over and its qualities assessed, but its function is often forgotten. To its designer, the piece of print in his hands is not some vital communication that will keep hundreds of people at Sausages-R-Us employed, it's a potentially award-winning use of distressed type layered over a mélange of abstract photography.

Another reason for the employer-employee confrontation not occurring more often is a particularly entertaining delusion that affects designers who are obsessed about their social status and would probably rather be lawyers. In this scenario, any client acceptable under the law of the land should have the right to appoint any design consultancy they so choose. The responsibility of the design consultancy is to provide the best possible service regardless of the owners' personal ethics. Like a lawyer representing a serial killer, prejudice must be put to one side and the skills and ideas gained from years of education, experience and plowing through awards annuals should be harnessed to give the client the best possible corporate clothes. This neatly sidesteps the thorny issue of whom it is right or wrong to work for. The guilt-free designer can happily apply himself to the challenge of presenting Company *X* in the best possible light, despite its predilection for putting toxic chemicals into the veins of affable young chimpanzees.

I find it remarkable that more designers haven't thought through the effects of their professional activity. I'm not advocating that each and every design consultancy should have a politically correct mission statement nailed to its front door. In fact, some of the dullest hours of my life have been spent listening to patronizing graphic "artistes" bleating on about how they feel a social obligation to kern text in the modernist tradition, or some such nonsense. However, I do believe everyone should step outside the hurly-burly of the studio once in a while and take a hard look at what they're producing. Whether your "project" is right or wrong, good or bad, beneficial or damaging is ultimately up to you to judge, but at least think about it as an object that has an effect on the world around you, not the cold result of an abstract, intellectual process. If you run a design consultancy and employ designers, consider initiating a debate about what is and isn't acceptable for you as a company to work on. If you think such a debate will destabilize your company—fine, but think through what it means for your employees not to have a voice (and for you not to have enough self-confidence to engage in debate). If you are an employee, consider the possibility of an objectionable company becoming your client. You don't care? OK. You do care? Well, how are you going to respond? Do you value your ethics above your paycheck?

Enough of this. A fax has arrived from Saddam Hussein asking me to pen a few words for *Creative Iraq,* a glossy new publication looking at what's new in Iraqi design. Mmm, not a bad fee, either . . .

HUMAN DIGNITY AND HUMAN RIGHTS: THOUGHTS ON THE PRINCIPLES OF HUMAN–CENTERED DESIGN

Richard Buchanan

As I walked on the shore of Cape Town to the opening ceremonies of a conference on design in South Africa, I saw through the rain and mist a small sliver of land in the bay.[1] Naïvely, I asked my host if it was part of the peninsula that

Originally published in *Design Issues* Vol. 17, no. 3 (Summer 2001). © 2001 Richard Buchanan.

extends south of the city or an island. With what, in retrospect, must have been great patience, she quietly explained that it was not "an" island, it was "the" island. I was embarrassed, but I knew immediately what she meant. I spent the rest of the evening thinking about the political prisoners who were held on Robben Island, human rights and the irony of a conference within sight of Table Bay that seeks to explore the reshaping of South Africa by design.

I was helped in these thoughts by the address of the Minister of Education, Dr. Kadir Asmal, who opened the conference by exploring the meaning of design, the need and opportunities for design in South Africa and, most importantly, the grounding of design in the cultural values and political principles expressed in the new South African Constitution. I have never heard a high government official anywhere in the world speak so insightfully about the new design that is emerging around us as we near the beginning of a new century. Perhaps everyone in the audience was surprised by how quickly and accurately he captured the core of our discipline and turned it back to us for action. Many of his ideas were at the forward edge of our field, and some were further ahead than we are prepared to admit. For example, I believe we all recognized his significant transformation of the old design theme of "form and function" into the new design theme of "form and content." This is one of the distinguishing marks of new design thinking: not a rejection of function, but a recognition that unless designers grasp the significant content of the products they create, their work will come to little consequence or may even lead to harm in our complex world.

I was particularly surprised, however, by Dr. Asmal's account of the creation—and here he deliberately and significantly used the word "design"—of the South African Constitution. He explained that after deliberation the drafters decided not to model the document on the familiar example of the U.S. Constitution, with an appended Bill of Rights, but rather to give central importance from the beginning to the concept of human dignity and human rights. Though he did not elaborate the broader philosophical and historical basis for this decision, it is not difficult to find. Richard McKeon, co-chair of the international committee of distinguished philosophers that conducted a preparatory study for the Universal Declaration of Human Rights, explains that the historical development and expression of our collective understanding of human rights has moved through three periods.[2] *Civil and political rights* were the focus of attention in the eighteenth century; *economic and social rights* were the focus in the nineteenth century; and *cultural rights*—formally discovered in the preparation work for the Universal Declaration—became the focus in the twentieth century. The U.S. Constitution begins with a statement of political rights, and the appended Bill of Rights is a statement of civil rights protected from government interference. The document was properly suited to the historical development of human rights in the late eighteenth century, and in subsequent evolution the United States has gradually elaborated its understanding of economic and social rights as well as cultural rights. The South African Constitution begins with a statement of *cultural rights*, suited to the current historical period in the development of human rights. It seeks to integrate civil and political rights, as well as economic and social rights, in a new framework of cultural values and cultural rights, placing cen-

tral emphasis on human dignity. The result for South Africa is a strong document, suited
to a new beginning in new circumstances. The opening article of the Constitution,
quoted by Dr. Asmal, reminded me of the Preamble of the Universal Declaration of
Human Rights, which announces "recognition of the inherent dignity and of the equal
and inalienable rights of all members of the human family."

Dr. Asmal's account was both historically important and a conscientious
reminder of the cultural context of the conference. However, the next step of his argument brought the room to complete silence. He made the connection between practice
and ultimate purpose that is so often missing in our discussions of design, whether in
South Africa, the United States or elsewhere in the world. Design, he argued, finds its
purpose and true beginnings in the values and constitutional life of a country and its
peoples. Stated as a principle that embraces all countries in the emerging world culture
of our planet, design is fundamentally grounded in human dignity and human rights.

I sensed in the audience an intuitive understanding of the correctness of this
view, though the idea itself probably came as a surprise because we often think about
the principles of design in a different way. We tend to discuss the principles of form and
composition, the principles of aesthetics, the principles of usability, the principles of market economics and business operations, or the mechanical and technological principles
that underpin products. In short, we are better able to discuss the principles of the various methods that are employed in design thinking than the *first* principles of design, the
principles on which our work is ultimately grounded and justified. The evidence of this
is the great difficulty we have in discussing the ethical and political implications of design
and the consequent difficulty we have in conducting good discussions with students
who raise serious questions about the ultimate purpose and value of our various professions.

The implications of the idea that design is grounded in human dignity and
human rights are enormous, and they deserve careful exploration. I believe they will
help us to better understand aspects of design that are otherwise obscured in the flood
of poor or mediocre products that we find everywhere in the world. We should consider what we mean by human dignity and how all of the products that we make either
succeed or fail to support and advance human dignity. And we should think carefully
about the nature of human rights—the spectrum of civil and political, economic and
social, and cultural rights—and how these rights are directly affected by our work. The
issues surrounding human dignity and human rights provide a new perspective for
exploring the many moral and ethical problems that lie at the core of the design professions.

What is important at the moment, however, is that we may recognize in Dr.
Asmal's argument the major tenet of new design thinking: the central place of human
beings in our work. In the language of our field, we call this "human-centered design."
Unfortunately, we often forget the full force and meaning of the phrase—and the first
principle which it expresses. This happens, for example, when we reduce our considerations of human-centered design to matters of sheer usability and when we speak merely
of "user-centered design." It is true that usability plays an important role in human-cen-

tered design, but the principles that guide our work are not exhausted when we have finished our ergonomic, psychological, sociological and anthropological studies of what fits the human body and mind. Human-centered design is fundamentally an affirmation of human dignity. It is an ongoing search for what can be done to support and strengthen the dignity of human beings as they act out their lives in varied social, economic, political and cultural circumstances.

This is why Robben Island remained in my thoughts on the first evening of the conference. It reminded me that the quality of design is distinguished not merely by technical skill of execution or by aesthetic vision but by the moral and intellectual purpose toward which technical and artistic skill is directed. Robben Island, site of the prison in which Nelson Mandela and other political prisoners were isolated so long from direct participation in the national life of South Africa, is another symbol of twentieth-century design gone mad when it is not grounded on an adequate first principle. It is a symbol of the wrongful use of design to shape a country in a system that denied the essential dignity of all human beings. Robben Island belongs with other disturbing symbols of design in the twentieth century, such as the one that my colleague, Dennis Doordan, chillingly cites. He reminds us that the Holocaust was one of the most thoroughly designed experiences of the twentieth century, with careful attention to every obscene detail.

Dr. Asmal's argument carried an urgent message for the work of the conference and for everyone in the design community. Not only is design grounded in human dignity and human rights, it is also an essential instrument for implementing and embodying the principles of the Constitution in the everyday lives of all men, women and children. Design is not merely an adornment of cultural life but one of the practical disciplines of responsible action for bringing the high values of a country or a culture into concrete reality, allowing us to transform abstract ideas into specific manageable form. This is evident if we consider the scope of design as it affects our lives. As an instrument of cultural life, design is the way we create all of the artifacts and communications that serve human beings, striving to meet their needs and desires and facilitating the exchange of information and ideas that is essential for civil and political life. Furthermore, design is the way we plan and create actions, services and all of the other humanly shaped processes of public and private life. These are the interactions and transactions that constitute the social and economic fabric of a country. Finally, design is the way we plan and create the complex wholes that provide a framework for human culture—the human systems and subsystems that work either in congress or in conflict with nature to support human fulfillment. These range from information and communication systems, electrical power grids and transportation systems to managerial organizations, public and private institutions and even national constitutions. This is what leads us to say that the quality of communications, artifacts, interactions and the environments within which all of these occur is the vivid expression of national and cultural values.

We are under no illusion that design is everything in human life, nor do we foolishly believe that individuals who specialize in one or another area of design are necessarily capable of carrying out successful work in other areas. What we do believe is that design offers a way of thinking about the world that is significant for addressing many of the problems that human beings face in contemporary culture. We believe that conscious attention to the way designers work in specialized areas of application such as communication or industrial design is relevant for work in other areas. And we believe that general access to the ways of design thinking can provide people with new tools for engaging their cultural and natural environment.

As we work toward improving design thinking in each of our special areas of application, we also contribute to a more general understanding of design that others may use in the future in ways that we cannot now anticipate. The urgent message of Dr. Asmal is that we must get on with our work as designers in all of these areas if we are to help in sustaining the revolution that has been initiated in South Africa and the wider revolution in human culture that is taking place around us throughout the world.

Notes

1. This essay is based on a paper delivered at a national conference organized by the Design Education Forum of Southern Africa, "Reshaping South Africa by Design," held in Cape Town from June 22 to June 24, 2000.
2. Richard McKeon, "Philosophy and History in the Development of Human Rights," in *Freedom and History and Other Essays: An Introduction to the Thought of Richard McKeon,* ed. Zahava K. McKeon (Chicago: University of Chicago Press, 1990).

A MANIFESTO OF INCLUSIVISM
Paul J. Nini

The Graphic Designer pursues much of his or her work in a mostly solitary manner, manipulating and arranging word and image on a computer, or in the past, by hand on a drafting table. The very nature of the profession is somewhat isolationist, as designers tend to tuck themselves away from the world, working in offices far removed from the maddening crowd. While there are, of course, meetings with clients, co-workers, suppliers and others who assist in the completion of our work, the man on the street often does not enter into the daily concerns of the typical graphic designer. We often speak vaguely about "target audiences" or "users," but in reality have very little to do with them. Certainly we don't typically engage them to participate in creating communications that are meant for their ultimate use.

This unspoken code of exclusivity has its roots in the acknowledged masters of our profession and their writings. Paul Rand, in his book *Paul Rand: A Designer's Art,* states in the section titled "Politics of Design:"

Originally written in 2000 for AIGA/Chicago's *Inform* and adapted for this book.

The smooth functioning of the design process may be thwarted in other ways: . . . by the insecure client who depends on informal office surveys and pseudo-scientific research to deal with questions that are unanswerable, and answers that are questionable.[1]

Many of us would immediately agree with this statement. None of us appreciates our work being ripped away from us and shown to the so-called uninitiated and uneducated, who are then asked to pass judgment on its worthiness. But this situation may also leave us with a somewhat uneasy feeling. It is, after all, the so-called uninitiated and uneducated who do end up experiencing the fruits of our labors, whether we like it or not. Shouldn't we consider ways to allow input from those on the receiving end of our work, so that everyone (the client, the user and the designer) might benefit from the process?

Much current graphic design seems to be "client-centered," where those paying the bills call the shots—or "designer-centered," where the strong personality of the designer holds sway. A "user-centered" approach has the potential to benefit all stakeholders, however. If users receive information that meets their needs and expectations, then our clients have provided added value to their products and services, and one benefit of our expertise as graphic designers becomes obvious.

While it's clear to us that the potential value graphic designers bring to communication can be great, shouldn't we perhaps agree that what we deem to be a "successful" project must at least meet the basic needs of those for whom it was created? We routinely celebrate work in our profession's publications based mainly on how it looks. What if these competitions also required designers to demonstrate how they interacted with users or audience members, and how input from those groups helped shape communications that successfully met their needs? The results of such a collection of work might not necessarily look much different from what we see today, but one could argue that such criteria for inclusion might move us away from an emphasis solely on the aesthetic and at least acknowledge some sense of the functional.

Slightly further in the earlier-cited passage, Paul Rand also writes:

Unless the design function in a business bureaucracy is so structured that direct access to the ultimate decision-maker is possible, trying to produce good work is often an exercise in futility.

Obviously this statement is true. No doubt we've all experienced the frustration of working with organizations that haven't enjoyed support for design efforts from top management, and have seen the wastefulness that results in such situations. But the remarkable thing about the above statement is its "designer-centeredness," if you will. It's assumed that if designers are just given the proper client support, then good design will naturally result.

But if the ultimate receivers or users of designed communications are ignored, are we truly creating "good" design? The results may be pleasant enough to view, but if the needs of those who will experience the information are not met, then what we're left with is simply aesthetically pleasing ephemera. Don't our clients, the users of our work and our profession all deserve a higher standard?

Graphic designers must recognize that they shoulder the responsibility to open the lines of communications with users and audience members. Paul Rand is correct when he, in the first quote cited, refers to the unsuitability of market research to design. Most market research is about discovering what conditions are necessary to convince potential customers to purchase existing products and services, and in the end, tells us very little that we can put to use in our efforts.

Good design research should be about listening to what people have to *say*, so that we can attempt to meet the needs and expectations that they voice. We must also recognize that what people say and what they *do* may be different things, and that they may not recognize the contradictions in their words and actions. We must develop the ability to observe users when necessary, so that their behavior can speak to us as well. We must also allow users to participate in the organization and structuring of messages and communications, so that the patterns apparent in what they *make* can be applied in our design efforts. In short, we must create a user-centered design process that is our own, and that meets the research needs specific to graphic design.

Many of us have started creating interactive communications in recent years and are familiar with the concept of "usability testing" in this context. While it's obviously very important to make sure that users can navigate such information spaces, this type of research represents only one limited opportunity for user input. Users can participate in helping to *generate* content at the beginning of the design process. They can also help *evaluate* communication prototypes throughout the development process, and *experience* finished solutions to help refine future generations of the project. We should strive to establish a sustained "dialogue" with users and audience members as an integral part of our design process.

I would like to assert, finally, that truly "good" design most likely cannot happen without input from the ultimate end-users of our work. We ignore them at our own peril and should take steps to allow their voices to be heard, and to address their needs in more significant ways. We must attempt to move beyond our at times contemptuous view of users, and instead see them as "collaborators" or "partners" in the process of creating useful communications. The age of exclusiveness must come to an end. For our profession to fully contribute to a democratic society, it must become as inclusive as possible. We must not be afraid to come down to the level of the common man—who, if we're listening carefully, will always have important things to tell us.

In closing, I would like to offer this insight from Elizabeth B. N. Sanders, President of SonicRim, a firm specializing in participatory design research. This passage appears in her paper entitled "Postdesign and Participatory Culture," which was presented at the "Useful and Critical: The Position of Research in Design" conference, and which is included in the proceedings. The conference was held in September of 1999 in Tuusula, Finland, and was hosted by the University of Art and Design, Helsinki.

End-users can and should be the most important players in the design process. In fact, other stakeholders in the process such as producers, distributors, sellers and buyers should also participate directly in the process. The inclusion of all the relevant stakeholders changes the nature of design activity from one of individual creativity to one of collective generativity. It is this domain of collective generativity that, when practiced as an ongoing activity, I will call Postdesign.

Note
1. Paul Rand, *A Designer's Art* (New Haven: Yale University Press, 2000).

GREASING THE WHEELS OF CAPITALISM WITH STYLE AND TASTE, OR, THE "PROFESSIONALIZATION" OF AMERICAN GRAPHIC DESIGN
Mr. Keedy

The role that commerce has played in American graphic design, and how it has determined what is valued in design practice, is one of the most interesting and least discussed topics. Questions of an ethical nature seldom arise in design discourse because designers are used to deferring responsibility to their clients, who are ultimately accountable for what is produced. Designers are for the most part subordinate to the client, obedient to society and patronizing to each other. The ethics of design are largely informed by a simplistic "politically correct" morality on one hand and a "bottom line" efficiency on the other, making for an easy value system for practice. It's a value system in which design is implicitly understood as a benign service, in which it is the designer's responsibility to anticipate and satisfy the expectations of the client and audience.

The problem with this arrangement is that the audience is for the most part silent, indifferent and undifferentiated entity, thus necessitating a surrogate (usually self-appointed) "expert" to become the spokesperson for the audience. This surrogate audience expert is usually the client, or worse, a marketing consultant hired by the client. This eliminates the possibility of the audience's desires contradicting the client's goals. On the other hand, the graphic designer as representative of the audience is just as likely to act with a

Originally published in *Emigre*, no. 43 (Summer 1997).

fair dose of self-interest. Neither the client armed with a team of marketing experts, nor the designer with the best of intentions, is a credible representative of the audience.

But what is the alternative? The designer's and client's confidence that "we know what's best for you" is based on the fact that they do know and care a lot more about design than the audience does. The fact that the audience is often unwilling to concede this point is proof of the ignorance and contempt they have for any specialized knowledge and expertise in design. Perhaps that's why designers don't use the word "audience" very much anymore; now they call them "users." The term "user" is a recognition of the fact that design and designers are supposed to be used up by the users.

1. JUST SHOW ME THE MONEY!

In spite of the general indifference most people have toward design, designers are hardly indifferent toward their users; in fact, they can't get enough of them. Who would have guessed that post-industrial capitalism would lead to so much selfless service to others' desires? But the "others" that designers are now so eager to please are not just *some* others, or *most* others; now we want to please *all* the others. Because nowadays, it often seems there is no point in recording music, making a movie or publishing a book without the guarantee of a huge audience, or maximum usability.

Motivated by greed and laziness, this crowd-pleasing attitude has infected design. Now exposure has become more important than what's being exposed. The number of hits your Web site gets, the number of fonts you sell, the number of design awards and magazine articles you can rack up, and how big your clients are, are what designers value most. Now bigger is better, particularly in regard to clients and users. Getting more users means getting younger users. Just like music, film, clothing and tobacco companies, now design companies are aiming lower for higher returns. It is without any sense of irony that designers now consider clients like Nike, Burton, and MTV the most desirable. AIGA design annuals that were once filled with great books, exhibition designs and public signage systems, now look more like sporting good catalogs for preteens.

Just because pop culture is ruled by adolescent taste, does that mean design culture has to follow the money? Since a designer's clients can never be too big, nor their audience too young, it would be logical to conclude that the really important design work of the future will be done for baby food and diapers, and the most desirable clients will be Gerber and Playskool.

In design circles you often hear designers use the expression "selling," but what does that mean in a practice in which the selling always precedes the production? And what exactly is being sold out? The designer's integrity and standards? What are those based on? Is design that doesn't attempt to make money somehow better than that which does? There has certainly never been a shortage of really crappy free design. The designer who believes that "selling out" is somehow easier than sticking to presumably higher principles has obviously never really sold out. Selling out is as much work and probably more aggravating than abiding by ones own self-fulfilling principles.

When it comes to the relationship between design and money, no one-to-one equation of value survives. Except maybe for the one that states: the bigger jerk the client is, the higher the charge. Or from the client's perspective: the bigger jerk the designer is, the higher the fee. But why would a client spend more money to work with a bigger jerk? It's like psychotherapy; if you don't pay for it, it doesn't work—no pain, no gain. "Just look at this fancy office, and all those employees and design awards, it's got to be worth the price? Right?"

2. ECLECTICISM *AND* MODERNISM

In the early days, the commercial artist's aesthetic ideology was formed largely by the demands of the market place—whatever sold the best and was cost-effective and expedient. That market-driven aesthetic was slightly tempered by the designer's personal experience that varied from print shops, sign painting, copy writing and illustration. The aesthetic ideology of the commercial artist was a vernacular hodgepodge that had no preference for either high or low cultural style. Good or bad was only a matter of how well something was done. The only thing that was deemed unethical was to do amateurish and inept work for professional wages. Well crafted, or slickly produced work, was highly regarded no matter whom it was for. It would be a gross generalization to say that the situation is exactly the opposite now, but things are certainly a lot more complicated today.

Not only was the commercial artist's approach to style iconoclastic, but their relationship to commerce was equally individualized. Not regarded as professionals, it was up to each individual to establish their own place between art and commerce. This democratic approach to style and practice, typical of the unschooled commercial artist, is now generally referred to as "eclectic" in the design community. The ethical standards of the eclectic designer were equally eclectic in that they varied according to whom the designer worked for—it was every man for himself (since they were mostly all men). They tended to be independent designers working on smaller scale projects, and they were often close acquaintances of their clients.

Because there was no prevailing aesthetic or ethical ideology, American designers were receptive to new ideas. The consumer-based economy was also receptive to new ideas, as long as they could be commodified, or added value to existing products. That was the fertile American soil that the seeds of modernism, blown from across the Atlantic ocean, were to root in. And that was also the beginning of the decline of American eclecticism in design.

Today, American graphic design is generally thought of as consisting of two basic currents of practice: eclecticism and modernism. The eclectic designer is a descendant of the commercial artist who learned on the job or in a trade school. The eclectic's work runs the gamut of stylistic vernaculars from classicism to contemporary. But today, the most pervasive model of practice is the modern professional designer, whose work is based on the ideas of European émigrés who were educated by artists in art schools. The modernist designer's work is defined by the designer's understanding and interpretation of modernism.

These two currents of ideology, eclecticism and modernism, have been widely accepted as the basic paradigm for the development of graphic design in America. The old eclectic and the new modern serve as a kind of historical continuum that concludes with the triumph of corporate modernism. However, the past decade has added a new third paradigm: postmodernism, a reaction to, or, as some would say, a confused disillusionment with, the first two.

Since most designers today are college-educated and have at least a rudimentary understanding of design history, the eclectic approach to design today is mostly an affectation of willful ignorance. Although greater claims are sometimes made by the designers, the overall effect of today's eclectic designer is mostly one of nostalgia and kitsch. Which is, as such, a very lucrative style. It is a lot easier to sell your clients on something familiar than to convince them to take a chance with something new. Although pandering to the tastes of the lowest common denominator is eclecticism's greatest commercial asset, it has also become the greatest aesthetic and conceptual liability, the American designer's albatross. There is something inherently cynical about exhibiting a naïveté that is not genuine, but as the saying goes, "No one ever went broke underestimating the taste of the American public."

The difference between the new eclecticism and the old is that the new eclectic designer has higher production values (due to new technology), and the old eclectic designer had better craftsmanship and formal skills (also due to new technology). Today eclecticism in design is viewed as the flip side of modernism; it is that catchall phrase for everything outside of modernism's majestic reach. The main function of eclecticism is to be everything but modern; it is the pre-modern as opposed to the postmodern. Little is known about the old eclectic designers; they are not considered important or interesting enough to warrant study. The commercial artists were supposed to be anonymous, while modernist designers are always autonomous. The old eclectic designers of America's past are a cipher on which we project everything we think we have lost, and everything we think we might like to lose.

3. WINNERS *AND* LOSERS

In *A History of Graphic Design*,[1] the *de facto* textbook for design history in America, William Addison Dwiggins, one of the most important American graphic designers, barely rated one paragraph in the "Arts and Crafts" chapter, with absolutely none of his work reproduced. In the most recent edition, he has been upgraded with an additional four sentences in "The Modern Movement in America" chapter, which lists three of his typefaces, reproduces a title page he designed and identifies him as a "transitional" designer.

By contrast, Herbert Bayer fills four pages (two in the second edition) with numerous reproductions of his work and all of his experimental alphabets reproduced. All this despite the fact that Bayer's typefaces were never used much, were not as influential to type design as Dwiggins's, and he was less prolific. However, Bayer's work is obviously considered substantially more important to the development of graphic design than Dwiggins's. Why? Because even though Dwiggins was a modern designer with modern values, he wasn't a *modernist* designer like those "Bauhaus boys" he used to make fun of, so he is relegated to oblivion. Obviously, when you do a history book, you can't include everyone and everything. Oz Cooper, for example, doesn't even warrant a mention. History is written by and for the winners. But how did designers as talented and important as Dwiggins and Cooper get to be the losers?

Designers like Dwiggins and Cooper were every bit as talented and arguably more innovative and original in their work than their canonized modernist counterparts. Although their design was based on the values of craftsmanship and tradition, they were committed to producing new work for the Machine Age. Their work was idiosyncratic because it was shaped by the force of their personal convictions. Perhaps they lost out because these "bumpkins from the Midwest" were difficult to categorize and were usually lumped together under the generic heading of eclecticism.

However, the real reason the eclectics were the losers in design history isn't just because they were ideologically diverse and more difficult to assimilate (copy); it also has to do with their values, or why and *who* they were working for. Although Dwiggins wrote one of the first good how-to books on design, *Layout in Advertising* (1929), he was very skeptical of advertising. So when he learned that he had diabetes, he decided to drop advertising work for good. "I am a happy invalid and it has revolutionized my whole attack. My back is turned on the more banal kind of advertising, and I have canceled all commissions and am resolutely set on starving. I shall undertake only the simple childish little things that call for compromise with the universal twelve-year-old mind of the purchasing public and I will produce art on paper and wood after my own heart with no heed to any market. Revolution, stark and brutal."[2]

Dwiggins also wrote rather critical essays about the poor quality of books, badly designed typefaces and a satirical spoof of systematic theoretical approaches to design. He designed typefaces that were highly speculative and unique, and many considered his use of color bizarre. Dwiggins, perhaps one of the most underrated graphic designers of the twentieth century, represents an alternative model for design practice to that of all the overrated corporate tools, whose financial and self-promotional success have eclipsed all other concerns.

The old eclectic designers were so absorbed in their work that they didn't bother sucking up to big business, and they weren't afraid to bite the hand that fed them if the integrity of their design was at stake. Hardly the kind of calculated crowd-pleasing gestures typical of designers today—it's no wonder they are considered a bunch of losers.

Unlike the local yokels, the debonair émigrés from Europe marched in the ideological lockstep of modernism. Compared to the homegrown aesthetic that evolved in a piecemeal fashion from the American "eclectics," the modernist ideology was much easier to grasp. You didn't need to know any history and you could get it in a few choice sound bites. The designers who were in the know knew that "less is more" and "form follows function," so that "the more uninteresting the letter, the more useful it is to the typographer," to create "the new typography." Wasn't that easy? Now just put on some black clothes, cop an attitude and you're a modernist designer.

The modernist ideology was perfect for schools because it was formulated in schools. Now all the new design programs that started springing up to meet the increasing demands of the market place had clear guidelines and an easy list of do's and don'ts to follow. They weren't overburdened with too much conflicting history; it all started with the Bauhaus and ended with Paul Rand.

In stark contrast to the old eclectic designer, the modernist designer worked on large scale projects in big studios for big corporations making bit profits. Clearly they were the big winners. However, even though the modernists were cloaked in their own pseudoscientific visual language, it was obvious to the outdated old eclectics that the new emperors would eventually be left out in the cold, in their underpants.

4. CORPORATE MODERNISM AND OBLIVION

"But, above all, I want to be aware that art and business must converge and cooperate in the new visual experience towards total integration." —Herbert Bayer, Magazine of Art 18 (1951)

The new modernist émigrés from Europe were not interested in improving and developing American design traditions; they wanted to put an end to the past and start over as the patriarchs of their own domain. But they couldn't build this brave new world alone, because basically they were just a bunch of starving artists with an attitude. What they needed was cash. Fortunately for them, the emerging corporate culture in America would provide cash in exchange for a look of respectability and sophistication—so it would look like they deserved the money they were making. Thus began the tawdry affair that presumably legitimized and professionalized the design trade in America.

The popular mass-market acceptance of anything is always contingent on its ability to be easily assimilated. The more useful and desirable something is, the better it will sell. American designers bought modernism from Europe lock, stock and barrel, and re-sold it to American corporations for a quick profit. Starting in 1951, all the way to the present, the Aspen International Design Conference's primary objective has been to sell modern design to corporate America by celebrating the success of corporate design, a theme that was to preoccupy most American design organizations for the next forty years.

The Aspen Design Conference set the stage for the successful design stars of the competitive, money-grubbing, golden years of the 80s, when corporate design was at its zenith. As an idealistic young designer at the time, the corporate design stars who I was supposed to emulate looked like a bunch of hustlers, tripping over each other to kiss corporate America's ass, hoping for a few farts of fortune and fame. In hindsight, I have more empathy for what some of them were doing, but not much respect.

Is it any wonder designers starting out today are trying to make it on their own and define design practice on their own terms? We can only hope they make more progress in establishing design as a meaningful endeavor for the next generation instead of just grabbing as much of the American pie as they can stuff in their mouth. However, if the next generation only does its own thing, it will ultimately be even more short-sighted than the last. Design will be defined as anything and everything, and will ultimately amount to nothing.

By constantly promoting the utility and the ubiquity of design, designers have unwittingly decreased their cultural cache. The average person has more respect and admiration for someone who can decorate a pair of boxer shorts than they do for a designer who can make the mass transit system of a big city intelligible and appealing. The more convincing the case that designers make for themselves, the more invisible they become. Once corporate America had modernism, what did it need designers for?

This is actually a very old problem, one that designers may never reconcile because the marginalization of design has been an essential component in the advancement of Western culture. In the beginning, everyone was a designer because everything was designed or made by hand. Later, in the Middle Ages, the "specialists in making things" gained rank and were called "artisans." With increased urbanization and technological advancements, the artisans diversified and regulated their work through Medieval guilds, which instigated commerce or trade with others, then "the Renaissance introduced an intellectual separation of practical craft and fine art. Art came to be held in higher esteem. The transition took a long time, but slowly the word 'artisan' was co-opted to distinguish the skilled manual worker from the intellectual, imaginative, or creative artist, and artists emerged as a very special category of cultural workers, producing a rare marginal commodity: works of art. Meanwhile artisans often organized their labors to the point where their workshops became factory-like."[3]

By the time the Industrial Revolution started, the subservient rank and diminished value of low end cultural workers (i.e., designers) was firmly inscribed in the culture. Today, the use of the word "designer," as in "designer jeans," often designates something superficial and of dubious merit, while the use of the word "art" or "artist" always connotes high quality and prestige.

This cultural legacy, combined with the designer's own aggressive boosterism, has led corporate America to view design as a cheap, endlessly renewable, natural resource. If you think that is an exaggeration, then ask yourself, "What has corporate America done to sustain and develop its design resources?" Corporate support of design usually amounts to little more than thinly veiled recruitment and self-promotion efforts, like awards given for the best use of their products, or the sponsorship of creative solutions to problems they can capitalize on.

One notable exception is the Chrysler Award for Design Innovation, now in its fifth year of celebrating innovation in design. But what about other corporations that rely on design for their continued success? Most corporations spend millions in support of the fine arts, not the design arts. After all, if the creator or designer is invisible, then nothing stands between the continuous feed loop between the consumer and the company; it's just you and it. "Just do . . ." "Just be . . ." it.

For all the hard work designers have invested in making crappy products and stupid ideas look interesting, they have been repaid by being marginalized into oblivion. "And everything that is *designed* will melt into air." I wish I could remove every bit of graphic design from the planet for a couple of hours. Great ideas would still be communicated, but the sensibilities that connect us to them, and make them real, would be gone.

5. INDEPENDENT VALUES

Money and status are inextricably linked—nothing elevates one's status as quickly and effectively as money; unless of course, you happen to be a designer. As commercial artists, designers are presumably "in it for the money" anyway, and as skilled manual workers they are held in lower esteem than the fine artist. So designers will never elevate their cultural status no matter how much money they make. And the monetary worth of design will always be low in accordance to its perceived cultural value. Designers will always be damned for being commercial when they make money, and failures when they don't. It will be a long time before this cultural bias changes, if ever.

When it comes to influence, contribution, success and recognition in the cultural arena, or the commercial world, designers are screwed. Like Rodney Dangerfield, they "don't get no respect." Instead of banging our heads against a cultural and commercial glass ceiling, perhaps it's time to look elsewhere for acknowledgment. Maybe designers should stop looking for public adoration and start working on mutual respect.

Up to this point, I have discussed design as a primarily passive and reactive service—reacting to clients, the economy and pop culture. Earlier, I asked if design culture must always follow pop culture, and I think the answer is "yes." Because of the ephemeral nature of graphic design, it will always be linked to pop culture. That, in no way, implies that design can't develop a culture of its own; a proactive design culture that determines its own values in its own best interest. If design is defined as a generative proactive activity, instead of a secondary reactive service, the arbiter of value is the individual creator, not the user. As such, the creator is responsible for developing and assessing values that are consistent with the best ideals of their time. But this may be more responsibility than most designers are willing to accept, particularly in light of the fact that designers have historically deferred credit and responsibility to their clients.

Is it wrong for designers to determine for themselves what constitutes quality work outside of economic realities? Or to set standards that exceed the expectations of the pragmatic ephemeral realities of day-to-day practice? Is it a waste of time to transcend imagined possibilities and continuously rewrite history as an endless source of inspiration? Is there nothing to gain from being reflective and critical of our theories and practices? If we have no conception of excellence without compromise, then how do we know when we are getting closer to excellence?

Falling short of excellence is not failure; not trying for it is. Designers' values today have been eroded by a commercialized pop-culture simulation of success that is too easily obtained. Does it really matter how many clients, design awards, Web site hits, fonts, faxes, Ferraris or fish a designer has accumulated? At the end of the day, and the end of your career, all that really matters is your body of work, your intellectual and aesthetic contribution, your skill, craftsmanship and humanity.

Notes

1. Philip B. Meggs, *A History of Graphic Design* (Bethesda, Md: Van Nostrand Reinhold, 1983; Second Edition, 1992).
2. W. A. Dwiggins, W. A. Dwiggins to Carl P. Rollins, Rollins Papers, June 6, 1923.
3. Malcolm McCullough, *Abstracting Craft: The Practiced Digital Hand* (Cambridge, Mass: M.I.T. Press, 1966).

NO PROBLEM
Julie Lasky

I know a designer whose working habits were shaped by years at a daily newspaper. "I can't get out of the habit of just solving the problem and moving on to the next thing," she once confided. Though she has weeks, not hours, to do layouts now, she is panicked by the thought of lingering experimentally over her designs. To her, "solving the problem" means arranging words and images so that they are reasonably visible, reasonably legible. She doesn't feel she has the luxury to dally with process. She doesn't take delight in running the obstacle course of size, budgetary or time constraints. She doesn't think of decision-making as a smorgasbord of possibilities, each imparting its own subtle flavor. Instead, she reaches for each layout scheme the way one reaches for the first container at hand to collect water from a leaky roof: a stainless steel bowl, a mixing bowl, a pitcher, the aquarium tank you put away after the tropical fish died— no, not the Ming vase; that's inappropriate. Any of the others can do the job, though. The problem's solved, move on.

I think of this woman whenever I encounter those well-worn graphic design metaphors "problem" and "solution." They're legacies of the days when designers needed to persuade clients that the work they did was scientific, requiring special skill. Most important, the goal-directed arrow of problem-solution suggests that design produces results. From the client's point of view, results are what really matter. Clients aren't much interested in the road between problem and solution. But are designers also running the danger of losing sight of process? Do the ideas of "problem" and "solution" help the end overshadow the means?

When I first encountered the term "problem" applied to graphic design, I was a staff editor for a publisher of professional books. My background had been in English literature and academic publishing. I circled the word and stuck a gummed flag to the manuscript with a question mark, just in case the author had made a mistake.

It was jarring because "problem" carries three associations, and none seemed to

Originally published in *Print* Vol. 52, no. 1 (January/February 1998).

fit. The first is an exercise in math or physics applying theoretical rules to concrete situations. When students master a problem set, they demonstrate understanding of the principles underlying calculus or quantum dynamics. After enough problem sets and a degree, the student is ready to take on real-life problems. Only they generally aren't called problems any more, unless they exist in an abstract realm and seem more like games—the Three-Body Problem in physics, for example. Designers work very much in the real world. This kind of problem-solving didn't seem to apply to them.

The second association to "problem" is similar: a puzzle. There may be different means of getting to the solution, but ultimately every square must be filled in with the right letter, every piece locked into the right position. Only one right solution? Hardly an appropriate metaphor for design.

Finally, there's "problem" in the sense of problem child—something troublesome. This is how people generally use the concept. It's the leaky faucet keeping you awake all night. If you can solve the problem, you can put the world back in order, and it hardly matters whether the washer on the faucet is replaced, or you wrap a rubber band around the spigot and tap, so long as the infernal thing stops dripping. There is a goal here. It is very simple and clear. Stop that obnoxious sound. But is this what designers mean when they say they solve problems? Of course not.

Here's the funny thing. Problem-solving is basically what any person with a Social Security number does—from a waiter figuring out how to balance a dozen trays on his arm, to a biologist trying to understand why a cancer cell divides uncontrollably—yet designers are alone in claiming it as a job description. Isn't the surgeon in the operating theater solving a problem? Yes, but the problematic nature of her profession is taken for granted, and it seems foolish to mention it. "We've got a problem, Houston," means that something is wrong, not that a cosmonaut has punched the timeclock.

Designers need not insist so much on the intellectual rigor of their work. Design is analytical. It doesn't have laws, exactly, but rules and limitations narrowing the creative pyramid from infinite possible ways of completing an assignment to, say, only a few hundred thousand. Problem: Design, on a budget of $18,000, a brochure that will be distributed to 20,000 tree surgeons at a convention. Solution: Could you predict one in your wildest dreams? Winnowing down the possibilities through the sifters of finance, audience, materials, suppliers' capabilities, time, appropriateness and personal taste, you arrive at something that is probably not printed on virgin paper. But who knows? Maybe it is. In the meantime, the effective designer has put a great deal of thought into the matter.

My problem with the publication designer's use of the word "problem" is that she doesn't *have* a problem. There's no negative situation that requires redressing through any possible means. Careful trial and deliberation may be called for, but a layout isn't a puzzle. The "problem" is filling up the page with words and images that elucidate the content and complement one another and inspire readers to continue reading. Now tell me, when will we know that those conditions have been met? Define, if you will, "elucidate," "complement" and "inspire." Or for that matter, define "words," "images" and "read"? Does skimming count?

I'm not a total relativist. I agree that it's possible to say when pages are well designed and when they aren't. It's even possible to reach a consensus. But to cast this elusive scheme, with its many opportunities and outcomes, into the language of problem-solution is to risk defining the "problem" too broadly or narrowly and "solving" it too hastily. When one is facing a problem, constraints are roadblocks that must be knocked down rather than a kind of gentle pressure fostering creativity. One is almost by definition in a negative state that needs solving, though it might be better to think of it as an indeterminate state that needs resolving. It's fine to be goal-oriented in our description of what designers do, but there are so many goals. Can't we also say: exercise taste, flaunt imagination, organize data, leave a mark, take a stand, raise curiosity, heighten senses?

Does anyone see a problem in that?

TERMINAL TERMINOLOGY
Katherine McCoy

"Information architect" has become the term of choice these days for communications designers working in Web design, e-commerce and interactive media. Richard Saul Wurman is often credited as the father of this term, although he did not use it originally to indicate interactive electronic communications. Wurman's new terminology was an attempt to create a more high-minded description of graphic design, something that eschewed style in favor of the more noble goals of clarity, objectivity and rational functionalism. These days, designers often use the phrase to indicate their serious intentions and solid professional grounding. Everyone seems to want to be an information architect, from Massimo Vignelli to Clement Mok, and especially new-media designers.

I find this term "information architect" troublesome, a very narrow description that omits a world of design strategies, especially those required for the design of resonant user experiences.

In this current use, the term "architect" apparently refers to the planning and structuring of a site or software application, the syntactical dimension of the design process. It also suggests a pathetic attempt to gain credibility and respect on the coattails of a more venerable and prestigious profession. This use of "architect" indicates a serious misunderstanding of the discipline of architecture, since that field includes far more than structure, organization and circulation.

Originally published in *Print* Vol. 55, no. 1 (January/February 2001).

While "information" is used as an overarching modifier, the word itself is extremely specific. Why "information" and not "communication"? Information design is a subset of communication design. The term "information" implicitly references a school of thought called Information Design, its adherents a distinguished lineage stretching from Otto Neurath to Michael Twyman and Robin Kinross. In that approach, the values of clarity, objectivity, rationality and ordered organizational hierarchy (most frequently based on a Swiss grid) are connected to the "crystal goblet" school of graphic design and the modernist ideal of culturally neutral, value-free design. Order the content, and it will speak for itself. "Information" underscores that traditional divide between information and persuasion.

However, in today's world of interactive media and the design of experience, graphic design's old dichotomy of information versus persuasion is no longer pertinent and imposes a limited and outmoded framework on the current landscape. Information is one type of content and cannot possibly describe the entire scope of interactive electronic design. Interactive media content is one big bowl of soup that includes computation, information, data, entertainment, learning, gaming, dating, relating, propaganda, shopping and advertising. All communications design—and now product design as well—must be consciously persuasive and seductive to create memorable experiences and resonant brands.

Cool, detached communications design might have been occasionally effective when it had the advantage of a continuous physical presence. But now dematerialized, temporal and nonlinear communications are more experience than artifact. They need all the viscous juice we can give them, including subjective emotion and sensual experience. "Stickiness" is a useful term to describe the resonance of a rich user experience, the quality that good design must now aim to achieve. This is generated by persuasive, seductive character and behavior that defines the sum total of the user's experience and interaction with the message, product and service.

What theories can help us create persuasive and resonant communications, considering that character and behavior would seem to be key attributes to animate our users' experiences? The semantic category of semiotics, the science of signs, describes some aspects of character and behavior, but neglects others. As described by semiotics, semantic associative meaning is an encoded language process. But character also has to do with nonverbal, non-language expression by means of preverbal, subverbal or subconscious experience. The term "information design" has the same flaw, describing a language-based process and omitting nonlinguistic aspects of communications. Non-language theories, like phenomenology, can contribute to design and guide us toward richly haptic, sensory and nonrational modes of experience. "Affective human factors" is an interesting new area of research that is exploring the role of pleasure and emotion in interface design. Its proponents call this "hedonic design."

To achieve stickiness, experience designers can use other, sensual dimensions beyond vision and hearing. Sight and sound are contemplative senses that deliver somewhat distanced, abstracted and more cerebral stimuli, which tend to be more culturally mediated. The contact senses of touch, taste and smell are more primal, evidencing some sort of hard-wired link to memory. Smell, in particular, is a powerful mnemonic trigger that stirs rich, spontaneous associations from past experience. Emerging media technologies promise to deliver kinesthetic body sensations that design can harness to create characterized user experiences.

To inform our process for these additional sensory dimensions of design, designers must investigate additional theories. Cognitive and perceptual psychology and an array of language theories are already applied in the more rigorous design schools. In addition, perhaps we should investigate behavioral psychology, the psychology of personality and animal behavior.

The ultimate goal in all this must be to ensure that persuasive character and user relationships evolve. This will be possible for character created by digital media. Computer technology allows a software application to evolve and learn from its interaction with the user. Random vectors and unexpected interactions may have some appropriate roles in interaction design for a generation of users raised on computer gaming conventions. We need to provide users with the experience they expect, and more utility, value and function heightened by delight.

How can user experience design create that essential stickiness, developing branded character rather than a superficial veneer? This must be an organic, inside-out process, an outgrowth and culmination of intrinsic, embedded character to achieve any authentic brand identity. An integration of the designed product's affordances and the user's response, utilization, appreciation and participation creates an effective branded identity.

Branded character in interactive electronic experience is like a car's character; the latter affects the user's driving style and creates a rich user interaction. Think of driving five different vehicles to town—the experience will be different each time, even though the activity, the route and the destination are the same. So when we design an interactive electronic experience, we could ask, "How does it drive?" Is it brisk and tight, low to the ground with instant response like a BMW roadster? Is it cranky and recalcitrant like an old pickup truck? We could also ask, "How does it smell?" Think of the pleasure of that "new car smell," the smell of leather seats, or the musty smell of a garaged old car.

How does this analogy extend to a Web site or a software application? The experience in both cases needs to go beyond superficial imitations of personality like AOL's "You've got mail," or overly rendered personalities like the computer Hal in *2001: A Space Odyssey*.

This is a revised vision of the designer's role. Networked pervasive products, for example, are more about behavior and less about graphic and product form. Thinking of the car analogy, we realize that much of a car's character comes from engineering choices that affect the contact senses—the drive train, suspension, brakes and engine compression. Too often, traditional design has been about the aesthetic senses triggered by the reflection of light on a car's surfaces. Perhaps "character engineering" would be a more descriptive and appropriate term. But I hope not. Design needs to define its own identity rather than playing the "wannabe."

So what's in a name? What we call ourselves influences how we see our roles and how our colleagues relate to us in cross-disciplinary teams. Too often, designers have been categorized as the look-and-feel specialists that are brought in at the end of the process. Hence the ambition of "information architects" to participate in a project from the beginning. But neither look-and-feel nor "information architect" adequately describes this new discipline. We need a term that includes these components, and more.

Even before interactive communications arrived, the traditional term "graphic design" was troublesome, too; librarians always shelve our books under "printmaking." "Industrial design" has also been problematic. People think these professionals design factories. Computing is also having trouble with terms: "Ubiquitous computing" and "pervasive computing" are mystifyingly vague.

"Experience design" is a little better, but still vague. But if we and our peers continue to think of ourselves as information architects—or industrial designers or graphic designers—we will never be positioned to design branded behavior and character experiences for our audiences, or to acquire the theories and skills necessary to do so.

THE HOLE IN ART'S UMBRELLA
Roy R. Behrens

More than eighty years have passed since the founding of the Bauhaus, the most famous art school in history. The school's name was a sandwich of two German words, *bau* (building) and *haus* (house), to indicate, as its founder Walter Gropius explained, that "to embellish buildings was once the noblest function of the fine arts" and "the ultimate aim of all visual arts is the complete building." In coining that name, as design historian Frank Whitford has noted, Gropius wished to evoke other associations. The German word *bauen,* for example, means "to grow a crop," which brings to mind Friedrich Froebel's kindergarten ("child garden"), the preschool system in which Gropius was raised, where children are treated metaphorically as seedlings while each of them also must nurture a plant. The name also alludes to *bauhütten,* the term for the guilds of artisans who worked together on the great Gothic cathedrals during the Middle Ages.

On the cover of the Bauhaus manifesto, published in 1919, was a woodcut of a cathedral by Lyonel Feininger, an American living in Germany, known for his Kinder

---

Originally published in *Print* Vol. 54, no. 4 (July/August 2000).

Kids comic strip in the *Sunday Chicago Tribune*. Inside, in a now familiar text, Gropius called for the abandonment of "salon art" and, following the example of the Arts and Crafts Movement, for the unification of fine art and applied art, of art and design. "Architects, sculptors, painters, we must all return to the crafts!" urged Gropius. "Let us then create a new guild of craftsmen without the class distinctions that raise an arrogant barrier between craftsman and artist! Together let us desire, conceive, and create the new structure of the future, which will embrace architecture and sculpture and painting in one unity and which will one day rise toward heaven from the hands of a million workers like the crystal symbol of a new faith."

As a graphic designer who began as a fine artist, I am often and easily moved by a call for unity among artists and designers. But having tolerated the insensitivity, unfairness and imperiousness of fine-art faculties for nearly three decades, the phrase that stands out for me now is "an arrogant barrier."

Simply, the neglect, mistreatment and marginalization of graphic design faculty and students in university art departments and art schools is an ever-worsening, nationwide problem. Despite the phenomenal growth of design student enrollment, design faculty in many schools (perhaps most) are impossibly outnumbered and outvoted by fine-art colleagues, with the result that design students are often deprived of the most basic components of their training. In universities and art schools across the country, as tuition is diverted to the needs of fine-art faculties, graphic design programs are regularly getting soaked through a hole in the so-called umbrella of art.

This is not a new problem. As design historian Philip Meggs said recently in an interview, "Academics and fine artists have been marginalizing graphic designers for a long time. In the past, this related to social class." Its origins go back at least to the Renaissance, and particularly to two important innovations. First, with the inception of painting on canvas and board (as an alternative to site-specific wall paintings and stained-glass windows), painting became portable. No longer an inherent physical part of an architectural setting, it became categorically separated from architecture. Freed from the "noble," subservient role of "the embellishment of buildings," painting could align with sculpture (and soon after with printmaking) in the formation of a new category called "fine art."

Second, and of wider consequence, was the emergence of the concept of *ingenium,* the Latin term for artistic "genius." The Renaissance, as music historian Edward Lowinsky has explained, made "a clear distinction between craftsman and genius," in which a craftsman, however talented, achieves only what he *can* (as the saying goes) while a genius is someone who does what he *must.*

According to this tradition, the artistic temperament is inevitably saturnine. Like a manic-depressive madman, writes Lowinsky, the fine artist is "driven to his art by a natural impetus so strong that it overcomes hunger and thirst, so powerful that it may put the [artist] into a state of ecstasy, and . . . in such a state of heightened awareness and activity the [artist's] mind can achieve more than in long periods of ordinary work."

These and other factors brought about the distinction between *artist* and *designer,* along with the glorification of "art" as a quasi-religious activity, less prosaic and far more exalted than "craft." Other consequences continue to this day: unlike craftsmen and designers, whose output is largely anticipated, the "self-expressions" of artistic geniuses cannot to regulated by clients, nor can they be censored or altered at all.

Indeed, artistic geniuses cannot even be paid by the hour. After all, their finest efforts spew out of them in frenzied, unexpected fits, while only their lesser productions are slow, thoughtful, and, God forbid, even designed. If artistic geniuses are extraordinary, so are their moments of inspiration. Both rarefied and portable, artworks have gradually become myth-laden investment opportunities, with the result that today's fine artists (and the fine-arts faculties who propagate that tradition) are the handmaidens not of architecture, but of a corrupt commercial behemoth—or better, behe*myth*—that is now the artistic equivalent of the Military Industrial Complex. (For more on this, from an art critic's viewpoint, see Deborah Soloman's article, "How To Succeed in Art," in the *New York Times Magazine,* June 27, 1999.)

The Arts and Crafts Movement, which began in nineteenth-century England, was an attempt to reconcile art with craft, and, using the Gothic cathedral as its symbol, to convince the most talented artists to turn to the applied arts as a profession. The Bauhaus inherited that cause, with the result that its workshops were frequently taught by both a "form master" (artist) and a "workshop master" (craftsman), while most of the things that the students produced were utilitarian architectural components, such as murals, pottery, furniture, wall hangings, stained glass windows, and so on.

If such attempts at reunification held any promise, they were inadvertently sabotaged in this country by the U.S. Congress in 1944, when it passed the Serviceman's Readjustment Act. Better known as the G.I. Bill of Rights, it provided military veterans with financial assistance to attend college, learn a vocation or purchase a home. No one could have anticipated that more than half of all World War II veterans would return to school on the G.I. Bill, so that by 1947, enrollment in American colleges and universities had doubled, producing a sudden, severe shortage of college instructors.

As a result, starting in the early 1950s and continuing for more than a decade, there was an unprecedented rise in the number of tenure-track art faculty positions at colleges and universities. The majority of these were given to the studio areas of painting, sculpture and printmaking, to art history and (for the purpose of certifying teachers) to art education programs. On the periphery of these departments were a small number of craftsmen in such applied-art areas as ceramics, jewelry and metalsmithing, and weaving.

If graphic design was offered, it was commonly known as "commercial art," the artistic equivalent of prostitution, implying, of course, that professional fine art is inherently pure and noncommercial, and that a genuine artist would never submit to art direction. (An irony of all this is that only the slightest minority of these fine artists had ever practiced art as a profession, since nearly all were college trained and had always earned their living not from art-making but from classroom teaching.)

By the early 1970s, it became apparent to those in the "crafts" category that, like graphic designers, they too were facing discrimination. But instead of protesting the preferential treatment of fine artists, academic craftspeople decided to migrate into the same category. As a result, weavers began to call themselves "fiber artists"; potters, recast as "ceramic artists," turned away from wheel-thrown dinnerware and promoted non-functional sculpture instead; and jewelers and metalsmiths working under the new label of "metals" or "metalry," also increasingly produced small-scale, nonwearable sculptural forms.

Nearly all the fine-arts faculty members who were first hired fifty years ago have either died or are no longer teaching. As they retired, they were usually replaced by younger artists in the same fine-art studio areas (or newer areas like photography, paper-making and glassblowing). As a result, despite an overwhelming shift in enrollment toward graphic design, the number of fine-arts studio positions has often held steady or even increased.

As the second generation of these artists nears retirement age, they too are now generally being replaced, not by graphic design or art education faculty (whose class-room and advising loads are legendary), but by a third generation of fine artists. Burdened by college loans, and fearful of being unemployed or employed in jobs outside of art, they align with their tenured colleagues (who will decide their tenure) in supporting the unfair diversion of funds toward the latest trends in fine art, such as performance art, installation art and the misuse of art for political gain.

As Deborah Soloman was told by conceptual artist Chris Burden, who now earns $102,000 as a professor of fine art at the University of California at Los Angeles, "People think collectors support artists, but it's the universities that support artists." However candid, Burden is still off-target: typically, it is not just the university but the tuition of graphic design students that pays for the whims and the salaries of the fine-arts faculties. No wonder that in the spring semester of 1999, despite the relative scarcity of fine-art faculty positions, an estimated two thousand postgraduate art students were granted M.F.A. degrees in studios other than graphic design—the vast majority (of course) in the areas of painting, sculpture, printmaking and photography.

"Design should never, ever be taught under the umbrella of an art program," design educator Joe Godlewski warned more than a decade ago. Meanwhile, graphic design programs throughout the country have become, to use Katherine McCoy's term, the "cash cows" of art departments (the slightly more civil and usual term is "bread and butter"), in which heavily enrolled but neglected design programs provide the funding for sparsely enrolled but well-endowed fine-arts programs.

Is there a solution? At some schools, the number of design faculty has increased sufficiently to afford them greater political clout. At others, where the design faculty remains a minority, benevolent deans and other administrators have stepped in to ensure that all decisions benefit the entire department, not just the traditionally privileged few.

Sadly, in many art schools and universities, perhaps most, the marginalization of design faculty and students is as prevalent as ever. Toppling the fine-art aristocracies in those schools to restore balance and fairness will require patience, courage and, very likely, the intervention of the parents of graphic design students. After all, it is they who unknowingly pay for the bricks that make up the "arrogant barrier."

GRAPHIC NEWS
John Hockenberry

In the early hours of the morning of May 12, 1996, NBC News graphic artist Rick Samartino has a typical inspiration: a plane crash. Confident that his work will be exhibited literally moments after he completes it, Samartino quickly assembles the materials for his latest image: a corporate logo, a picture from the crash scene and some clip art of a DC-9. Immediately, he realizes that the corporate logo—a pudgy-looking plane with eyes and a big smile—is too cute for this image. So the logo is out. And there is another problem: The picture of the crash scene turns out to be nothing but a green swamp that looks about the same as it did during the Jurassic epoch. "There's nothing to show it's a swamp, even," Samartino complains. In the end, all he has to work with is the file picture of the DC-9 and the airline name: Valujet. With less than an hour before air time, he puts the finishing touches on the "over-the-shoulder" graphic for the lead story of *NBC News at Sunrise*.

Valujet was the top story on May 12, and remained the lead "disaster" news item for weeks to come, until another plane, TWA Flight 800, crashed off the coast of Long Island, followed quickly by a bomb at the Olympics in Atlanta. Each subject generated scores of subsequent network graphics incorporating pictures of wreckage, regulatory agency logos, maps and animated re-creations of where and why the events took place. Each image was carefully reconciled with the known facts just like any element of text.

Robert Samartino's twelve-year body of work is replete with plane crashes, earthquakes, floods, diseases and other natural disasters. The thirty-nine-year-old Samartino is also undoubtedly one of the few artists in history to have been well paid to construct images about the federal deficit and other arcane twists and turns of policy in Washington, D.C., images seen by millions. But this is news graphics, after all. "Most of the stories are horrible," Samartino says, sketching on the digital pad of a Quantel Paintbox classic, the workhorse of television news graphics for more than a decade. "But there's an adrenaline in your gut you feel with news. Like you're at the center of the universe."

Samartino is the first to agree that his work isn't exactly the Sistine Chapel, but graphic images associated with television news stories, especially the biggest stories, can acquire a certain timelessness, lingering in memory like trademarks. Events beget television logos, which in turn beget a kind of historical record unique to our age. Sometimes the graphic for an event is dominated by a single still photograph, as in the Tiananmen Square disaster, defined by a man facing a tank. Other times the graphic is

Originally published in *I.D.* (September/October 1996).

more abstract, as in CNN's "War in the Gulf" logo for its coverage of Operation Desert Storm. History is captured, encapsulated in a quick sketch and the occasional notes of canned music. Samartino likes it that way. "All of it is instant. You don't have that much time for design. That's the challenge."

TELEVISION DISCOVERS DESIGN

For most of its half-century of existence, television has produced little in the way of graphical expression. Catching action in TV's little window was all that was required to make a television program, and "action" has always been fairly loosely defined, covering anything from a moon landing to people (men mostly) sitting around desks in well-stuffed chairs. Before television discovered graphics it had already become its own logo, its blank screen instantly the symbol for an unannounced cultural revolution. The cathode ray tube cluttered science-fiction movies and advertisements long before there was much of interest to put on it.

Now, however, moving and still images composed by graphic designers are beginning to dominate television news and coverage of special events like the national political conventions and the Olympics. The trend is driven by technological advances as well as by the maturity of television as a visual medium. While some might puzzle over the notion of "television aesthetics," the profound evolution in technology has transformed the composition of the image on the screen.

There has also been a shift in emphasis from the global, instantaneous transmission of any image to a more selective approach. Today, the use of advanced techniques to enhance the quality and content of the image itself has accelerated as digital tools for network designers have proliferated. The popular Quantel Paintbox, for example, allows for high-resolution sketching on a digital surface, full-screen editing and image enhancement; it then matches graphic color tones with the federally regulated and somewhat restricted color spectrum of broadcast video.

"For twenty years we were cardboard and contact cement," recalls Ben Blank. "Now the high tech is in graphics." Blank has been around long enough to have seen this entire transformation—indeed, to help make it happen. A seventy-four-year-old retired graphic designer, Blank is the television graphic artist's equivalent of Homer, Marshall McLuhan and Edward R. Murrow rolled into one. Blank's career at CBS and ABC spanned five decades, beginning in the 1950s, when he got his start painting the posters that sat on easels on the sets of long forgotten shows like *Hollywood Screen Test* and *Stop the Music*. He is credited with inventing the idea of putting a graphic image over the shoulder of a news anchor as he or she read each story. "We were looking for a logo so people could follow these stories over time," he says. Blank retired in 1992. His last big logo—i.e., news story—was Operation Desert Storm at ABC News, which broadcast the first fuzzy pictures of the air war over Baghdad.

"Until the war with Iraq, television technology was all about transmission," says Blank. "The graphic designers were always just the decoration. Now we are part of the editorial process."

Ben Blank's treasures—which include a fat black portfolio full of pictures from television's earliest days—belong in the Smithsonian. In the beginning, as he tells it, network management had no feel for and little interest in graphics. "I had to sell graphics to them. I would go around to the programs and get them to use a map here, a nice font there. It was hard going."

Blank recalls that it was Don Hewitt, then the executive producer of the CBS Evening News with Eric Sevareid, who was most interested in incorporating graphics into television news. "Hewitt always stayed around the graphics area looking for something we could do." (Ironically, Hewitt today presides over *60 Minutes,* probably the most anti-graphic of the network magazine shows: after twenty-five years, *60 Minutes* is still defined by its ticking second hand, primitive clock and blocky poster graphics. Each network magazine show has a distinct visual: *48 Hours* is known for its animated twirling camera. The ABC programs *Prime Time* and *20/20* open with crane shots through infinite vistas of blue. I work for *NBC Dateline,* the orange guys. With its 3D rotating universes and moving murals of red and orange, *Dateline* is the most graphically intense of the magazine shows, a far cry from Hewitt's stopwatch and soundtrack.)

During the 1950s, Ben Blank says, television graphics technology usually consisted of what he had lying around in his workshop, or what he could get cheaply down the street. When the Soviet Sputnik satellite was launched unexpectedly in 1957, Hewitt and Blank wanted something to underscore the drama of their lead story. Blank pulled a five-dollar turntable from his shop, affixed a globe to it and mounted the rotating model Earth inside a black background cutout spangled with stars. "I took a black wire coat hanger and a golf ball, which we made to look just like Sputnik using the wire stories as our guide," remembers Blank, who held this little Sputnik on a stick with his own arm wrapped in blue tape to prevent it from being seen on camera. "We filmed it for a minute, edited it into a loop and it led the evening news."

A LONG WAY FROM GOLF BALLS

Nearly forty years later, NBC lead graphic designers Scott Pressler and Zoa Martinez sit in front of a 24" monitor and work on images for the Atlanta Olympics. (See *I.D.,* May/June 1996.) In their editing room, tables are stacked with equipment and CRT screens, including a 3D area with a brace of Silicon Graphics terminals paused in midrotation of an NBC Peacock. Pressler operates a Hal Express Quantel workstation capable of holding seven-and-a-half minutes of uncompressed video in instantly accessible storage—a couple of billion Sistine Chapels worth of graphic information. Each still image is a million bytes, so at thirty frames per second the Hal keeps track of 810 billion bits of information. A more advanced animation workstation nearby, the Henry, holds roughly double the information and allows full animation of six screens (or "cels," in animation terms) that can be altered or combined at the designer's whim and composited for broadcast in real time.

"We can do anything here, really," Pressler says with pride at the images before him. The hum of hard disk drives is accompanied by a castanet percussion of point and click as Pressler rearranges Martinez's cels on a Waycom digital tablet and, with dazzling speed, rotates a caption and highlights a border, adjusts a tint and in an instant gives the whole image a completely different feel.

With the superb resolution on fifth- and sixth-generation Quantel machines, the Olympic graphics affect a greater sense of dimension—and appear more animated—than the familiar video billboards that lead into and out of commercial breaks. Paul Pauley, NBC's director of engineering, explains the significance of so much computational power: "We can do almost everything you see here in real time and send it to the control room during the broadcast." Pauley oversaw an equipment investment of over $20 million for the 1996 games. And after the Olympics? "All this goes to the news division," he says. "And believe me, they're drooling already."

It is no accident that the 1996 Olympics were the impetus for a huge investment in a new generation of video graphics technology (especially given the $456 million spent for the broadcast rights). Since the 1960s, each Olympiad has provided a stable, predictable setting, a narrow range of content and a long lead time, allowing for the experimentation that eventually ends up on the evening news. Maps, charts and frames for keeping track of athletes' standings are essential for focusing an event as large as the Olympics. "And unlike news," Pauley remarks, "it happens more or less on schedule."

In general, advances in news graphics have been driven by sports, weather and other well-defined events where the need for graphics is great and editorial uncertainties are at a minimum. Ben Blank recalls the 1960s NASA mission to the moon as a boom period for graphics: "We were always doing something new for each space shot." Blank pulls out a thick stack of black-and-white stills showing Mercury and Gemini capsules in orbit. He calls them "animations," but in fact they are more like studio creations. In a kind of staged performance piece, CBS designers created elaborate (and expensive) fake space ships and used actors on tethers to represent astronauts, filming the "missions" for later broadcast. Real animation for news production was not possible in the 1960s because lead times were too short. "Any animation we needed had to be shot in film in the studio well ahead of the launch, all strictly according to what NASA told us would be happening," says Blank. And, he adds, without the benefit of any photographic documentation.

BLUE PANTS AND BROWN SOCKS

Ralph Famigliatta, who heads up NBC's Broadcast Creative Services, the graphics department on the ninth floor of Thirty Rockefeller Plaza, has watched his department grow from a single office and seven people in 1977 to a booming wing of edit suites, control rooms, animation studios and post-production facilities employing more than sixty people today. Electronic graphics has driven every bit of this growth. "In the beginning it was a little intimidating for the designers," he recalls. "Some people were saying 'What am I going to do with my watercolors?'"

Famigliatta knows the technology inside and out and is regularly courted by digital luminaries and inventors who have new products to demonstrate. But Famigliatta says that the real revolution caused by electronic graphics has not occurred among designers or technical people. "It's the editorial side that has changed the most," he explains. "Technology has made every producer into an art director." He describes with a smirk how he sometimes has to listen to suggestions he would never have heard in the old cut-and-paste era. Producers, he says, think nothing today of asking for an image to be cooler, darker or to punch it up with some orange. He pauses and looks cautiously around. "As a designer for three decades, I sometimes have a problem with a producer wearing blue pants and brown socks telling me that something needs to be color-corrected." Suddenly graphics, a medium that has always been completely foreign to television producers, has been demystified. "It's not a secret anymore," Famigliatta says with a sig as I look down to see if my own socks match.

Upstairs and down a long hall from my own office, in an *NBC Dateline* video suite, a group of designers play a twenty-second animated depiction of a bus bombing in London that was the subject of a recent *Dateline* story. Graphics are increasingly used in this way to substitute for unobtainable video pictures. Designer Paul Bennet clicks through the animation that he and one other designer composed on at least four separate cel backgrounds over twenty-four hours on a so-called crash deadline. At each point, he shows how the position of the animated bus coincides with specific facts reported by wire services and eyewitnesses.

This kind of animation has only recently been available on quick-turnaround news deadlines, and all the network magazine shows take full advantage of it. With software that allows a designer to set lighting sources and points of view, these quick animations have become central to the storytelling process, especially in disasters and crime stories, staples of the news magazine shows. With current technology, the animation is generally vector-based 2D, but with artful use of editing cels and background dissolves, a credible 3D look is possible, and full three-dimensional animation is just around the corner.

Ever since the first focus groups back in the 1960s indicated that, to the great surprise of network producers, viewers were paying attention to news graphics, the visual style of television has been evolving at an accelerating rate. The outgoing logos of network news—the talking heads—are shrinking in the frame, competing with the limitless possibilities of digitally composed graphics and animation. Today each television news image can be as composed and thought out—some might say as staged—as the famous World War II news photograph depicting the raising of the flag at Iwo Jima. In the battle between strict content and the need to get viewers to retain images over time, news graphics have become an important visual mediator.

As I watched Ben Blank packing up his portfolio of filmed animations for the ABC News coverage of NASA's missions, I asked him about the old tabloid conspiracy theory that claims the space program was just a hoax filmed on a back lot somewhere and that there never was a landing on the moon. Ben looks at me and winks. "You know, we could have done it all with graphics. All they had to do was ask."

MOVIE TITLES: MUCH ADO ABOUT LITTLE
Peter Hall

Like a long-awaited feast, the film titles event at New York's Walter Reade Theater last April held great promise for designers and aficionados of the typokinetic craft. Nearly four hours of back-to-back film titles, from Saul Bass to Kyle Cooper, plus roundtable discussions of the neglected "art form." Yet the actual experience of "For Openers: The Art of Film Titles" was strangely dissatisfying. Emerging, dazzled and weary onto the windswept walkways of the Lincoln Center, I suddenly felt as though I had been sitting in a restaurant for four hours, being shown a succession of different menus, without ever actually eating.

Having contributed a few thousand words on the titles art myself, with an essay on Fifties and Sixties titles in a new book coming up, and a roundup in last spring's *I.D.* magazine, it was a sobering epiphany. No one was to blame: a standing ovation—or more appropriately, a credit sequence—should have accompanied the end of the titlethon to recognize David Peters's indefatigable commitment to collating and curating the relevant spools of celluloid, not to mention the gargantuan task of gaining permission from film studios. This was a definitive night in film titles history.

If only I were convinced that film titles history were a standalone discipline. But titles without films are like frames without paintings. The history of frames might provide an interesting device for looking at the history of art, but if the art weren't present, the story would start to seem a little limited. One easy test is to list five acclaimed movies and then try to visualize the title sequences: *Citizen Kane* (1941), *Apocalypse Now* (1979), *A Bout de Souffle* (1960), *Chinatown* (1974) and just about any Woody Allen movie. As far as I can recall, none of these films had a memorable title sequence. The movies, clearly, get along fine without motion graphics.

Titles can, however, cast a revealing light on the history of film. The medium was born, effectively, in the late Fifties and Sixties, when the film studios were running scared from the advent of television, audiences were plummeting and newly empowered directors were doing the best they possibly could to overwhelm their audiences with the largesse of the cinematic medium. They commissioned lengthy, dramatic opening sequences from designers like Saul Bass and Maurice Binder as a way of accentuating the similarities between film and theater or the opera (watch Bass's now-tedious visual overture to the 1961 movie version of *West Side Story*.) The last film titles boom, sparked in 1996 by R/GA and Kyle Cooper's twitching, jump-cut introduction to *Se7en*, came out of the age of the fast-cut, Gen-X music video, the "new typography" movement—

Originally published in *AIGA Journal of Graphic Design* Vol. 18, no. 2 (2000).

in which designers were using computers to distress and distort classic letterforms—and, well, the advent of digital effects. Although *Se7en* was created with traditional opticals technology, it came from the same effects studio—R/GA—that was using digital composition to insert Forrest Gump into historical footage, and neatly anticipated the digital manipulation that Cooper was subsequently to apply to film titles with his firm Imaginary Forces, from *Twister* to *Fight Club*.

I recently heard an employee of Imaginary Forces declare that the film titles boom is now over, that just about everything has been done and that his company is focusing its attention on other fields, notably commercials and environmental signage. This seemed to echo a comment in Sarah Boxer's oddly self-defeating report in the *New York Times* on the "sprouting" of a new genre of film titles history. Boxer first cited evidence of a growing interest in the discipline of film titles, then, in her conclusion, announced that it was already over. "With desktop filmmaking on the horizon," writes Boxer (April 22, 2000), "the very notion of auteur title designers seems quaint. The writing of history begins when an era is ending."

It's a depressing idea only if you consider film titles as an art form in their own right. It seems obvious to anyone who has seen Imaginary Forces' titles for *The Island of Dr. Moreau* (1996), *Mission: Impossible* (1996), and *Fight Club* (1999) that there are only so many tricks you can make letters perform before the tricks begin to look the same. If designers continue to perform the subservient role of packaging and setting up the film with the opening sequence, their limits are pretty clearly defined. Their work will set the right mood (*The Ice Storm*, 1997) or the wrong mood (*Dr. Moreau*); it will settle the audience down (*Alien*, 1979) or completely overpower the film (*Walk on the Wild Side*, 1962); or it will float by completely unnoticed (most movies).

Graphic designers can do a lot more than that, however. Despite the much-ballyhooed convergence of interactive media and TV and film and whatever, there has yet to be a film that successfully incorporates typography throughout. Director Jean Luc-Godard's *Week End* (1967) hinted at the possibilities with his use of typographic chapter headings, and Tony Kaye was reported to have been working on a typographic film, but generally the work of graphic designers within the body of a movie has been confined to incidental details (the Ikea scene in *Fight Club*, for instance) or subtitles. You may counter that it would be just too distracting or annoying to have words popping up around the live action, but that never stopped TV or Web designers.

Better still would be for us to pull graphic design out of its self-imposed ghetto at the beginnings and ends of movies and recognize that design is present throughout a film. It's why they list art directors in the credits, and costume and set designers. Directors, too, are designers—Sofia Coppola's *The Virgin Suicides* (2000) is a shallow story made into an exquisitely composed film, clearly directed by someone with a the visual sensibility of a photographer and designer. Occasionally, designers even make films, as in Mike Mills's new short *The Architecture of Reassurance* (1999), in which the former poster, T-shirt and record cover designer has made every scene look like a film poster. One thing I like about Mills is that, as soon as he got into film and video work, he avoided motion graphics like the plague. "I didn't want to be stuck in that hole," he says.

It would be nice to imagine that desktop filmmaking would put an end to the design community's need to have events like "For Openers," which elevate the profession by association with film. If in the video-digital future, anyone can make films, and that anyone includes graphic designers, then perhaps the sequel to "For Openers" could be "For Entrées: The Art of Film."

THE NAME GAME
Ruth Shalit

When Hewlett-Packard decided last year to spin off its instrumentation and measurement division into a separate company, executives at the computer hardware giant did everything they could to smooth the transition. Shareholders had to be notified. A topflight management team hired. The trades brought on board. But such housekeeping duties were a minor matter compared to the vast existential task that loomed—a five-phase, cross-unit "identity project," intended to unearth a suitably momentous name for the $8 billion enterprise. The name had to be a grand, monstrous, powerful thing—broad-shouldered yet luscious, tempered by oaky bass notes of maturity, courage, characters—like a 1961 Cheval Blanc. "This was similar to the Lucent process," says David Redhill, global executive director for Landor Associates, the identity firm hired last year to supervise the project. "We needed a tremendous name that really was magisterial and compelling, and had a certain amount of stature right away."

As with Lucent, Redhill and his team approached the problem with ingenious thoroughness, devising a naming module that would eventually cost the client more than $1 million and involve up to forty Landor executives around the globe. The first step was to interview key executives at the massive new entity, then known only by its code name of NewCo. "We wanted to know what the company needed to be; what it was aiming to be," says Redhill. "The aim was not to manipulate them, but really to draw out of them exactly how they visualized people feeling about their brand."

The exercise got off to an unpromising start. NewCo executives volunteered that they wanted the company to be perceived as strong, innovative, dynamic and caring. "We've done this process with hundreds of companies," Redhill says wearily. "They all say, 'We want to be perceived as strong, innovative, dynamic and caring.'" And therein, it seemed, lay the problem. Though top NewCo executives had avowed their intention

Originally published in *salon.com*, 30 November 1999.

to be different, to change the paradigm, to think outside the nine dots, "the qualities they were aiming to project were in fact common currency," Redhill sighs.

Fortunately, the Landor identity crew had come prepared for exactly this possibility. "We did mood boards," Redhill says. "We did random visual associations, attached to sequential words. And so, when they said, 'We want to be strong,' we would show them a picture of an ocean wave breaking. And we'd ask: 'Do you want to be strong like a force of nature?' Then we'd show them a picture of a metal chain link fence. And we'd ask, 'Do you want to be strong like a chain? Strong but breakable?'" The final slide was a close-up of a human face. "We said, 'Perhaps you want to be strong like human nature—indomitable and immutable.' And they said, 'Yes, that's us. That's exactly how we imagine people feeling about our brand.'"

After four months of this sort of intensive brand therapy, the group settled upon the only name capable of conveying such protean emotions—"Agilent." They took the name into focus groups, where, to their great delight, it was received with admiration, approval and total open-mouthed attention. "I've never seen anything like it," says Amy Becker, who works alongside Redhill in Landor's verbal branding and naming group. "This was a pretty rarefied crowd. We're not talking about the mass-consumer, chips-eating sort of person. This was a very particular sort of business-to-business decision-maker. A hard group to impress. And they were just delighted." The name was also a hit among the NewCo rank and file. "It's funny, because 'Agilent' isn't even a real word," muses Redhill. "So it's pretty hard to get positive and negative impressions with any real basis in experience. But I'm pleased to say that when we unveiled the name last month at an all-company meeting, a thousand employees stood up and gave the name a standing ovation. And we thought, 'We have a good thing here.'"

But did they? Among Landor's rival name-slingers around the Bay Area, the choice of Agilent was immediately greeted with snorts of derision. "The most namby-pamby, phonetically weak, light-in-its-shoes name in the entire history of naming," declared Rick Bragdon, president of the naming firm Idiom. "It's like a parody of a Landor name. It's insipid. It's ineptly rendered . . . It ought to be taken out back and shot."

Steve Manning of A Hundred Monkeys, a San Francisco naming firm, was also appalled. "What a crummy name," he says. "It sounds like a committee name. 'Who's your competition?' 'Lucent.' 'Well, we want to play off Lucent—only we're *agile*. I mean, if you wanted a name like that, I could have come up with that kind of name in about four seconds."

Naseem Javed, president of ABC Namebank in New York, tries to be more charitable in his assessment. "Mm-hm. Mm-hm. Yes, I did hear about the Agilent mess," he says. A long sigh escapes his lips. "Perhaps it would be best if Landor just closed up shop," he says quietly. "I don't want to trash them too badly. It's just that their last four, five naming projects have been total disasters."

Landor, for its part, is quick to defend its handiwork. "To our critics, I can only say, *vive la différence, vive* the competition and *vive* individual entrepreneuralism," says Redhill, in his gentle, grandfatherly voice. "We have the utmost confidence in our model." To drive home that point, Redhill put me in touch with Darius Somary, the research director who had confirmed to an empirical certainty the allure of names like Agilent. "From a quantitative standpoint, it's a very appealing name," Somary told me. "On all the scalar measures of distinctiveness and appropriateness, it tested right off the charts."

Welcome to big-league corporate naming, a Pynchonesque netherworld of dueling morphemes, identity buckets and full-scale linguistic sabotage. What was once a diverting sideline for mild-mannered grad students has become an increasingly lucrative and increasingly cutthroat profession, as blue-chip consulting firms schedule raids on college English departments and linguistics nerds scramble to shift their focus from the syntax of negation in the Anatolian languages to the murkier precincts of corporate identity.

The professional back-stabbing is a bit puzzling, given that professional naming, above all, is supposed to be fun. The literature of the namers brims with references to "joy," "play," and to the capacity for childlike wonderment. This image of naming gurus as paragons of corporate delight would be more believable, however, if the namers didn't spend so much time tearing each other to shreds. "You should call up Ira Bachrach of NameLab," breathes one namer. "He doesn't even have meetings with clients. It's just taking a bunch of morphemes and phonemes, and crunching them through the computer. Unbelievable." Another whispers honeyed words of ill counsel about Enterprise IG. "Their names are nothing more than a bunch of concatenized prefixes and suffixes—totally soulless," he insinuates. "I'd love to see you blow this wide open."

In the extreme sport that is modern corporate nomenclature, trust is in short supply, and paranoia reigns. "I used to work by writing names on individual pieces of paper and sticking them up on the wall," says Steve Manning of A Hundred Monkeys. "I don't do that anymore." The reason? "People were walking around the room with cameras, taking pictures of my names," Manning says blearily. "It got a little creepy. I mean, this is Silicon Valley. People move around a lot . . . If they liked one of my names, they might be drawn to register it as a URL. And that would be very bad. Because, you know, I *own* those names."

What can explain this tense, sour mood? Part of the reason is increased competition. While the corporate-identify racket used to be dominated by a few big players—Landor, Interbrand, Enterprise IG—the market is now glutted with professional namers, all scrounging for the same clients. In addition to Lexicon, Idiom and Metaphor, the discriminating brand managers may now choose between NameLab, NameBase, Name/It, NameTrade, Namestormers and TrueNames. Each of the firms has its own jealously guarded methodology, a signature "naming module" that distinguishes it from its competitors. Enterprise IG has its proprietary NameMaker program, good for generating thousands of names by computer. Landor uses a double-barreled approach; deploying both its "Brand Alignment Process" and a "BrandAsset Valuator." Others find that their module must be described in more than a few words. "We have a wonderful approach," says Rick Bragdon of Idiom. "We use an imaginative series of turbo-charged naming exercises, including Blind Man's Brilliance, Imagineering, Synonym Explosion and Leap of Faith . . . We find that when clients are playing, literally playing creative games, they create names that come from a place of joy, a place of fun. A place that allows them to transcend the drudgery of naming, and come up with names that are fresh and different." Bragdon's most recent naming project? "I-Motors," he says sheepishly.

But a cutthroat marketplace isn't the only reason for the jaundiced mood. Among ad agencies and corporate marketing departments, and even at the naming companies themselves, there is a grim consensus that, despite all the frantic bonding and interfacing, despite the morpheme-munching computer modules, names today are worse than ever. "I tend to steer clients away from hiring naming companies," says Marc Babej, a brand planner at Kirshenbaum, Bond, & Partners, a New York ad agency. "As naming has become professionalized, it's led to a certain norming standard. The names have come to sound more and more alike." Babej explains what he means by this. "You can imagine how, at one time, Livent might have sounded new and hot," he says. "Well, but now we have Lucent. And we have Aquent and Avilant and Agilent and Levilant and Naviant and Telegent. What's next, Coolent? What you have here is clients being taken for a ride."

Naseem Javed, president of ABC Namebank in New York, speculates that someday, historians will look back on the late Nineties as a low point in the annals of naming. "There were periods in history of terrible architecture," he says. "But this architecture was actually presented to popes and kings and lords. And they actually went out and lived in this type of housing! Why, then, should we be surprised that corporations are going out and spending $5, $10, $15, $20 million promoting these dumb names? And then going out and changing them to names that are even dumber?"

Javed elaborates: "As I see it, there is a real malpractice issue," he says. "If you've just developed a great stereo system, I can see paying $1 million for a great name—Sony. But what if you hire the same company for another naming project? And the names they come back with are Bony, Cony, Dony, Zony? At what point do you say, forget it, this is not worth $1 million? This is not even worth $5."

At no point, responds Landor. "We don't have an issue at all" with soundalike names, Redhill tells me. "Think of the names Larry and Mary," he says soothingly. "They have the same suffix. But the meaning is completely different!" So, too, he says, with Landor creations Livent, Lucent, and Agilent. Other top naming firms, aware that their names have come to resemble each other, have taken to attaching lagniappes of meaning to individual letters. Think of it as a couture touch, the syntactical equivalent of scalloped stitching on an inside hem. Michele Lally, global marketing director for Reuters-Dow Jones Interactive, recently renamed Factiva, is grateful to her naming company, Interbrand, for helping her stand out in a world of Factevas and Actevas. She has sought refuge in, as she puts it, "the semiotics of the letter *i*." "Have you seen our letterhead?" she asks. "We do the *i* as a biacron. An *i* with a circle on top. Or 'the bubble,' as we call it internally." Lally herself is bubbling over with enthusiasm for the bubble. "The brand circle denotes infinite possibilities," she says. "We very much hope that bubble, that icon, will come to symbolize business information in airport lounges worldwide."

Ron Kapella, head of Enterprise IG, seems to be pursuing a similar tack with Naviant, an online data-mining company. Eager to distinguish his brainchild from its soundalike cousins Agilent and Navigent, he, too, has honed in on the letter *i*. "Notice that the letter *i* is exactly in the middle of the word," he says. "Notice also that it has a circle over it. An *i* with a circle over it is the international symbol for information. It's a visual symbol we've created. Consumers will come to associate it with endless inspiration, endless possibility."

Unless, that is, they associate it with googly-eyed teenage girls who dot their *i*'s with hearts and smiley faces. And indeed, among some companies, a backlash against the naming companies has taken hold. For some, the fact that they came up with their names all by themselves, without recourse to professional help, has become a point of pride. "I love our name," Jeff Mallett, president and CEO of Yahoo, recently told an industry newsletter. "It's fun, irreverent and consumer-focused. And it wasn't conjured up by Landor, or some huge naming agency."

It's this sort of chutzpah that makes the namers at Landor see red. "The Internet is filled with arrogance," says Amy Becker coldly. "You might have a provocative, fun name. But do you have the basis for a lasting brand? We still don't know how compelling a brand Yahoo will be ten years from now. I sense a real missed opportunity."

"Let's put it this way," says Redhill. "Over the years, we have created and sustained many of the world's most durable brands. We make a lot more hits than companies who think up their own symbols and names. I'm not suggesting that a company couldn't get it right with a stroke of insight or genius or luck. But if it's your own brand, how can you possibly be objective? I mean, would you name your own baby?" Redhill thinks for a minute, then backpedals. "I mean, of course you would name your own baby. But wouldn't you ask your friends and family for suggestions and recommendations? Perhaps they would open your eyes to a name you'd never considered."

Redhill is not alone in warning against the dangers of dilettantism in naming. Other namers are quick to deplore the proliferation of amateurs—naming arrivistes who don't know the difference between denotative and connotative meaning, and who hilariously confuse brand equity with brand awareness. "A typical naming process costs about $75,000," says Ron Kapella of Enterprise IG. "Now, that might sound like a lot of money. But naming is very difficult and challenging. There are rules to follow. Rules of linguistics. Rules of trademark. Rules of international corporate nomenclature . . . It's not just a process of pizza and beer around the table."

In hushed tones, Naseem Javed of ABC Namebank talks of the seamy underbelly of naming—of squalid, Dickensian naming mills operating late into the night. "I've heard of those outfits," he says. "They've piled up thousands, zillions of names, which they'll sell for a buck each. For $1,000, they'll give you a thousand names. But look at the names! It's garbage in and garbage out." His voice lowers ominously. "Names like 'Oasis,' 'Advanta,' 'Advantia,' 'Advantia Plus.' Clients don't realize how many times those names have been recycled and recycled. Then, all of a sudden, it's Friday afternoon, and the press release has to go out on Monday." Apparently unaware of Redhill's description of the arduous process, culminating in an outburst of mass euphoria, that generated the name of Hewlett-Packard's new division, he speculates, "That's how you end up with a name like Agilent."

The naming pros love to trade stories of shortsighted CEOs who attempt to go it alone before finally turning to them in humble desperation. "Our system really is a quite powerful system to make new words out of English," says Ira Bachrach of NameLab. "We comprehend how identity structure works. We're creating natural language solutions from a morphemic core . . . When clients try to do it themselves, out of word fragments, they end up throwing their hands up in disgust. Luckily for us," he adds, laughing uproariously.

Bachrach recently completed a renaming project for MacTemps, a specialized talent agency that provides print production experts who are proficient on Macintosh computers. Bachrach didn't much care for the name. "It didn't function well," he says. "It didn't suggest a brand." Bachrach thought he could help. "What MacTemps needed," he says, "was a name that was aggressively novel, shockingly different. A name that grabbed the perceiver by the throat and shook him."

Bachrach and his team of constructional linguists rose to the occasion. They presented MacTemps executives with their recommendation—Aquent. Aquent? "It doesn't mean anything," Bachrach cheerfully explains. "But if it did mean something, it would mean, 'Not a Follower.'"

Bachrach elaborates. "This is a company that advocates for independent professionals," he says. "They have asequential career paths . . . 'A,' as in 'not,' comes from ancient Greek. 'Quent' comes from the Latin 'sequor,' meaning, 'to follow.' These are people who are striking out on their own, charting their own course."

At MacTemps—Aquent—the name change went into effect last month. Befuddled employees are struggling to get with the program. "Let's see if I'm explaining this correctly," says Nunzio Domellici, an Aquent vice president. "The root of 'sequential' is 'quent.' 'Quent' itself is not a Latin word. But if it *were* a Latin word, it would mean, 'follower.' Or 'not a follower.' They share the same root." Domellici pauses. "Anyway, it's not something we stress when we pick up the phone."

You could be forgiven for thinking that a functional, descriptive name such as MacTemps, for all its pedestrian clunkiness, might be preferable to a name like Aquent, which to the casual observer evokes something vaguely liquid, perhaps a mouthwash, and whose meaning only becomes clear, if then, when parsed by a listener who is profoundly familiar with the morphemic structure of Latin and ancient Greek. But to the new pros of nomenclature, such quibbles are irrelevant. To hear Bachrach tell it, he couldn't care less whether company executives actually *like* the name he has bestowed upon them. "We're not really interested in what the client wants," he says. "What we do reflects what the clients *needs*. We have our own analytic system for looking at what the structure of a name should be, and actually, tend to ignore the client's wishes."

Bachrach is joined in this view by many of his naming compatriots. Some go so far as to say that it's actually better if the client doesn't like the name. "We actually prefer that clients don't fall in love with the name," says Rick Bragdon of Idiom. "If they fall in love with the name, it's a good sign there's something wrong with the name."

"By establishing criteria, and by developing names against those criteria, we've taken the arbitrariness out of the process," says Ron Kapella of Enterprise IG. "And so, when a client says, 'I don't like it,' I say, 'It doesn't matter whether you like it or not. The question is: does it meet the criteria?'" In addition to Naviant, Kapella's brag book includes Navistar and Tempstar, Telegy and Telegent, Verbex and Azurex, Nortel and Meritel.

Despite all the complaints about unlicensed amateurs, the true threat to great naming may come not from the slapdash fumblings of anarchic freelancers, but from something close to the opposite. In their zeal to professionalize and standardize what used to be a goofy, freewheeling, fly-by-night enterprise, the naming conglomerates tend to produce names that are reflective not of the client's corporate culture, but of their own. The result: a slew of names that are sterile, antiseptic, talcum-powder bland.

To find the soul of the Agilent generation, you need look no further than Darius Somary, a bright, eager research director at Landor. Somary is a firm believer in the need to subject all names to the rigors of quantitative and volumetric research. "The advantage we see in quantitative research in name testing is that it yields definite statistical results," he tells me. "It's easier to pick a winner."

But language, of course, is not digital, but organic. It comes from that wet, sticky place that we call our brain. How, I ask Somary, can Landor quantify an emotional response to a word? Easy, he says. "We set up phone interviews in which the interviewer has a very clear script to follow. And she can't really interact outside of that script. The questions are quite straightforward. She might say something like, 'On a scale of one to ten, how strongly does the name 'Agilent' communicate the following attributes: 'high quality,' 'very strong customer focus,' 'adapted to my needs,' 'truly cares about its customers.'

"Then we look at the results," Somary tells me. "We chart it all out. We make name graphs. And we go back to the client, and we say, 'Here's our winner.'"

Lu Cordova, president of *TixToGo.com,* is among the CEOs who roll their eyes at this sort of hubris. "Let's face it," she says. "We know who's in these big naming companies. We went to college with some of them. They say they're experts at this and experts at that. But they're really just our peers. They don't have any special mystical powers."

Cordova learned this the hard way earlier this year, when she sought out a new name for TixToGo, a popular online booking, ticketing and reservations service. After several months of probing and crunching, the naming firm she'd hired came back with a strong recommendation: *YourThing.com.* "The first ten people we mentioned it to all said, 'It sounds like your, um *thingy,*'" Cordova says dryly. "So we said, whoops, okay, that one's gone."

Finished with the naming companies, TixToGo decided instead to sponsor a contest. Last month, the company picked a winner, David Nader, from over 128,000 entrants. In return for his winning submission, "Acteva," Nader received the keys to a Porsche Boxter. The shy young software engineer was thrilled—and so was Cordova. "We love the name," she says. "And we're especially delighted it came from a civilian. The [naming companies] are unbelievable. I had one guy from a naming firm ask me how I expected to get a name from a nonexpert. He literally said, 'I charge $150,000 just to sneeze.' His whole attitude was, 'How could you go to them when you have me?' The snobbery, the credentialism was incredible."

Cordova casts her decision to snub the namers in populist terms. "We bet on America, and the bet paid off," she says. "We spread awareness. We grabbed a lot of creative names . . . The whole thing was tons of fun. What a vindication of the American population—to show that they could do it."

For those corporate souls not brave enough to put their brand in the hands of the American citizenry, another option is to turn to a renegade naming firm. A Hundred Monkeys, headed by Danny Altman and Steve Manning, is leading the fight against terminal blandness in corporate naming. "We don't do names like Agilent," Manning tells me. "And so we have to pass on a lot of big contracts. We'd name a car for GM for free, if they'd just let us do something cool. Something with some emotional connectivity. It'd be such a fucking public service."

"No one names a car Mustang or Thunderbird or Monte Carlo anymore," Altman chimes in. "Instead, you have Acura, Alero, Xterra, Integra. All thoroughly researched committee decisions. All emotionally empty . . . By the time they've been laundered, and pressed, and packaged there's nothing left."

Altman and Manning, whose clients include Nickelodeon, Apple and Matchbox toys, are contemptuous of their morpheme-crunching rivals. "It's like using a computer program to write a song," Manning says. "You can do it, but why? Why go there? Why do that?" They regard their names as organic, throbbing beings, deserving of courtesy and respect. "I think all the time about the names that didn't make it," Altman says mournfully. "I think about what those names would have been like had they lived."

"It's like the names are our foster children," Altman says eagerly. "We have to give them up to someone. But we want to make sure they go to a good home. And that they're going to be used in a good way."

Some would say they love their names a little too much. "It's like [the names] are these little creative pearls, and they're casting them before us swine," says one advertising executive who has worked with the pair. The executive puts down the phone. "Lorraine," he yells, "what were some of those names that A Hundred Monkeys kept trying to shove down our throats? Oh yes. Jamcracker, Calabash, Wallop, Kitamba, which is apparently some kind of Hindu cloth. Totally inappropriate for our client."

"Who told you about Jamcracker?" Manning asks. "If you printed that, there would be legal issues. No one's taken that name yet! That name is our intellectual property." Later, however, Manning relents and allows me to publish the name. "There's actually been an issue with Jamcracker," he admits.

It seems that when Altman and Manning presented the name Jamcracker to a client recently, the reception was not everything they had hoped for. "I put the name up in front of their creative people," Manning says. "There were a couple of women sitting in. One of them got up and said, 'Oh, that's disgusting.' Another said, 'This is really sick.' I said, 'Excuse me, what are you talking about?' They said, 'We can't explain it, but that name is just creeping us out. We don't know what it is, but could you take it off the wall, please?'" Manning remains mystified by the incident. "There's apparently some strange, uncomfortable meaning attached to it in the minds of some women," he says. "God knows what that could be."

But while the Monkeys' methods aren't universally popular, some people can't get enough. Satisfied clients describe their experience as akin to the religious epiphany that follows an agonizing exile in the desert. "It's not all fun and games with the Monkeys," says Robin Bahr, marketing director for MedicaLogic, a healthcare Web site. "At the end, you see the light. But early on, when the primordial soup is still being stirred, there's a lot of contention. There's fear and trepidation."

"They just kept digging and digging," says Gary Siefert, the company's director of Internet services. "There's a Walter Payton confidence about what they do. They were actively, if not aggressively, challenging our business model and our thinking. They were asking questions and more questions. Until they got to the essence of what we do. It was like digging into a huge watermelon on a summer day, just breaking it down, piece by piece. They kept drawing us back and back, from the playground of our inner child to the reality of our business model. It was an almost mystical experience."

Bahr and Siefert are thrilled with their Monkey-furnished name—"98point6." "It's perfect," says Bahr. "It's just what we wanted. No Latin roots. No suffixes of any kind. I mean, these guys are good."

The Monkeys don't come cheap. "We charge $65,000 per name," says Altman. "But we work with you for a month. And for that month, we are basically yours. It's actually a much lower price point than many of our competitors."

He's right. What's more, at A Hundred Monkeys, $65,000 will buy you an entire word. Some rival firms charge more than that for a mere suffix.

Consider Luxon Cara's $70,000 "identity program" for US Air. The airline "wanted to be repositioned and perceived as a major United States airline," says John Hudson, Luxon Cara's president. "And so we researched this. We checked it out globally. We basically lived with them for nine months to a year. It was one of the most exciting things we ever did."

Tom Lagow, US Air's executive vice president of marketing, says it was exciting for him, too. "They did an extensive amount of research," he says. "A hundred to a hundred fifty hours of interviewing. And I'll tell you, I was very impressed. They peeled the onion back to the point where they were able to define what business we were in. They determined that we were in the business of proficiency. And that, very unfortunately, that message of proficiency was not conveyed by the name US Air."

What was the new name? I asked. And when would it be unveiled? I was guessing Skystar, Glident, Proficienta. "Oh, it's already been unveiled," Lagow explains. I was perplexed. "But isn't US Air still US Air?" I asked. "I was just in an airport the other day, and I could have sworn . . ."

"No, no," Lagow says. "It's been changed to US Airways."

"That's it?" I asked.

"That's all we needed!" he said eagerly. "What we found was that airlines that end in 'Air' tend to be thought of not as major. What we found is that if you stretch the name a little bit—don't throw it out, just stretch it a little bit—you create the perception of a larger, more substantial airline. Strategically and structurally, we are now oriented toward the international."

The renaming, which was announced in April 1997, was worth every penny, says Lagow. "We've heard comments from around the industry that it's one of the best identity programs ever done," he says.

If $70,000 seems like a hefty price for a word fragment, consider the chutzpah of Ira Bachrach. Several years ago, he charged Infiniti $75,000 for a single letter. Or, to be fair, two letters.

"We wanted to express the idea that [Infiniti] was a philosophically different kind of car," Bachrach explains. Proclaiming E, X, Z or X to be yesterday's news, Bachrach recommended that the company adopt different letters for its model identifiers. "I told them to use letters that weren't conventional," he says, "that were, in fact, aggressively unconventional."

Bachrach decided he was sweet on "q" and "j." "Utterly unused letters," he says. "Aggressively novel letters which didn't necessarily parse to luxury and performance. These were marketing guys with courage."

One model became the Infiniti J30, another the Q45. "I know it doesn't sound like much," Bachrach admits. "But I'm prouder of that than anything I've ever done in the model business. It was a marvelously condensed way to convey something that would have taken millions of dollars in advertising to convey." Instead, they scraped by with a mere $37,500 per letter. Lucky Infiniti.

In the end, however, attempting to quantify the benefits of a naming project may be just as small-minded as, well, attempting to quantify the benefits of a name. For the lucky client who truly clicks with his or her namer, the collateral benefits go far beyond nomenclature. There are new words to learn. Fun games to play. And, in the case of the Monkeys, unimpeachable warmth and love. "We got so much more than a name," says Robin Bahr of 98point6. "I mean, I got a name for my daughter. One of our senior executives identified strongly with 'Mescalanza.' No one calls him Jim anymore. His name is Mescalanza." Meanwhile, she says, "our senior manager for Internet development just fell in love with the name 'Jamcracker.' And so today, the Harvey meeting is known as the Jamcracker meeting. There are three hundred people at this company who identify Jamcracker with Harvey."

Bahr claps her hands over her mouth. "Oh my God," she says. "I forgot. I shouldn't be mentioning these names to a reporter. Technically, we don't have ownership of those names. Jamcracker is still the Monkeys' property."

Bahr stops for a moment, as if listening to herself. Then she bursts out laughing. "Listen," she says. "I take it back. You write whatever you want to write. If someone out there wants to name their company Jamcracker, God bless them. And good luck to them."

AUTHORSHIP

H istorically, designers have often looked to language as a way to extend their visual thinking. William Morris, Bruce Rogers, Paul Rand and Josef Müller-Brockmann are among many twentieth-century designers who wrote extensively about design. In the same tradition, Ellen Lupton and J. Abbott Miller (Design Writing Research), Rudy VanderLans (*Emigre*) and Robin Kinross (Hyphen Press) are examples of contemporary design practitioners who write, design and publish on their own. Beyond the ideas and the work itself, what distinguishes their contributions to design scholarship is their approach to the *ownership* of the medium itself: no longer content to merely write and design, these designers combine critical discourse with entrepreneurial ambition. In the truest sense, they are expanding the definition of design authorship.

The historical tension between graphic designer and artist had found a new outlet for expression: designers and students yearning for the credibility and authority associated with the "authorship" of making something original—in the classic model of the writer, architect or filmmaker—embraced this concept as never before. In the spirit of a new design criticism, Michael Rock wrote a seminal essay in *Eye* magazine in 1996 on the subject of design authorship, arguing the merits of film *auteur* theory as another model. In the years since, *Eye* has championed work by designers who exemplify the designer-as-author. (Interestingly, while the concept remains strikingly relevant to contemporary design criticism, the editors of this volume were surprised to find little that continued the critical discourse initiated in Rock's original essay.)

What has emerged is a series of monographs characterized primarily by their heft. (In general, however, the trend in page-count escalation may have owed more to indulgent photography than to extensive prose.) Among the designer-authors embracing the genre of "The Big Book" are Bruce Mau, Tibor Kalman, Vaughan Oliver, John Maeda, Milton Glaser, Wolfgang Weingart, Bill Cahan, Steve Tolleson and Stefan Sagmeister. Rick Poynor has been on both sides of this equation, authoring a monograph of Vaughan Oliver at one point and commenting on the phenomenon of the oversized book at another: both of his essays appear in this section, as does an article offering his perspective on authorship from another direction: that of a writer designing his own novel.

Certain designers—Tibor Kalman and Bruce Mau, for example—had ambitions that extended beyond simple documentation, seeking instead to articulate ideas and philosophies that repositioned design discourse within a larger social and political arena. Interestingly, both were publicly critiqued by highly penetrating reviews in the mainstream (read "non-design") press. These reviews are included here as an indication of the kind of progress that has been made in recent years: designers acting as authors, with critics addressing design no longer as a secularized or exotic discipline, but instead, on an equal playing field with other topics.

William Drenttel

THE DESIGNER AS AUTHOR
Michael Rock

Authorship has become a popular term in graphic design circles, especially in those at the edges of the profession: the design academies and the murky territory between design and art. The word has an important ring to it, with seductive connotations of origination and agency. But the question of how designers become authors is a difficult one, and exactly who qualifies and what authored design might look like depends on how you define the term and determine admission into the pantheon.

Authorship may suggest new approaches to the issue of the design process in a profession traditionally associated more with the communication than the origination of messages. But theories of authorship also serve as legitimizing strategies, and authorial aspirations may end up reinforcing certain conservative notions of design production and subjectivity—ideas that run counter to recent critical attempts to overthrow the perception of design as based on individual brilliance. The implications of such a redefinition deserve careful scrutiny. What does it really mean to call for a graphic designer to be an author?

The meaning of the word "author" has shifted significantly through history and has been the subject of intense scrutiny over the last forty years. The earliest definitions are not associated with writing *per se,* but rather denote "the person who originates or gives existence to anything." Other usages have authoritarian—even patriarchal—connotations: "the father of all life," "any inventor, constructor or founder," "one who begets," and "a director, commander, or ruler." More recently, Wimsatt and Beardsley's seminal essay "The Intentional Fallacy" (1946) was one of the first to drive a wedge between the author and the text with its claim that a reader could never really "know" the author through his or her writing.[1] The so-called death of the Author, proposed most succinctly by Roland Barthes in a 1968 essay of that name, is closely linked to the birth of critical theory, especially theory based in reader response and interpretation rather than intentionality[2]. Michel Foucault used the rhetorical question "What Is an Author?" in 1969 as the title of an influential essay which, in response to Barthes, outlines the basic characteristics and functions of the author and the problems associated with conventional ideas of authorship and origination.[3]

Originally published in *Eye,* no. 20 (Spring 1996). The author thanks his partner Susan Sellers and colleague Jenny Chan for invaluable assistance with this essay.

Foucault demonstrated that over the centuries the relationship between the author and the text has changed. The earliest sacred texts are authorless, their origins lost in history. In fact, the ancient, anonymous origin of such texts serves as a kind of authentication. On the other hand, scientific texts, at least until after the Renaissance, demanded an author's name as validation. By the eighteenth century, however, Foucault asserts, the situation had reversed: literature was authored and science had become the product of anonymous objectivity. Once authors began to be punished for their writing—that is, when a text could be transgressive—the link between author and text was firmly established. Text became a kind of private property, owned by the author, and a critical theory developed which reinforced that relationship, searching for keys to the text in the life and intention of its writer. With the rise of scientific method, on the other hand, scientific texts and mathematical proofs were no longer seen as authored texts but as discovered truths. The scientist revealed an extant phenomenon, a fact anyone faced with the same conditions would have uncovered. Therefore the scientist and mathematician could be first to discover a paradigm, and lend their name to it, but could never claim authorship over it.

Post-structuralist readings tend to criticize the prestige attributed to the figure of the author. The focus shifts from the author's intention to the internal working of the writing: not *what* it means but *how* it means. Barthes ends his essay supposing "the birth of the reader must be at the cost of the death of the Author."[4] Foucault imagines a time when we might ask, "What difference does it make who is speaking?"[5] The notion that a text is a line of words that releases a single meaning, the central message of an author/god, is overthrown.

Postmodernism turned on a "fragmented and schizophrenic decentering and dispersion" of the subject, noted Fredric Jameson.[6] The notion of a decentered text—a text which is skewed from the direct line of communication between sender and receiver, severed from the authority of its origin, and exists as a free-floating element in a field of possible significations—has figured heavily in recent constructions of a design based in reading and readers. But Katherine McCoy's prescient image of designers moving beyond problem-solving and by "authoring additional content and a self-conscious critique of the message . . . adopting roles associated with art and literature" has as often as not been misconstrued.[7] Rather than working to incorporate theory into their methods of production, many so-called deconstructivist designers literally illustrated Barthes's image of a reader-based text—"a tissue of quotations drawn from innumerable centers of culture"—by scattering fragments of quotations across the surface of their "authored" posters and book covers.[8] The dark implications of Barthes's theory, note Ellen Lupton and J. Abbott Miller, were fashioned into "a romantic theory of self-expression."[9]

Perhaps after years as faceless facilitators, designers were ready to speak out. Some may have been eager to discard the internal affairs of formalism—to borrow a metaphor used by Paul de Man—and branch out into the foreign affairs of external politics and content.[10] By the 1970s design had begun to discard the scientific approach that had held sway for decades, exemplified by the rationalist ideology that preached strict adherence to an eternal grid. Müller-Brockmann's evocation of the "aesthetic quality of mathematical thinking" is the clearest and most cited example of this approach.[11] Müller-Brockmann and a slew of fellow researchers such as Kepes, Dondis and Arnheim worked to uncover a pre-existing order and form in the way a scientist reveals a natural "truth." But what is most peculiar and revealing in Müller-Brockmann's writing is his reliance on tropes of submission: the designer submits to the will of the system, foregoes personality, withholds interpretation.

On the surface, at least, it would seem that designers were moving away from authorless, scientific text—in which inviolable visual principles arrived at through extensive visual research were revealed—towards a position in which the designer could claim some level of ownership over the message (and this at a time when literary theory was moving away from that very position). But some of the institutional features of design practice are at odds with zealous attempts at self-expression. The idea of a decentered message does not necessarily sit well in a professional relationship in which the client is paying the designer to convey specific information or emotions. In addition, most design is done in a collaborative setting, either within a client relationship or in the context of a studio that utilizes the talents of numerous creative people, with the result that the origin of any particular idea is uncertain. The ever-present pressure of technology and electronic communication only muddies the water further.

IS THERE AN AUTEUR IN THE HOUSE?

It is perhaps not surprising that Barthes's "The Death of the Author" was written in Paris in 1968, the year students joined workers on the barricades in a general strike and the Western world flirted with real social revolution. The call for the overthrow of authority in the form of the author in favor of the reader—i.e., the masses—had real resonance in 1968. But to lose power you must already have worn the mantel, which is perhaps why designers had a problem in trying to overthrow a power they never possessed.

The figure of the author implied a totalitarian control over creative activity and seemed an essential ingredient of high art. If the relative level of genius—on the part of the author, painter, sculptor or composer—was the ultimate measure of artistic achievement, activities that lacked a clear central authority figure were devalued. The development of film theory during the period serves as an interesting example. In 1954 film critic and budding director François Truffaut had first promulgated the "politique des auteurs," a polemical strategy developed to reconfigure a critical theory of the cinema.[12] The problem was how to create a theory that imagined a film, necessarily the result of broad collaboration, as the work of a single artist, thus a work of art. The solution was to determine a set of criteria that allowed a critic to define certain directors as auteurs. In order to establish the film as a work of art, auteur theory held that the director— hitherto merely one-third of the creative troika of director, writer and cinematographer—had ultimate control of the entire project.

Auteur theory—especially as espoused by the American critic Andrew Sarris— speculated that directors must meet three criteria in order to pass into the sacred hall of auteurs.[13] Sarris proposed that the director must demonstrate technical expertise, have a stylistic signature that is visible over the course of several films, and through his or her choice of projects and cinematic treatment show a consistency of vision and interior meaning. Since the film director often had little control of the material he or she worked with—especially within the Hollywood studio system, where directors were assigned to projects—the signature way a range of scripts was treated was especially important.

The interesting thing about auteur theory is that film theorists, like designers, had to construct the notion of the author as a means of raising what was considered low entertainment to the plateau of fine art. The parallels between film direction and design practice are striking. Like the film director, the art director or designer is often distanced from his or her material and works collaboratively on it, directing the activity of a number of other creative people. In addition, over the course of a career both the film director and the designer work on a number of different projects with varying levels of creative potential. As a result, any inner meaning must come from aesthetic treatment as much as from content.

If we apply the criteria used to identify auteurs to graphic designers, we yield a body of work that may be elevated to auteur status. Technical proficiency could be claimed by any number of practitioners, but couple this with a signature style and the field narrows. The designers who fulfill these two criteria will be familiar to any *Eye* reader; many of them have been featured in the magazine. (And, of course, selective republishing of certain work and exclusion of other construct a stylistically consistent oeuvre.) The list would probably include Fabien Baron, Tibor Kalman, David Carson, Neville Brody, Edward Fella, Anthon Beeke, Pierre Bernard, Gert Dumbar, Tadanori Yokoo, Vaughan Oliver, Rick Valicenti, April Greiman, Jan van Toorn, Wolfgang Weingart and many others. But great technique and style alone do not an auteur make. If we add the requirement of *interior meaning,* how does the list fare? Are these designers who, by special treatment and choice of projects, approach the issue of deeper meaning in the way a Bergman, Hitchcock or Welles does?

How do you compare a film poster with the film itself? The very scale of a cinematic project allows for a sweep of vision not possible in graphic design. Therefore graphic auteurs, almost by definition, would have to have produced large, established bodies of work in which discernible patterns emerge. Who, then, are the graphic auteurs? Perhaps Bernard Van Toorn, possibly Oliver, Beeke and Fella. There is a sense of getting at a bigger idea, a deeper quality to their work, aided in the case of Bernard and Van Toorn by their political affiliations and in Oliver by long association with a record company that produces a consistent genre of music, allowing for a range of experimentation. In these cases the graphic auteur both seeks projects that fit his vision and approaches projects he is commissioned to work on from a specific, recognizable critical perspective. Van Toorn will look at a brief for a corporate annual report from a socioeconomic position; Bernard evokes an image of class struggle, capitalist brutality and social dysfunction; and Oliver examines dark issues of decay, rapture and the human body. Jean Renoir observed that an artistic director spends his whole career remaking variations on the same film.

Great stylists such as Carson and Baron do not seem to qualify for admission to the auteur pantheon, at least according to Sarris's criteria, as it is difficult to discern a message in their work that transcends the stylistic elegance of the typography in the case of Baron and the studied inelegance in that of Carson. (You have to ask yourself, "What is their work about?") Valicenti and Brody try to inject inner meaning into their work—as in Valicenti's self-published AIDS advertising and Brody's attachment to post-linguistic alphabet systems—but their output remains impervious to any such intrusion. A judgment such as this, however, brings us to the Achilles' heel of auteur theory. In trying to describe interior meaning, Sarris resorts to "the intangible difference between one personality and another."[14] That retreat to intangibility—the "I can't say what it is but I know it when I see it" aspect—is one of the reasons why the theory has long since fallen into disfavor in film criticism circles. It also never dealt adequately with the collaborative nature of cinema and the messy problems of moviemaking. But while the theory is passé, its effect is still with us: the director to this day sits squarely at the center of our perception of film structure. In the same way it could be that we have been applying a modified graphic auteur theory for years without being aware of it. After all, what is design history if not a series of critical elevations and demotions as our attitudes about style, meaning and significance evolve?

OTHER MODELS OF AUTHORSHIP

Auteur theory may be too limited a model for our current image of design authorship, but there are other ways to frame the issue based on different kinds of practice: the artist's book, concrete poetry, political activism, publishing, illustration and so on. Could a theory of poetics be a functional model? Use is a major sticking point in trying to view designed work as poetic: traditionally the poem or artwork is a self-contained artifact, while design refers to some exterior function or overt intention.

This poetic-practical opposition is resolved in two examples of design production: the artist's book and activist design. The artist's book offers a form of design authorship from which function has been fully exorcised. The artist's book, in general, is concrete, self-referential and allows for a range of visual experiments without the burden of fulfilling mundane commercial tasks. There is a long tradition of artists' books through the historical avant-garde, the Situationists, Fluxus and experimental publishing in the 1960s and 1970s. Its exponents include an eclectic mix of designers and authors (Diter Rot, Tom Phillips, Warren Lehrer, Tom Ockerse, Johanna Drucker) as well as visual artists (Robert Morris, Barbara Kruger, Mary Kelly, Jenny Holzer, Hans Haacke). Diter Rot has produced a monumental and consistent body of books which explore, in a self-reflexive way, the nature of books. Lehrer has focused on production processes, such as printing and binding, and aspects of dialogue and narrative. He has recently produced a new group of graphic portraits, distributed in the form of a trade paperback, perhaps the most ambitious recent attempt at wide distribution.

Artists' books—using words, images, structure and material to tell a story or invoke an emotion—may be the purest form of graphic authorship. But the odd thing about the genre is that many of the most skilled designers have avoided it and much of the work produced under the rubric is of substandard graphic quality (not in terms of production values, which are often necessarily low, but in typography and composition). The singularity of the artist's book, the low technical quality and the absence of a practical application may alienate the professional graphic designer.

If the difference between poetry and practical messages is that the latter are successful only when we correctly infer the intention, then activist design would be labeled as absolutely practical. But activist work—including the output of Gran Fury, Bureau, Women's Action Coalition, General Idea, ACT-UP, Class Action, and the Guerrilla Girls—is also self-motivated and self-authored within a clear political agenda. Proactive work has a voice and message, but in its overt intentionality lacks the self-referentiality of the artist's book. Yet several problems cloud the issue of authored activism, not least the question of collaboration. Whose voice is speaking? Not an individual, but some kind of unified community. Is this work open for interpretation, or is its point the brutal transmission of a specific message? The rise of activist authorship has complicated the whole idea of authorship as a kind of free self-expression.

Perhaps the graphic author is one who writes and publishes material about design—Josef Müller-Brockmann or Rudy VanderLans, Paul Rand or Erik Spiekermann, William Morris or Neville Brody, Robin Kinross or Ellen Lupton. The entrepreneurial arm of authorship affords the possibility of a personal voice and wide distribution. Most split the activities into three discreet actions: editing, writing and designing. Even as their own clients, the design remains the vehicle for the written thought. (Kinross, for instance, works as a historian then changes hats and becomes a typographer.) Rudy VanderLans is perhaps the purest of the entrepreneurial authors, since in *Emigre* all three activities blend into a contiguous whole. In *Emigre* the content is deeply embedded in the form— that is, the formal exploration is as much the content of the magazine as the writing. VanderLans expresses his message through the selection of material (as an editor), the content of the writing (as a writer) and the form of the pages and typography (as a form-giver).

Ellen Lupton and her partner J. Abbott Miller have almost single-handedly constructed the new critical approach to graphic design, coupled with an exploratory practice. A project such as "The Bathroom, the Kitchen and the Aesthetics of Waste," an exhibition at the M.I.T. List Visual Arts Center, seems to approach a new level of graphic authorship. The message is expressed equally through graphic-visual devices and text. The design of the show evokes the issues that are its content; it is clearly self-reflexive. (The exhibition catalog, by contrast, does not embody the same level of graphic authorship. Here Lupton and Miller seem to have slipped back into the more familiar, functionally separate roles of author and designer.) But much of their other work demands to be reckoned with, visually and verbally.

While Lupton and Miller's work is primarily critical—a reading of exterior social and historical phenomena directed at a specific audience—the illustrated book, often overlooked by the design community, is almost entirely concerned with the generation of a creative narrative. Books for children have been one of the most successful outlets, but author-illustrators such as Sue Coe, Art Spiegelman, Charles Burns, Ben

Katchor, David McCaulley, Chris van Allesberg, Edward Gorey and Maurice Sendak have also used the book in wholly inventive ways and produced serious work. Books such as Spiegelman's *Maus* and Coe's *X* and *Porkopolis* expand the form into new areas.

Other models that may indicate a level of graphic authorship include projects of such a scale that the designer is called on to make sense of a sea of material and construct a narrative. Bruce Mau's work with Rem Koolhaas on the gigantic *S,M,L,XL*, an architectural and typographic "novel" (see *Eye*, no. 20), and Irma Boom's five-year commission from a powerful Dutch corporation to create a commemorative work of unspecified form, scale and content are two such projects. Here the designer—working like a film director on the unfolding cinematic structure of the work—assumes a primary position in the shaping of the material.

The final category is that of designers who use the medium of professional graphic design to create self-referential statements and compositions. Examples include April Greiman's special issue of *Design Quarterly* (no. 130, 1985), a full-scale image of her pixilated body with a personal text full of dreams and visions, and any number of intricate and enigmatic works by the likes of Tom Bonauro and Allen Hori (for instance, Hori's graphic interpretation of a Beatrice Warde essay in a recent Mohawk paper promotion). Operating in a space between service-oriented projects and free expression, these works eschew the parameters of a client relationship while retaining the forms dictated by the needs of commerce: the book, poster, exhibition and so on. In the case of Hori's visual essay, the client pays for a graphic work to embellish a corporate project and the designer lends his avant-garde credentials to the corporation.

FORWARD OR BACKWARDS?

If the ways a designer can be an author are complex and confused, the way designers have used the term and the value ascribed to it are equally so. Any number of recent statements claim authorship as the panacea to the woes of the brow-beaten designer. A recent call-for-entries for a design exhibition entitled "Designer as Author: Voices and Visions" sought to identify "graphic designers who are engaged in work that transcends the traditional service-oriented commercial production, and who pursue projects that are personal, social or investigative in nature."[15] The rejection of the role of the facilitator and call to "transcend" traditional production imply that authored design holds some higher, purer purpose. The amplification of the personal voice legitimizes design as equal to more traditionally privileged forms of authorship.

But if designers should aim for open readings and free textual interpretations—as a litany of contemporary theorists have convinced us—that desire is thwarted by oppositional theories of authorship. Foucault noted that the figure of the author is not a particularly liberating one: the author as origin, authority and ultimate owner of the text guards against the free will of the reader. Transferring the authority of the text back to the author contains and categorizes the work, narrowing the possibilities for interpretation. The figure of the author reconfirms the traditional idea of the genius creator; the status of the creator frames the work and imbues it with mythical value.

While some claims for authorship may be simply an indication of a renewed sense of responsibility, at times they seem ploys to gain property rights, attempts to exercise some kind of agency where there has traditionally been none. Ultimately the author equals authority. While the longing for graphic authorship may be the longing for legitimacy or power, is celebrating the designer as a central character necessarily a positive move? Isn't that what has fueled the last fifty years of design history? If we really want to go beyond the designer-as-hero model, we may have to imagine a time when we can ask, "What difference does it make who designed it?"

On the other hand, work is created by someone. (All those calls for the death of the author are made by famous authors.) While the development and definition of artistic styles, and their identification and classification, are at the heart of an outmoded modernist criticism, we must still work to engage these problems in new ways. It may be that the real challenge is to embrace the multiplicity of methods—artistic and commercial, individual and collaborative—that comprise design language. An examination of the designer-as-author could help us to rethink process, expand design methods, and elaborate our historical frame to include all forms of graphic discourse. But while theories of graphic authorship may change the way work is made, the primary concern of both the viewer and critic is not *who* made it, but rather *what* it does and *how* it does it.

Notes

1. W. K. Wimsatt and Monroe C. Beardsley, "The Intentional Fallacy," in *Critical Theory since Plato*, ed. Hazard Adams (New York: Harcourt Brace Jovanovich, 1971).
2. Roland Barthes, "The Death of the Author," in *Image-Music-Text*, trans. Stephan Heath (New York: Hill and Wang, 1977).
3. Michel Foucault, "What Is an Author?" in *Textual Strategies*, ed. Josué Harari (Ithaca, N.Y.: Cornell University Press, 1979).
4. Barthes, "Death of the Author," p. 145.
5. Foucault, "What Is an Author?" p. 160.
6. Fredric Jameson quoted in Mark Dery, "The Persistence of Industrial Memory," *Architecture New York*, no. 10: 25.
7. Katherine McCoy, "The New Discourse," *Design Quarterly*, no. 148 (1990): 16.
8. Barthes, "Death of the Author," p. 146.
9. Ellen Lupton and J. Abbott Miller, "Deconstruction and Graphic Design: History Meets Theory," *Visible Language* 28, no. 4 (Autumn 1994): 352.
10. Paul de Man, "Semiology and Rhetoric," in *Textual Strategies*, p. 121.
11. Josef Müller-Brockmann, *Grid Systems in Graphic Design* (Stuttgart, Germany: Verlag Gerd Hatje, 1981), p. 10.
12. *Cahiers du cinéma*, no. 31 (January 1954).
13. See Andrew Sarris, *The Primal Screen* (New York: Simon & Schuster, 1973).
14. Andrew Sarris, "Notes on the Auteur Theory in 1962," in *Film Culture Reader*, ed. P. Adams Sitney (New York: Praeger Publishers, 1970), p. 133.
15. "Re:Quest for Submissions" to the "Designer as Author: Voices and Visions" exhibition, Northern Kentucky University, 8 February to 8 March 1996.

BATTLE OF THE BIG BOOKS
Rick Poynor

Traditionally, books signify cultural value. Simply stated, if there is a book about you, your work must be more important than most. For designers, the lavish, self-designed, celebratory monograph, produced by a reputable publisher, is first and foremost a sign that they have made it. Whether about Paul Rand or Pentagram, Neville Brody or David Carson, books are the single most effective assertion of design-world significance—an unbeatable way of cementing a pre-eminent position for present-day colleagues and for design historians to come.

Fall 2000 saw the biggest seasonal crop of designer monographs in years—perhaps ever—with new books on Bruce Mau (Phaidon), John Maeda (Thames and Hudson), Milton Glaser (Overlook), Wolfgang Weingart (Lars Müller) and Vaughan Oliver (Booth-Clibborn). New titles from Bill Cahan, Ed Fella, Steven Tolleson (all from Princeton Architectural Press), Fuel (Laurence King), Art Chantry (Chronicle) and another Seattle-based design provocateur, Shawn Wolfe (Gingko), have also hit the stores in recent months. *Made You Look*, the collected inspirations of Stefan Sagmeister, is scheduled for delivery any moment now (Booth-Clibborn), and it's a safe bet that many other designers will be plotting to document their brilliance between hard or soft covers in the coming year.

Looking at this seductive parade of titles, it's easy to forget that the honor and privilege of the full-blown monograph was once accorded to only the most Olympian and unanimously acclaimed designers. From 1946 to 1996, Rand published four new titles and one reissue, and Steven Heller's weighty 1999 posthumous monograph for Phaidon (a much rarer category of design book) underpinned his unassailable place in the pantheon. Operating at a slightly brisker clip, Pentagram's ever-expanding phalanx of partners continue to record their design conquests at six- to eight-year intervals, with escalating lavishness, though their latest volume's title, *Pentagram Book Five* (Monacelli, 1999), suggested a certain weariness had set in.

In recent years, the cycle has accelerated. The drive for publicity is much stronger, and monographs now arrive mid-career, or even earlier. In 1988, jaws dropped when a youthful design maverick called Neville Brody released a commanding retrospective survey of his work—at the tender age of 30. Six years later, in 1994, it was joined on the shelf by a second, equally confident and substantial Brody tome. This is a comparatively laid-back publishing program, though, compared to David Carson's. His self-generated output includes monographs that have come out in 1995, 1997, 1999 and

---

Originally published in *Trace: AIGA Journal of Design* Vol. 1, no. 1 (2001).

2000 (a re-issue). It took Paul Rand almost forty years to get around to publishing this number of titles.

That the market can sustain such an embarrassment of riches confirms the speed with which the international design book audience is currently growing. But the phenomenon also contains inherent problems and dangers. As more designers produce monographs and the monograph shows signs in some quarters of becoming a biennial reflex, so its power as a signifier of achievement and value is reduced. How, then, can new arrivals to the publishing pantheon distinguish their own volumes from the now routine, 200-page, large-format softback? The answer: by making theirs thicker, heftier, more serious-looking. In 1998, *Tibor Kalman: Perverse Optimist*, edited by Peter Hall and Michael Bierut, readily sacrificed the customary big page, normally chosen for showing pictures, for sheer quantity of pages—420 all told—and width of spine, accentuated by a no-nonsense hardback binding. *Pentagram Book Five*, published the following year, was even chunkier.

If these heavyweights seemed to have been inspired by Bruce Mau's approach to the Rem Koolhaas collaboration *S,M,L,XL* (Monacelli, 1995), it was left to Mau himself to wheel bigness into action with the flourish of a man who feels he owns it. Mau's recent *Life Style* is 624 pages long, has a spine width of two-and-a-quarter space-consuming inches and a choice of eight glossy satin covers. If scale alone were a reliable guide to intrinsic merit, Mau would appear to be the most important graphic designer the world has ever seen. As an object, *Life Style* is preposterously overblown, but as a media attention-getter it worked brilliantly. By the end of 2000, *Time* was nominating it as one of its ten best designs of the year—the only item of graphic design to be featured—alongside Jim Polshek's Rose Center for Earth and Space, Herzog and de Meuron's Tate Modern gallery and the NIKEiD customized sneaker. To designers, it might not seem especially strange that a book's style of binding should assume such centrality. From this perspective, Mau's fetching collection of liveries could even be seen as a triumph for design over drab book-industry convention.

What it also illustrates, in the most tangible terms, is the way that the designer monograph is no ordinary genre of book. Filmmakers, photographers or artists might expect to have a say in the way their visual material is presented in book form, but they could never control the visual format and delivery as fully as a graphic designer can. Nor would they be likely to see the book itself as an extension of their oeuvre. Yet that's how designers quite naturally tend to treat their monographs, and they and their publishers are doubtless right to assume that many fellow designers will buy the books partly for this reason, rather than simply because they want to look at and read the content.

Some books, such as Mau's *Life Style*, Glaser's *Art Is Work*, John Maeda's *Maeda @ Media* and Wolfgang Weingart's *Typography*, are written, as well as designed, by the designer, perhaps with the help of in-house assistants and editors. Others are effectively authorless, with brief, upbeat, flavorless introductions commissioned by the designers themselves (as opposed to the publishing house's editor), as in the British firm Why Not's *Why Not?* (Booth-Clibborn, 1998). Sometimes, as with the Vignellis' *design: Vignelli* (Rizzoli, 1990) or *Perverse Optimist*, there is a range of editorial contributions by different writers. Kalman's book has credited editors; the Vignellis' doesn't. Either way, designer monographs present unusual, if not inherently dubious, editorial situations, with the texts passing through their subjects' hands. One is entitled to ask how independent—let alone argumentative—such pieces of writing could possibly be.

In the case of the Kalman book, I can offer an answer because I was one of the contributors. No attempt was made to influence or alter the writing of my text. If it had been, I would have argued the case and, if necessary, withdrawn. On the other hand, if, as a writer, you wanted to attack the subject of the monograph (which I didn't), this is hardly the forum to pick. A writer's presence between the book's covers necessarily signals some degree of sympathy and support. That doesn't mean the text can't be robust, independent-minded and written in a spirit of detached critical inquiry.

For the writer, these problems grow in proportion to the size of the text. To date, despite the vogue for monographs, few independently authored studies of graphic designers have appeared. Even those with a high degree of involvement by a single writer have elements of ambiguity that are almost inevitable when the subject is involved in creating the book. For instance, Jon Wozencroft, a collaborator of Brody's on other projects, wrote the lengthy texts for both Brody books, but his name doesn't appear on the front covers, where this would be most clearly signaled, though it does on the spines and title pages. The books are obviously about Brody, but Brody is also implied coauthor, with back-flap "author" blurb, in addition to front-flap and back-cover copy. It's unclear to what degree Wozencroft's authorial views influenced the books' visual form. Yet the selection and placement of visual examples is critical to any interpretation of a design subject.

Again, I have experienced these issues from the inside. *Vaughan Oliver: Visceral Pleasures*, my book about the British music graphics designer, is an attempt to produce a unified, independent, critical view of a designer's body of work. The text is fairly long for this kind of book—18,000 words, divided into three essays. It was understood from the outset that Oliver would read the completed text and indicate any factual errors, but that all matters of opinion and interpretation were my own. Considerable trust is necessary, on both sides, before such an agreement can be reached. I devised the book's structure, and selected and positioned the images within the essays, with design input from Oliver's studio. The picture editing, visual sequencing and pacing of the rest of the book is a collaboration between author and subject.

When we first discussed the project, it was assumed by both designer and publisher that the book would be a spectacular "Vaughan Oliver" in its own right. Yet, too often in self-designed monographs, the designer's inability to let the material speak for itself gets in the way. Designers find it hard to believe that just showing the work that made them famous in the first place, with some space around it, is frequently enough for the reader. They are terrified of being "boring." As a result, it's often impossible to see the work—the book's supposed subject—properly at all, while frenetic, jigsaw-puzzle layouts sabotage all attempts to concentrate on the accompanying text. Even a book as apparently lucid in its typography and design as Mau's *Life Style* is guilty of distorting the imagery. Mau's immersive approach to page layout—with huge, full-bleed, blow-up details—makes it hard to gain a sense of what many of these projects are really like, unless one happens to know them already, which cannot be assumed. In the end, after much debate, Oliver came round to the view that both oeuvre and reader were best served by showing his designs clearly, in relationships that illuminated, rather than masked, recurrent approaches, tropes and themes.

Much as graphic designers would love to be taken seriously as cultural producers, the monograph remains, even at its purest, a compromised form. It mingles motivations—the desire for critical credibility, the need for self-promotion, the urge to show off to colleagues and cut a dash—that cannot ultimately be reconciled. For all design book publishing's conventions—the monograph as ready-made design opportunity, the designer's habitual wish to reinvent the wheel—the preconceptions of readers and reviewers in the world outside design carry more weight. Books do have to look reasonably serious if they aspire to be more than transient eyewash and hope to stand a chance of finding a place at culture's high table. Seriousness can, of course, be stylish, but a degree of restraint must be accepted if critical credibility is truly the goal.

My own view—I recognize it has few takers at this point among those aiming to be monographed—is that design criticism will only mature when designers let go of their material and allow others to design, as well as edit and write, the books. The monographs with most authority—Heller's *Paul Rand*; Roger Remington's *Lester Beall*; Martha Scotford's *Cipe Pineles*; Robin Kinross's recent *Anthony Froshaug*—are almost always about designers who are no longer with us. Why? Because only then do the authors have a largely free hand (though there are usually still family members to satisfy). A superb example of the same treatment, applied for once to a living designer, is Frederike Huygen and Hugues Boekraad's *Wim Crouwel—Mode en Module* (010, 1997), sensitively designed by Karel Martens and Jaap van Triest. Crouwel, one of the finest post-war Dutch designers, ended his career as a museum director, and perhaps this is how he acquired the perspective to see that permitting others to do the job makes for a more convincing and durable book. Too bad it's only available in Dutch.

Perhaps it would also help if designer monographs, having reached some kind of wild apogee with *Life Style*, now began to contract. The Crouwel and Froshaug books combine modest, readerly dimensions with an exceptional, well-ordered density of content. They retain, in both meanings of the word, a sense of proportion and eschew tiresome, distracting hype. In these books, small is not only beautiful—it's serious, too.

ALL HAIL MAU THE MAGNIFICENT
Robert Fulford

When nearly everyone agrees on any given proposition, there's certain to be a flaw in it. Most of the people who write on design and related matters have decided that Bruce Mau, the Toronto graphic artist, has vital things to say about mass society, consumerism, and the way we live. This view of him as a thinker began appearing last spring, after journalists saw a large-scale art work called *STRESS*, which he did for a festival in Vienna; its main point was that contemporary society is pretty damn stressful. Last autumn [in 2000] his status as philosopher was heightened by the appearance of his book *Life Style* (Phaidon Press), in a burst of publicity. Now he's entrenched as a guru, with the clippings to prove it.

But to qualify as a thinker it's usually necessary to put forward ideas that have not already been published, thoughts that are new to readers interested in your subject. I have carefully searched Mau's work (*STRESS, Life Style,* his Web site, and various interviews and feature stories) without discovering a single thought that has not already been widely stated and explored.

Life Style expresses, in a worried and fretful sort of way, the familiar belief that commercial imagery has invaded our collective imagination, forcing us to live under the power of brands and logos. Along with that main point, the book contains several distinct elements. One is a manifesto containing Mau's suggestions for encouraging creative growth, a collection of notions that he's published before and on one occasion read in public. He and his editors have spread it across four pages of *Life Style,* apparently unaware that it's crammed with brain-numbing banality.

"You have to be willing to grow" is a typical piece of wisdom. Another is "Go deep. The deeper you go the more likely you will discover something of value." He gets more complicated when he says, "Don't be cool. Cool is conservative fear dressed in black. Free yourself from limits of this sort." From Mau that's an odd (and unexplained) remark, since his work defines cool for many designers and appears calculated to look as cool as possible.

Mau has a way of picking ideas out of the air without necessarily knowing their origin. He advises us, "Work the metaphor. Every object has the capacity to stand for something other than what is apparent." Does he realize that this is a paraphrase of Freud? If he does, he doesn't say so. One statement must have been clipped from an old *Reader's Digest*: "Today is the child of yesterday and the parent of tomorrow."

He tells us how to absorb a book: "Read only left-hand pages." Marshall

Originally published in the *National Post*, 13 March 2001, Arts and Life section.

McLuhan claimed he read that way, and Mau reports that it limits the information entering our heads, thereby leaving room to think. Would this be one of the passages that
made Herbert Muschamp of the *New York Times* call Mau a friend of the book?

Last October, Muschamp, a Mau admirer, declared that "*Life Style* is a designer's
celebration of the book . . . While perceived by some as trendy, Mau has a staunchly traditional attachment to the printed page." But you do not celebrate books with a
leviathan like *Life Style,* a work so massive that it's far more likely to intimidate than
stimulate.

It's so heavy that only athletes can hold it in their hands; it causes discomfort if
it sits on your lap for more than fifteen minutes; and you wouldn't dream of reading it
on a subway or a plane. It requires total commitment: you put it on a desk, lean over
and pick your way through it. In other words, treat it like a precious medieval manuscript in a library. A note on the back describes it as "a singular album of playful and
critical statements." Playful? A book this heavy-handed is about as playful as a rhinoc-
eros. Whatever Mau's message, it's overwhelmed by his medium. *Life Style* may be the
most pretentious piece of bookmaking since Yousuf Karsh's last search-for-greatness
collection of portrait photos.

Those who make the effort to read it will discover they are spending all this
time on an elaborate exercise in self-congratulation, a designer's promotion piece.
Mainly, it catalogues Mau's work. He discusses at length many projects completed for
distinguished clients (Zone Books, the Andy Warhol Museum, *I.D.* magazine, the Getty
Research Institute, Indigo Books), explaining the problems he and his colleagues faced
and what they learned by solving them.

The designs that emerge from his studio are indeed impressive, though perhaps
not impressive enough to bear the weight of Mau's self-regard. Speaking of *S,M,L,XL,*
the 1,376-page book that he and Dutch architect Rem Koolhaas produced on the subject of Koolhaas's work, Mau writes: "I have simultaneously expanded the role of the
designer and made it invisible" (*Life Style*).

Expanded, yes. Invisible, no. With that book, Mau became the first designer ever
to receive equal credit on the jacket with the person who was both author and subject,
Koolhaas.

Life Style is expertly designed in most ways, but the images tend to be repeti-
tive, and sometimes it falls into the kind of art director errors in readability that drive
readers crazy, like printing text in white on colored backgrounds (at least it's his own
text, so maybe he feels entitled to make it inaccessible to the rest of us).

Mau's career has turned into one of the more bizarre stories in the history of
graphic design. He starts out (in the 1980s) as the kind of designer that writers, editors
and publishers dream about and love to work with: he understands much of what they
do and actually wants to read their texts. But he slowly twists this dream into a night-
mare by Mary Shelley. In the story as Mau re-enacts it, Dr. Frankenstein's creation not
only comes triumphantly to life but takes over the laboratory and announces that he
will henceforth use it as the basis of his own scientific career.

No one should suggest that Mau is an emperor without clothes. My point is that he wears the wrong clothes. He's a talented designer who now stands before us costumed as a philosopher, a social critic and an artist. In these roles he appears to have nothing to say.

HALF EMPTY
Thomas Frank

T ibor Kalman is a graphic designer, a crafter of corporate logos, a producer of presentation materials, a maker of menus and restaurant posters. But Tibor Kalman is so much more than that.

According to most of those who judge such things (with whom I concur, by the way), he is accomplished, even brilliant at what he does. He may even be the greatest graphic designer of his generation. Certainly his output of the last twenty years, just collected in the three-and-a-half-pound book *Perverse Optimist* (Princeton Architectural Press), sparkles with witty solutions to the problems typical of corporate presentation. But why stop there? Kalman is, we are told, a *radical*—a breaker of rules, a dealer in astonishment, a deft questioner of the corporate order. In a manifesto coauthored in 1990, he insisted that graphic designers be "bad," "disobedient," "insubordinate," that they refuse to be "a cog in the machine," that they must make clients "think about design that's dangerous and unpredictable." It's no surprise that accounts of Kalman's oeuvre take pains to note his SDS exploits in the late '60s.

The question that inevitably arises, though, is why a corporation should be so keen to hire a "radical" graphic designer. What makes Kalman's radicalism, such as it is, a desirable quality in what is possibly the most constrained branch of creative endeavor? What does "radicalism" even mean in such a field? It certainly isn't readily apparent from his work. What impresses one first about *Perverse Optimist* is not Kalman's radicalism but his weird omnipresence in the most modish precincts of corporate-sponsored culture of the last two decades. Here is his work for the Talking Heads, here his ironic celebration of the commercial "vernacular," here his packaging of David Byrne's latest world-beat exoticisms, here his work for some hip restaurant or gentrification scheme, for *Interview* magazine, for the movie *Something Wild,* for the Times Square redevelopment project, for the Benetton clothing company's magazine *Colors*. (Here is even late-'80s *Artforum!*) All that's missing is *Wired* magazine—for whom, it turns out, Kalman did indeed work, although it is not included in the book.

Originally published in *Artforum* (February 1999).

It's an amazing track record, an almost flawless string of loud but empty gestures. Beyond Kalman's brilliance, the book is a parade of horrors, a reminder of all the things that were celebrated as authentic and transgressive over the last twenty years—each looking hollow, craven, and embarrassingly wrong with age. Look, for example, at Kalman's 1989 work for "Red Square," the spiffy housing project that was plunked down right in the middle of the Lower East Side. Brochures celebrated the neighborhood's authenticity, its hardness, its bohemian goings-on ("It's not to be confused with the *Upper East Side*" declared one brochure; another fantasized about ready access to "after-hours clubs," "Dutch models," "semifamous guitarists," and "young account executives . . . out to conquer the world"). "Red Square" permitted affluent folks to participate in the neighborhood's fun lifestyle radicalism—poetry slams, expensive leather jackets, safe deviance, bars with Talking Heads records on the jukebox—while forcing the nasty nuts-and-bolts radicals who made the neighborhood "colorful" in the first place off into the hinter boroughs. The project functioned as an efficient factory for the domestication of dissidence, all while a towering zany Kalman-trademark clock whimsically transgressed temporal boundaries overhead. Now *that's* what I call culture war.

Kalman may be best known for *Colors* magazine, that triumph of agitprop emptiness published by Benetton and edited by the graphic designer from 1991 to 1995. It carried almost no advertising and was made up largely of startling photographs overprinted with bombastic slogans, most of them hectoring readers in several tongues and at several decibels on some simple lesson in elementary-school civics. Many have pointed out that *Colors* served fairly transparently as an extension of the famous Benetton advertising campaign, in which the sweater manufacturer, like so many other concerns in recent years, sought to identify its products with some unmistakably good bit of goodness. The consensus is that Kalman's "radicalism" shines through nevertheless, that somehow *Colors* subverts the corporate project. What I found, though, was the opposite: Powerful images and strong language skillfully combined in the service of fatuous corporate sentiment. A consistent tendency to reduce every question to a gesture, to something you don as easily and as unproblematically as a Benetton sweater. A bullying species of what critic Chris Lehmann has called "lifestyle Leninism," in which a simplistic, ultra-virtuous multiculturalism is presented repetitively as the solution to almost everything. But are we really confronting corporate interests when we trumpet the cultural benefits of open borders (a position so transgressive that *The Wall Street Journal* shares it)? Or was Kalman's *Colors*—its pages crowded with businessmen-heroes and schoolboy pranks (the designer once retouched a photo of the queen of England so that she appeared to be black; *Perverse Optimist* revels in how this gesture "outraged" various prudes)—simply an effort to capture the smug righteousness of Reform for the globalizing corporate world, another machine for separating the glam of lifestyle "radicalism" from any actions that might actually pose a challenge to the Benettons of the world?

Were one to restrict his or her reading of *Perverse Optimist* to Kalman's writing and remarks in interviews, though, one might easily take him for the dead-on (if less than subtle) critic of capitalism he purports to be. He begins the book with a double-barreled blast at the culture industry, declaring that "consumer culture is an oxymoron" and "most media, architecture, design and art exist for the sole purpose of creating wealth." "Corporations have become the sole arbiters of cultural ideas and taste in America," Kalman tartly observes in an essay titled "Fuck Committees." "Our culture is corporate culture." We hardly need him to tell us this, but given his embeddedness in the center of it all, we begin to expect great revelations.

But we are disappointed almost immediately. Kalman actually argues that the only capable challenge to the total-corporate world is from . . . corporations. Or, to be precise, good-hearted entrepreneurs and CEOs, those Benettons who are willing to sink enormous money into the work of people like Kalman. His manifesto concludes by mourning the disappearance of the really, really big philanthropists and advising readers to seek out "lunatic entrepreneurs," persuade them to bankroll our projects, "treat them well and use their money to change the world." There's Rolf Fehlbaum of the Swiss office-furniture concern Vitra, whose adventurous projects and openness to innovation are the subject of a 590-page montage-homage that Kalman put together in 1997. That book was whimsically entitled *Chairman Rolf Fehlbaum* and designed to resemble those little red books from the '60s, but that is where Kalman's romance with Marxism ends. "I think you can be political only when you're privileged," Kalman opines at one point in *Perverse Optimist*. "The agent of social change," he declares in *Wired,* "is the corporation." Historical agency is a thing reserved for capitalists and their hired pens, whom Kalman suggests that we "trick . . . into doing socially responsible things." This may seem like a fairly realistic vision of culture and corporate responsibility to those whose world is underwritten by foundations and errant millionaires, but as a description of the way history works, it stinks.

Beneath this curious "radicalism" is an oddly dated view of the world of business. In "Fuck Committees," Kalman vents that the "struggle" now is "between individuals with jagged passion in their work and today's faceless corporate committees," and complains that "TV scripts are vetted by producers, advertisers, lawyers, research specialists, layers and layers of paid executives who determine whether the scripts are dumb enough to amuse what they call the 'lowest common denominator.'" But in fact, while it's true that business imperatives determine mass-cultural content, those imperatives are vastly different from what they were in the '60s, when Kalman's passion-versus-hierarchy rap first became popular. Today it's a different story. Embracing nonconformity, practicing transgression, smashing the existing order—these are the clichés of organization these days, repeated every year thousands of times over in hundreds of business magazines and management books, translated into countless pictures and charts and formulas, each one struggling to convince you of the same thing that Kalman apparently believes to be his special revelation and his alone.

What Kalman overlooks is that it is not simply a fluke that a "radical" like him has become one of the most sought-after architects of the corporate facade. It's not even a new phenomenon: All through *Perverse Optimist* one hears echoes of George Lois and Howard Gossage, two of the superstar graphic designers of the '60s (famous for their campaigns for *Esquire* and Irish Whiskey, respectively) who were also fierce critics of American business and who, curiously, were at the height of their powers when

American business actually *was* dominated by the bean-counters and creativity-quashers that Kalman imagines, wrongly, still to be in power today. The best admen, publicists, and designers of the last thirty years have been the self-hating producers, idealistic folk whose disgust with the system for which they toil gives their vision of redemption-through-products an invaluable ring of authenticity. That business allows "radicals" to do its graphic design is not the inexplicable exception, the "crack in the wall" that Kalman believes to be such an opportunity for disruption; it is the rule. And it is the rule for reasons that *Perverse Optimist* makes abundantly clear.

LOST IN SOUND
Rick Poynor

The graphic designer is, by definition, a talent for hire. Designers offer a service and most of them work for a succession of clients. They might do a single job, a small series of jobs or work for several years, off and on, for the same client, but a measure of uncertainty—not knowing where the next commission will come from—is one of the basic conditions of the life. The designer's workload will consist of any number of these relationships, interwoven with each other throughout the week, competing demands that have to be juggled and met. Designers are free to determine the course of their careers, but personal preoccupations and artistic ambitions will need to be adjusted to meet the ebbs and flows of the work that comes through the studio door. Every designer hopes for an ideal client, a relationship that will blossom into a long-term creative union, but in practice these perfect matches are hard to achieve. They require a sympathy, shared taste and understanding between client and designer that is as unpredictable, at the personal level, as the chemistry that makes lasting friendships, or causes people to fall in love. Of course, for this to happen at all, the client must have a steady stream of projects to offer the designer.

Designers who operate in-house for a single organization can often find themselves even more tightly constrained. Any client large enough to afford to maintain its own design department is likely to have definite, if not limiting, ideas about what it expects from its designers. It is not unknown for designers who work in-house to build public reputations for highly personal bodies of work, but such cases are newsworthy exceptions rather than the professional rule.

Originally published as the introduction to *Vaughan Oliver: Visceral Pleasures*, by Rick Poynor (London: Booth-Clibborn Editions, 2000). © 2000 Rick Poynor.

In 2000, Vaughan Oliver's relationship with the independent record label 4AD, based in a south London suburb, was two decades old. Apart from his early days as a young designer new to London, at the start of the 1980s, he has devoted most of his creative passion and energy to the 4AD project. For fifteen years, he was based at 4AD's Wandsworth office in Alma Road and, even though he was a full-time employee for only four years, this remained his studio until 1998. Although Oliver was freelance and worked for other clients during this time—publishers, record labels, theater companies and TV stations—there was never any question that 4AD lay at the heart of his concerns. His eventual departure was undeniably traumatic, but even this did not signify the end of a remarkably durable alliance.

At the age of twenty-three, just starting out, Oliver had the luck to meet his ideal client—Ivo Watts-Russell (known as Ivo), founder of 4AD. Ivo offered him a degree of continuity and a creative freedom that comparatively few designers experience over so many years, if at all. When he took on Oliver, in 1983, there were only two of them on the label. Ivo hoped that Oliver might assist him in a range of tasks, from shifting boxes to record promotion, as well as sleeve design, but Oliver had little intention of doing anything other than design, and Ivo did not complain.[1] They shared a fanatical devotion to independent rock music, and Ivo believed that the label's commitment to quality and respect for its audience should be reflected in the standard of its packaging. Oliver was treated as an artist in his own right, like one of the musicians. Ivo might venture his opinion of a design, when he came across it on the drawing board, but he did not interfere in the design process and still believes that Oliver's strongest work for 4AD came from allowing him to follow his own path.

Designers are often heard to say that they see it as part of their role to "educate" clients about the value of visual communication. In Ivo, Oliver discovered a patron who readily acknowledges that working with him really did amount to a design education. "He made me realize that you can communicate with the packaging a record or CD comes in, both sympathetically and separately from the music," Ivo explains. "As a fan of the music, who enjoys beautiful things, that was a revelation. I love the idea that you're buying a new album and it's something you can love and cherish, not just for the music but also because of the packaging. . . . Funnily enough, I think that contributed heavily to the 4AD sound because it meant there was an identity, both visually and sometimes aurally, coming from this label."[2]

Oliver found it natural to dedicate himself to a project as heartfelt, impassioned and continuously stimulating to him as Ivo's record label. Today, he is one of a handful of contemporary British graphic designers with a genuinely international reputation. Yet to many in design, who perhaps know his name, the exact nature of his achievement remains mysterious. Oliver's primary audience is the legion of music fans around the world, who bought records by the Cocteau Twins, Colourbox, This Mortal Coil, the Pixies, Lush, His Name is Alive and many other 4AD groups, and gradually became aware of the designer behind this extraordinary series of sleeves and posters. To this day, Oliver is as likely to be written up in a music magazine as a design publication. The poster sets and calendars he creates for 4AD and v23 invariably sell out. There aren't many graphic designers whose work is known, sought after and collected by people who aren't designers, and this intimate connection with 4AD's fanbase, as well as his love for the music and freedom to pursue his own path, is what kept him at a tiny record label tucked away in south London for so long.

In recent years, the body of work created by Oliver has acquired a new retrospective significance. The idea that the graphic designer could function as a kind of "author," using client-given work as the vehicle for a personal vision or message, has been implicit in the practice of some designers from the earliest days of the discipline. In the 1990s, these possibilities were theorized in the design schools and vigorously debated in the design press, particularly in the United States.[3] The discipline has now reached a point where many graduating designers take it for granted that a graphic communication should ideally include a measure of self-expression. Away from the safe haven of the degree show, however, out in the commercial world, graphic authorship remains an intoxicating though still largely untested theory. What it would mean in terms of real client relationships goes more or less unexamined, as do the criteria the work itself would need to fulfill before one could say that the designer was fully present in it as an author in the sense that novelists or fine artists are present in their work.

Oliver's designs for music stand out not just because they ravish the eye with their graphic invention and production quality, but because they appear to exhibit the consistency of vision across a body of work that one might expect of a genuine authorial presence. Fellow designers have been quick to recognize—and sometimes to criticize—the powerful sense his projects transmit of private concerns being worked out in the designs, and of a deeper underlying structure of meaning that goes beyond the promotional needs of a group's identity and packaging. "It almost seems as if the vast output from his studio forms part of some grand vision, each element but one piece from a larger canvas, whose ultimate scope is in all probability known only by Vaughan himself," notes Oliver's contemporary, the sleeve designer Malcolm Garrett.[4] The 4AD bands have on occasion made no secret of feeling the same way and have resented, or rejected outright, his highly recognizable graphic signature. Oliver himself is ambivalent on the subject, insisting diplomatically on the "eclectic" nature of his approach. Like any graphic designer acclaimed for being wayward and distinctive, he is caught in a paradox. There is a continuing expectation among clients that designers will have the versatility, and professional humility, to interpret the client's needs *before* doing anything else, but it is the exploration of his own personal vision within a framework where *he* is the constant that has given Oliver creative fulfillment and won him his reputation.

Although he is reluctant, these days, to make personal claims for his position as a graphic author—in the 1980s, determined to be recognized, he was less reticent—Oliver continues to insert himself into his work in an almost Hitchcockian way. On Clan of Xymox's *Medusa* (1986) his face appears as a stone cast, emerging from a pool. On *Pod* by The Breeders (1990), he dances wildly for the camera, adorned in a belt of flailing eels. Few perhaps realized that the bashful young bridegroom with the moustache, on the back of *Universal Frequencies* by His Name is Alive (1996), is none other than

Oliver, seen at his own wedding in 1978. He reappears on the compilation album *Anakin* (1998), a husky montaged onto the back of his familiar shaven head.

Despite Oliver's literal presence in some of his designs, the issue of authorship is far from clear-cut. Graphic design is by its nature a collaborative art. While some of Oliver's sleeves and covers are entirely his own work, many others incorporate the creative contributions of other people. From 1981 to 1987, Oliver operated as a loose alliance with the photographer and video-maker Nigel Grierson, under the deliberately enigmatic title 23 Envelope. The shared credit simply read, "Sleeve by 23 Envelope." There were no individual credit lines until the final days of the partnership when Grierson insisted on a photography credit. Later, the question of who had done what became a source of contention and this book (*Vaughan Oliver: Visceral Pleasures*) attempts to set the record straight, so far as Oliver's and Grierson's memories allow, by retrospectively assigning detailed credits to each project.

From 1988, operating under the new title v23, Oliver worked closely with a number of photographers, among them Simon Larbalestier, Kevin Westenberg, Jim Friedman, Richard Caldicott and Dominic Davies, and used art by Terry Dowling—his former design teacher—and the Japanese artist Shinro Ohtake, who returned the favor by asking him to collaborate on *Tokyo Salamander*, an artist's book. Chris Bigg first visited Oliver at the 23 Envelope studio in 1983, as a student researching album cover designs, and occasionally assisted Oliver over the next few years. He was taken on as a full-time member of v23 in 1988 and has become an increasingly significant contributor to the studio's output in recent years, running many of the projects himself.

The most significant of these collaborations will be discussed in the course of this book. What should be noted here is that Oliver's partnership with Nigel Grierson— the closest and most sustained of his creative relationships with photographers—is a special case. When questions of shared background, education, taste and mutual influence are taken into account, it seems safest to conclude that the artistic vision was also shared and that the original 23 Envelope credit line, by blurring their separate creative identities, functioned as they originally intended, for the most part, by expressing this union.

In the case of the later collaborations, however, a slightly different argument must be made. Even if a photograph already exists in the photographer's portfolio and is not specially commissioned for a design, its meaning will change when it is incorporated alongside other elements (words, typography, rules, boxes, borders and other images), treated as a percentage tint or over-printed by metallic inks. This does not detract from the artistic integrity and power of the photograph when seen in its own right—for instance, on an art gallery wall. But in the design it becomes a new thing. The photograph's contextual relationship to the music it represents, and its place within 4AD's evolving visual identity, add other layers of meaning, moving it even further from its original "pure" state.

The process by which an object or image is transformed by the act of selection, and by its insertion into a new context defined by the artist, is a recurrent theme of twentieth-century art, from Duchamp's urinal to Warhol's boxes of Brillo pads, from Cubist collage elements cut from the daily paper to the Appropriation art of the 1980s, where an artist would simply repaint an earlier artist's picture, without bothering to come up with something "original." There is no reason, in essence, why the same process should not apply to a photograph, whether "found" or commissioned. But it is not easy for the photographer to accept this idea, especially when photographs are generally seen to enjoy higher artistic and cultural status than design in the first place. There is a tendency for the photographer to deal with this implicit demotion and subordination to design by regarding the image as being simply presented or "curated" by the designer and by discounting the mediating effects of the design, even when the picture is overtly manipulated and transformed. Somehow the photographic image is supposed to survive its new, lower context with its intrinsic higher value intact.

If it is accepted that the meaning of a photograph changes when it is introduced into a design, an obvious question arises. Since this will happen regardless, in what way is Oliver's work different from the norm? The argument made in *Vaughan Oliver: Visceral Pleasures* is that one of the factors, among others, that makes Oliver a graphic author is the consistency of vision that emerges from the way that he goes about selecting and commissioning his collaborators, and the way that he then uses the images they provide. The process could, after all, be arbitrary. It might be determined by factors that have little or nothing to do with the designer. Even if the designer were relatively free, there might be no personal continuity at all in the choices made. Being an art director does not automatically make you an artist. Indeed, the traditional rhetoric of design suggests that the designer or art director's personal preoccupations should not play a decisive role if the "objective" needs of the communication are put first. Given the inherently constrained nature of commercial design, even Oliver's portfolio reveals its share of projects compromised by external influences, or lack of full commitment on his part, that cannot be said to display the organic unity of his most personal work.

For graphic authorship to occur in a collaborative commercial setting, all inputs will need to be harnessed to a single synthesizing vision in a way that transcends the randomness of conventional art direction. In this sense, the teamwork of film production, under a director's leadership, is a more useful model for understanding graphic authorship than the practice of fine art (unless it happens to be conducted along Warholian "factory" lines). In the 1950s, the French film director François Truffaut, writing in the film journal *Cahiers du Cinéma*, formulated the so-called politique des auteurs to distinguish between filmmakers responsible for the entire conception of their films—*auteurs*—and those who merely staged and filmed a given script. The idea was taken up by American critics such as Andrew Sarris, author of the essay "Notes on the Auteur Theory in 1962," which identifies three essential conditions of film authorship. At the most basic level, the *auteur* must demonstrate technical competence as a director and his or her films must show recurring characteristics of style that function as a signature. "The way a film looks and moves," explains Sarris, "should have some relationship to the way a director thinks and feels."[5] But these qualities, which can be found in the work of many established directors, are not sufficient to define the *auteur*. To qualify, a director must transform the material of a given project by imposing, visually, his personal preoccupations and enduring themes. It is the ability to imbue a film with interior meaning that separates the *auteur* from the journeyman director. Each of the *auteur's* films can be seen as a development or variation of this central structure or vision.

This is not the place for a long digression on the history of the *auteur* theory as applied to film. Many critics have questioned it, though as one film writer noted, the issue seems less resolved than suppressed.[6] Meanwhile, the assumption of individual authorship, where none perhaps exists, underpins the publicity, presentation and discussion of films. Movie titles proclaim "a film by . . ." in even the most questionable cases, and reviews and interviews routinely promote and celebrate films as the *de facto* creations of their directors. In a culture that applauds every variety of individualism, it should come as no surprise that the author, far from being "dead" as theorists once insisted, is enjoying a field day. An unacknowledged version of the *auteur* theory also seems to underlie the judgments made about the work of some of the more acclaimed designers. Yet while the existence of magazine articles, exhibitions and sometimes even monographs might seem to constitute indisputable proof of authorship, in reality its presence is simply assumed, as though the answer has been given before the question has been asked. An auteurist analysis of an individual designer's body of work, which sets out to discover whether the conditions of authorship have been met, is rarely if ever attempted; to do so would require a working hypothesis as to what those conditions might be.

Oliver is a designer whose most characteristic work is about music. At their most expressive, his designs embody his intense emotional responses to his sensations as a listener. This is by no means always the case with designers of music graphics. Reid Miles, creator in the 1960s of many classic covers for the Blue Note jazz label, never had much enthusiasm for Hard Bop, even though fans regard his graphic rhythms as perfectly in sync with the music. Peter Saville, designer of sleeves for Factory Records, was engaged more by the sub-cultural, stylistic and fashion aspects of the post-punk milieu than by the music itself, and this detachment can be seen in the conceptual control of his designs. For Oliver, the connection with music is much more visceral and intimate. Music is a way of twisting the moment, leaving the mundane reality of the here and now, the world of bills on the doormat, and attaining a more vital state of being beyond rational understanding, beyond the comfortable habits and orderly procedures of everyday life, where reality can be experienced anew, as if looking back from the other side.

"That's generally where music takes me," says Oliver. "That's why I listen to it: to change or enhance my mood, to take me elsewhere. It tickles things in me and takes me into a different state of mind—a dreamlike state. When I'm at a gig, music affects me totally physically and I don't think rationally about how I'm going to describe it. I get images and I would like to leave enough mystery and vagueness in those images for someone else to bring their experience to it. That's why I've been with 4AD for so long, because it has been so natural to me. I would get inspiration from virtually everything that Ivo was giving me. Voosh! It would affect me. I was full. I was somebody else. Inspired."[7]

This intensification of ordinary experience, the sense of being possessed by music, lost in sound, the ego dissolving, blissfully or sometimes darkly adrift in a primal zone of color and image, recurs throughout Oliver's work. Many of these lustrous designs are metaphors for psychic states—reverie, dream, abandonment, ecstasy—attainable through surrender to music. There is a constant emphasis in his selection and use of images on the body as the locus of these physical sensations and on the senses as their transmitters. When Oliver hears music, he sometimes visualizes sound in terms of color, and in his designs aural sensations are often transferred, synaesthetically, to images representing the other senses: sight, touch, taste, even smell—as in a Venus Flytrap, which reeks of meat. Bodily images to which Oliver returns include eyes, hands, the thumb, the toe, the tongue, teeth, hair (shaped as heart, vagina and skull), sexual parts (clitoris, penis) and various kinds of meat—heart, pig's liver, eel, ox tongue, bull's eyes, human stomach lining. As editor of the exhibition catalogue for *This Rimy River*, Oliver gave himself the anagrammatic pseudonym "Vulva O'Reighan." To intensify the sensation of nerve endings in sharp or even painful contact with tactile reality, he uses devices such as bandaging (a preoccupation that first emerged when he was a student),[8] gloves, injury to a thumb, prosthetic devices, surgical instruments, a drill, and a shattered knife, a recurrent image at the mid-point in his career.

Sometimes the body itself is laid bare for the viewer as conductor and conduit. In a poster for a 4AD festival, Oliver uses a photograph of a young woman, naked except for gloves and a blindfold that covers her eyes but not her nostrils or mouth. It isn't an overtly sexual or predatory image, but a metaphor for a private interior state. You can sense the woman's alertness, as her hands reach out to touch air she cannot see. She is listening, but whatever it is she "sees" as she listens, it is concealed behind the blindfold, unfolding on a screen in her head. She is posed against a neutral backdrop—it might be a sheet—and in places the lines of her body begin to soften and blur. Oliver didn't take the photograph himself. He chanced upon the image in a photographer's portfolio, saw its possibilities, chose it and then applied it here, in this way. In another key series of images, shot for Oliver by Kevin Westenberg in 1990, the sensation that the viewer is being plunged into a realm of trance-like inner experience is even more acute as the naked designer, dressed in a belt of eels, enacts his own abandonment to the music. Any sense of the real location in which this is taking place is lost as the dead eels jerk and writhe and his physical features and awareness of self dissolve in the rapture of the moment. His body vibrates in a demented dance and begins to leak away and merge with swirling clouds of color.

For Oliver, these devices originate at a level below conscious apprehension and, like the music that inspires them, they act on the receiver in ways that feel "right," but cannot be rationally explained. Oliver's early experiences as a graphic designer, before committing himself to Ivo and 4AD, convinced him that the discipline, as conventionally taught and practiced, was too orderly and rational to satisfy his longing for other levels of experience. As a teenager, he was drawn to surrealism, and though he would not now describe himself as a surrealist, the movement's visual strategies and favored lexicon of images offer keys to help unlock his work. The surrealists, too, discovered intimations of the sublime in the corporeal reality of the flesh. Surrealist photographers of the 1920s and 1930s explored many of the visual themes towards which Oliver (and his collaborators) also gravitated, sharing the same sensibility, without ever having seen these earlier images. Jacques-André Boiffard, who had been Man Ray's apprentice, photographed a big toe and an open mouth, the tongue glistening with saliva, to illustrate texts by Georges Bataille published in the magazine *Documents*. "[O]n important occasions," writes Bataille, "human life is still bestially concentrated in the mouth."[9] Oliver used similar images by Simon Larbalestier and Dominic Davies for a ballet poster, titled (in a surrealist coincidence) *Paysage après la bataille*, and for His Name is Alive's CD single *Can't Always Be Loved*. In 1935, Raoul Ubac photographed a woman clamping a long piece of liver between her teeth, like an engorged tongue.[10] Oliver put an ox tongue from the butcher on a digital scanner to create the poster for *This Rimy River*. "For me, the tongue is the most important organ," he says. "Speech, language, sex, food: it's used in all those fundamental activities."[11]

In his image-making, Oliver has an instinctive craving for the mysterious convulsive beauty and for the deeply gratifying state of being and heightened awareness that the surrealist poets and painters termed *le merveilleux*. "When seeking the object of its fulfillment," wrote André Breton, "the demands of desire exert a strange power over external phenomena, tending egoistically to admit only that which can serve its purpose."[12] At 4AD, working at the meeting point of design, art, music and popular culture, Oliver was given, and seized, an exceptional opportunity to embrace the "demands of desire." In the mid-1980s, he was one of a handful of design explorers who, by pursuing an intensely personal vision, made a lasting contribution to our understanding of the expressive possibilities of the graphic image.

Notes

1. Copies of draft press releases in Oliver's handwriting in the 4AD files show his involvement in press release writing in the label's early days. He was a sounding-board for Ivo and always ready to offer an opinion. It was Oliver, for instance, who urged Ivo to take on Dead Can Dance, which proved to be one of the label's most successful bands.

2. Quoted in Desmond Sampson, "Do Not Remove This Label," *Pavement*, no. 31 (October/November 1998).

3. See Michael Rock, "The Designer As Author," *Eye* 5, no. 20 (Spring 1996); and a revised version, "Graphic Authorship," in *The Education of a Graphic Designer*, edited by Steven Heller (New York: Allworth Press, 1998), pp. 149–58.

4. Quoted in Vulva O'Reighan, editor, *This Rimy River: Vaughan Oliver and v23* (London: 4AD/v23, 1994) [unpaginated].

5. Andrew Sarris, "Notes on the Auteur Theory in 1962," in *Film Theory and Criticism: Introductory Readings*, ed. Gerald Mast and Marshal Cohen (New York: Oxford University Press, 1974), p. 512.

6. Bill Nichols, editor, *Movies and Methods: An Anthology* (Berkeley and Los Angeles: University of California Press, 1976), p. 221.

7. Interview with the author, 30 June 1999.

8. As a student, Oliver saw photographs of the extreme performances ("actions") staged in the mid-1960s by the Viennese Actionist artist Rudolf Schwarzkogler. He displayed Schwarzkogler's images of bandaged performers in his studio space at Newcastle Polytechnic.

9. Georges Bataille *et al.*, *Encyclopaedia Acephalica* (London: Atlas Press, 1995), p. 62.

10. See Rosalind Krauss and Jane Livingston, *L'Amour Fou: Photography & Surrealism* (London: Arts Council, 1986).

11. Interview with the author, 30 July 1999.

12. Quoted in Roger Cardinal and Robert Stuart Short, *Surrealism: Permanent Revelation* (London and New York: Studio Vista/Dutton, 1970), p. 57.

MEDITATIONS

A t its core, graphic design is all about observation. We look, we notice, we see something others do not, or we see it in a way that others do not. *How* we see what we see is framed by both pragmatic perceptions and prosaic gleanings: if graphic design practice is defined by the former, then its discourse sometimes veers toward the latter, where language itself becomes a visceral mode for expressing visual ideas. Such writing is all about style: the rhythm of the author's voice—like an internal metronome capturing observations and metering their introduction into a text—conjures up images that captivate even as they instruct. To paraphrase Véronique Vienne's engaging view of consumer culture, such writing benefits from the reckless abandon of right-brain creativity with the organizational strengths drawn from the left. Between these two extremes, however, are many kinds of writing: design history, design criticism and perhaps a newer form, and the focus of this section, the design essay.

Graphic designers, as it turns out, observe much more than the visual environment. They question reality and representation, critique language and consider values and moral issues. They examine content, context and the intangible spaces between them. They embrace issues of considerable cultural breadth—the intractable symbolism of the American flag, for instance. And conversely, they target the specificity of topics as seemingly narrow as a single color, hoping to find a window onto larger themes. Thus, this section includes essays as far-ranging as Ralph Caplan's probing look at the sculptures of Duane Hanson, Todd Lief's thoughtful reflection on graffiti and Andrea Codrington's wonderfully obsessive mediation on the color beige.

At their best, the essays collected in this section share the presence of penetrating insights expressed through personal observation: using language to illuminate the vicissitudes of contemporary culture, these writers show us that no subject is too small, no reflection unworthy. They show us inspiration, exasperation, meditation. They show us what becomes of design writing when it is laced with observation that is smart, original and personal. They show us that God is, in fact, in the details.

William Drenttel

GETTING REAL
Ralph Caplan

A poster in a Toronto graphic design competition consisted of two elements: a drawing of a bugle and the following copy:

Is this a bugle?
If not, why not?
If it is, blow it.

I don't know of a more charming expression of the perennial conflict between representational art and objective reality.

Bishop Berkeley, in *Principles of Human Knowledge,* argued that, since representation was all we had to go on, matter does not really exist. This led James Boswell to observe that while Berkeley's position was plainly nonsense, it was just as plainly irrefutable. To which Samuel Johnson replied by kicking a stone in the road and declaring, "Thus I refute Berkeley."

But the dramatic validity of Johnson's demonstration that the stone was real rested on the premise that his foot was real, a proposition easy to believe but difficult to prove to the satisfaction of Berkeley, who remained preposterous but unrefuted.

They cared about such things in the eighteenth century. Do we still? Marshall McLuhan told the story of a woman sitting on a park bench while her children played in the sandbox. A man sitting next to her remarked, "You have such beautiful children." Waving the compliment away disparagingly, she opened her purse and said, "Wait till you see their pictures!"

Wallet-sized and suitable for framing, pictures are always easier to handle than reality, which is messy even when we can't identify it.

Emigré, a new novel by Joan Brady, begins, "Reality? What's so good about it? Where's the structure in it? Nobody wants it. Nobody buys it."

Well, I'd buy it, if I could afford it. To eschew reality carries the penalty of never fully coming to life. Look—as we may have to if he runs again—at Dan Quayle, who is basing his present campaign on the boast, "He was right about Murphy Brown. Family values do matter." Since families matter and values do too, of course he was right. But the slogan misses the point. Quayle was not lampooned for being wrong in defending

Originally published in *Print* Vol. 53, no. 3 (May/June 1999).

the sanctity of families. He was lampooned for picking a fight without noticing (or, since he admitted he had never seen the show in question, without having been told by his sound-bite writers) this his chosen antagonist was a fictional character, while he himself was being presented to the public as a real one. When this was called to his attention, Quayle acknowledged Ms. Brown's unreality but refused to accept it as an excuse for her behavior. Some of us have principles. Jerry Falwell, on the other hand, having become a fictional character himself in *The People vs. Larry Flynt*, was fully qualified to attack the Teletubbies on their own turf.

Lately my interest in reality has been stirred if not shaken by an encounter with the startlingly prosaic sculpture of Duane Hanson. My experience was rooted in a root canal. On the way home from the dentist, I passed the Whitney Museum, where a Hanson retrospective was on view. I have always found his work fascinating for what I assumed were the usual reasons: admiration for photorealistic achievements that, like the J. Seward Johnson sculptures in front of urban buildings around the country, are more real than photos because, being three-dimensional, they can be walked around and bumped into. As with a magician's performance, you know there is a trick to it, but it is no less intriguing for that. Figures like this, I figured, were to be enjoyed one at a time and briefly. It had not occurred to me that a retrospective would heighten their effect, and I had no plan to see the show.

Yet here I was and here they were. I went in. And now that the swelling induced by the root canal has subsided, I am prepared to eat crow. There is more to Hanson than meets the I. A Hanson standing alone is too fleshy to look like sculpture exactly, and too inelegant to pass as the higher form of life that once inspired the dreams our stuff was made on. In *The Tempest*, Miranda, seeing for the first time a man who was neither her father nor a beast, cries "Oh, brave new world, that hath such people in't." Could such a response be elicited by a piece of sculpture? Adonis or David maybe, but never the schlumpy denizens of Hanson's universe. Whatever his creations evoke, it is not the Pygmalion impulse, although that impulse lives on. Open a fashion magazine—and they are almost all fashion magazines—and you see portfolios of people who want to look like manikins and do. Readers in their turn want to look like the models who look like manikins. But no one wants to look like a Duane Hanson. His predilection for bluecollar subjects has been called patronizing (he has been called much worse) on the grounds that he caricatures people who are safely mocked because they are not the kind of people who go to art museums. Don't bet on it. At the Whitney, at least when I was there, the visitors looked unnervingly like the show. So much so in one case that I mistook a man for a work of art. He was, to be sure, an unprepossessing person, and he was standing still in a roomful of what I think were Hansons.

The roomful makes a difference. However individual they seem, these are not representations of particular persons. They are abstractions, just as George Segal's people are. But instead of taking what is there and reducing it by the selective removal of individual attributes as Segal seems to, Hanson reduces the way a chef does, by intensifying essence until nothing is left but the eerily recognizable. If, as has been said, Segal's figures look like ghosts, Hanson's look like ghosts who have retained color and flavor, and are thereby able to show us something about ourselves. His artistry is not in the verisimil-itude but in the shared depth of observation.

Once, in the Nelson Atkins Gallery Museum in Kansas City, I mistook a Hanson for a janitor—but only for a moment. That is apparently so common an experience, there is no point in remarking on it, except that at the Whitney I made the same mis-take, but stayed with it more rewardingly. A wall caption designated a piece entitled "Policeman," but there was no policeman in place there. Usually in such cases, a cura-torial apology explains that the captioned art object has been temporarily removed. As there was no such notice on display, I turned to the guard and asked when the police-man would be restored. He did not answer. He was not a guard. He was "Policeman."

As I turned away in embarrassment from the art cop I had thought was a guard, the man I had thought was a work of art came into the gallery. I was equally embar-rassed to see him, although he could not have known I had thought him unreal any more than "Policeman" could have known I had thought he was a Whitney guard. The man, who was lethargic at best, stood still again. I looked from one to the other. Clearly there was a difference between them, but I could not have said what it was. I had gone through something like this before, and suddenly I remembered where and when.

During my sophomore year in college, I lived and worked in the Klute Funeral Home in Richmond, Indiana. For the most part, living there *was* the work—someone had to be on hand at all times because either state regulations or industry ethics pre-cluded leaving a corpse unattended. As college jobs went, mine was considered a plum. It was better than waiting on tables, and there was plenty of quiet time for study and contemplation. What I studied and contemplated was the corpse in the next room. I had seen dead bodies before but had never had any of them all to myself. They were unlike anyone else I knew, but how exactly? Anyone could see that they were not alive, not asleep, not unconscious, not faking. Something had gone out of them, but what?

I didn't know and still don't. There is an enormous difference between the quick and the dead. Hansons, neither one nor the other, never having lost what was never theirs to lose, may, in time, help illuminate the difference. But I'm not going to hold my breath. They don't.

LEAST DESIGNED AND MOST READ
Quentin Newark

I am ashamed to say that I have said it myself during meetings with clients: "Yes," I say, "people don't read anymore." This phrase is accepted wisdom. The argument behind it goes like this: we are living in the a visual age; in Maurice Blanchot's phrase we are "tireless voyeurs of images," because of MTV and the proliferation of television channels, video games and the Internet; reading is old hat; we just don't have time; and the younger generations, well, they just don't know what reading is.

You can see the effects of this way of thinking in almost all contemporary graphic design. The modern designer and her client utilize an armory of devices, many developed in the world of magazines but now used everywhere to break up any nasty, boring gray text: whopping "headlines," big introductions in child-size type, lots of "pull quotes," subheads, highlighted words, selections of enlarged-type words, second-rate pictures with meaningless captions, icons, abstract graphic shapes (which for some reason are usually pieces of the corporate logo). And if all else fails, use the solution beloved of Web designers: a lovely tint picture all over the background.

Of course we all know the real reason this gets done. It's because a busy, graphically complicated layout is much, much faster and easier than the alternative: good writing with layout and pictures in support. My argument is not in pursuit of a particular style—I don't mean readable design has to look any specific way. Plenty of the most adventurous experimental typographers produce fabulous, easy-to-read magazine, book and Web designs. But within any stylistic approach, its depressingly common for lots of graphic activity on the page having nothing whatsoever to do with helping people understand a news story or a narrative. And decoration is useless when you get past it to read the text—that is either clear or it's not, refreshing or cliché ridden, wry or garbled.

There are exceptions to the domination of graphic flak, mostly in areas that have not yet yielded to whatever the latest in typographic fashion happens to be. Almost all newspapers utilize typography that has only evolved gently over the last 250 years. Novels continue to offer us unrelentingly gray text, untouched by pull quotes, justified in long measures, in painfully unchic typefaces like Centaur, Blado and Plantin. School textbooks, specialist publications, most newsletters, scientific and academic publications, handbooks and manuals, all these tend towards conveying their content to readers with the minimum of typographic trumpet blowing.

Is it any surprise that it is all the material that is least "designed" that is most read?

Originally published in *Design Week*, January 2001.

To say that no one reads anymore is, of course, absolute nonsense. A brief look at book sales is one indication—paradoxically the most popular retailer on the literacy-busting Internet is Amazon, offering its visitors a choice from over one million books. The top hundred selling paperbacks in the United Kingdom last year sold well over a total of 30 million books. And as for the illiterate young, the latest Harry Potter hardback, weighing in at 638 pages, sold 978,993 copies. When was the last time you rushed out to buy a 600-page book?

I think when designers say, "People don't read," they mean, "I don't read." In my experience designers don't read, they glance. We all read briefs, (some of) the "copy" that has to be flowed into layouts, the captions and a couple of articles a month in *Design Week*, the Sports pages in the newspaper. It's like Samuel Goldwyn said: "I read part of it all the way through." We put *Eye* magazine aside, saying, "Mmm, I'll read that later." Only a few read actual books, one a year, two, three? And almost certainly light novels.

The roots of this are twofold; it is partly to do with design being perceived as non-intellectual, and partly to do with the genuinely non-literary way that we develop visual skills. I strongly believe that reading has to be learned, especially the stamina to read difficult texts, and designers are often allowed to forgo this effort early on. Compare the amount a designer reads on art A-level or on a degree course with what a Sociology or English student has to read. Why should it be different? Why should designers know less, and not exercise the best way to know more? If designers really do want to change the world, we ought to know more about it.

The reading of the late Paul Rand serves as an example of self-expansion. He published a partial bibliography for his last book *From Lascaux to Brooklyn*; it covers some very diverse and difficult reading—mysticism, manifestos, sociology, history, the literary criticism of I. A. Richards and Harold Bloom, the philosophy of Hegel and John Dewey, the art history of Erwin Panofsky and Michel Foucault. There seems little doubt that his influence on several generations of other designers, and clients, is as much due to the thinking espoused in his books as to his design. Or put another way, his influence has been greatly intensified by his writing, which could not have been written without his reading.

If designers read more, the way they designed would be more conscious of being read. What designers considered important would change; instead of "design as content," we would be much more interested in making the content into content worth reading.

THE HANDWRITING IS ON THE WALL, BUT WHO CAN READ IT?
Todd Lief

One of the prices we pay for knowing English so well is that we don't even know what English looks like any more. We can recognize Arabic, say, by its delicate curls and swoops, or Hebrew, by its engaging little turrets and drips, or French, or Chinese, and many other languages we don't speak, by their familiar—if content-free—shapes.

But if the look is familiar, the meaning is opaque. There's no apparent difference between the most dreadful curse, a sweet love poem, or directions to a bar.

On the other hand, you can't so much as glance at any text in the particular language you are now reading without immediately comprehending it.

I think this may be why I sometimes find myself really enjoying the graffiti I see in a foreign country, in a foreign language. Yes, sure, like everyone else I abhor the property abuse, the public scatology and the expressions of violence and intolerance. Traveling abroad, I get to encounter the dazzling, monumental letterforms as pure visual impressions, full of color and power and individuality, blissfully ignorant of what any of it "means."

WE CAN'T SEE IT BECAUSE WE GET IT

For English speakers, English-speaking graffiti are all about content. Unfortunately, this is usually filthy, incendiary, divisive, offensive or otherwise disturbing.

No doubt the same thing is going on in the other languages, too. But severing the connection between the pure letterforms and their information content frees me to appreciate something quite energetic and extraordinary there—the self-trained inventiveness and virtuosity shown by so many graffiti artists, most of whom are teenagers.

Besides, the real culprit is not the graffiti per se, is it? Rather, isn't it the failure of the larger culture to have found ways to more usefully mobilize all that outside-the-lines energy? Actually, the global ubiquity of graffiti reveals as much about the youthful impulse toward aesthetics and self-expression as it does about anything political. There's a lot of young talent and intensity out there. Maybe we should start fretting less about recycled paper and soy ink and more about the universal squander of human creativity.

Without young talent and intensity, we wouldn't have civilization in the first place. Or language, either.

Originally published in *AIGA Journal of Graphic Design* Vol. 17, no. 1 (1999).

Think about it. What was the life expectancy of those earliest humans? Fifteen? Twenty? You can almost see them out there, bands of roaming teenagers, messing around in the woods and the caves, yelling, pointing, scribbling on the walls. Prehistoric graffiti. Visual hip-hop.

Appropriation (which is giving the intellectual property lawyers such a headache in cyberspace these days) was the big thing back then, too. Familiar objects were the original graphic reference. The very first human-made images were representations: marks made to look like the horns of a bull, for instance, or a human figure—or magically even to *be* these things.

Over the next umpteen hundred thousand years, the linear alphabet evolved. Eventually the rough designs came to encode the sounds of individual spoken syllables. Somewhere inside this innocent and playful coupling of arbitrary noises and meaningless shapes was the DNA of Shakespeare, the *New Yorker* and your new Web site.

According to the *American Heritage Dictionary*, the Phoenicians and other Semitic peoples began to use graphic signs about 1,000 B.C. to represent individual speech sounds instead of syllables or words. One of the first was called "aleph," their word for "ox." Later, the Greeks adopted the Phoenician alphabet, turned the aleph letterform on its side, renamed it, "alpha," and used it as a sign for the sound "a." It all happened haphazardly, randomly, with no mission statement or teambuilding exercises. Today's oh-so-precious alphabetical order was yesterday's hieroglyphic mishmash, an unruly jumble of visual puns.

STUCK IN THE AMBER OF OUR NATIVE TONGUE

The scientist Murray Gell-Mann has described such phenomena as "frozen accidents," a cool phrase in any language. This is what happens: some random event draws attention to itself and begins to attract interest, like iron filings around a magnetic field, eventually crystallizing into the way things are forever more. The procedure explains the persistence of the QWERTY keyboard from the days of jamming typewriter keys. It's also why VHS beat Beta in the VCR department, why Windows continues to outsell the Mac OS, and why we have the Spice Girls, purple dinosaurs, fake wood grain and a lot more high-level interest in branding.

By now, of course, whether they're chiseled in old stone or dancing in the quantum soup, our twenty-six English letters are the sacred ground beneath all the information storage and communications structures of the present age, for linear thinkers and holistic grokkers alike. They are drenched with so much significance we scarcely notice that they also obscure more than they reveal, as anyone who knows a pictographic or iconic language can attest.

What's to be done? Go sit by a lake with someone you care about and roast a marshmallow. Get real quiet. Try not to think of anything. Reach inside yourself to before you learned to talk. When something happens, don't try to name it.

LET THE BUYER BEWARE
Véronique Vienne

A s soon as you walk into a store, your attention drifts to the right. Even left-handed people like me can't help but glance starboard. It's instinctive. You always make a beeline for whatever happens to be on the right side as you walk in. No matter what it is—a pile of cashmere sweaters or a special on umbrellas—it gets your attention. Knowing this, merchants bait their customers with nothing short of dexterity, a word that comes from the Latin *dexter,* meaning "to the right."

Nature or nurture? Retailers have always noticed that the right side, which is, coincidentally, the creative, nonverbal side of the brain, is more conducive to impulse buying. Well-established cultural conventions, which favor clockwise movements over counterclockwise ones, reinforce this neurological tendency. Outside of England, making a right turn is a lot easier than making a left turn. The trick is to find the exact spot in a store (not too close to the entrance, but not too far inside) where people will go without being prompted. At Bloomingdale's, in New York, shoppers love to wander aimlessly among cosmetic counters located on the right side of the main aisle. At Tiffany, they can't help but stare at engagement rings. At the Gap, they size up T-shirts. At the Metropolitan Museum—the ultimate cultural mall—they investigate the crowded gift shop on the right side of the grand staircase. In almost every store in this country, the bulk of the foot traffic happens in a comfort zone located on a fuzzy diagonal to the right of the main entrance.

Does this mean that the stuff on the left side of a store simply gathers dust? No way. The left side becomes the right side as soon as you turn around. This is where retailers catch stragglers—shoppers walking back empty-handed toward the main entrance. There, on the right side on their way out, these sluggish consumers must tangle with belts, scarves, costume jewelry, sunglasses, hats, T-shirts and souvenirs—spoils that will turn their fruitless spree into a triumphant ransacking expedition.

All people need in order to navigate retail mazes is the foolproof compass of their peripheral vision. Like sleepwalkers, they can cross the main selling floor, ride up and down escalators and find the right merchandise at the right price without ever having to know where they are. In retail dreamland, wayfinding is a no-brainer: something that requires almost no consciousness. It's meant to be that way. The more you have to think about where you're going, the less likely you are to use your credit card.

To favor right-brain receptivity over left-brain linear thinking, in-store navigational information is transmitted through the senses—through ceiling heights, smells,

---

Originally published in *AIGA Journal of Graphic Design* Vol. 15, no. 1 (1997).

sounds, temperature changes, lights and shadows. For example, from the corner of your eye, you notice a brightly illuminated area, somewhere ahead and slightly to the right. You know, without having to be told, that there you'll find stuff for less than $99. Behind the escalators, muffled classical music tells you that you are approaching the men's store—it's time to think leather accessories and spicy colognes. Beyond the watch department, thick carpeting slows you down. This is a restricted area—you've probably wandered by mistake into the fine-jewelry department.

Walking into a store is the closest thing to appreciating what it's like to be legally blind. Retailscapes are laid out in such a way as to discourage visual scrutiny while encouraging total body awareness and open-ended, head-to-toe receptivity. They map out the emotional territory of the shopping experience, emphasizing its main through-ways, busy intersections, quiet shortcuts and hidden rest stops. They are designed to shut out the rational mind and help shoppers get in touch with their creative side. That's why cosmetics products are sold near the main entrance—with the hottest vendors stationed on the right side. Buoyant color palettes and glittering mirrors, brushes, testers, jars and bottles make these beauty counters look like artists' studios.

Forewarned is forearmed. From this ominous gateway, shoppers are inspired to proceed upward into a right-brain world ruled by artists, stylists, designers and arbiters of elegance. As you rise from floor to floor, the taste level of the décor rises with you. Chandeliers replace recessed lighting. Aisles get wider. Noise reverberation diminishes, while merchandise grows sparse. Greater opulence is implied by a process of elimination. You know that you've reached the store's luxurious inner sanctum when the only signs of exuberance are the exorbitant price tags.

But sleepwalkers beware: never venture beyond the fur salon on the proverbial third floor. In most department stores, the upper levels require you to wake up. It's mass versus class. At about one hundred feet above ground, visual clues prompt you to switch from right brain to left brain. The colors are lighter, the hallways narrower and the racks more numerous. Here, the merchandising strategy promotes comparative shopping. You are encouraged to investigate things counterclockwise. Winter coats on sale are on the other side of the aisle while close-out comforters are behind you on the left side. At this altitude, you read directional signage: stark billboards with bold prices and loud percentage signs.

Navigating through a store is like negotiating our collective assumptions about who we think we are and who we would like to be. People choose stores for their merchandise, but also for their special geography. Where things are displayed is more telling than the way they are displayed.

In Barneys original flagship store in Chelsea, women used to walk through the men's department to get to their section—almost as if they had to sneak behind men's backs to buy a couple of deliciously frivolous garments. At Barnes & Noble bookstores, espresso bars are strategically located on a mezzanine, providing bookworms with an ample perch where they can hide to nibble on their literary finds. In the new Chanel megastore on 57th Street in New York, shoes are sold at the bottom of a soaring grand staircase—the very spot where Cinderella lost her glass slipper. Staunch consumerism is dead. Today, the most rewarding buying sprees are compelling mythical journeys.

Because of my French accent, I am often asked to elucidate one of fashion's greatest mystery: how come Parisian women manage to look chic even though they are often wearing plain outfits. "They don't shop for clothes, they shop for locations," I usually answer. No one knows what I am talking about. "Frenchwomen are as confused by trends as anyone else—they don't have the faintest idea of what to buy," I explain. "But they always know where to go. They can pinpoint exactly where they will find their next purchase. What street, what store, what floor, what rack." Next time you go shopping, take your internal compass. Be ready to travel inside your mind.

BEIGE
Andrea Codrington

Beige is the color of evil, or at least that's what Aaron Priven thinks. Priven, the author of the Internet's only Web site dedicated to that most unassuming of hues, writes:

> Most people think if colors have attributes such as good or evil, that the color of evil is either the red of arterial blood gushing from a wound, or the deepest black of the darkest night sky. While these are certainly evil colors, they are not as evil as beige . . . The most evil color has to appear benign.[1]

Priven might just have a point.

At first blush, of course, the color beige might have all kinds of comforting associations—from oatmeal, that pabulum of wintertime childhoods, to a worn-to-softness pair of trousers. But beige is also the color of deceit and oppression. Khaki, after all, originated in mid-nineteenth-century colonial India, where it took its name from the Urdu term for "dusty." It was in the altogether different—but no less exotic—locale of Transvaal that the British first realized that donning dun-colored uniforms while fighting the Boer locals would help them sneakily blend into their dried-out South African surroundings. Thereafter, khaki replaced regimental blues and reds and became a military staple the world over—as well as the building block of any hot-climate camouflage pattern.

One can easily find other examples of beige's pernicious ability to blend into the background at the political and sociocultural level. Just consider the Hannah Arendt–John Mellencamp continuum.

Originally published in *Cabinet*, no. 2 (Spring 2001).

What does a German-born left-leaning political critic hold in common with a hard-living Midwestern rock star? Arendt, whose 1963 book *Eichmann in Jerusalem* gives a first-hand account of the trial of Nazi war criminal Adolf Eichmann, was one of the first twentieth-century thinkers to set forth the idea that evil was represented as much in this world by banality as by anything that could be called sinister. She based this observation on Eichmann's behavior during the trial, which was marked by total thoughtlessness: cliché speech patterns, a lack of critical ability and unthinking obedience to authority. (As a Nazi, of course, Eichmann also tended to wear beige uniforms.)

Exactly thirty years later, John Mellencamp came out with a song that further implicated the relationship between banality, evil and the color beige:

> It's just beige to beige
> That's all it is these days,
> Little windows for you to crawl through.
> You just do what's expected of you.
> It's just beige to beige to beige
> These days.

Of course, Mellencamp's formula that routine ("beige") equals constraint equals evil is a rock-and-roll staple. It is also at the very core of the advertising techniques that drive contemporary consumerism, as Thomas Frank has pointed out in *The Conquest of Cool*. "Commercial fantasies of rebellion, liberation and outright 'revolution' against the stultifying demands of mass society," he writes, "are commonplace almost to the point of invisibility in advertising, movies and television programming."[2]

In a cultural moment predicated on visual flamboyance, beige is indeed the enemy. It is a truism that when the economy is doing well, colors brighten (hence the Great Depression's nickname as the "Taupe Age"). According to the Color Marketing Group, the country's most influential color forecasting organization, colors like Mazenta ("A new twist on magenta that leaps from retro right into the future") and Fuschion ("An active, unisex pink that is both sporty and glamorous") will be dominant in 2001—which leaves beige beyond the pale.[3]

Apple Computers, one of the most obvious progenitors of the consumption-as-rebellion method of advertising, is now in the position of distancing itself from decades of cranking out what tech aficionados disparagingly term "beige toasters." These days, Apple heralds each season with a splashy introduction of new colors for its lollipop-reminiscent iMac. An interview with iMac designer Jonathan Ive on Apple's Web site even bears a headline that reads "Sorry, no beige"—thus shifting blame from the company to the color. (Interestingly, when German designer Hartmut Esslinger first created the original Macintosh in 1984, the company lovingly referred to the beige box as "Snow White.")

Of course to every revolution there is a counterrevolution, and recent years have seen a return of low-key colors in fashion. But far from representing suburban normality or old-school comfort, high-style beige is all sharp tongue and urban angularity.

"Beige is like the martini of color," says New York–based club organizer Erich Conrad in a 1997 *Esquire* article called "Ecru Brut." "It's quiet but toxic."

There is certainly some evidence to the contrary. Those frenetic jitterbugging commercials for Gap Khakis seem to reposition beige as the *methamphetamine* of color. But whatever your poison, too much of either might land you in the infirmary. And according to Sir Elton John—who knows a thing or two about substance abuse and sartorial extravagance—beige is one color that should be kept in the clinic. At a VH-1 Fashion Awards show a few years ago, John spoke out against "boutiques looking like hospitals, selling a lot of beige suits."

Evil. Toxic. Hospital-like. Could these terms really apply to a hue that Webster's describes as "the color of undyed wool?" Could the wolf really be dressed in sheep's clothing? A quick numerological evaluation of color chip 468C in Pantone's ubiquitous matching system reveals an astounding answer. Adding the color's three numbers amounts to the number eighteen. And we all know that the number eighteen results when you combine 6 + 6 + 6.

Notes

1. See *www.geocities.com/Paris/93861*.
2. Thomas Frank, The Conquest of Cool: Business Culture, Counterculture, and the Rise of Hip Consumerism (Chicago: University of Chicago Press, 1997), p. 4.
3. Editors' note: As this essay was written prior to 2002, the new color has probably come and gone.

THE FLAG WAVERER
Steven Heller

Two days after the World Trade Center tragedy, I bought a U.S. flag to hang from my apartment window. It was the first flag I'd displayed since before the Vietnam War, and I did it as a gesture of solidarity with the victims, their families and, of course, the rescuers. We all know how important symbols are, and in the aftermath of the terrorist assault on our nation, I embraced the flag as a symbol of resolve and unity with my fellow Americans.

But I'm ambivalent. I've long been suspicious of flag-waving and what it connotes. It's probably a difficult symbol for many of my generation that grew up during the era of Vietnam protest. That was a time when the U.S. flag was as much a symbol of division as accord. Despite attempts to claim it for themselves, opponents of the war

Originally published in *Print* Vol. 55, no. 6 (2002).

lost the flag to a so-called silent majority whose mantra, referring to flag and country, was "love it or leave it." During the critical period of anti-war protest in the late Sixties and early Seventies, it seemed that all the symbols of patriotism, Old Glory primarily, had been ceded to "true" Americans, leaving the rest of us to find alternate signs of allegiance.

So the flag became something to rebel against. When the hardhats and police took to wearing tiny flags on their work clothes and uniforms as a means of distinguishing themselves from us, the opposition countered by wearing peace signs and related accouterments. If the flag was used in anti-war protests, it was usually flown upside down or with a peace sign in place of the stars. Or worse, it was ritually burned—an act I could never condone.

With the traditional symbol of American freedom denied us, protesters like me felt increasingly detached from the nation's heritage. Red, white and blue came to symbolize the injustice that the civil rights and anti-war activists were trying to redress, all the while knowing in our hearts that this protest was possible only in a democratic society like ours. We wanted the flag, but felt forced to reject it.

Even after the Vietnam War ended, the flag remained a charged symbol—a vivid reminder of polarization—and continued to provoke profoundly ambivalent responses. I remember a visit I made to East Berlin a few years before the wall came down, walking along the drab main boulevard just yards away from the Brandenburg Gate. The wall was punctuated with a score or so of gray guard booths manned by uniformed officers peering through waist-high eye slits. The only color on the street was the green of a few lonely trees and, to my surprise, the red, white and blue of an American flag hanging from a consul building. I admit feeling comforted—indeed proud—when I stumbled upon this sight. Amid this dreary Iron Curtain landscape, our flag was luminescent.

I have something of the same feeling when I return home from other countries. No matter how alluring those countries may be, the sight of our flag provides a welcome sense of security that, during the Sixties, I never dreamed it could offer. In 1986, as a means of reclaiming the flag, Kit Hinrichs mounted an AIGA exhibition for which he invited a slew of designers and illustrators to come up with their own versions of the national symbol. He invited me to write the introduction to the catalog for the show. It was a cathartic event in that it was the first time in what seemed like eons that the flag belonged to everyone again.

Still, I cannot totally forget the feelings evoked from my past. So when phrases like "God Bless America" and flag images cropped up on T-shirts, caps, buttons and even crucifixes in the aftermath of the terrorist attack, I balked. There are a couple of reasons for this. One was the fear that some zealots would use the flag as a battering ram to suppress difference and dissent. (I recall the famous photograph from the Seventies of an anti-busing protester in Boston wielding a flagpole like a spear against his enemy—a fellow American. The savage anger on his face was chilling.)

The second reason for my unease was the outpouring of cheesy, over-priced flag products that flooded the streets and stores of New York and other cities around the country. From a street vendor near one of the makeshift memorials in Union Square in downtown Manhattan I bought one of these products: a T-shirt with the American flag shown behind the twin towers with the words, "America Under Attack." (Another of her T-shirts for sale read, "I survived the Trade Center Bombing.") When I gave the shirt to my twelve-and-a-half-year-old son, he indignantly refused it, saying, "Those people shouldn't sell that; it doesn't help anyone but themselves."

Recently a reporter I know asked me why so many patriotic products are cheap-looking and ugly. I replied that it was the easiest thing in the world to apply the colors red white and blue to any kitschy product to make it seem patriotic. We do not have standards that govern our symbols in the same way that, say, Nazi Germany prohibited the swastika from being used in commercial endorsements. Any U.S. company can appropriate the flag—which, of course, is what distinguishes the United States from a totalitarian regime. Our colors, icons, and symbols are democratically available, free for the taking, and there's a long history of their use on buttons, banners, fans, hats, etc., that goes back to the nation's inception. Over-used, they easily become trivial clichés. The one thing we're admonished not to do is burn the flag; although doing so is not a federal offense, its prohibition is regularly debated in Congress.

Ours is a nation of symbols, and all of us turn to them at one time or another, whether they be yellow ribbons, red ribbons, pink triangles, black armbands, or red, white, and blue anything. The terrorists understood the power of our symbols, which is why they attacked two of the foremost of them: the Pentagon and the World Trade Center.

As we compulsively reach for a symbol to express our solidarity in this critical time, we rely more than ever on the American flag. We want it to figuratively bind our collective wounds and tie us together as one nation. We own it. It's ours. And so I will proudly hang the flag from my window—just as long as it does not become a symbol of us against you, you, you, and me.

CONTRIBUTORS

ROY R. BEHRENS, a contributing editor of *Print* and editor of *Ballast Quarterly Review*, teaches graphic design and design history at the University of Northern Iowa.

MICHAEL BIERUT is a partner in the New York office in the international design consultancy Pentagram and a past president of the American Institute of Graphic Arts.

MAX BRUINSMA is the former editor of *Eye* magazine and an independent critic and editorial designer who currently teaches design at the Sandberg Institute in Amsterdam.

RICHARD BUCHANAN is a professor and head of the School of Design at Carnegie Mellon University.

RALPH CAPLAN has been looking closer at design for decades, and writing and speaking about what he sees. He is at present writing a novel about World War II.

ANDREA CODRINGTON is a New York–based writer and editor specializing in design and visual culture. She is currently writing a book about motion-graphics designer Kyle Cooper.

WILLIAM DRENTTEL is a designer and publisher who works in partnership with Jessica Helfand in Falls Village, Connecticut. Their design consultancy, Winter House Studio, concentrates on graphic design, new media, publishing and education. He is president emeritus of the American Institute of Graphic Arts and a board member of the Cooper-Hewitt National Design Museum.

JOHANNA DRUCKER is the Robertson Professor of Media Studies at the University of Virginia. She has lectured and published widely on the history of writing, typography, graphic design, visual language, artists' books and digital media.

THOMAS FRANK is founding editor of *The Baffler* and author of *One Market under God* (Doubleday, 2000).

ROBERT FULFORD is a Toronto author, journalist, broadcaster and editor. He writes a weekly column for the *National Post* and is a frequent contributor to *Toronto Life*,

Canadian Art and CBC radio and television. His books include *Best Seat in the House: Memoirs of a Lucky Man* (Collins, 1988); *Accidental City: The Transformation of Toronto* (MacFarlane Walter & Ross, 1995); *Toronto Discovered* (Key Porter Books, 1998); and *The Triumph of Narrative: Storytelling in the Age of Mass Culture* (Broadway Books, 2001).

KEN GARLAND is principal of Ken Garland & Associates in England. He is the author of several books including *Graphics Handbook* (Studio Vista, 1966), *Illustrated Graphics Glossary* (Barrie & Jenkins,1980) and *Mr. Beck's Underground Map* (Capitol Transport Publishing, 1994). He is also the author of the original, 1964 First Things First Manifesto.

MILTON GLASER, artist, illustrator, author and restaurant critic, is the co-founder of Push Pin Studio and principal of Milton Glaser Inc. He is the author of *Art Is Work* (Overlook, 2001) and the creator of the "I ♥ New York" logo.

PETER HALL is a contributing editor for *Metropolis*. He is the writer of *Sagmeister: Made You Look* (Booth-Clibborn Editions, 2001) and *Tibor Kalman: Perverse Optimist* (Princeton Architectural Press, 1998) and co-author of *Pause: 59 Minutes of Motion Graphics* (Rizzoli/Universe, 2000). He is a faculty member at the Yale University graphic design master's program and a research fellow at the University of Minnesota Design Institute.

JESSICA HELFAND is a partner of William Drenttel/Jessica Helfand, a multimedia and print media company. She is the author of *Six Essays (to 12) on Design and New Media* (William Drenttel, 1997) and *Paul Rand: American Modernist* (William Drenttel, 1998).

STEVEN HELLER is art director of the *New York Times Book Review* and co-chair of the M.F.A./Design program of the School of Visual Arts. He is the author of more than eighty books on design and popular culture and the 1999 recipient of the AIGA Medal for Lifetime Achievement.

JELLY HELM is an Associate Professor at Virginia Commonwealth University Adcenter, a graduate school of advertising in Richmond, Virginia. Previously Jelly was a senior vice president and group creative director at The Martin Agency, and before that a creative director at Wieden & Kennedy in Amsterdam. Jelly is from Louisville, Kentucky.

JOHN HOCKENBERRY, a contributing editor of *I.D.*, is a correspondent for *NBC Dateline* and the author of *Moving Violations: War Zones, Wheelchairs and Declarations of Independence* (Hyperion, 1995).

ANDREW HOWARD runs his own design studio in Portugal, where he specializes in work for cultural and educational organizations. He teaches design communication at the Escola Superior de Artes e Design.

NATALIA ILYIN is a writer and designer with a design consultancy that specializes in communications for nonprofit cultural organizations. Her articles on design and media have been published internationally. Her first book is *Blonde Like Me: The Roots of the Blonde Myth in Our Culture* (Simon and Schuster, 2000).

TIBOR KALMAN, who died in 1999, was the co-founder with Maira Kalman of M&Co and editor of *Colors* magazine. He brought a restless intellectual curiosity and subversive wit to everything from album covers for the Talking Heads to the redevelopment of Times Square. Kalman used his work to promote his radical politics and used his talent to question the status quo of his profession.

MR. KEEDY is a designer, writer, type designer and educator who has been teaching in the graphic design program at the California Institute of the Arts since 1985. His designs and essays have been published in *Eye, I.D., Emigre, Critique* and *Idea*, as well as in numerous collections, including *Looking Closer, Looking Closer 2* and *Texts on Type* (all published by Allworth Press).

NAOMI KLEIN is the author of *No Logo: Taking Aim at the Brand Bullies* (HarperCollins, 2000) and a columnist for the *Toronto Star*.

JULIE LASKY writes frequently about design and visual culture. She is the author of *Some People Can't Surf: The Graphic Design of Art Chantry* (Chronicle Books, 2001).

KALLE LASN is editor in chief of *Adbusters* magazine.

TODD LIEF is based in Chicago as a writer, communications planner and professional troubleshooter on the creative process for individuals and organizations.

NICO MACDONALD (*www.spy.co.uk*) is a London-based writer, event programmer and consultant focusing on the overlap of design, business and technology. Along with *New Design* contributor Kevin McCullagh, he co-founded the think tank Design Agenda in 1994.

BRUCE MAU is the author of *Life Style* (Phaidon Press, 2000), a 627-page manifesto, monograph and virtual museum, and he is co-author with Rem Koolhaas of *S,M,L,XL* (Monacelli Press, 1999). With Frank Gehry, he designed the signage and typographic identity for the Walt Disney Concert Hall in Los Angeles. His many collaborative projects have led to work with the artist-composer Gordon Monahan, filmmaker Michael Snow and choreographer Meg Stuart.

KATHERINE McCOY, a senior lecturer at Illinois Institute of Technology's Institute of Design in Chicago, co-chaired the Department of Design at Cranbrook for twenty-four years. She is a partner in McCoy & McCoy and High Ground Tools Strategies for Design.

QUENTIN NEWARK is co-founder of Atelier Works. The studio's projects include the Labour Party manifesto for the last election, rebranding the Royal Institute of British Architects and a stone sundial outside the Houses of Parliament. He is the author of *What Is Graphic Design?* (Rotovision, 2002).

PAUL J. NINI is an associate professor in the department of design at Ohio State University. He has written for *Eye, Information Design Journal*, ACD's *Statements* and *Design Issues*. A former Chicagoan, he is an alum of the Institute of Design at IIT's master's program and onetime instructor at the School of the Art Institute.

MONIKA PARRINDER teaches design and cultural theory at London College of Printing, the Royal College of Art and Central St. Martins in London. She trained as a graphic designer and is currently the designer of *Things* journal.

RICK POYNOR writes about design, media and visual culture for *Eye, Print, Metropolis, Frieze, Artbyte* and many other publications. His books include *Typography Now* (Booth-Clibborn, 1991); *Design Without Boundaries* (Booth-Clibborn, 2000), *Vaughan Oliver: Visceral Pleasures* (Booth-Clibborn, 2000); and *Typographica* (Princeton Architectural Press, 2001), a study of the post-war design journal.

TIM RICH is a London-based writer and editorial consultant. He is a contributing editor for *Print*, a columnist for *Design Week*, and ex-editor of *Graphics International*.

CHRIS RILEY is a chief strategic officer with Wieden & Kennedy. He works with all W & K offices worldwide (New York, London, Amsterdam, Tokyo, Portland). His role is to help them think strategically about the relationship between the consumer and client brands.

MICHAEL ROCK is a founding partner, with Susan Sellers and Georgianna Stout, of the multidisciplinary studio 2×4 in New York City. In addition he is a partner in the design strategy collective AMO and an associate professor of design at the Yale University School of Art.

SOL SENDER lives and works in Chicago. He is an adjunct faculty member at the School of the Art Institute of Chicago and director of business and creative integration at Designkitchen, a hybrid brand strategy and design company.

RUTH SHALIT is a New York writer. Her work has appeared in the *New Republic*, the *Wall Street Journal* and *Details*. She is currently at work on a book about brands.

MATT SOAR is currently visiting assistant professor of video at Hampshire College. From 1996 to 2001 he was the resident graphic designer at the Media Education Foundation (*www.mediaed.org*).

LORETTA STAPLES has practiced as a graphic, exhibit and interface designer for the past twenty years. She has written and lectured extensively on design, digital technology and visual culture.

RUDY VANDERLANS is the editor and designer of the quarterly design journal *Emigre* and author of two books of photographs, *Palm Desert* (Emigre, 1999) and *Cucamonga* (Emigre, 2000).

VÉRONIQUE VIENNE is the author of short essays on culture and lifestyle and has written *The Art of Doing Nothing*, *The Art of Imperfection* and *The Art of Growing Up* (Clarkson Potter, 1998, 1999 and 2000, respectively). Also available is a collection of her design essays, *Something to Be Desired* (Graphis, 2001).

LORRAINE WILD has a design practice in Los Angeles and teaches in the graphic design program at CalArts.

INDEX

Books from Allworth Press

Looking Closer 3: Classic Writings on Graphic Design
edited by Michael Bierut, Jessica Helfand, Steven Heller, and Rick Poynor
(paperback, 6¾ × 9⅞, 304 pages, $18.95)

Looking Closer 2: Critical Writings on Graphic Design
edited by Michael Bierut, William Drenttel, Steven Heller, and DK Holland
(paperback, 6¾ × 9⅞, 288 pages, $18.95)

Looking Closer: Critical Writings on Graphic Design
edited by Michael Bierut, William Drenttel, Steven Heller, and DK Holland
(paperback, 6½ × 10, 256 pages, $18.95)

AIGA Professional Practices in Graphic Design: The American Institute of Graphic Arts *edited by Tad Crawford* (paperback, 6¾ × 9⅞, 320 pages, $24.95)

Graphic Design Humor: The Art of Graphic Wit
by Steve Heller (paperback, 6¾ × 9⅞, 288 pages, $21.95)

Design Issues: How Graphic Design Informs Society
edited by DK Holland (paperback, 6¾ × 9⅞, 288 pages, $21.95)

Graphic Design and Reading: Explorations of an Uneasy Relationship
edited by Gunnar Swanson (paperback, 6¾ × 9⅞, 256 pages, $19.95)

The Graphic Design Reader
by Steven Heller (paperback with flaps, 5½ × 8½, 320 pages, $19.95)

The Education of an E-Designer
edited by Steven Heller (paperback, 6¾ × 9⅞, 352 pages, $21.95)

The Education of a Graphic Designer
edited by Steven Heller (paperback, 6¾ × 9⅞, 288 pages, $18.95)

The Education of an Illustrator
edited by Steven Heller and Marshall Arisman (paperback, 6¾ × 9⅞, 288 pages, $19.95)

Business and Legal Forms for Graphic Designers, Revised Edition
by Tad Crawford and Eva Doman Bruck (paperback, 8½ × 11, 240 pages, includes CD-ROM, $24.95)

Careers By Design: A Business Guide for Graphic Designers, Third Edition
by Roz Goldfarb (paperback, 6 × 9, 232 pages, $19.95)

Please write to request our free catalog. To order by credit card, call 1-800-491-2808 or send a check or money order to Allworth Press, 10 East 23rd Street, Suite 510, New York, NY 10010. Include $5 for shipping and handling for the first book ordered and $1 for each additional book. Ten dollars plus $1 for each additional book if ordering from Canada. New York State residents must add sales tax.

To see our complete catalog on the World Wide Web, or to order online, you can find us at *www.allworth.com*.